DELIGHTS AND DISQUIETS OF LEISURE IN PREMODERN INDIA

DELIGHTS AND DISQUIETS OF LEISURE IN PREMODERN INDIA

Edited by

Seema Bawa

B L O O M S B U R Y
NEW DELHI • LONDON • OXFORD • NEW YORK • SYDNEY

BLOOMSBURY INDIA
Bloomsbury Publishing India Pvt. Ltd
Second Floor, LSC Building No. 4, DDA Complex, Pocket C – 6 & 7,
Vasant Kunj, New Delhi, 110070

BLOOMSBURY, BLOOMSBURY ACADEMIC INDIA and the Diana logo are trademarks of Bloomsbury Publishing Plc

First published in India 2023
This edition published 2023

Bloomsbury Academic India
An imprint of Bloomsbury Publishing Plc

ISBN: HB: 978-93-94701-26-7; eBook: 978-93-94701-28-1
2 4 6 8 10 9 7 5 3 1

Typeset in Manipal Technologies Limited
Printed and bound in India by Replika Press Pvt. Ltd

CONTENTS

FIGURES

PREFACE

Jī dhūñdtā hai phir vahī fursat kī rāt din
baithe raheñ tasavvur-e-jānāñ kiye hue
The heart seeks again the same days and nights of leisure
Given over to the imagining the beloved.

—Ghalib

This edited volume is planned as a companion volume to the recently published *Locating Pleasure in Indian History: Prescribed and Proscribed Desires in Visual and Literary Culture* (edited by Seema Bawa, Bloomsbury Academic India, 2021).

While leisure studies have been an intrinsic part of sociology as a discipline for a long time, research on leisure activities and spaces in history has been a relatively recent phenomenon and has sparked a lively debate. Did leisure as a concept exist in premodern societies, or is it an invention of industrial work? If it did exist, what were the kind of ideas and activities that could be used to define the concept of leisure in these premodern societies? The current book takes up this challenge to excavate the ways in which leisure was viewed and experienced in early and medieval Indian history. However, like most scholarly pursuits, it is just a partial exploration of a very vast theme, and much research can be done in this direction.

First, I am very grateful to all the contributors who took up the challenge of writing on the visual, literary, performative and environmental histories of leisure with enthusiasm and creativity. Marion Frenger and Suchandra Ghosh look at hunting and wrestling as aspects of divinity as well as through the lens of quotidian life in the mundane world. That gender and power are embedded in acts of entertainment and play is evident and established in the manner in which leisure is projected in various cultural artefacts. Smita Sahgal explores the masculine aspects of projection of leisure activities in literary productions. I (Bawa) have explored the agency of wine and femininity and womanhood that is represented through the visual culture of the early period. Patrick Kruger delves into the Jaina tradition to retrieve the contradictions inherent in the religious and social discourse of the Jainas regarding the notion of work and leisure on one hand and sin and salvation on the other.

Cultural performances, be it dance, drama or music, are the very definitions of entertainment that ensures pleasure of the senses and enhances the idea of leisure, which has been analysed with aplomb by Mrittyunjay Prabhakar, who looks at the classical Sanskrit drama, which often emplots leisure to amplify notions of class, gender and status. Music as history has been brought to scholarly attention by T.K. Venkatasubramanian who looks to Tamil music to trace the evolution of an activity from service to leisure, from singing praises of the patron to courtly and social entertainment, thereby also tracing the formation of a sub-regional music tradition.

The other major act of relaxation and enjoyment examined is the quintessential sleep, which Farhat Nasreen explores in all its dimensions, giving it a historical perspective and recreating its milieu within the Indo-Persian literary tradition. Her unique perspective places the history of sleep within a real and imagined inscape where the dream world collides with the mundane.

Vipul Singh looks at state and society's interface with forests and the social environment of clubs and courts where leisurely sports and activities took place in the medieval and early modern period. Prescribed and proscribed leisure activities could take place in a contained environment at the cusp of the medieval and modern eras. Prem Kumar brings alive the gardens, the parks and the orchards of early Indian history where romance and picnics of early Indian drama and poetics took place in exalted pastorals.

The mushairas of the early modern and modern period are examined by Raziuddin Aquil where the extraordinary lives of the poets and, more importantly, the poetesses see these personages rise above the barriers of class and gender through their poetic creations that refer to the space of *ishq*, *mohabbat* and *tehzeeb* (etiquette). The mushaira trope is continued by Rakhshanda Jalil, who delves into the dying world of the late Mughals to bring to fore the imagined last mushaira of Delhi where all the great poets gather in the glittering evening to revel in the last vestiges of the vanishing world of *fursat* (leisure) and tehzeeb.

I would like to reiterate my gratitude for the rich and insightful scholarship of the historians who have contributed to weave this evocative tapestry of pursuits of leisure and pleasure in times past. A special acknowledgement is due to my postgraduate students whose curiosity and questions led me to explore the theme of leisure in Indian history further, partly to enhance the study material available to students and researchers and partly to answer their and my own queries. Of all these students, Janica Paul has taken a keen interest in the subject and helped in the layout of some of the figures. Arijeet Chatterjee provided photographs of sculptures/figures in the Indian Museum.

This book was written at a singularly unleisurely time in my career, which made me yearn for freedom from work and the stresses thereof.

I am, therefore, doubly grateful for all those who treated my intermittent absences and silences with patience and indulgence. R. Chandra Sekhar of Bloomsbury Publishing India is one such partner who showed immense forbearance and supported this endeavour consistently. I also take this opportunity to thank my husband, Ashish, who read and reread my writings and corrected these repeatedly.

Seema Bawa
Delhi, 2023

INTRODUCTION : DELIGHTS AND DISQUIETS OF LEISURE IN PREMODERN INDIA

Seema Bawa

The idea of leisure invokes myriad emptions, ranging from longing to nostalgia, not to speak of the commerce. This volume delves into premodern leisure forms and practices, especially the relation of leisure to notions of individual freedom, choice and self-determination. It interrogates select aspects of social and cultural theory, ranging from cultural representation of leisure to a state of voluntarism or free-time behaviour within the realm of human behaviour and state of mind. Here the revitalisation of human life is premised on unfolding how leisure forms and practice enhances the storage capacity and repertoire of accomplishments in terms of the multiple meanings accumulating pleasure acquires across eras.

There are multilayered scholarly debates ranging from the invention of modern 'industrial' leisure to leisure activities that permeated the life experiences of people in the past clearly visible in premodern literary and visual cultures. There is also a debate—does premodernity define its leisure time differently, according to cyclical time rather than linear time? A time that is more in tune with nature, seasons and moods. The folk and visual culture of the Baramasa, the *rāgamālā* and the *abhisārikā* within these[1] would suggest so (Bawa 2021, 12). That there are some 'times' (monsoon?) that are more conducive to leisure activity, when productive activities such as agriculture require less effort, when picnics, rendezvous with lovers or staying indoors is more possible. This is often counterposed with a sense of nostalgia attributable to postmodern anxiety and pressures of work where leisure time, concepts and activities are structures defined and sometimes even mandated.[2] Some of the debates on whether and how premodern societies viewed work and leisure are discussed below.

This volume studies the embedded discourse of leisure in Indian social and cultural pasts through three forms—visual, literary and performative; leisure that is frequently performed as a spectacle, to enhance the status of the consumer. The spectacle of leisure and spectacle as leisure are salient aspects of social manifestations of leisure projected in political and cultural spaces in the ancient and medieval period. The popular perceptions of leisure tend to push it to the level of elite luxury, *rājasi śauq*, rather than see it as an everyday activity. In history textbooks, leisure activities are usually discussed at the end of the volume under the heading of 'Daily Life' or 'Arts and Entertainment' and are not mainstreamed in scholarly debates. Yet, there is a huge canvas of enjoying and being seen enjoying extolled in visual, literary and performance productions, whether it is the king in the bedchamber, the banker and his wife at a picnic, the *hoi polloi* at the theatre or wrestling match or attending or hosting a banquet of epicurean delights, being entertained with dance and music, gambling, watching sports; most importantly, being observed and projected as indulging in these leisurely pursuits. Here one could explore the class and gendered nature of leisure. It privileges elite male leisure which gets described, celebrated and projected; on the other hand the producers and providers of the same, the toiling lower classes and women are marginalised or voyeuristically projected.

How do cultures deal with leisure and work? Can a culture sustain itself without some sort of leisure? Did different civilisations and *weltanschauungs* view leisure and work differently? These are the questions seeking a general response. In the Western tradition, leisure is considered at the 'fountainhead of all creativity ... fundamental to the creation of anything beautiful' (Modi 2012, 386–403), also popularly referred to as free time, state of freedom or an absence of obligations. An important component of premodern leisure studies have been the focus on entertainment, both specular and participative. In many ancient societies such as that of Athenian polis, entertainment had a place of pride and privilege (Balme 1984, 140–52, 151; Turner 2020, 209–36, 210). The polis ideal, the locus of social and political organisation of the Greek, it is believed, was based on leisure (Sylvester 1999, 14). Aristotle further argues that the polis is an achievement of social organisation (ibid., 14, 212) while households and villages facilitated mere living, the polis is for 'the sake of living well' (ibid., 14). Bearing in mind the centrality of the polis to the character of all the citizens, leisure may be seen as a desirable cultural archetype (ibid). Pericles too says: 'We provide more recreation from toil for the mind than any other state, enjoying competitions and sacrifices throughout the year' (ibid.). Entertainment included drama, music, dancing, athletic, games, processions, where citizens participated and anyone 'could attend for nothing' (ibid.). Alternate entertainment was related to chattering in the *agaora* (ibid.).

Ancient Greek attitudes towards work and leisure, it appears, suggest a dichotomy. While certain cultural ideal in Greece during the 4th and 5th centuries BCE devalue work and praise leisure, others see work as both a necessity and a virtue (Tilgher 1930; Mosseâ 1969; Sylvester

1999, 3). Kraus explains that 'for the Athenians particularly, leisure was the highest value of life, and work the lowest' (1990, 49; Sylvester 1999, 3). Sessoms states that 'to the Greeks, work was a curse, an obligation from which free men should escape' (Sessoms 1984, 35; Sylvester 1999, 3). For Greek citizens eschewing work, treating it as antithetical to freedom, excellence, and citizenship (Sylvester 1999, 14) and esteeming leisure was a normative. Considering slaves unfree by nature, Aristotle categorically concludes that there is no leisure for slaves (*Politics*, 1334a20). Maurice Balme, on the contrary, in documenting the ancient Greek contempt for idleness, sees an ethic that saw work as both necessary and virtuous. For Hesiod, the archetype of the Greek peasant work is a leading motif of his 'Works and Days'; 'Work, foolish Perses' is the recurrent theme in his advice to his erring brother. As a matter of example, Socrates presents to his audience the example of king of Persia (Cyrus) whose main concerns are farming and war. When Lysander, a good Spartiate, exclaimed: '…Did you really plant some of these trees with your own hands?', Cyrus replies: 'I never sit down to dinner without first sweating at either martial exercises or farming work' (Balme 1984, 135). 'Even the wealthiest', Socrates says, 'cannot refrain from farming'.

Thus, the west often sees in leisure a lens into the societal norms. According to Max Kaplan, 'in our leisure we stand exposed. Through our leisure we provide the element for diagnosing our culture … how deeply we are in age of leisure' (Kaplan 1960, 4; Modi 2012, 387). In a similar vein, Sebastian de Grazia claimed in his 1964 masterpiece 'Of Time, Work and Leisure' that 'you tell me your leisure, I shall tell your culture' (Modi 2012, 8). Hunnicutt explains that Greeks used the word *schole* for leisure in two ways. One was the ordinary sense of having free time; the other was used in a comparative or superlative sense as 'freedom from a less important activity for a more (or the most) important activity (Hunnicutt 1989, 215)'. One of the first scholars to take the idea of play into serious consideration Johan Huizinga in Homo Ludens: the Play element in Culture too says that for the Greeks, 'the treasures of the mind were the fruit of his leisure.' He explores how the meaning of school from leisure has changed to mean the opposite to connote systematic work and training (Huizinga 1950, 147–48).

The changing conceptions of time make leisure a subject of interdisciplinary studies, which attain importance and salience from the 1960s. Closely related with the notion of work, time and status, leisure in modern society has been a subject of many sociological studies. While Peter Burke (Burke 1995) contends that the invention of leisure starts in early modernity the same is contested by other historians some of whom argue that leisure as the 'constitutive other' of work is a perennial human personal and social need. Even as leisure becomes a prominent status marker in the industrialised West, leisure and recreational activities did exist and were often celebrated as such during premodern times. The debate between Burke (1995, 1997) and Marfany (1997) seeks to address the existence and contours of premodern leisure.

Burke states that:

> Implicitly or explicitly, most recent work has been based on one central hypothesis, that of a fundamental discontinuity or great divide between pre-industrial and industrial society (Dumazedier 1967).[3] According to this view, in medieval and early modern Europe, as in other pre-industrial societies, the modern idea of leisure was lacking. (Burke 1995, 136–137)

This is seen as particularly germane as it is around this time that the economics of leisure is seen to undergo a shift away from leisure being seen as individual 'residual time' (Melvin 1974, 251–67) to what is seen as an economically material 'mass leisure' (Larrabee and Meyersohn 1958; Elias and Dunning 1986). There is also the perspective that there is a clear dichotomy, rupture or gap between premodern concept of leisure and the postindustrial/modern one. It is emphasised that it is only after industrial capitalism does a clear work-leisure dichotomy get established. According to the perspective, 'Pre-industrial societies had festivals (together with informal and irregular breaks from work), while industrial societies have leisure, weekends and vacations' (Burke 1995, 137). According to this perspective, while some sort of sporting, entertainment existed in the premodern world and there was a dominant social group with ample time for leisure or that the lower classes to had some access to what is not termed 'leisure preferences'; the engagements were built into ritual, ceremonies or training and were not practiced as a stand-alone activity. The dichotomy discourse also seems to identify that modernity brings into focus a new concept of time where time is largely linear and, therefore, nature and time both need to be appropriated to human will, albeit here for a structured planned leisure. This is seen in distinction to an imagined premodern world of seasonal festivals predicated on cyclical time and harmony with natural rhythms.

Marfany contests Burke's contention about the invention of leisure and argues instead that not leisure per-se but a tendency to theorise leisure emerges with modernity:

> Though Burke is quite right in detecting an awakening of interest in leisure at the beginning of the early modern period, what he fails to emphasize, however, is that this is, first, an intellectual interest and, as such, secondly, an interest of the upper classes. (Marfany 1997, 195)

Marfany further argues that the work–non-work dichotomy can be located in premodern times and cites numerous examples. In his response, Burke (1997) warns against the ahistorical tendency to relate modern notions of leisure to a 'tradition' that harks back to the past without excavating 'the meanings which contemporaries gave to their activities'; he, however, concedes as deeply problematic the tendency to create a series of hard-coded binary oppositions between preindustrial 'festival culture on the one hand and post-industrial "leisure culture" on the other as some continuities and commonalities remain'. The dichotomy discourse, further, Burke[4] believes, may reduce the richness of 'ideas, assumptions and practices' of premodern leisure to a monolithic trope. Burke highlights that both Nietzsche in *The Gay Sciences* (1882) and the Annales Historian Lucien Febvre in his oeuvre have not identified the themes of boredom or leisure in their histories of emotions as worthy of excavating and compiling.[5]

Civic Humanism in Europe impelled by bio-politics and what Foucault terms 'discipline' is evinced in the drive towards, what may be seen as sanitised, lawful or utilitarian leisure-recreation for the larger population. Norbert Elias places the rise of regulated leisure as part of a civilisational process of economic interconnectedness that industrial society brings about (Elias and Dunning 2008, 260–90). Foucault too sees a connection between regulation and the rise of leisure where 'some real existent in the world' is required to be 'the target of social regulation at a given moment' (Foucault 1994, 123; 2001, 171). For Foucault, 'the absence of work' can be madness (Foucault 1995) and not necessarily leisure. Thus, organised leisure seeks to withhold the right to be different and impels the individual to revert to a regulated social self (Foucault 1982, 781, 777–78). It is no surprise that what Deleuze terms the contemporary post technological 'control society "gamifies" unpaid labour whereby blurring the gap between labour and leisure'. For Deleuze and Guattari, leisure is both a 'becoming' and a negation of difference; a zone where a body-self can to an extent be conceived as a state of being, a period of empty time or an activity. Guattari suggests that while the assemblage or apparatus of social performance for the leisure may have varied at different points in history but within their own relational space these allowed for legitimate spaces of leisure as non-work as a retreat to the body or to an activity out of work and perhaps into timeless time.

Mihaly Csikszentmihalyi in his 1981 article 'Leisure and Socialization' critiques contemporary sociologists (Csikszentmihalyi 1981, 332–40). He argues that early 'optimal' experiences in everyone's life's journey partake nurturance, feeding and play. These primary experiences are inherently pleasing and set out a benchmark against which later occurrences are measured. Thus, with maturity, the most fulfilling experiences are seen to transpire contextualised with expressive leisure such as through games, sports, intimate interactions, artistic and religious activities. The early experiences, argues Csikszentmihalyi, stipulate a benchmark of fulfilment for later experiences. The dialectic between instrumental and expressive activities, Csikszentmihalyi argues, is innately see in the context of connotations established in leisure settings (Csikszentmihalyi 1981, 334). For him, 'leisure' comes to be seen to 'work' in certain sociological conditions. In primitive hunter-gather or subsistence farming societies, work and play are inseparably entwined: through song, dance, play or ritual (Firth 1929, 332; Csikszentmihalyi 1981, 332). In fact, Csikszentmihalyi concludes that gratification is not just the 'frosting on the cake' (Csikszentmihalyi 1981, 332); for a healthy society, it is essential for long-term survival as a boring system is not sustainable.

What Agamben (1998, 3) terms 'bare life' as against the philosophical 'form-of-life' can be used to excavate notions as to why leisure is denied in premodern societies. As bare life is produced from the gap between inherited conventional meaning (*phusis*) and the 'nature out there' (*nomos*), the form-of-life construct suggests that, for most premoderns, 'a life that can never be separated from its form, a life in which it is never possible to isolate and keep distinct something like a bare life' (Agamben 2015, 207).

Agamben says that, in the Aristotelian paradigm, humans are motivated to constitute a *polis* for survival while maintaining their natural life. The *polis* allows some of the priestly classes the leisure for philosophic contemplation, which for Aristotle is the highest possibility of free human life. In premodern times, this mode of leisure, it is believed by some, is, thus, not accessible except to exclusive classes that have taken care of necessities. The lives of the non-priests/ exclusive class are 'used' so that the exclusive are given the highest, free life, but the non-priests are excluded from this form of life (ibid., 2–23). Agamben instead argues that while classes use each other's bodies, the same does not lead to exclusion of lives from leisure the good life or, what amounts to the same.

Within this universal paradigm, one is required to locate and situate within premodern archives, Indian rejoicings, celebrations, aspirations and dynamic engagements with the notions of leisure. As regards the Indian Sociological perspectives on leisure, Ishwar Modi, a pioneer, believes leisure is an 'all pervasive phenomenon' (Modi 2012, 386), synonymous with culture and life itself. Does the excavation of leisure lay bare the cultural basis of the Indic Past? Here various categorisations have been applied and most popular of these, leisure and labour, are modern expressions. Labour enables man and Leisure makes good life possible. As regards the Indian notion of leisure, Modi's pioneering works traces how leisure practices have evolved in India in relation to social transformations. In the mid-1960s, Modi says that while people including academic colleagues around him were largely unaware of the common dictionary meaning of the term leisure, his rural respondents told him that *gup shup* or gossiping was their main leisure-time activity; in fact, for many of them leisure and gossiping were synonyms (Modi 2012, 386). For Durkheim, the cultural concept of leisure has two broad and specific dimensions: the religious dimension (Durkheim 1961; Modi 2012, 388) and the time dimension (ibid.). Modi argues that while religious rites and traditions impact leisure, given that the conception of time varies among different cultures, so does their role in determining attitudes towards leisure (Evans-Pritchard 1940; Brightbill and Meyer 1952; Paul 1953; Margaret 1955; Hughes 1961; Linder 1970, Modi 2012, 388).

For Modi, leisure activities in most traditional societies, particularly in India, were 'hierarchical, group institutionalised, group participation oriented, normative and rhythmic' (Modi 1985, 262). He says that in the traditional society subsuming of leisure in culture was integral to its worldview. 'Leisure was culture; the basis of culture was leisure' (Modi 2012, 390). Modi further argues that social structures influence the nature, form and extent of participation in leisure. 'Who participates in what, with whom, when, where, and to what extent is determined by the structure of a society according to its nature and organisation' (ibid.). Leisure, however, as Modi argues, helps create new structures and social norms (Modi 1985). As against this, the socio-psychological critique of leisure privileges the role of the individual and his personality in determining leisure activities (ibid., 262). This makes leisure a modernity linked individualistic phenomenon (Becker 1955; Havighurst 1957; Veblen 1957; Reisman 1961).

The premodern Indian attitude to leisure, while conforming to the general delineation by Modi, is perhaps more nuanced.[6] Interestingly, there is no single term in Sanskrit for leisure; it vaguely approximates *avakāśa*[7] or akarmanan that are states of non-activity. Bhoga and vilāsa[8] are twin terms that connote to enjoy and to luxuriate. In popular imagination, these are often conflated with *śauq'* or indulgences, when elevated as *rājasi* then as royal tastes and sports. Johan Huizinga not only looks at the roots of Western notions of play but also its Sanskrit roots (Huizinga 1950, 31–32). He recovers four root words *Kridati*, of playing in the classical sense of the word; *Divyati* in sense of gambling, dicing and mocking, joking etc; *las* (from which the terms *vilasa, alasya, alasata* are derived) which mean, movement and shining and pursuing: and *lila* (a term used for often for the actions of Indic gods) to denote 'light, aerial, frivolous…'as if 'appearance' (ibid., 32).

The trivarga and four *purusarthas—dharma*, *artha*, *kāma* and *mokshạ—* are not mutually exclusive but are supplementary and complementary (Bawa 2021, 4). *Dharma*, at a cosmic level, may have referred to an overarching world order and at the individual level to a mandated righteous way of living for each class; the *dhārmin* living is seen to bring about a spontaneity in actions and joy in what is done; whether work or leisure. While a certain discourse valorises austerity, *artha* suggests that all should work, often to create wealth and leisure. *Kāma* suggests gratification of the five senses and the mind and refers not to sensuality alone but to leisure, art, music, dance, beauty, affection, love and intimacy (Bawa 2021, 10–14). *Mokshạ*, while signifying liberation from the *samsara*, suggests eternal bliss. For Abhinavagupta, the emotional repose as suggested in *śānta-rasa* is predicated upon creative leisure that carries the subject beyond the mundane to higher domains (Timalsina 2020). Laziness or indolence as exemplified in the Sanskrit term *alasatā* too has widely varying connotations. In *Nāṭyaśāstra*, it is also known as *ālasya* and is amongst the thirty-three 'complementary or transitory states' (*vyabhicārimbhāva*) that accompany *sthāyinbhāva* or permanent state/dominant emotions. In the Indian sacred tradition, indulgence in *līlā*, sportiveness, which was ascribed as a supreme attribute, had profound consequences for the mundane.

It is in this context that the *nāgarakas* of *Kāmasūtra*, quintessential men of leisure, need to be seen. They cultivated and partook of fine arts like music dance and other sense pleasure were source of amusement (*vaihārika-śilpa* or *vinodasthāṇa*). In fact, it is believed that such *nāgarakas* along with other connoisseurs of the arts and courtesans debated on the texts on aesthetics and brought to the public debate art critiques as in *alaṅkāraśastra* (Bawa 2021, 55).

Seema Bawa explores the representation of the world of urbane men and women, *nāgarakas* and of gods who indulge in drinking wine, in leisurely surroundings through visual, literary and performative sources that suggests that wine drinking and even wine making was very much part of the 'imagined' daily life of people and of some gods who were associated with earth, prosperity and mirth such as Kubera Balarāma and the Nāga devatā. There are drinking parties, drinking vessels, drinking couples in courtly or domestic settings and intoxicated protagonists, which can be seen through not just bas relief narrative depictions but also material remains. The association of drinking with leisurely luxury is also indicated through its association with Greek, *yavana*, origins of wine and 'foreign' Greek women who drink and serve it. A study of the visual culture of drinking transmits and reifies ideas about values and behaviours that were implicit, if not explicit, within the early Indian cultural context that reflected shared social experiences.

The visual evidence also gives a gendered perception of women and wine drinking as part of the discourse of leisure and pleasure.

Looking at leisure and play in art forms, Huizinga refers to the Greek idea of a pastime providing both recreation and cognition (understanding). For Aristotle, music was not only for pleasure but also a means of education, because 'nature requires us not only to be able to work well but also to idle well' (Huizinga 1950, 160–61). In the Indian context, T.K. Venkatasubramanian, using Tamil musical texts and performances as a case study, has shown how leisure evolved from the idea of service. He asserts that, though leisure and labour are modern expressions, labour enables man and leisure makes good life possible. When we attempt to look for it in primitive conditions, the distinction is not sharp. The line between Leisure and Labour is seen as tenuous and shifting, especially in primitive societies and was not sharply drawn. Labour produced wealth and, when wealth got concentrated in few hands, leisure became the prize. It is believed that extended leisure depended on some kind of surplus wealth. Looking at the case of Tamil music in an evolutionary perspective, it is possible to track the trajectory of Labour (social) evolving into courtly entertainment from singing the praise of patron (chieftain) to lord is discernible. It is also the story of formation of subregional music traditions to live and for Leisure. He tracks the evolution of Tamil music, and its transformation as an ingredient of court culture, focusing on a single activity, namely, singing the praise of patrons. This development is examined across three stages, up to 300 CE, 300–750 CE and 750–1250 CE as it develops into courtly entertainment.

Mrityunjay Prabhakar observes that the elite, the *nāgarakas*, are shown as a category who have a lot of leisure; through entertainment provided for them, such as gaming, hunting, debating or socialising with same order of people, while at more personal level, they enjoy dancing, singing and other recreational activities in their personal spaces. He excavates the works of playwrights like Bhāsa, Kālidāsa, Harśā, Śūdraka, Bhavabhūti who devised a whole new act of leisure which has been portrayed in most of their plays like *Swapanavāsavdatta*, *Abhijñāna Śākuntalam*, *Mālavikāgnimitram*, *Vikramorvaśīyam*, *Priyadarśikā*, *Ratnāvali*, *Uttararāmacarita* and many others. Dramatic performances provided elite and popular entertainment, though most of these had an underlying moral and ethical message, there were always passages and episodes that were meant for pure entertainment. Another element often seen in most of the ancient Indian dramas is that these follow the narratives of the royalty, courtesan, merchants and other high-class people. These are set in garden/palace park/*samudra gṛha* or other private spaces where the protagonists could find solitude for their romances. These actions were used to fulfil one's goal of *artha* (political ambitions), *kāma* (*srngara*) or *moksha* (spiritual). Robert E. Goodwin terms this phenomenon as 'about creating an imaginative pleasure garden where the ultimate goal, attaining Siddhi could be nursed.' These leisure scenes carry romances, chance meetings of the lovebirds, coming closer of the loved ones through suggestive means, opening of one's heart to a close friend and through that to the lover.

Indic classical literature and folk narrative often privilege an elusive idyllic past of unlimited leisure where often laziness wins the day, over the zealous industry. Thus, characters like Kumbhakāran, Chillum Shoru (the name itself indicates his euphoric, intoxicated state), Shaikh Chilli or Mullah Nasruddin are demi heroic figures in the folk retelling of their exploits. A question emerges how and why there is an imagined past where leisure was unlimited and untrammelled by the burden of work? In the realm of divine boons and blessing, the mythical Kāmadhenū, an ever-giving wish fulfilling cow and Kalpatārū, the evergreen giving tree too valorise a world of toil-lessness, where work and luxuries are provided without labour, leaving time for untrammelled leisure. There is also the Indic idea of the Uttarakuru heaven where there is toil-less leisure, where fires burned and cooked food by themselves, crops grew without human effort, children drew nurture from the hands of the parents, etc. gives us a picture of the ideal world where work is not required to survive. These ideas incentivise leisure as a goal in the afterlife, if socioeconomic order and defined stations of life were maintained in the present.

Farhat Nasreen in her chapter explores the notion of sleep as offering free and precious time and perceptions around sleep that are built as epitomising leisure through Persian literature. She examines how sleep, though comparable with death, is vital for life and it also presents a rare paradox of repetition, which is not boring. Despite the notion that the overall availability of free time increased with the increasing use of machinery, leisure was available to the rich even in the preindustrial age. She presents the connection of sleep with leisure as having a complex and layered history, which she traces from Pauranic times to the Mughal rule. The fear of being labelled as 'lazy' invoked sleep related guilt in many, while the truly lazy ones slept feeling guiltless. However, for the rich, it was a ritual of luxurious leisure. Getting into philosophy beyond economic structures, sleep could postpone sorrow, pain, worries, guilt, boredom and decision making for everyone. It could shorten almost anything associated with consciousness—whether good or bad. For example, Emperor Akbar believed that a hack for increasing life is reducing sleep. If death could be an escape for people, sleep—the temporary death—could well be a temporary escape. On the other hand, it could also be a route to a destination that the sleeper looked forward to. No wonder human perceptions about sleep remain quite conflicted.

Her paper takes the reader into the Persian literature full of beautiful descriptions of not just setting up sleep but also giving it up. There were characters that cut a remarkably thin slice for sleep from their share of leisure. Maulana Jami's Zulekha dreamt of her beloved Yusuf in a dream and then lost her sleep for years, as she chased this dream. Nizami Ganjavi's Majnun lost his sleep over Laila. Ziauddin Nakshabi's Khojasta kept awake for many nights for a rendezvous with her lover while her husband was away on a business trip. So, it is not only about why people sleep, it is also about why they do not or cannot sleep.

The premise that in premodern Indian history the discourse of leisure is not only ambivalent in terms of censure or approbation but is also deeply gendered, with differential access to 'free time', and the history of recreation and relaxation too begs scholarly attention. Especially, in the textual tradition, leisure activities of women are usually invisible or vilified. In *Manusmṛiti*, the so-called essential nature of women, *strīsvabhāva*, is seen as entirely dedicated to leisure, laziness, gossip, jewellery, etc. (Manu, 9.17) *Kāma*, on the other hand, in the visual culture the feminine is epitomised by languor or *ālasya*, beautiful in indolence (*Silpa Prakasa* 46–47).[9] In *Kāma* texts and visual discourse, there is this imagination of the languorous leisure-able female (*Natyashastra* 6.45–6.48; Bawa 2021, 72). Men are identified through strength in masculine sporting activities such as wrestling or hunting. Even 'cultured' activities such as playing the lute project skill and knowledge of the civilised male rather than leisure.

Smita Sehgal asks the question whether leisure could be associated with a particular class or was it a phenomenon experienced across caste and class in early India? She tries to interrogate how an activity like 'hunting' is understood in early literary traditions and sees the links between a masculine sport for the king and elite in contradistinction to as an essential activity for survival by forest tribes. Similarly, she problematises gambling or '*dhyūta krīdā*' too as it appears as fun-sport that men across caste and class dabbled in but at the same time it could often be strategised into ruining an opponent not just financially but socially and politically too. All the activities have been portrayed in early Indian literature as *krīdā* or sport but in early India these were charged with significant masculine attributes. The two 'sports' of hunting and gambling were both gendered in terms of spectatorship as well as participation, which were largely reserved for men but had serious consequences for others including women such as Draupadī, Damyantī and Pārvatī associated with them. She intertwines the representation of leisure activities of 'hunting', and 'dice game' with masculine aspirations of power, wealth and status to unearth its deeper social implications towards material and gender inequities. Huizinga views dice playing as 'play' which makes it an integral part of ritual and religion (Huizinga 1950, 57–58).

Among the variety of sports and games, dicing too has embodied the masculine leisure and has been seen as being a primary part of urban leisurely life. According to Suchandra Ghosh, by the 2nd century CE, gambling-houses occupied an important role in the urban landscape. Winning a game of dice was largely a matter of chance with some amount of skill. She shows how the game of dice finds a pride of place in various texts and is represented in visuals as well. Besides the indoor games, she focuses on wrestling, another sport which became popular in the post-Mauryan period. Wrestling was a combative sport, between two persons, but watched by spectators, played within an arena and, thus, formed a part of public space. Through the reference to the presence of a gymnasium (*vyāyāmaśālā*) at Bandhogarh, in an inscription of about 165 CE, she shows that this was used for recreation for the travelling merchants. She illustrates this through the art of Gāndhāra, Bhārhut, Bodhgaya and Sāñchī where there is evidence of the practice of physical exercise in the form of wrestling and weightlifting. Weightlifting stones from Gāndhāra are evocative of preparation for wrestling. Wrestling, as a sport, received much patronage from the royal court and elites. Besides in art, there is plethora of literary examples in the *jātaka* stories of the practice of dicing and wrestling along with other texts. Suchandra Ghosh, therefore, ventures into the male world of dicing and wrestling, navigating through different genre of sources to document their transition from urban elite forms of leisure to popular pastimes. She raises the issue of spectatorship and audience in the act of watching a bout of wrestling or gambling as a form of spending leisure hours seen through sculptures from the Gāndhāra region. Through text and art, she raises the issue of the intersection between leisurely pursuit and sports turning into a professional endeavour also, bringing to light the multivalence of meanings of leisure in early India.

Hunting by gods and kings being one of the suitable leisure occupations where many narratives are set against the background of the ruler, hunting in the wilderness has been read by Marion Frenger in premodern South Asian contexts. Literary sources for these narratives include the stories about the former births of the Buddha (*jātakas*) and depictions of hunters—both professionals and leisure seekers—can be found in the earliest representations of these stories in reliefs at Buddhist sites. She contends that the attitude towards hunting as reflected in literature is, however, ambivalent. While its positive effects on the rulers physical and strategic abilities and usefulness as a display of his virility and military competence are generally appreciated, hunting, together with drinking, gambling and womanising, is also counted as one of the essential vices that are able to distract the attention from the core tasks of governance and can potentially have devastating consequences both for the ruler and his realm. Against this background, Frenger studies how the hunt became an integral part of the iconography of a deity particularly associated with and probably venerated by rulers—the god Revanta—who according to myth is a son of the sun god Sūrya whose representations appeared all over North India from the 6th century CE.

A significant element extolled in modernity and postmodernity is leisure travel but was viewed very differently in ancient and medieval eras. Travelling for broadening the mind was seen as an aberration. *Yātrās* or journeys (probably to holy places) undertaken by women were condemned by Aśoka as waste of time and effort. *Tīrthayātrās* or pilgrimage were extolled later in the *Purāṇas*. Travels for procuring luxury items by merchants while visible in textual and epigraphic traditions is more vocation oriented, though there are instances where merchants do indulge in exotic lands.

If there is one religion that is known for its strict adherence to ascetic and frugal ideals, then that would be the Jaina path of salvation. The Jina as the assumed founder or renewer of the doctrine is, therefore, considered the ideal ascetic. The life story of the Jina Mahāvīra and his predecessors is described in the Kālpasūtra, a text written around the middle of the 1st millennium AD. Countless illustrated manuscripts of this text were prepared in western India, especially in the 15th and 16th centuries. Patrick Krüger based on his study of these observes a dichotomy within the many of these *Kālpasūtra* that describe the life of an ascetic; paradoxically, the illustrations in these manuscripts focus primarily on leisure and recreational activities at court, where the future Jina grew up before his world renunciation. The descriptions in the *Kālpasūtra* text reflect the life of a royal upper class during the era of the creation of the text; the illustrations take up this theme and focus on the leisure activities of the elites whose representatives had the manuscripts produced and donated them to religious institutions. Consequently, the text and especially the illustrations reflect a tension between leisure and ascetic renunciation that characterises the Jaina communities consisting of ascetics and laymen until today. Krüger explores this contradictory motif and shows how leisure and pleasure are used to describe and emphasise the contrasting lives leading to the ascetic path of salvation of the Jina Mahāvīra and his predecessors. In Buddhist renunciatory discourse also, *alasatā* has negative connotations of sloth and laziness.

Designated spaces for leisure and recreation, courtly or public such as orchards, garden and performance spaces or transitional such as *baithaks* and roofs or semi-pubic areas existed across eras from early periods to the medieval. In these spaces dance, drama, banquets and *dastarkhwans* and *goṣṭhī* or *addās* of like-minded cultured people, dissipates and dissolute characters took place. The *bhāṇas* such as *Caturbhāṇī* describe the streets of town such as the *sarvabuama nagara* (Pāṭaliputra) as having many such places. Somadeva's *Kathāsaritsāgara* and Mankhala's *Srikantcharita*, attributed to the 11th and 12th centuries CE describe banqueting halls, drinking clubs (*pānagoṣṭhī*) which were visited by both men and women. The banquets and spaces such as these were centres of discussion, performance as a spectacle and critique of the arts.

Prem Kumar, whose paper explores early literary tradition as providing a meaningful representation of leisure and leisure spaces, has examined these in terms of early urban history. He excavates the words and their meaning used for 'having at leisure' such as *vinoda, kṣaṇa, prakramah, avakāśa, vitāna, vīchī* and *sāvakāśa, labdhāvakā, kahaṇita, kṣemya*. He places the varied activities they represent within physical landscape (spaces and places) that determine the patterns of relaxation and leisure experiences. Such leisure landscapes or leisure-scapes were the significant sites of the city. Various gardens in the city indicate enough space for leisure setup within the cityscape. The gardens were deeply embedded into the urban culture and intimately related to the urban landforms, architecture, arts, food, dress, festivity, politics, social interaction, leisure, pleasure and public and private lives. The gardens dominated the leisure and pleasure landscape of a city. Most of these gardens carry architectures associated with leisure as described in sources are well cognisant of the significance of paraphernalia of the garden as being interrelated with leisure and beauty, such as rows of plants, trees, bowers, pavilion swings, benches, ponds, artificial hills, birds, animals, etc. All aspects of leisure and pleasure, such as view, smell, sound, feel, etc. were considered essential to planning an urban garden. Recreation, leisure, romance, aestheticism and eroticism were integral to the garden landscapes and were for all urbanites along with other public or social leisure spaces of the city were along with gardens, highways, roads, streets, gambling salons and courtesan's quarters.

Vipul Singh explores the medieval spaces and spectacles as providing an antidote to work and goes on to see the transition and transformation of these spaces and activities in the colonial period. He has located these spaces in beautiful gardens for leisure that Lodis and the Mughals constructed around their monuments. The kings often went hunting with all their paraphernalia looking for wild animals in the dense forest. They also held various courtly performances in Agra and later in Delhi. The local communities lived away from the walled areas of the court, inhabiting the huge areas with dense forest in the surroundings and riverfronts of rivers to enjoy the cool evening breeze. Rituals, prayers, dance, community feasting, plays and *melas* often accompanied their daily work, and were, thus, major components of commoners' leisure activities. Under the colonial rule, the British officials continued the practice of hunting for their leisure, but for the common people the whole concept of leisure underwent a major transformation. While the parks and garden were developed, proclaiming healthy environment, public space performances were brought under the ambit of state supervision. The Dramatic Performance Act of 1876 censored the public space performances that were against the oppression of the colonial rule. Through the development of parks, recreational areas, clubs and circuses, an attempt was made by the British to make the local population to be part of amusement. Singh's chapter looks at the way the state facilitated commoners' leisure, but with some other unsaid intent. The other questions raised in the chapter include—was the state trying to achieve certain social outcomes through display of unknown sports and animals from different parts of the world? Did it work as an antidote to colonial resentments? How the parks, sports and circuses resembled the precolonial spectacles and leisure in some way and, thus, became easily acceptable to the public; and did leisure become more circumscribed because of it now being managed in a fixed space?

Raziuddin Aquil studies women poets who dabbled in emotional genre of Urdu poetry that focuses on the spirit of love—*ishq* and *muhabbat*—but have been kept on the margins in the history of arts and literature—these include wives and daughters of Mughal nobles, some who worked as courtesans, and were independent women known for their taste for nicer aspects of life such as poetry, music, dance and other art forms. Poetry was not their work; it was an activity in leisure. For courtesans, it was an extension of their work, showcasing their excellent attributes to enhance their credentials as public figures, artists and performers. It emerges that some of these personalities—professional or otherwise—conformed to traditional ideals, but some others defied traditional norms and could be thoroughly subversive. The histories of lives of poets and other excellent men and women are called *tazkiras* that provide an account of important events of the past and and take the form of literary-history. Aquil distills the compositions of some of these women poets presented by Nawab Mustafa Khan. Shaifta in his *tazkira*, *Gulshane Be-Khaar* who presented their work in such a way that the reader could easily understand their value. Shaifta retains the poets' independent mindedness and free flow of imagination, feelings and emotions. It could be highly romantic, less devotional and certainly not prudish. Aquil presents some enchanting examples of the place of women poets in Urdu biographies, women who were writing for pleasure or were articulating their emotional expressions through fine art of poetry, displaying their literary taste and flavour while also commenting on their trials, tribulations and situation.

The book ends with Rakshanda Jalil's exploration of imagined *Dehli ki Aakhri Shama*, The Last *Mushairā* of Delhi of Farhatullah Beg, set in the fictional date of 14th of Rajab, the year 1845, which is a fictional-historical account of what *might* have been the last *mushairā* of its kind held in Delhi, just before it was ravaged by the Mutiny. Its culture, poets and, above all, its language, the *zaban-e-Dehlī* was threatened by extinction. Rakshanda Jalil attempts a close reading of the text and uses it to make some observations about *mushairā*, public spaces and the tradition of reciting poetry before live audiences and fellow poets, bringing to life the *haveli* of Mubarakunnisa Begum in Hauz Qaz where the fictional *mushairā* takes place. It is here that the greatest poets of this age are about to come together—a bit like a rare astronomical alignment. The *haveli* is transformed into the ultimate spectacle of leisure, filled with the dazzling light from countless candles, lamps, lanterns, expensive woollen carpets, *gao-takhiyas* and cushions and white *chandni*-covered *farsh*. Burnished *huqqās* polished *pīkdān*, *khāsdan* and *pāndāns* mingled scent of musk, amber and *kewra* instruments of somatic pleasure and leisurely pursuits are described at length and the entire composition evokes a feeling of nostalgia for an age where leisure was treasured and privileged.

Within the mundane elite leisure is described, celebrated and projected; it is often provided by the toiling lower classes. Class and gender determine this interplay of leisure. Leisure is a calibrated activity and appropriate as per class, caste, gender, position and status and available in this world or vouchsafed in a promised after world. Alternately, surfeit of leisure leading to pathologies, as in the case of Mohammad Shah Rangila and Wajid Ali Shah, is also depicted and vilified in popular imagination. While indulgence is valid and legitimate for some, it is proscribed for others. Often pastimes of divine and human elite, like the royal hunt, or the visual pleasures of dancing girls, are romanticised. The underlying labour and the transactional nature that caters to this leisure is invisiblised. While some popular recreational activities are more participative, egalitarian and inclusive in their representation in literary and performative cultures, what comes across is the mutual exclusivity of notions and types of leisure. Thus, leisure is often imagined as a collective, though the experience may be individual.

Notes

1 Baramasa is a folk and devotional tradition of narrating the passage of seasons as seen through the twelve months, of which seasons such the summer and rainy season are given over to leisure activities. The *rāgamālā* is a painterly tradition of personification of *ragas* and *raginis* as young women and the moods of the raga are evoked though this. The protagonist is the *abhisārikā* who is shown in many poses of indolence and leisure that reflects the mood of the raga.

2 There is even an acronym for this amongst the Millennial Generation—FOMO, Fear of Missing Out.

3 Joffre Dumazedier's definition and redefinition of leisure has led to much debate it was originally published in 1962 and based on three functions of leisure identified in his empirical research in France. Three issues are addressed in this paper. First, aspects of the English translation of the definition, published in the USA in 1967, are found to be inappropriate and misleading. Second, attention is drawn to the unexplained omission of experiential features of leisure, also identified in Dumazedier's research. Third, it is observed that, in the 1970s, Dumazedier disavowed his original definition and replaced it with a more exclusive perspective identifying him with the 'Leisure Aristotleans'. Possible reasons for the original omission of experiential dimensions and for Dumazedier's decision to replace his definition with a very different one are discussed, together with consideration of why these matters have been largely ignored by leisure studies scholars. J. Dumazedier, *Towards a Society of Leisure*, translated by S.E. McClure (New York, 1967).

4 Burke also sites Lucien Febvre's thesis on the importance of excavating meaning from archival sources through examining gaps and 'absences' as also how words were understood in contemporary contexts; especially words that expressed the notions of a time or activity which indicated other than 'work'. Words such as Aristotle's distinction between *theoria* and *praxis*, 'the French loisir', the Latin terms otium as the opposite of the political negotium, *vița contemplativa* as against *vita active*. The contemplative vacatio has been seen in history as restorative, recreational and even redemptive at different points by different discourses. The dichotomy discourse also seems to identify that modernity brings into focus a new concept of time where time is largely linear and therefore nature and time both need to be appropriated to human will albeit for a structured planned leisure. This is seen in distinction to an imagined premodern world of seasonal festivals predicated on cyclical time and harmony with natural rhythms.

5 This given that there exist an entire class of literature in the west especially as the cusp of modernity, such as Boccacios's Decamerone and Castiglione's Cortegiano, where people are seeking to do something to pass the time. That the desire for 'pass time' is seen as both a pejorative and a positive has been highlighted by Burke who suggests that there at least four discourses that sought to deal with leisure and pastimes, viz., the educational, legal-political, theological-moral and medical discourses. The educational discourse included '(T)reatises on the training of children, or books on the ideal courtier, noble-man, housewife and so on' argue on the use or denial of leisure for education the legal-political debate includes the 'seventeenth-century England' one between Ben Jonson, Milton and Marvell 'in defence traditional holidays and pastimes, which were under threat for mixture of religious and economic reasons'. The theological-moral discourse sought to proscribe and restrict leisure keep them within strict limits while the medical discourse suggested the positives of 'psychological need for relaxation'.

6 An apocryphal joke/parable mentioned below illustrates the conflict between premodernity and its notion of leisure and the industrial age of toil.

Once there was a *jāt* (belonging to the north Indian farming community) who was sleeping on a charpoy under the shade of a tree. A representative of a potato chips making factory woke him and told him,
'You must introduce modern agricultural methods. Buy a tractor and a harvester, plant better seeds, dig another tubewell, put in more labour.'
The bewildered farmer asked, 'But why?'
The industrial man replied, 'So that you get more and more yields of potatoes.'
The farmer wanted to know, 'What will I do with more potatoes?'
The other man replied, 'You will sell these to us at a profit and then you can buy more land and equipment and then you will get rich. With all that money you can retire and can have more leisure.'
The *jāt* asked, 'You woke me up to tell me this. What do think I am doing now?'

7 (*-śaḥ*) 1. Leisure, opportunity. 2. Interval, space. 3. An open or wide space. 4. A receptacle, a repository, a place in which anything is kept. 5. A place, a spot, a situation. E. *ava* between, &c. *kāśa* to shine, *ac* aff.

8 Vilāsa (विलास) refers to pastimes, especially the playful amorous pastimes of Śrī Rādhā-Kṛṣṇa. [v.s. ...] sport, play, pastime, pleasure, diversion [especially] with women etc.; but also applied to any playful action or gesture), [*Mahābhārata*; Kāvya literature] etc. (*sāya*, 'for sport')
[v.s. ...] sport, play, pastime, pleasure, diversion ([especially] with women etc.; but also applied to any playful action or gesture), [*Mahābhārata*; Kāvya literature] etc. (*sāya*, 'for sport').

9 Local terminology it is called Naribandha and is indispensable in architecture. *Gandharvas*, *Yaksha*s, Raksasas, *Pannagas, Kinnaras* become enchanted on seeing the graceful postures of women. Woman is the most beautiful, when adorned with all ornaments. Contemplated in various postures, she is known as *Alasa,* indolent.

References

Agamben G. 2015. *The Use of Bodies*, translated by Kotsko A. Stanford. CA: Stanford University Press.

Aristophanes. 2012. *Clouds*. New York: Cambridge University Press.

Balme, Maurice. 1984. 'Attitudes to Work and Leisure in Ancient Greece'. *Greece & Rome*, Vol. 31 (2): 140–52.

Bawa, Seema. 2021. *Locating Pleasure in Indian History: Prescribed and Proscribed Desires in Literary and Visual Cultures*. New Delhi: Bloomsbury Publishing.

Becker, Howard S. 1955. 'Becoming a Marihuana User'. In *Mental Health and Mental Disorder*, edited by Arnold Rose. New York: W.W. Norton.

Brightbill, Charles K. and Harold D. Meyer. 1952. *Recreation: Text and Reading*. New York: Prentice-Hall Inc.

Burke, Peter. 1995. 'The Invention of Leisure in Early Modern Europe'. *Past & Present*, no. 146: 136–50.

Castiglione, Baldesar. 1967. *The Book of the Courtier*, translated by George Bull. London: Penguin Books.

Csikszentmihalyi, Mihaly. 1981. 'Leisure and Socialization'. *Social Forces*, Vol. 60 (2): 332–40.

Daud, Ali. 2004. *Courtly Culture and Political Life in Early Medieval India*. Cambridge: Cambridge University Press.

De Grazia, S. 1962. *Of Time, Work, and Leisure*. New York: Twentieth Century Fund.

Dumazedier, J. 1967. *Toward a Society of Leisure*, translated by S.E. McClure. New York: Free Press.

Durkheim, Emile. 1961. *The Elementary Forms of the Religious Life*. New York: Collier Books.

Elias, N. and E. Dunning. 1986. *Quest for Excitement: Sport and Leisure in the Civilising Process*. Oxford: Basil Blackwell.

———. 2008. *Quest for Excitement: Sport and Leisure in the Civilizing Process*, Collected Works, Vol. 7. Dublin: UCD Press.

Evans-Pritchard, E.E. 1940. *The New: A Description of the Modes of Livelihood and Political Institutions of a Nilotic people*. Oxford: Clarendon Press.

Firth, R. 1929. *Primitive Economics of the New Zealand Maori*. New York: Dutton.

Foucault, M. 1982. 'The Subject and Power', translated by L. Sawyer. *Critical Inquiry*, Vol. 8 (4): 777–95.

———. 1994. 'Problematics: Excerpts from Conversations', in R. Reynolds and T. Zummer (eds), *Crash: Nostalgia for the Absence of Cyberspace*. New York: Third Waxing Space, pp. 121–27.

———. 1995. 'Madness, the Absence of Work', translated by P. Stastny and D. Şengel, *Critical Inquiry*, Vol. 21 (2): 290–98.

———. 2001. *Fearless Speech*, edited by J. Pearson. Los Angeles, CA: Semiotext(e).

Hain, Kathryn A. 2020. 'The Prestige Makers: Greek Slave Women in Ancient India'. *Journal of World History*, Vol. 31 (2): 265–94.

Havighurst, Robert J. 1957. 'The Leisure Activities of the Middle-Aged'. *American Journal of Sociology*, Vol. 62 (2): 152–62.

Hughes, Charles C. 1961. 'The Concept and Use of time in the Middle Years: The St Lawrence Island Eakimos'. In *Ageing and Leisure*, edited by Roberts W. Kellmeier. New York: Oxford University Press.

Huizinga, Johan. 1950. *Homo Ludens: A Study of the Play Element in Culture*. New York: Roy Publishers (republished 2014 by Marino Publishing, Mansfield Centre CT).

Hunnicutt, Benjamin Kline. 1989. 'Leisure and Play in Plato's Teaching and Philosophy of Learning'. *Leisure Sciences, an Interdisciplinary Journal*, Vol. XII (2): 211–27.

Kaplan, Max. 1960. *Leisure in America: A Social Inquiry*. New York: John Wiley and Sons.

Kaulacara, Ramacandra, Alice Boner and Sadasiva Rath Sarma (eds). 1966. *Silpa Prakasa: Medieval Orissan Sanskrit Text on Temple Architecture*. Leiden: Brill.

Kraus, R. 1990. *Recreation and Leisure in Modern Society* (4th ed.). New York: HarperCollins.

Larrabee, E. and R. Meyersohn (eds). 1986. *Mass Leisure*. Glencoe: Free Press.

Linder, Staffan Burenstam. 1970. *The Harried Leisure Class*. New York: Columbia University Press.

Marfany, Joan-Lluís. 1997. 'The Invention of Leisure in Early Modern Europe'. *Past & Present*, 156: 174–91.

Mead, Margaret (ed.). 1955. *Cultural Patterns and Technical Change*. New York: UNESCO Report, Mentor.

Melvin, James R. 1974. 'A Theory of Leisure'. *Eastern Economic Journal*, Vol. 1 (4): 251–67.

Mendoni, Lina G. 1989. 'More Inscriptions from Keos'. *The Annuals of the British School at Athens*, 84: 291–92.

Miller, Toby. 'Michel Foucalt and Leisure'. Online available at: https://linkprotect.cudasvc.com/url?a=https%3a%2f%2fmedia.tobymiller.org%2fimages%2f-Sports%2fMichel%2520Foucalt%2520and%2520Leisure.pdf&c=E,1,eU-7VRDaYlhrpRddDoVjfYBqdh1Too9p3P6im9kWMHiLl0OvwrjiV6gtSiI-YDjJasVToR9bJPcaPKmD9_8KPlpFuHpR_nGBdvCA4PqAK4&typo=1" \t "_blank"; https://media.tobymiller.org/images/Sports/Michel%20Fou-calt%20and%20Leisure.pdf (accessed on 20-10-2023).

Modi, Ishwar. 1985. *Leisure, Mass media and Social Structure*. Jaipur: Rawat Publications.

———. 2012. 'Leisure and Social Transformation'. *Sociological Bulletin*, Vol. 61 (3): 386–403.

Mosseâ, C. 1969. *The Ancient World at Work*, translated by J. Lloyd. New York: W.W. Norton & Co.

Nàtyasàstra ascribed to Bharata Muni, 2 Volumes, edited and translated by Manmohan Ghosh. Calcutta: Ganthalya Pvt. Ltd, 1967.

Olivelle, Patrick (trans.). 2005. *Manu's Code of Law*. New York: Oxford University Press.

Paul, Bohannan. 1953. 'Concept of Time among the Tiv of Nigeria', *Southwestern Journal of Anthropology*, Vol. 9 (3): 251–62.

Reisman, David. 1961. *The Lovely Crowd*. New Haven: Yale University Press.

Sessoms, D. 1984. *Leisure Services* (6th ed.). Englewood Cliffs, NJ: Prentice-Hall.

Sylvester, Charles. 1999. 'The Classical Idea of Leisure: Cultural Ideal or Class Prejudice?'. *Leisure Sciences*, Vol. 21 (1): 3–16.

Timalsina, Sthaneshwar. 2020. 'Abhinavagupta on Śānta Rasa the Logic of Emotional Repose', *Handbook of Logical Thought in India*. Available at https://www.academia.edu/43929896/Abhinavagupta_on_Śā_nta_Rasa_The_Logic_of_Emotional_Repose (accessed on 1 June 2023).

Tilgher, Adriano. 1930. *Homo Faber: Work through the Ages*. Chicago: Renery.

Turner, Christopher. 2020. 'Trouble in Paradise: Aristotle's Ideal Polis & Political Exclusion'. *Revista Portuguesa De Filosofia*, Vol. 76 (1): 209–36.

Vatsyayana and Mallanaga. 2003. *Kama Sutra*, edited and translated by Wendy Doniger and Sudhir Kakar. Oxford and New York: Oxford University Press.

Veblen, Thorstein. 1957. *The Theory of the Leisure Class*. London: Allen & Unwin.

1

WINE, GODS, MEN AND WOMEN: LEISURE IN THE VISUAL CULTURE OF EARLY INDIA

Seema Bawa

My continuing research into the social history of early Indian art, representing as it does a complex web of ritual, theology and representations of popular themes and interests, has attempted to read into emotions and experiences of the past as embodied in artistic productions, such as pleasure and, its subset, leisure.

Wine drinking, the leisurely attributes of the *mithuna*, *yākṣī* or young maidens or even gods may be conceptualised within the broader discourse of leisure which, like pleasure, is sited within the domain of *kāma;* one of the dimensions of *trivarga* that represent three chief spheres of human activities and pursuits that benefit those who perform them, that is, *dharma, artha, kāma*. In the ancient Indian worldview, a combination of all three 'similar' and 'beneficial' actions are favourable to a person's happiness (*prīti*) (Olivelle 2019, 381; Bawa 2021, 3–5).

Visual representations of leisure in the early period, as I have explored elsewhere, should be contextualised within a consistent and methodical iconographic programme that privileges the discourse of beauty, physicality (Bawa 2013, 23–28, 32–40) and pleasure (Bawa 2021, 54–93). This was displayed, celebrated and highlighted in Buddhist, Jaina and other architectural buildings in the post-Mauryan period. A survey of 1st–3rd-century art at both Gandhara and Mathurā reveals a plethora of sculptural evidence that suggests that wine drinking and even wine making was very much part of the imagined daily life of people. There are drinking parties, drinking vessels, drinking couples in courtly or domestic settings and intoxicated protagonists. An aspect of leisure that is located within performance or the 'performative' display in the visual culture during Kusāna times is also explored here. Leisure may be inferred from the activity depicted, the interactive exchange within the sculpted composition or the concept it tries to communicate. Often scenes of entertainment are shown which constituted leisure for the viewers of the same. One of the earliest depictions is from Bharhūt, where a scene with acrobats who are making a human pyramid (Fig. 1.1) seemed aimed at not only the entertainment of the imagined audience within the sculpture but also the viewer present.

The representation of such interactive scenes of leisure does not seem to continue into the subsequent centuries as art from the Gupta period onwards becomes conventionalised into an iconographic schema that lays lesser emphasis on the quotidian aspects. The distinction between premodernity and its relationship with leisure as a concept and idealised activity has been discussed in the introduction.

Drinking intoxicating liquor has been studied since the 19th century, especially in the context of the ritual drinks of *soma* and *surâ*. The early historiography on wine has concentrated on the origins, methods and materials of brewing, with an emphasis on literary sources with Rajendralal Mitra (1878), bringing out the most extensively researched work in this direction. D.N. Jha's edited book (Jha 2020), which includes Mitra's contribution (ibid., 69–98) is in the same direction. In terms of art history, Dionysian and Bacchanalian association of Gandharan art has been a focus, with Martha Carter (1968, 1982) and Seungjung Kim's (2011) works shedding light on this. In a recent intervention, Suchandra Ghosh (2019) has placed drinking scenes in visual and literary cultures

Figure 1.1. Acrobats, railing pillar, 1st century BCE, Bharhut, Satna district, Madhya Pradesh

as part of representing quotidian life. Ardhendu Ray (2014) has used drinking scenes from the Sanghol sculptures to discuss the brewing and other material processes that would have existed in the early times while McHugh has focused on the production and consumption of grape wine.

The Leisure of Gods, Men and Women

The imagery of Indra, the lord of *devas*, who lives in his heavenly palace enjoying the spectacle of dancing, music and feasting in his Indra-*sabhā*, with *apsāras* dancing and wine being imbibed by the male audience of *devas*, is an epitome of enjoyment of courtly leisure in popular visual culture. In early art and architecture, especially between the 1st and 3rd centuries CE, there is a plethora of sculptures that represent wine drinking. While there is a preponderance of such depictions at Gandhara and Mathurā, adjacent sites have also shown that wine-drinking culture was present and quite visible.

In the present study, I have tried to view drinking 'wine' and its consequences, that is, the state of intoxication as a leisure activity as a symbolic representation of the sociocultural milieu and attitudes through some sculptural types. That we often find more than one example with some changes in the composition or permutation and combination of characters proves not just the popularity of the themes but also the collective and cognitive understanding of its symbolism and semiotics. Locales, especially urban spaces where festivals (*utsava*), soirees (*goṣṭhī, samāja*), a music, dance and theatre performances (*sangītaka, preksā*) or on picnics (*gosthīyāna*) (Kaul 2010, 212), accompanied by wine drinking and serving are often shown in literary and visual culture within a socially complex organisation where leisure is regulated and celebrated.

Intoxicated Gods

A sculpture type found from Mathurā belonging to the Kuṣāṇa period is that of the oft-published double-sided piece made out of a block of stone that has a drinking scene and a drunken person on the panels. The finest example of this type is from Pālīkherā, which had been previously identified as Silenus and Dionysius[1] but now the identity of the main figure as Kubera has been widely accepted. Both sides show a potbellied, quite plump, male figure surrounded by attendant figures. On the obverse, we see the act of drinking where the main male figure is seated on a rocky throne holding a cup with a handle in one hand while the other is resting on his thigh (Fig. 1.2). To the right is a woman

Figure 1.2. Kubera drinking in company, Obverse, 1st century CE, double-sided panel, Pālīkherā, Mathurā, now in Mathurā Museum

holding a similar cup. The cups are decorated with a vine design and are quite ornamental in appearance (Fig. 1.3). On the left are three figures; there is a taller woman to the immediate right of the corpulent male who holds a similar cup while the other (shorter) woman to further right holds a bunch of grapes. There is a male figure at the back but his face and features are defaced and the diminutive figure of a boy is carved in the foreground touching the thigh of the main figure. The attendant figures are dressed in typical north-western attire seen in Gandharan sculptures of long pleated robes tied at the waist, which was inspired by Hellenistic and Roman clothing. The hairdo of the taller woman with a roll over the forehead is also very much in keeping with the fashion of depicting Hellenistic Scythian women at Mathurā such as the Kambojika sculpture (Fig. 1.4).[2]

On the reverse is the very evocative scene with the corpulent figure leaning towards the left as if overcome, inebriated or somehow not in possession of his full senses (Fig. 1.5). A female on the right and a male on the left are supporting him. The female figure wears similar clothes as those on the obverse and the male wears a cloak over a toga-like garment. The main corpulent figure is bare-chested and wears a *dhoti* but the obligatory ornaments associated with *yākṣa*'s are not visible. The diminutive child is again touching the knee of the seated figure here also. The main figure is shown seated on the same mound

Figure 1.3. Detail of cup, Kubera drinking in company, obverse, 1st century CE, double-sided panel, Pālīkherā, Mathurā, now in Mathurā Museum

Figure 1.4. Kambojika, a woman dressed in north-western Indian apparel, 1st–2nd century CE, Mathurā, now in Mathurā Museum

Figure 1.5. Kubera intoxicated and overcome, reverse, 1st century CE, double-sided panel, Pālīkherā, Mathurā, now in Mathurā Museum

as on the obverse that seems to show a rocky or hilly outcrop. This may represent Alaka, the kingdom of Kubera or just a garden setting.

The two sides are narrating two episodes from a story that involves drinking and inebriation from excess of the same. There is a grapevine and Aśoka leaves with fruits carved on the sides of the panels that connects the two sides into one composition. The whole is topped by a bowl with lotus petals carved on that also gives it an appearance of being a single object. There is another bowl dedicated to the Buddhist Mahāsamghīkā sect from Pālīkherā (Carter 1968, 125).[3] The purpose and function of these bowls is much debated as they were placed in religious establishments; these may have contained water for ritual ablutions or solicited offerings in kind or were meant for flower offering. Given the subject matter of some of the panels, these may have been used for keeping wine as offering or ritual use. Read with Falk's interpretation of inscribed wine vessels from Gandharan monastic complexes discussed below, the bowls as wine containers may be plausible (Falk 2009). In V.S. Agarwala's opinion, vines, grapes along with bough of Aśoka trees carved on the inside and outside of stone bowls is linked to the widespread import and use of wine in the times of the Kuṣāṇas, rather than indicating indigenous production (Agrawala 1936, 133).

Another double-sided panel from Mathurā is now housed in the Indian Museum, Kolkata. On the obverse (Fig. 1.6) is the same composition as the Pālīkherā panel's reverse with the inebriated pot-bellied figure, down to the last detail. On the reverse (Fig. 1.7), interestingly, are two couples in a garden setting; the one on the left, the

Figure 1.6. Kubera intoxicated and overcome, obverse, 1st century CE, double-sided panel, so called Silenus panel, Mathurā, now in Indian Museum, Kolkata

Figure 1.7. Frolicking couples, reverse, 1st century CE, double-sided panel, so called Silenus panel, Mathurā, now in Indian Museum, Kolkata

male is clasping the arm of the female while the other arm is wrapped around her shoulder. The woman holds up her *uttarīya* like garment, which has slipped down over the tunic and skirt. The man has a cloak around his shoulders and is standing in a relaxed attitude with one leg crossed behind the front leg. The couple on the right is in less interactive posture and stand facing the viewer. The genitals of the male can be seen through the clothes. A vessel containing some kind of liquid stands on the ground between them. A bowl tops the panels. This scene of revelry suggests a drinking party in a leisure garden, perhaps a part of the spring festival, the *vasanta maha* that invokes the Kāmadeva and involves sportive and leisurely activities (Agarwala 2015, 744, 812–15).

A double-sided panel with a bowl atop it, called the Maholī slab or the Vasantasenā depictions from Mathurā, now housed in the National Museum, shows a kneeling woman being helped up by her attendants/lovers, one of who holds a cup in his hands (Fig. 1.8). The popularity of this depiction can be discerned from the fact that multiple versions of these were made all over north India during the first two centuries of the Common Era (Bawa 2013, 269–294; Bawa 2021, 75–78; Stadtner 1996, 42). In a truncated version at Sanghol, a woman shown kneeling with a male companion helping her rise or keep her from falling down (Fig. 1.9), Monika Zin in a forthcoming publication has identified the male as *vidūṣaka* from the crow's feet or kaka pada design on his head. The scene is set under a flowering tree. This suggests a strong interrelationship between performative elements and sculptural art (Bawa 2021, 61, 73) as is demonstrated through sculptures such as these and those of *stambha yoṣītā*'s discussed below.

Figure 1.8. Drunk or woman kneeling, 2nd century CE, reverse of double-sided panel, Maholi, now in Mathurā Museum

Figure 1.9. Kneeling woman with a male companion, railing pillar, 2nd century CE, Sanghol, now in Sanghol Museum

Coming back to Kubera-Vaiśravaṇa-Jambhala clasping a 'wine' goblet or cup, he is shown in the manner depicting Kubera as the *yākṣa* king. This is also an attribute of his iconography be it his depiction as an individual and as a couple with his wife Hāritī (Bawa 2013, Figs 3.3.5, 3.2.7, 3.2.8, 3.2.9, 3.2.10, 3.2.11, 3.2.12) that evolves both at Mathurā and Gandhara (for the *yākṣa* origin of Kubera's iconography (see Banerjea 2002, 338–42). The difference is that unlike the Pālīkherā panels he is not shown as heavily intoxicated or in a narrative setting.

Nevertheless, Kubera is definitely shown associated with drinking activities, probably because of his status as *yākṣa raja* who enjoys worldly delights as part of his kingly as well as his *yākṣa* character. There are numerous depictions of Kubera seated in a squatting posture (Fig. 1.10), holding a cup with or without his spouse Hāritī. In a typical depiction from Mathurā, the pot-bellied Kubera sits on a platform (Fig. 1.11) in a squatting position. A ribbon from the back hangs over his chest and arms, with the right hand holding a goblet and the left probably holding something to cover the drinking cup. His expressions remain static and calm, with eyes closed, broad nose and locked lips. Two women seem to be peeping behind her left shoulder, while behind his right shoulder is a diminutive and smaller version of a pot-bellied *yākṣa*. His hair is arranged in curly ringlets combed at the back with

Figure 1.10. Kubera with a cup, 2nd century CE, Kankāli Tilā, Mathurā, now in Lucknow State Museum

Courtesy: AIIS.

Figure 1.11. Kubera with a cup, 6th century CE, Mathurā, now in Mathurā Museum

a large bowl crowning his head. In another example from Mathurā, he is seated on the right holding a cup with Hāritī on the left and a group of devotees on further left (Fig. 1.12). The more royal aspect of Kubera with a kantharos-like cup in his hand is seen in the Gandharan examples (Carter 1968, 127fn7; Bawa 2013, Figs 3.1.12, 3.2.13). Falk links consumption of young wine with the worship of Pāñcika and Hārītī, who were present as statues inside the monastery, who were shown drinking as well or holding a grape (Falk 2009, 75).

Kubera is not the only god who is shown with a cup. Balarāma–Sankarṣana has a wine cup as an attribute (Shaw 2004, 5–59).[4] Often, Kubera, Nāgas and Balarāma, as an embodiment of Seṣa Nāga, are associated with one another. In fact, in a Buddhist agricultural manual, Kubera recommends the worship of Nāga devatā at the time of drought with various rituals that include the use of liquor, incense, flowers, honey and other items used to entice the gods and men for pleasure.[5]

In a sculpture of *Samkarṣana* within the emanating figure of *Samkarṣana* Caturvyūhā Viṣṇu in the Mathurā Museum, there is a cup with a stand (Fig. 1.13), similar to the one held by Kubera in his hand. A similar cup is again noticed in another image now in Mathurā Museum (Fig. 1.14) where the cup with a stand is held by the handle in god's left hand. He is shown wearing a *vanamala* under the seven hoods of the Ananta or Seṣa Nāga, with a diademed turban on his head while his masculine aspect is clearly visible in genitals under the *dhoti*. In a similar standing image of Balarāma from the Norton Simon collection, he stands in front of the seven hooded coiled Ananta or Seṣa Nāga, the cup held in his left hand is a prominent attribute while the right hand is upraised. In a similar depiction in Yamunā Bagh in Mathurā, a graceful

Figure 1.12. Kuabera with a cup, along with Hāritī and devotees, 2nd century CE, Mathurā, now in Indian Museum, Kolkata

Figure 1.13. Detail of *Samkarṣana* with a cup, Caturvyuha Visnu, 1st century CE, Mathurā, now in Mathurā Museum

Figure 1.14. Balarāma with a cup under a Naga hood, 2nd century CE, Mathurā, Mathurā Museum

Courtesy: AIIS.

figure of Balarāma, attributed to the Gupta period, stands in front of Ananta holding a cup in his left hand. The iconography of Balarāma with a cup is well established and, in a composition from 9th-century, Bajna, he is again shown with a cup. Balarāma is an agrarian deity with hala or ploughshare as one of his attributes or āyudha, while in other hands he holds a musala or corn pounder and a drinking cup or vessel (*panapatra*) (Fig. 1.15), emphasising his inebriety (for iconography of Balarāma, see Banerjea 2002: 306). In the *Viṣṇudharmottara Purāṇa* among the many characteristics of Balādeva is the ploughshare, conch and/or drinking bowl-in his left hand of his representing a Sea of wine, *śūra ambhū dih* (VDM III.65, Maxwell unpublished translation). Maxwell comments that the drinking bowl, the sea of *surâ* (wine) indicate the god's characteristic drunkenness *mada-vibhramaḥ-locanaḥ*, which is also commented upon in Varāhamihira's *Bṛhat Saṁhitā* (58.36).

That this drunkenness is part of Balarāma's characteristic behaviour may be located within the discourse of pleasure and leisure is clearly delineated in the *Bhāgvata Purāṇa*. In the episode that happened

Figure 1.15. Balarāma with a cup and attendants, 10th century CE, Bajna

Courtesy: AIIS.

on the Gomanta hill, Kṛiṣṇa and Balarāma are shown roaming in the forest of the hill in search of sport, where they are separated. Sankarṣana is fanned by sweet-smelling wind and the smell of wine that awakens the desire to drink and soon he becomes drunk and consorts with the wine incarnate Vāruṇi and other goddesses.[6] He, in fact, is surrounded by goddesses, wine and frolic as he spends the day in picnic and enjoyment.

Women as Agents of Leisure

Of all the activities shown on railing pillars of Buddhist and Jaina religious edifices from Mathurā of the sculpted young women, drinking is often shown as a social spectacle, involving more than just one person. In the art historical literature, such 'damsels' are described in terms of indulging in Madirāpāna or wine drinking. Women in association with drinking vessels presumably associated with spirituous liquids may be shown alone, but most often men are shown in company of women. In fact, frequently, the depictions are quite interactive, inviting the onlooker to witness and participate, as will be seen under.

The association of women and wine as being the epitome of attractiveness and temptation can be seen Canto 4 of Aśvaghosa's *Buddhacarita* where Śuddhodana, Gautama's father, ordered the women of the palace to seduce and divert Gautama from abandoning the world by enchanting his senses with worldly pleasures, especially by women being intoxicated with liquor (*madanīya varījitah*) and touching him with their firm, rounded (*pina*), close-set (*sahatā*) and charming breasts (*stana*) (*Buddhacarita*, IV, 29–35).

The centrality of women to creating and participating in somatic pleasures and aiding it as being objects of leisure has been elaborated by Yaśodharā who says basic sex is centred on the unrestrained, beautiful, young, amorous women who are flirtatious, clever at flattery and skillful in drawing one to themselves. However, Kāmā is pleasure, and its limbs are jewellery, perfumed oils and garlands as well as forest groves, roof-top gardens, the playing of lutes and wine (*Kāmasūtra* xlviii–xlix). Thus, spaces and objects related to leisure that enhance the feeling of pleasure when located in the feminine is privileged.

In context of Gandharan wine-making representations, Falk significantly says that an amorous and erotic scene of a man approaching a woman always accompanies wine drinking. Wine consumption is read as 'legitimizing the popular practices' through organisational participation of monastic establishments which soon led to participation in general, 'with the concerned monks finding an excuse for drinking and erotic encounters by creating religious construction' (Falk 2009, 75).

Even up to the 11th century, it is stated in the *Mānasollāsa*, attributed to Someśvara III, that grape juice and its wine was the favourite of young women (McHugh 2021, 116).

The first examples of shared drinking activity between men and women are indeed not from Mathurā but from an early sculpture from Patna. A *mithuna* with the woman leaning against the stem a tree trunk, her left arm enfolding the man's shoulder and her right arm holds the waist band or the *mekhalā*. The man on her right embraces the woman with his right hand. In his left hand he holds a drinking cup, which he offers her, the cup touching her breast. The woman face is turned away in a coy gesture. The slab is perforated between the two figures above and below the arms of the couple where the cup is placed. Between the couple resting on the pedestal is a tall object made of woven cane, held together with a rope, with something, perhaps some small vessel, resting on top (Fig. 1.16). The whole composition is set under the bough of a tree. The museum catalogue says that it is made of buff sandstone with traces of red paint (Plate VI) (Acc No. 8178). In a railing pillar relief of *yākṣa-yākṣī* from Amin, dated to the 2nd century BCE, the male companion standing on the left hands *her* a cup with his right hand (Fig. 1.17).

At Bharhūt and Sanchī, there are no clear depictions of drinking activity, but, from 1st century CE onwards, there is a plethora of representations of wine vessels, drinking and perhaps intoxication from the Mathurā atelier. There are many versions of the composition as mentioned above; the similarity is so striking that it seems as if the

Figure 1.16. *Mithuna* under an Aśoka tree, male offering wine to female, 2nd century BC, Patna Museum, Bihar, Arch 8178

Courtesy: AIIS.

Figure 1.17. *Yākṣa* offering a cup to *yākṣī*, 2nd century BCE, Amin, now in National Museum, Delhi

patron asked for a copy of a sculpture he or she may have seen and wanted copied.

Since there is such similitude in representation, I have classified these according to types. Type one consists of *yākṣī-yoṣītās*, holding a *surāh*-like vessel (Fig. 1.18), offering it to the spectator figure carved above the main sculpture and also to the viewer who may perceive such a depiction as symbolising fertility, sensuality and visual pleasure. The main female figure of Fig. 1.18 series stands in a *tribhaṅga* posture in the first three images with the right leg maintaining the load of the entire body, while the left leg stands at ease bent at the knees or in the last image in a less pronounced *tribhaṅga* posture. The right hand either swings along the waist holding a bunch of grapes (in Figs 1.18.1. and 1.18.2) or bends at the elbow upwards carrying a mirror or below the waist bearing a flute-like object, diagonally positioned from the thighs up to the waistline (Fig. 1.18.4). Interestingly, the left hand in all four cases is bent at the elbow, facing upwards to hold a *surāhī*-like vessel capped with a drinking glass, which almost always has a design engraved with either a pattern of alternating and well-spaced six circular petal flowers and a heart-shaped design with a drop circle to its top (Figs 1.18.1 and 1.18.4) engraved. In contrast, in one example, there is a simple horizontal line running from the centre covering its entire width

Figure 1.18. Women holding a *surāhī*-like vessel fom Mathurā (Fig. 1.18.1), Ropar (Figs 1.18.2) and Sanghol (Figs 1.18.3 and 1.18.4), railing post, 2nd century CE. Below are the magnified images of the *surāhīs* in the same order

(Fig. 1.18.2) or engraved with three circles, two circles topped with the third in a pyramidal pattern. The drinking cups that top the *surāhī* have a single pattern of two horizontal lines closely packed together across the glass and repeating themselves at some space across the length of the cup. In two depictions, there is a bunch of grapes in one hand and, in Fig. 1.18.3, she holds up a mirror and the last depiction has her holding a flute like instrument. The grapes reinforce the idea of wine in the *surāhī*, while the mirror and the flute reinforce the idea of beauty and leisure.

The vessel and the cups become more noteworthy, as three of the four images show an interaction with the spectator figures in the upper register of the composition. In Fig. 1.18.1, the *mithuna*, the couple, with the female gazing at the male and both clasping each other across the shoulders are shown, the male figure to the left extends his left hand below the *vedikā* to clasp to the cup. In Fig. 1.18.2, though much abraded, one can see a single male figure above the *vedikā* who holds on to it with the right arm, as if struggling to climb out of its enclosing space, while the left hand drops down to grasp the glass. In Fig. 1.18.4, a dwarfish figure peeps from above a hanging curtain that is weighted down in curve at the centre and held up at both ends by pilasters. His diagonally directed gaze reinforces the importance of the *surāhī* as he looks at it perhaps displaying his temptation to drink from the latter. In all the depictions, the expressions of the *yākṣīs*' are gentle, with smiling faces and open eye set in roundish oval faces, slightly tilted to the right side (in Figs 1.18.1, 1.18.2 and 1.18.4) or facing straight, with a steady gaze at their audience (Fig. 1.18.3). The effortlessness with which, in all four cases, they hold the *surāhī* with the drinking cup in their left hand while simultaneously holding something in their right hand indicates the familiarity with image being part of social mores of the time.

The *yākṣīs* are shown standing on pedestals decorated with diagonal, plain and beaded lines with two flowers flanking the northern and southern corners (as in Fig. 1.18.2) with dwarf *yākṣas* with enlarged heads or a *makara*.

As is with the early Mathurā art tradition, the *yoṣītā-yākṣīs*' are shown as beautiful and youthful with slender waists, prominent round breasts and exposed genitals (in three of the four cases). Adorning their waists are five or four-tiered *mekhalā*, above which is either a knotted sash with its ends flowing up to the feet along the left thigh (Figs 1.18.1 and 1.18.2) or flowing at length with pleated folds on both sides of the waist Fig. 1.18.3). In the last figure, the *yākṣī* wears a sampot-type garment with seven pleats covering her lower half, flowing from the waistline up to the thighs and an *uttarīya* flowing from behind and moving across the front of the person reaching the left shoulder (in Fig. 1.18.4). All four figures have three and two-layered hāra or neckbands with flowers around their necks. They wear figure one *kaṅkaṇa* in each hand along with spiral bangles covering two-fourths of the arm, which is further adorned with an armlet or *keyura*. The hairdos, however, are distinctive in all four cases. While in the first case the hair is neatly combed without partitioning at the centre, adorned with a circular tiara, in the second case, the hair is combed with a knot on the forehead. A similar case is visible in the third image with an interesting deflection of a tree laden with fruits stemming from the *yākṣī's* forehead. In the last case, while the small bun remains at the forehead, there is a pearled hairband and the larger portion of the hair is combed back and allowed to sling at the back and is loosely embellished with six layers of pearl bands.

In a set of depictions from Mathurā and adjacent sites, female figures are shown as drinking from or holding a goblet, perhaps they enact drinking. In Fig. 1.19.1, a woman drinks from the goblet as a spectator looks on. While her entire body weight rests on the right leg, the other leg bends at the knees and crosses the right leg so as to have her stand on her toes. With her left hand, she raises a goblet to her lips, tipping the contents into her mouth, her face turned upwards and, in other hand, she holds a round object perhaps a fruit. The expression of enjoyment in her upturned face is clearly delineated. She wears a four-tied *mekhalā* below a waistband whose knots hang at length to its right up till the feat, while her genitals remain exposed. The hair is tied with a small bun on the forehead, braided towards the back and tied in a loose knot. The spectator above looks down with the right hand resting on the *vedikā*. He is slumped and sleepy as if intoxicated by the beauty, the drink or both. The description of a *yavanī* given in *Pādataditaka of Śyāmilaka* of *Chaturabhānī* comes very close to this depiction.

> This is our friend Varahadās's paramour *yavanī* Karpuraturiṣhthā (probably a resident of Ujjaiyini). She is holding up a bronze cup of *madhū*/wine (*madhūneh kansyam lingulitrayena*) with three fingers towards the moon (*pratīchandrabhimukha*, a Greek ritual). 114. With her other hand, she is holding a moon like earring that is casting a show on her cheek.... With hair and eyes like a *chakor* bird, the *yavanī* is looking at her reflection in the wine cup, spreading her waist long hair with her hands, white as *mahuā* flowers, wiping away wine inducing flush from her cheeks thinking it was a smudge of *alatā*. (*Chaturabhānī*: 115). (translation by author)

It goes on say that *yavanī* and *gaṇikā*, monkey woman and dancing girl, woman of *kāmuka*, donkey and singer, all their characteristics (*guṇa*) are similar (*Chaturabhānī*: 115). The play emphasises the 'foreignness' and the *gaṇikā* element of *yavana*. *Ibhyaputra* is used in sense of a rich person who is riding an elephant (*Chaturabhānī*: 116). Harry Falk has brought to light an inscription on the pedestal of a young maiden sculpted on a pillar which says that this *pratimā* or sculpture of *kāmukī ibhaye*, established by Sirsu (?) for the pleasure of the deity (lit. not to the dislike of the deity, *priyatā bhāgava mahatṛ* (Falk 2014, 13–17). The operative word here is the *kāmukī*, a desirous (for sexual or other

Figure 1.19. Woman drinking from or holding a goblet at Sanghol (Fig. 1.19.1, Fig. 1.19.2, Fig. 1.19.3), Mathurā (Fig. 1.19.4) and Kankāli Tilā (Fig. 1.19.5), railing post, 2nd century CE. Below are magnified images of goblets in the same order

material objects such as wealth), lustful or libidinous woman (Pāṇini, *Astadhyayi* 4–1, 42).[7] She is an *ibhī*, literary meaning an elephant mare, a woman of the *hastinī* type. In this context, *Ibhyaputra* may well have erotic connotations.

A railing pillar of the same period from Sanghol, carved in bold reliefs (Fig.1.19.2) portrays a female standing gracefully turned towards the left, resting her right leg on the trunk of a tree by gently pushing it, in an act known as Aśoka-*dohada*. Her body remains mostly uncovered, with just a four-tied *mekhalā* tied on her waist. Her left hand, positioned at a right angle, holds the stem of a goblet, and the other holds a small object. Viewed as left profile of the face, the peaceful and tranquil expressions on it reveal her at leisure and ease. The hair is tied up in a conical coiled knot covered with beaded lace or pearls, while long strands hang over behind her head.

Further, in a fragmentary railing pillar from Kankāli Tilā, the female figure holding a cup is shown under a tree. The cup with its small stand, like a goblet is clearly delineated (19.5). In a similar image from pillar now in the Los Angeles County Musuem of Art, the woman holds up a cup with a fluted design. This design is seen on kantharos from the Roman period. In the museum catalogue, Pratapaditya Pal has referred to the figure as performing the *bakula dohada* that describes a young woman trying to make a tree flower by spraying it with wine (Pal 1986, S55; Sivaramamurti 1970, 40). There is a spectator couple peering down carved on the uppermost register. The *dohada* rite has been best described by Kālidāsa in Meghadūta:

> … red tree with its waving foliage and a beautiful Kesura tree close to a bower of Mādhavī creepers having a hedge of Kurabaka plants. The former longs, with me, (like myself) for a kick of left foot, *vāmapadāghaṭa*, of your friend (my wife), and the latter a mouthful of wine, *madirā*, from her under the pretext of *dohada* (an operation necessary to make it bloom). (Kale 2015: Uttaramegha, 18)

The entire third act of *Mālvikāgnimitram* is focused on the *dohada* act and its consequences on the flowering of the tree due to the youthful sexuality of the Mālvikā, emphasising the popular belief of this symbiotic sexuality of the plant and the woman that gets translated into the *śālabhañjikā* motif in art.

Two other figures, though comparatively smaller compared with the above examples, may be holding a cup in similar vein. One depicts a royal/prosperous lady given the presence four-layered and U-patterned parasol dangling over her head in the background. She poses in a *tribhaṅga* posture wearing a diaphanous *dhoti* and a *mekhalā* around her waist, above which is a cloth waistband, knotted to the left side. Her right hand holds a small cup seems held close to her chest using her thumb and fingers. While the hair is tied together in a small bun on the top, the face expresses a delicate smile. Another image (Fig. 1.19.4) shows a *śālabhañjikā* standing cross-legged position, with the right leg crossing over the left on a dwarf who leans on his face to gaze upon the woman or probably her drinking cup held in her right hand, while her left hand stretches upwards to hold the branch of a flowering tree. The overall effect of these figures is one of elegance, refinement and beauty.

Hellenistic association in relation to wine, intoxication, frolic and women is very well illustrated in a four-sided railing pillar from Mathurā in the Cleveland Museum published by Martha Carter (1982). Along with the Hellenistic theme and composition, there are elements that point to the piece having been produced and consumed in the area around Mathurā. It is made of typical Sikri red spotted sandstone associated with the area and has many Mathurā *dramatis personae* in terms of their posture, hairdo and composition. Women in Hellenistic attire, partially disrobed due to inebriation, are dancing around a column. One of the celebrants is balancing a cup on her head. There are kantharoi, Greek drinking and mixing vessels lying between the figures along with a vessel that looks like a combination of an amphora and a *surāhī*. Above these are other revellers, some playing instruments, dancing and holding a cup, presumably drinking and making merry. There is also a couple doling out wine into a cup (?) from a large kantharos. Harry Falk (2009) is of the opinion that young wine was produced and distributed near monastic complexes 'with the *saṅgha*s being in possession of fermentation bowls and sieves presented to them also by local monks as pious donations.' A bowl with an inscription from Takht i Bahi monastery refers to intoxicating drinks as well as it describes it as a 'container for healthy (alcoholic) drinks.'

The relationship between *gaṇikā's* and their representation in sculptural forms has been brought forth in context of the Didarganj *yākṣī* by Doris Meth Srinivasan, who suggests that this does not represent a divine/semi-divine figure but rather a *gaṇikā*, a courtesan par excellence or deluxe. In another publication, I too have suggested a close connection between eroticism and women (Bawa 2013, 23, 32–40).

The spectator figures also become actors in the drama of wine drinking (Fig. 1.20). In some railing pillars, we see the spectator/performer bend down or hand down a goblet to the *yoṣītā-yākṣī* below. In one example, a woman standing with her back towards a viewer and drying her hair by squeezing out water from her locks and the drops being swallowed by a Hansā. Above her are two spectators gazing at her, with one on the left side hanging his left arm out of the *vedikā* and offering a small jar-like vessel or a mug with a handle. The woman wears a four tired *mekhalā* and a cloth waistband knotted at the centre with six pleated folds, also wears a skirt until her knees. The overall effect of the image appears lyrical and rhythmic with, glances pointed at the woman, her posture, her loosened hair brought to the front and her *tribhaṅga* posture is sensually delineated. A similar *mithuna* figure is found on the Bhūteśvara railing where the spectator drinking from a goblet with the *yoṣītā* figure standing below (Fig. 1.20.2).

Woman as purveyor of play and entertainment is shown in other ways also. A female figure balancing a ghata that reaches above the

Figure 1.20. Spectator couple with cups (Figs 1.20.1 and 1.20.2). Sporting women with a ghata, Sanghol, a railing post (Fig. 1.20.3). Below are magnified images of Mathurā cups in the same order

Fig 20.1 Fig 20.2 Fig 20.3

vedikā on her elbow, reaching out towards the two spectators whose eyes remain fixed on the pot along with the woman who glances at her ghata (Fig. 1.20.3), as if she herself is entertained by the act. While she seems to be offering the pot to the spectators, with their hands outstretched as in the case of the Fig. 1.18 series. She is seen in movement, standing in a *tribhaṅga* posture with both legs bent at the knees facing left, while the hips are deflected to the right, wearing a transparent *dhoti* with eight pleated knots at the centre, with its other elongated end flowing through her right side. Her hair is loose, with a slight partitioning at the centre, held together with a beaded hairband and loosely tied by three ribbons at the ends not unlike the *yavanī* women. The overall effect of the image showcases a childlike playfulness, swift movement and rhythm and, as Daud Ali suggests, games, toys and sporting events formed a sort of communicative idiom in courtship through which intentions and affections could be suggested indirectly to one's prospective lover amidst friends and companions (Ali 2006, 255).

In the *Arthaśāstra*, different kinds of leisure and their purveyors are depicted and become a category to be allowed but regulated. Wine, wine shops, prostitutes, dancers and other mediators of leisure are grouped together (*Arthaśāstra*: 54–5; II. 4.55). The *Arthaśāstra* suggests as to who all would live to the south of the city. This is the quarter where the superintendents of the city, of commerce, of manufactories and of the army would stay. The area would also house those who trade in cooked rice, liquor (*surâ*) and flesh (*mansā*) besides prostitutes (*rupajiva*), musicians (*stalavacārā*) and the people of the Vaiśya castes. Even in the section on prostitutes XXXVI, the rules framed for *gaṇikās* are to be applicable on actors, dancers, buffoon (*vāgājīvana*), a mimic player (*kuśīlava*), juggler (*śaubhika*), a rope dancer (*plavākā*) and so on. Purveyors of entertainment, sexual or visual or aural are all grouped together.[8]

In the urban landscape; the presence of the wine merchant would not have been unfamiliar given the ubiquitous references to wine in textual, epigraphic, archeological and visual sources. The material culture that underlay making, vending and consumption of wine can be presumed. It is no wonder that Vātsyāyana says that for a *nāgaraka*, a go-between, messengers or helper, a friend maybe a washerman, barber, florist, perfumer, wine-merchant, beggar, cowherd, betel-seller, goldsmith, libertine, pander or clown and so forth; and men-about-town can be friends with the wives of these men too (*Kāmasūtra:* 1.5.34). The same list is also meant for a *gaṇikā* though libertines are added to the list (*Kāmasūtra:* 6.1.9).

The suggested social landscape of Mathurā would have comprised most of these categories of entertainers be it courtesans, *gaṇikā*, actors, perfumers or garland makers; *śailalaka,* (MI: 62) and dancers or *nāṭaka's* (Kumar 2019, 144), goldsmiths or *hairaṇyaka* or *soavanīka*, *suvarṇakāra* (127, 129), perfumers or *gāndhikas* (LL. 39, 68, 76) dyers, garland makers or *mālākāra* (EL Vol XXXIIP 2110) barbers or *nāpita* (LL.MI, 111) and jewellers. Significantly, these social categories are also active donors to religious enterprises, be it to temples, shrines or monastic establishments, for example, the Sarasvatī image inscription from Kankāli Tilā was donated by Ranganarttano, a person related to the theatre (120)[9] and an *āyāgapaṭṭa* was donated by *gaṇikā* Lonāśobikhā and her junior Vasu (Bawa 2021, 80; Kumar 2019, 120).[10] Their presence as well as their trade as performers and entertainers is very visible in the visual culture of the area.

The epigraphic evidences in Mathurā and Sanchi may have mention of wine sellers. They are called *Kālavāda/la* who may be 'a seller of wine' (or a high-ranking official). The word possibly refers to a seller or distiller of wine (Sanskrit *kalyavāla, kalyapāla*, or *kallavāla*). Two such inscriptions include the Màtharaka *àyàgapata*, which says:

> Adoration to the *arhat* Mahāàvìra! The āyāgapaṭṭa of Mātharaka, a *kālavāda*, and his wife Svarakhitā"*namo arahato mahāvìrasa mātharaka(sa) (kā)lavāda sā (kaā) bhayāye Śivarakhitaye āyā[gapato].*[11]

The term *kālāvada* is also found in a donatory inscription from Sanchī Stùpa I (Luders 1912, 330, 522, 523). 'Gift of Datta, the *kālavada* from Vidishà,' Lüders also cites the usage of *M[ā]thuri kalavad[ā]* in the inscription on the base of the female figure of *Tośā* from *Morā*. The presence of wine sellers, as seen in the donative inscriptions, catering to the tastes of the urban elite, is significant because this presence and prominence in the social sphere also indicates the material milieu within which sophisticated tastes of the elite and the masses were not only catered to but were also represented in cultural productions.

The concern for the quality of alcohol being sold and served is expressed as part of political economy of the *Arthaśāstra* where the *surādhyakṣa* or the superintendent of wine is not only supposed to regulate the price, quality and potability of the liquor being served but also ensure that liquor is served in safe environment where the customers are not robbed of their dress or ornaments or money. Even more telling is that the wine-seller has to ensure pleasant and appealing surroundings in wine shops so that the consumers can get the full experience expected from consuming alcohol. The atmosphere tallies with some of the interior scenes represented in bas-relief from Mathurā. It says 'Liquor shops, *pānāgāra*, shall contain many rooms provided with beds and seats kept apart *vibhaktā sayāna āsana*. They (the drinking room, *pānoddhesani*) shall contain scents, garlands of flowers, water (*gandha, mālā*) and other comfortable things suitable to various seasons (*Arthaśāstra*: 132; XXV. 119), where the patrons may 'lie down in intoxication with their beautiful mistresses' (*rupabhiragaṇtū*) (*Arthaśāstra*: XXV. 120).

The entire fourth *adhyāya* or chapter of the first book of *Kāmasūtra* is devoted to *nāgarakavṛtti* (*Kāmasūtra*, 1.4, 5–26) that is the mode of life, behaviour, moral code, style or movements of the man about town, the sophisticated cultured man, the *nāgaraka*. The daily routine prescribed for him involves leisure activities that ultimately lead to fulfilment of intellectual and physical desires; 'the physical manifesting in the sculptural evidence and the intellectual in textual' (Bawa 2021, 86). The daily routine in the first half of the day is to be devoted to sport and games such as quail fights and cock fights, *kālākṛida* and then he goes to *goṣṭhī* and *sabhā's*, salons with amusing and intellectually stimulating companions, *viṭa* and *vidūṣaka*. He also participates in picnics, *udayānāgamana*, and theatrical auditions and performances. In the evening there is music and dancing, *saṅgīta*, where he waits, *pratīkṣā*, for the women, *abhisārikās*, who are slipping for a rendezvous. There is a reference to a salon (*goṣṭhī*) held in the house of a courtesan, where the *nāgaraka* goes to the house of courtesans who get the men to drink along with themselves. They drink wine made from honey, grapes, other fruits or sugar, with various sorts of salt, fruit, greens, vegetables as well as bitter, spicy and sour foods (*Kāmasūtra* 1.4.22–23).

Such pleasant space for leisured drinking can be seen in many sculptures of couples or *mithunas*. Two architectural fragments from Mathurā J.232 and J.627, now housed in the Lucknow Museum, show a seated male figure wearing a turban discoursing with a female figure on the left (Fig. 1.21) (Quintanilla 2007, 209, Fig. 269). There are two attendant females in the background, one carrying a *surāhī*-like pot and the other a palm leaf fan. A similar three-sided 2nd-century jamb from Mathurā, known as the *Saundaranandā* panel (SML J. 533, red sandstone, height 143.5 × 29 cm, 1st century AD, Kankāli Tilā, Mathurā) has been discussed elsewhere (Bawa 2021, 62–68). The significant element of this

Figure 1.21. *Mithuna*, drinking activity, Kankāli Tilā, Mathurā, 1st century CE

a couple seen seated on a couch is the man offering a cup to a woman on his right, and an attendant women standing carrying a *surāhi*-like pot. In a similar composition, also from Mathurā, a *surāhī*-like vessel is placed behind on a table behind a woman is seated on a stool (Bawa 2021, Fig. 2.7). Elements of intimacy between the male and female are often delineated. These are very much in the vein of the Patna double sided panel described above are many intimate *mithuna* scenes with wine cups were made at Mathurā from the 1st century. These scenes of intimacy and social drinking continued well into the Gupta and early medieval period in the literary[12] and visual tradition.

There is a considered difference in the shape, placement and size of vessels containing liquids at Mathurā having distinct symbolic significance. The pot placed at the feet of and between divine beings represent life giving water, the *pūrṇaghata*. It may also be offered for consecration as in the Gajā Lakshmî images. However, the *surāhī* is seen in context of the *mithunas* or *yākṣīs*, which would suggest its relationship with *kāmā* and *nāgaraka* traditions. That these *surāhīs*, like today, were probably made of fired clay and have, thus, not survived is likely. We have plenty of evidence of wine amphorae from excavations (Archaeological Survey of India: Annual Report 1972, 24; 1985, 141–42; 1986, 86–87; 1989, 86), however, none of these match the shape of the *surāhīs*.

Similarly, there are different types of cups and goblets. The use of cups is not specific to *yakṣīs* and women but is also represented as used by Kubera, Balarāma, Nāgas and the like. Broadly, two types of cups are shown in the sculptures: one is the cup with the *surāhī* which covers its mouth and has tapered straight lines; the other cup is like a goblet with a stand; sometimes it also has a handle to hold it. The stemmed goblets held by the Pālīkherā Kubera and ancillary figures are intricately carved with floral patterns and seem objects of luxury (Fig. 1.3). Like the goblets in hands of the *yākṣīs*, these have short stems with a small stand and a longish curved cup. We can correlate this with the metal cup found from the Rupanagara excavation now in the site museum (Fig. 1.22) that has a similar structure and shape. However, it seems that like the Greek Kanatharos seen in Gandharan sculptures illustrated by Martha Carter (Carter 1968, Fig. 12), this was two handled, one of which is broken off now. The goblet is one of the many devices used to suggest locale, activity and identity of not just the activity but also the cultural context underlying wine drinking.

As part of this cultural context, wine and wine drinking were, as discussed later, associated with 'foreign' luxury and leisure. Further, most wines amongst other luxury goods were imported into India from the Mediterranean region, especially from Rome since the early centuries of the Common Era. *Periplus Maris Erthryea* mentions special jars and utensils along with Italian, Laodicean (Syrian) and Arabian

Figure 1.22. Kantharos-like cup found from Ropar, Rupanagar Museum, Punjab, 2nd century CE (?)

wine being imported into Barygaza (modern Broach) for 'the king there was imported in those times precious silverware ... and fine wine' (Casson 1989, 81; Brancaccio 2011, 28). Words such as *yavana*, *yona* and *yavanar* too proliferate ancient Indian textual sources of many genres: the epics (*Rāmāyaṇa, Mahābhārata*), books on grammar, list of Buddhist literature, edicts of Aśoka and other stone inscriptions, drama, poetry and many more. Archaeological evidence of the existence of Greek slaves is available through two clay bullae marked with *brahmī* characters, dated to the 2nd century CE are inscribed with the legend, *yavanikānam*, 'of the *yavanikās*' (Ghosh 1990).

Further, cults that celebrate or ritualise drinking of wine and other inebriating drinks have been associated with Dionysian or Bacchanalian Cults and, thus, with *yavanas*, which for Indians was a generic term to refer to people from north-west, Bactria, Rome and Central Asia. In addition, *yavanikās* or Greek women were highly prized as slaves, in part because of their exotic nature and also as having markers of licentious sexuality being located in them. In fact, it is my premise that these two vectors associated with *yavanas* became aspects in creating a leitmotif when referring to leisure and pleasure centred in *yavanikā*. On the other hand, the ritual nature of wine drinking cannot be discounted as well.

The Periplus Maris Erythraei too refers to the export of concubines to India:

> For the king, there was imported in those times precious silverware, slave musicians, beautiful girls for concubinage, fine wines, etc. (Casson 1989)

Roman lists as seen in bills of lading and other documents also attest to slave women being an oft traded commodity. In Bihar, India, circa 5th century BCE, a royal Jain harem while celebrating the birth of a prince refers to multiethnic women (Hain 2020, 271).

There is also significant evidence of women, including those of *yavana* origin being used as currency, to buy peace or influence; these include slaves marked by foreign racial origins (ibid., 273). A Vedic era list of rules for kings' commands that the prince's entourage should comprise only women.[13] Sanskrit drama posits the *yavanī* as a preferred bodyguard to accompany the prince for his favourite leisure activity of hunting.

These foreign slaves were, however, perhaps valued for providing exotic sex or as status marking courtesans as evinced from many sources. Indian texts, too, affirm the close relationship in consumers' minds between wine and women, especially *yavanī* women. The *Purananuru* (Tamil text 4th century CE) praises foreign wine. In Kālidāsa's *Raghuvanśa*, a renunciant 'could not bear the flush caused by wine in the lotus-faces of the *yavana*-women'.

Wine drinking and its association with *Yavanas*[14] finds depiction at Ajantā in other contexts. One such depiction relates to the 'Persian Embassy on the cave 1 ceiling (Brancaccio 2011, 82, Fig. 112). Here a man dressed in 'Central Asian' clothes is seen drinking wine being served by two servants. These figures are placed in a panoramic landscape peopled with imaginary/mythical animals, *ganas*, etc. Pia Branaccio terms such scenes 'genre scene' that 'comment on the distant world where wine was made and abundantly consumed'. Unlike the Mathurā imagery of wine drinking where female presence is emphasised, at Ajantā, there are scenes of two men drinking wine together. Pia Brancaccio also refers to another scene, probably Viśvantara *Jātaka* in the porch of cave 17 where an attendant in Central Asian attire is holding a metal ewer resembling a *surāhī* and serving a *mithuna* couple, while an Indian servant also holds a cup very much like the spectator couples atop Mathurā railing pillars (ibid., Fig. 111). Whether the couple is royal or a *nāgaraka-gaṇikā* pair is difficult to say, but the trope is that of world of *kāmā* of the *nāgarakas*.

Why should we consider wine drinking a leisure activity at all, and not part of ritual and religion as many Brahmanical texts suggest? After all, drinking spirituous liquor outside of religiously sanctioned spaces is always condemned. Survey of Brahmanical, Buddhist literature on intoxication is given in many other scholarly works; I will confine myself here to examining the main strands related to attitudes towards this to enable some kind of contextualisation of the visuals in terms of compliance or alterity.

In normative literature, be it Brahmanical, Buddhist or Jaina, leisure, drinking intoxicating liquids and feminine wiles are equated as being equally appalling and sinful. I am giving select references here to illustrate the negative attitudes towards drinking intoxicating liquor. *Chandogya Upanisad* says that (5.10.9-10) 'A man who steals gold, drinks liquor, and kills a Brahman; a man who fornicates with his teacher's wife—these four will fall as also the fifth—he who consorts with them' (Deuseen 1980: *Chandogya Upanisad* 5.10.9–5.10.10). This is elaborated upon in the *Nārada Parīvrajaka Upanishad* where householder not engaging in productive work and mendicant monk busying himself with work are condemned. However, non-work of the monk is in not to be taken as freedom to indulge in leisure. In fact, there is a warning that '(o)n seeing a young handsome woman (he) becomes inflamed with passion and drinking liquor he becomes intoxicated. Therefore, he shall avoid from afar a woman who is poison to the eye' (VI-36). Conversing with women, as well as chatting with them and sending them on errands, even their dance, music and laughter and scandals about them—these (the ascetic) shall avoid (VI-35). Further, it says that 'a thief, a drinker of spirituous liquor, a seducer of his preceptor's wife and one treacherous to his friend get purified by expiation; (but) one who abandons the sign of Vishnu, external or internal, which he was possessing, will never be purified in spite of all his self-exertions (Deussen 1980: *Satyayaniya Upanishad* 28).

The injunctions given in *dharmasāstric* literature are quite prohibitory when it comes to wine being partaken by women, especially upper-caste women, even though there is plenty of evidence of men and women both drinking wine in pleasant environs. Manu (IX.13) enjoins that drinking spirituous liquor is one of the six causes of ruin of women. Going a little further, Vasiṣṭha says that half the body of the husband falls off if his wife drinks alcohol. If a wife drinks, then Manu would have her superseded by another (Manu, IX.80). Of course, in case the husband is an alcoholic, the wife will not disrespect him (IX.78). Women who drank wine were not be allowed to participate in ritual (Cf. Jha 2020, 190). Intercourse with women who drank spirits was punishable (*Viṣṇu* XXXVIL.33, *Vasiṣṭha* XXI.5). The man who sees a woman of good family drinking *surâ* must purify himself by looking at the sun, pronouncing the name of Viṣṇu and bathing in the same clothes as he wore when he saw the woman (*Mahänirvänatantra* XI.163, Meyer, p. 244) (Cf. Jha 2020, 191). Another author mentioned in the *Kāmasūtra* as a source of its composition is Śvetaketu Auddalakī who was the son of Uddalakā. This writer (the seer, Uddalaka's son) is so anxious about the seduction of other men's wives that he forbade not only Brahmans to drink wine, but even the common people (*Kāmasūtra* 4, fn 9).

In Aśokan inscription, there is no direct references to drinking per se but in the first, eighth, ninth major edict at Girnār, Aśoka makes it a point to condemn the behaviour of those who go on useless travels (*vihara yatras*) and participate in useless festivals and ceremonies

(*Maṅgalām*) during illness or marriages of sons and daughters. Women especially are condemned for practicing vulgar and useless ceremonies (Corpus Inscriptionum Indicarum, Vol. I: pp. 1–17).

The Jaina text *Ratnakarandaka-śrāvakācāra* by Ācārya Samantabhadra is a work that elaborates on rules and regulations for the householder, instructs that those who wish to give up *hiṃsa*, violence, should first give up wine, flesh, honey and the five *uḍumbaraḥ* fruits. This is because of the belief that 'wine is the birthplace of many creatures that owe their origination in liquor and those who drink wine, necessarily commit hiṃsa' (Jain 2006, 110–11). *Hiṃsa* and wine produce other vices like pride fear, disgust, laughter, etc.

In the non-religious literary tradition, especially of the *bhāṇas* and *parīhāsas*, drunk religious leaders are often parodied and their hypocrisy exposed (Abrol and Paul in Bawa 2021, 94–105). Even in a Buddhist drama, entitled Nāgānanda, attributed to King Harṣā, a scene occurs, the plot of which depends upon the vagaries of a drunkard, who had for his lady-love a maid of honour of the queen. In plays such as the *Mattavilāsa*, the cult of *Kāpālikas* are shown as hedonists who indulge in drinking liquor and eating meat and sexual play with beautiful female companions.[15] In the *Mattavilasa*, the *Kāpālikas* Satyasoma's beautiful consort/ritual companion Devasoma is the object of lust of a Buddhist monk and the Pāśupatā ascetic. Satyasoma and Devasoma are shown as drinking liquor out of the ritual skull alms bowl and eating meat. Drinking spiritous liquor out of the skull bowl should be seen in context of Tantric practices that five *makars* or things that begin with M—*madya, mâmsa, matsya, mudrā, maithuna*—liquor, meat, fish, parched grain and sexual intercourse (Lorenzen 2020, 260).

Padātilaka after saluting Kāmādeva, and the chief prostitute (*vara*) the protagonist salutes those intoxicating youthful, leisured women (*vilāsinī*) whose laughter spreads on the cheeks from the ears, salutations to their staggering gait (probably from being intoxicated and vivacious nature (*citavana*) (*Chaturabhānī*: 124).

Śilpa Prakāśa composed by Rāmacandra Kaulācāra Bhattaraka mentions sixteen *alasakanyās* in various emotional and physical states of being (Cf. Śilpa Prakāśa of Rāmacandra Kaulācāra 1996: 63).[16] The term *alasa* itself translates into indolent, leisured, unhurried young woman who is the epitome of this state of beauty. By the early medieval times, the iconographical and sculptural and architectural prescriptive text as the one mentioned above start using the figure of young women in languorous poses to represent the entire discourse of beauty which in turn is related to fertility and apotropaic functions.

Lest it be thought that wine was the monopoly of prostitutes, rogues, *viṭas* and *nāgarakas*, the ubiquitousness of wine and its regulations

Figure 1.23. Seated couple with the male offering a drink in a leisured environment, Gupta period, National Museum, Delhi

by women is echoed in *Kāmasūtra* that says that good wives are also involved in making sure that wine is very much part of the household. She sees to the stocking and use of pots of wines and liquors, and to selling and buying them, and she keeps track of the income and expenditure from them (*Kāmasūtra* 4.1, 35). Mitra has cited many cases of wives like Sīta, who are shown as offering drinks in the literary tradition (Mitra 2020, 77–83).

There has been a tradition in literature and art of showcasing the men as controlled, firm and balanced, while the women are shown as slaves of their senses (Bawa 2013, 23–28). Especially in literary culture, women are represented as intoxicated or agents leading to loss of senses. However, a deeper study of sculptures related to drinking, be it of offering drinks, drinking itself, intoxication of women, men and spectator figures fractures this discourse. It reveals that both men and women are shown as enjoying drinking or the spectacle of it thereof within social settings that seem familiar in their urban and suburban locales (Fig. 1.23). The sensual portrayal of drinking activity, the leisured environs of palaces and gardens enhances the atmosphere of pleasure and desire.

A study of the visual culture of drinking transmits and reifies ideas about values and behaviours that were implicit, if not explicit, within the cultural context of the periods. They may through this kind of depiction of drinking, intoxication and the agents thereof have given visibility to shared social experiences. The visual evidence also gives us an insight into how the viewers, men and perhaps women as well, viewed women and wine drinking as part of the discourse of leisure and pleasure.

Notes

1 In 'Dionysiac Aspects of Kushān Art', Ars Orientalis, Vol. 7, 1968, Martha Carter cites various Kubera-type figures, often accompanied by females and usually holding some sort of cup. In some cases, grapes and vineleaves appear in the image.

2 Saptarshi-Tila (Saptari Mound), Mathurā City (find-spot). Schist. H. 1.5 m. Mathurā Museum. See R.C. Sharma, *Buddhist Art of Mathura* (Delhi: Agam Kala Prakashan, 1984), 67, 165, Fig. 4.

3 A large stone bowl (Mathurā Museum, 00.662) found in a village bears an inscription (L. I43d) saying that it was given 'for the acceptance of the (Maha)samghlyas (Mahasanghikas) ...' (Luders-Janert, p. I65)

4 The Hindu agricultural deity, Balarāma, usually depicted in Naga guise, in Mathurā, often bearing a wine cup, which was one of his attributes.

5 Gergely Hidas, A Buddhist Ritual Manual on Agriculture Vajratuṇḍasamayakalparāja – Critical Edition and Translation: Open Access published by De Gruyte Creative Commons Attribution-NonCommercial-NoDerivatives 4.0 License. https://doi.org/10.1515/9783110621051-002 [2.23] Then Vaiśravaṇa, the Great King, addressed the Bhagavān, 'O Bhagavān, teach the detailed offering manual.' [2.24] Then the Bhagavān taught the offering manual, 'At the time of drought one should prepare a *maṇḍala* with clay and cow dung measuring three *hasta*s on a mountain, in a forest, at a monastery, a spring, a pool, a tank, a well, a lake, or the residence of the Nāgas. It should be sprinkled with perfumed water all around… Four Nāga kings should be prepared in the middle of the ditch. Having ground sandal, red sandal, fragrant sandal, padmaka wood 67 and saffron, it should be scattered along with fumigation. 68 Flower garlands should be offered. Parched grain and mustard seeds should be scattered there in the middle of the [Nāga] residence…Buddha images with relics, and *caityas* with relics should be placed in the four directions. Decorations should be made with ribbons and banners Worship should be performed. One should perfume *agaru*, 69 sandal and olibanum, and combine tagara, nalada, kunduruka, 71 liquor, parched grain, mustard seed and *sarja*-resin with honey.

6 *Harivamsha Purāṇa* by Manmatha Nath Dutt, 1897, Chapter 41. II ('Vishnu Parva') of the *Harivamsa* 41.II. 11. The powerful Balarāma was over-powered by thirst, so drinking that wine again and again, like a sick person drinking water he grew inebriate and his body began to reel. 12. On account of his being drunk his eyes and face, resembling an autumnal moon, began to roll. 13. The Goddess Varuni, who was the churning rod of ambrosia unto the gods, was born in that Kadamva cave in the shape of wine. And so she passed by the name of Kadamvari.14-16. Inebriate with Kadamvari wine while Kṛṣṇa's elder brother began to speak in indistinct but sweet words the wine incarnate Kanti, the beloved spouse of the moon, the Goddess Shri the foremost of damsels having the emblem of a cloud on her flag, these three celestial ladies approached him with sweet words.

7 Also, *Mrchh* as mistress; in the *Devi Bhagvata Purāṇa* translated by Swami Vijnananda, Chapter 30, verse 53–102, the Devi is called Kamuki in the

region of Gandha Madana, the fabled mountain from where Hanuman carried the Sanjivini plant.

8 There are also many such entertainments described among the 64 *kalas* or arts described in *Kāmaṣūtra*, some are for adornment and others for intellectual pleasures such as the ability to speak in sign language; understanding languages made to seem foreign; knowledge of local dialects; skill at making flower carts; knowledge of omens; alphabets for use in making magical diagrams; alphabets for memorising; group recitation; improvising poetry; dictionaries and thesauruses; knowledge of metre; literary works; and cultivating the self such as skill at rubbing, massaging, and hairdressing; performative arts such the art of impersonation playing the lute and the drum; telling jokes and riddles; completing words; reciting difficult words; reading aloud; staging plays and dialogues; the art of using clothes for disguise; special forms of gambling; the game of dice. But the most significant for us is the skill at staging leisure such as preparing wine (KS.1.3.15).

9 Smith 2010, 55; Vijay Kumar, 2019–20, 'Catalogue of Antiquities of State Archaeological Museum, Lucknow, U.P. India; Part i: Jain (from Kankali tila, Mathura & Other Places of Mathura), Bauddha (from Mathura) & Gandhar Antiquities'. *Indian Journal of Archaeology*, Vol. 4 (4): 62–1167.

10 These refer to slabs of honour, or respect that depict auspicious symbols and the figure of the Tirthankara, donated by Jaina laity as well as monastic community.

11 Luders, EII, Appendix II.12, Mathurā ca. 20 BCE, red sandstone H. 34" × W. 34" (87 × 87 cm) State Museum, Lucknow SML J.248; H. Lüders, 'Seven Brahmi Inscriptions from Mathura and its Vicinity,' p. 204, fn. 3.

12 For example, this passage from *Kathasaritasagara*, Chapter XXI:

> And while the roof of the palace was white with moonlight as with his own glory, he drank wine in plenteous streams as he had swallowed the pride of his enemies; beautiful women brought him, as he sat retired, in vessels of gold, wine flaming with rosy glow, as it were the water of his appointment as ruler in the empire of love; he divided between the two queens the cordial liquor red, delicious, and pellucid, in which danced the reflection of their faces; as he did his own heart, impassioned, enraptured and transparent, in which the same image was found; his eyes were never sated with resting on the faces of those queens, which had the eyebrows arched, and blushed with the rosy hue of love, though envy and anger were far from them; the scene of his banquet, filled with many crystal goblets of wine, gleamed like a lake of white lotuses tinged red with the rising sun. (https://www.gutenberg.org/files/40588/40588-h/40588-h.htm - xd20e7327)

13 Fuhrer, A.A. 1882. *Vasishtha-Dharma-Sastra*, translated by G. Buhler. Oxford. Sutra D II-9 in Devraj Chanana, *Slavery*, 57, 159. As cited in Hain. 'The Prestige Makers', 273.

14 James McHugh, 'Grape Wine in Ancient and Early Medieval India: The View from the Center', *IESHR*, 58, 1(2021), p. 114. Wine was foreign in both practice and representation, and its exotic nature contributed to its prestige. He argues that wine was assimilated into a complex varied drinking culture that long predated wine.

15 'Kapalika: My love, just look. This liquor shop equals the majesty of the sacrificial enclosure. Here the flag pole equals the sacrificial post; the liquor equals the *soma*; the drinkers, the priests; the liquor glasses, the soma cups; the snacks such as meat kabobs, the various oblations; the drunken chatter, the sacrificial formulas; the songs, the sacrificial hymns; the liquor vats, the sacrificial ladles; the thirst of the drinkers, the sacrificial fire; and the owner of the shop, the sponsor of the sacrifice.'

16 These are enumerated as: *alasa,* indolent, *darpana* holding a mirror, *torana,* leaning on the door, *dalamalika* the gesture of touching a branch of a tree, *padmagandba* enjoying the fragrance of a lotus *ketakibbarana* wearing *ketakibharana, wearing ketaki* flower, *matrimurti* image of a mother, *cbamara,* holding a *fly* whisk, *nartaki* dancer, *shukrasarika* playing with a parrot or *maina bird, nupurapadika* tying ankle bells, *mardala* drummer, *mugdha* young and innocent, *manini* haughty and offended, *vinyasa* pensive, *gunthana* bashful. Similarly a 15th century Gujarati text *Ksharарnava* adds some new names to the list. Prescribing thirty-two types of females, *devakanyas* or *devanganas,* on the projections and recesses of the *jangha* (wall of the temple). Many of them are in dance postures. The text prescribes that these *surasundaris* should be placed in a certain order so that the devotee who circumambulates the temple experiences them in a certain fixed relation to other images in the temple. Starting from the *ishana* (the north-east) it places Menaka, Lilavati, Vidhichitta, Sundari, Shubhagamini, Hamsavali, Karpuramanjari, Putmvallabha, Patralekha and so on. Lilavati is like *aktsa* of the *Shilpa Prakasha,* Vidhichitta looks into a mirror like *darpana,* Putravallabha is like *matrimurti.* In addition, we see in the text *Kshirarnava,* a *surasundari* removing a thorn, who is called Shubhagamini. Patralekha or a *surasundarl* writinga letter is a favourite motif in central Indian temples. Karpummanjari or the *surasundarl* that has freshly bathed and seen with a *hansa* drinking the water dripping from her hair is also another motif.

References

Agarwala, V.S. 1936. 'Vine Motif in Indian Art'. *Journal of the Indian Society of Oriental Art,* Vol. 4 (2): 130–33.

———. 1939. *Mathura Museum Handbook.* Allahabad: Superintendent Printing and Stationery.

———. 1963. *Catalogue of The Mathura Museum: Architectural Pieces.* Varanasi: Prithvi Prakashan.

Agarwala, V.S. 2015. *A Selection*, edited by Kapila Vatsayana. New Delhi: Sahitya Akademi.

Ali, Daud. 2006. *Courtly Culture and Political Life in Early Medieval India*. Cambridge: Cambridge University Press.

Banerjea, J.N. 2002. *Development of Hindy Iconography*. Delhi: Munshiram Manoharlal Publishers.

Bawa, Seema. 2013. *Gods, Men and Women: Gender and Sexuality in Early Indian Art*. New Delhi: D.K. Printworld.

———. 2021. *Locating Pleasure in Indian History.* New Delhi: Bloomsbury Publishing.

Bhatta, Somadeva. 1880. *Kathá Sarit Ságara; or, Ocean of the Streams of Story*, edited and translated by C.H.Tawney. Available at: https://www.gutenberg.org/ebooks/author/40720 (accessed on 16 September 2023).

Brancaccio, Pia. 2011. *The Buddhist Caves at Aurangabad: Transformations in Art and Religion*. Leiden/Boston: Brill.

Bruce, Long J. 1971. 'Siva and Dionysos: Visions of Terror and Bliss', *Numen*, Vol. 18, Fasc. 3: 180–209.

Buddhacarita. 1972. Edited and translated by E.J. Johnston. New Delhi: Motilal Banarsidass.

Carter, Martha L. 1968. 'Dionysiac Aspects of Kushān Art'. *Ars Orientalis*, Vol. 7: 121–46.

———. 1982. 'The Bacchants of Mathura: New Evidence of Dionysiac Yaksha Imagery from Kushan Mathura'. *The Bulletin of the Cleveland Museum of Art*, Cleveland Museum of Art, LXIX (8): 247–57.

Casson, L. 1989. *The Periplus Maris Erythraei*. Princeton: Princeton University Press.

Chanana, Dev Raj. 1990. *Slavery in Ancient India as Depicted in Pali and Sanskrit Texts*. New Delhi: People's Publishing House.

Chaturbhani. 1960. Edited and translated by Moti Chandra and V.S. Agarwala. Bombay: Hindi Granth Ratnagar Karyalaya Pvt. Ltd.

Corpus Inscriptionum Indicarum, Vol. I, Inscriptions of Aśoka 1925, edited by E. Hultzsch. New Delhi: Archaeological Survey of India.

Deussen Paul. 1980. *Sixty Upanishads of the Vedas*, Volume 1–2, translated by V.M. Bedekar and G.B Palsule. New Delhi: Motilal Banarsidas.

Devi Bhagvata Purana. 1922. Translated by Swami Vijnananda. Allahabad: Allahabad Panini Office.

Dutt, Manmatha Nath (ed.). 1987. *A Prose English Translation of Harivamsha (Translated Literally into English Prose)*. Kolkata: Printed by H.C. Dass.

Errington, Elizabeth and V.S. Curtis (eds). 2007. *From Persepolis to the Punjab, Exploring Ancient Iran, Afghanistan and Pakistan*, contributed by Joe Cribb et al. London: The British Museum Press.

Falk, Harry. 2009. 'Making wine in Gandhara under Buddhist monastic supervision'. *Berlin, Bulletin of Asia institute. Essays in honour of Richard Salomon's 65th Birthday*, New Series/Volume 23: 65–77.

———. 2014. 'An Inscribed Statue of a Lustful Woman from Mathura'. *Indo Asiatsche Zeitschrift*, 18: 13–17.

Ghosh, A. 1990. *Encyclopedia of Indian Archaeology* (Vols. I and II). New Delhi: Munshiram Manoharlal.

Ghosh, Suchandra. 2019. 'The Quotidian Pursuit of Leisure: Hellenistic Way of Life and North-Western Borderlands of India (3rd century BCE to 3rd CE)', *Presidential address, Section 1: Ancient India, Proceedings of Indian History Congress*, Kannur.

Hain, Kathryn. 2020. 'The Prestige Makers: Greek Slave Women in Ancient India'. *Journal of World History,* June: 265–94.

Hidas, Gergely. 2019. *A Buddhist Ritual Manual on Agriculture Vajratuṇḍasamayakalparāja*—Critical Edition and Translation: Open Access published by De Gruyte Creative Commons Attribution-NonCommercial-NoDerivatives 4.0 License. Available at: https://www.degruyter.com/document/doi/10.1515/9783110621051-002/html (accessed on 1 January 2023).

Jain, Vijay K. (ed.). 2016. *Ratnakrandaka-sarvacara by Acharya Samantabhadra*. Dehradun: Vikalp.

Jha, D.N. (ed.). 2020. *Drink of Immortality: Essays on Distillation and Alcohol Use in Ancient India*. Delhi: Manohar Publishers.

Kapila, Vasudeva (ed.). 2015. *Agrawala Vasudeva Sharan (A Selection)*. New Delhi: Sahitya Akademy.

Kaul, Shonaleeka. 2010. *Imagining the Urban: Sanskrit and the City in Early India*. Delhi: Permanent Black and New York: Seagull Press.

Kim, Seung Jung. 2011. 'The Beginnings of the East-West Dialogue: An Examination of Dionysiac Representations in Gandharan and Kushan-Mathuran Art'. *Beyond Boundaries: East and West Cross-Cultural Encounters*, edited by M.Y.L. Huang. Newcastle upon Tyne: Cambridge Scholar Publishing, pp. 16–34.

Kumar, Vijay. 2019–20. 'Catalogue of Antiquities of State Archaeological Museum, Lucknow, U.P. India Part I: Jain (from Kankāli Tilā, Mathura and other places of Mathura), Bauddha (from Mathura) & Gandhar Antiquities'. *Indian Journal of Archaeology*, no. 4: 62–67.

Lorenzen, David N. 2020. 'A Parody of the Kapalikas in the Mattavilasa'. In *Drink of Immortality: Essays on Distillation and Alcohol Use in Ancient India*, edited by D.N. Jha, Delhi: Manohar Publishers, pp. 251–72.

Luders, H. 1912. 'A List of Brahmi Inscriptions from the Earliest Times to about AD 400 with the Exception of those of Asoka' (Appendix to *Epigraphia Indica* 10), no. 1276.

———. 1937–38. 'Seven Brāhmī Inscriptions from Mathurā and Its Vicinity.' *Epigraphia Indica*, XXIV: 194–200.

McHugh, James. 2021. 'Grape Wine in Ancient and Early Medieval India: The View from the Centre'. *The Indian Economic & Social History Review*, 58 (1): 113–44.

Malavikagnimitram of Kalidasa. 1985. Edited and translated by M.R. Kale. Delhi: Motilal Banarsidass Publishers.

Mṛcchakaṭikā. 1962. Translated by M.L. Kale. Delhi: Motilal Banarsidass Publishers.

Mitra, Rajendralal. 2020. 'Spirituous Drinks in ancient India'. In *Drink of Immortality: Essays on Distillation and Alcohol Use in Ancient India*, edited by D.N. Jha. New Delhi: Manohar Publishers, pp. 69–98.

Olivelle, Patrick (trans.). 2005. *Manu's Code of Law*. New York: Oxford University Press.

Pal, Pratapaditya. 1986. *Indian Sculpture: A Catalogue of Angeles Country Museum of Art Collection. Vol. 1, Circa 500 BC–AD 700*. Berkeley: University of California Press.

Pisharoti, K. Rama. 1935. 'Dohada or the Woman and Tree Motif'. *Journal of the Indian Society of Oriental Art*, Vol. III (2): 110–12.

Quintanilla, Sonia Rhie. 2007. *History of Early Stone Sculpture at Mathura, ca. 150 BCE–100 CE*. Leiden, Boston: Brill.

Ray, Ardhendu. 2014. 'Wine Production and Consumption: Archaeological Evidences from Sanghol'. *Proceedings of the Indian History Congress*, Vol. 75: 1135–40.

Shamashastri, R. (ed. and trans.). 2012. *Kautilya's Arthsastra*. New Delhi: Low Price Publications.

Sharma, R.C. 1984. *Buddhist Art of Mathura*. New Delhi: Agam Kala Prakashan.

Shaw, Julia. 2004. 'Naga Sculptures in Sanchi's Archaeological Landscape'. *Artibus Asiae*, Vol. 64 (1): 5–59.

Stadtner, Donald M. 1996. 'The Little Cart in Early Mathura'. *Orientations*, Vol. 27 (1): 39–46.

Sivaramamurti, C. 1970. *Sanskrit Literature and Art, Mirrors of Indian Culture*. New Delhi: Lakshmi Book Store. (First published, Archaeological Survey. Memoirs, no. 73, 1955.)

The Meghadutam of Kalidasa. 2015. Edited and translated by M.R. Kale. Delhi: Motilal Banarsidass Publishers Pvt Ltd.

The Malvikagnimitram of Kalidasa. 2018. Edited and translated by M.R. Kale. Delhi: Motilal Banarsidass Publishers Pvt Ltd.

Varāhamihira's Bṛhat Saṁhitā. 2021. Translated and edited by M. Ramakrishna Bhat. Delhi: Motilal Banarsidass Publishers.

Vatsyayana and Mallanaga. 2003. *Kama Sutra*, edited and translated by Wendy Doniger and Sudhir Kakar. Oxford and New York: Oxford University Press.

Vasishtha-Dharma-Sastra. 1982. Edited by A.A. Fuhrer and translated by G. Buhler. Oxford.

Vishnudahrmottara Purana. 1958–61. Edited and translated by Priyabala Shah, 2 vols. Baroda. Oriental Institute.

Vishnudahrmottara Purana, translated by T.S. Maxwell, unpublished.

Zin, Monika. Forthcoming. 'About Visual Language, Drunken Women, Jesters and Escaping the World'. *Cracow Indological Studies*, 24.

2

DICING AND WRESTLING: PURSUIT OF LEISURE THROUGH CHANCE AND COMBAT IN EARLY INDIA

Suchandra Ghosh

The simple dictionary meaning of 'leisure' is the use of free time for enjoyment and it is opposed to labour or work. The monotony or drudgery of everyday activities leads one to the pursuit of leisure. Leisure hours could be enjoyed in a public space as well as in a private sphere. Among the various kinds of leisure, indulging oneself in sports activities was quite common across time and space. The world of early Indian male was not an exception and, of the variety of sports and games, dicing was the most popular. The game became an integral part of urban leisurely life, by the 2nd century BCE.[1] Gambling-houses gradually began to occupy an important role in the urban landscape. Winning a game of dice was largely a matter of chance with some amount of skill. Game of dice finds a place of pride in various texts and is represented in visuals too. While a game like dice was more favoured, one cannot ignore another sport, wrestling, which became popular in the post-Mauryan period. Wrestling was a combative sport, between two persons, played within an arena, viewed by spectators and, thus, became a part of the public space. We have the visual evidence of the practice of physical exercise in the form of wrestling and weightlifting. Weightlifting stones from Gandhara and Mathurā are evocative of preparation for wrestling. Wrestling, as a sport, received much patronage from the royal court and the elites. The *jātaka* stories (Cowell 1895–1907) are also repositories of the practice of dicing and wrestling along with other texts. Thus, an attempt is made here to venture into the male world of dicing and wrestling, navigating through different genre of sources. The essay would try to understand their transition, if there is any, of these sports from urban elite forms of leisure to popular pastimes. Watching a bout of wrestling or gambling could also be a form of spending leisure hours as we see represented in the art of Gandhara. How far these sports could retain the character of a leisurely pursuit and not turn it to professional endeavours will be another area of discussion.

Games played with dice was very popular in India from early times as pieces of dice were unearthed from many excavation sites right from the time of the Indus valley civilisation. Dice were played with *aksas* and *salakās*. Square terracotta dice pieces and oblong ivory pieces have been found at Mohenjodaro and many other Indus Valley sites and are on display in various museums now[2] Many of these were unearthed from archaeological sites. Not only mere mortals but even deities reveled in the game of dice. Thus, we have representation of Śiva and Pārvatī playing the game of dice in the veranda of Rameshwara temple, Ellora, among few others and, as the story goes, Pārvatī defeated Śiva. This is, however, an exception in the mortal world. We generally have narratives of men indulging in a game of dice. Dicing more often transformed from a mere leisurely activity to an act of gambling which could make or mar a person. This affliction was a phenomenon right from the Vedic times. Thus, in one of the hymns of *Ṛig Veda* (Book X, 34), a charm to cure a habitual gambler is found (Griffith 1999). A fatal fascination for the game is also narrated, leading finally to the enslavement of a dancer's family (Book X, 54). Gradually, the game became associated with kingship and so the consecration ceremony included a game of dice (Heesterman 1985). This was, however, more of a ritual. From around the post-Mauryan period, dicing took the character of an amusement which included both chance and skill, as the knowledge of throwing a dice became essential. The dice was made of guided shells, of wooden or ivory cubes or of the nut of the *vibhītaka* fruit (*Terminalia bellerica*) which was the size of a hazelnut (Auboyer 1994, 243, 700).

Dicing as an activity of pure leisure, with or without some economic gain and fun, are both represented in our textual and visual sources. Jeanine Auboyer talks about a rock from Bharhut which has the inscription 'the gamer who likes to play at the square table' (Auboyer, 1955, 123–37). It shows a rocky mountain with a kind of chessboard with thirty-six squares drawn at its summit. There are two couples, all men, and it appears like they were enjoying the game. According to her, the scene remains unidentified with any story but the fact remains that men playing a game of dice is being represented. This was undoubtedly a common recreation for the people in general.

Now taking the *jātaka*s into consideration, there are three specific *jātaka*s which take one to the world of dicing. These are the Vidhurapaṇḍita *Jātaka*, the Aṇḍhabhūta *Jātaka* and the *Liṭṭa Jātaka*. There are visual translations of Vidhurapaṇḍita *Jātaka* and *Liṭṭa Jātaka* on the caves of western Deccan and the Bharhut stūpa railings. In the stories described in these *jātaka*s, element of gambling predominates rather than leisurely pursuit. I begin with the *Liṭṭa Jātaka* (Cowell 1895, 221–22). The story depicts Bodhisattva, who was born in a well-to-do family in Varanasi, grew up as a dice player (*akkha dhutta*). With him, another player used to play who was a cheat dice player (*kuṭṭaka dhutta*) (Fausboll 1877, 379). Whenever the cheat gambler was on the verge of being defeated, he used to put one of the dices in his mouth and claim that the dice was lost. As the story goes, in no time, the Bodhisattva caught the trick and decided to make the gambler suffer. He smeared the dices with poison and let the gambler gulp it. Later, however, he saved the gambler by its antidote. The gambler promised not to cheat again. What is evident from the story is that a game of dice was a common pastime which eventually turned into gambling. The story of the *Liṭṭa Jātaka* is depicted on a panel from Bharhut where Bodhisattva is depicted as a common man, seated in a sedate manner for the game and the gambler is seating in the opposite with a cunning look and holding the dice, almost ready to throw (Fig. 2.1).

One of the stories in Aṇḍhabhūta *Jātaka* (Cowell 1895) throws light on the game of dice as a pastime. Here, the king who was the Bodhisattva used to play the game regularly with his minister and used to utter a catch for luck and always win, while the poor minister was left to sulk always. The story then goes on to describe how the minister beat the king by devising a new formula.

Vidhurapaṇḍita *Jātaka* (Cowell 1907) highlights how through a game of dice the Kuru king lost to the Yākṣa Punnaka and had to part with his favourite minister and adviser, Vidurapaṇḍita. Offer of a dice game as a means of obtaining some kind of power or property has a long lineage which is so well reflected in the *Mahābhārata*. Thus, Yudiṣthira after the *rājasūya* sacrifice indulged in a game of dice as desired by his kinsmen and finally lost his kingdom. In the story, there is an interesting description of the gaming room decorated with carpets and fine cloths. The dice was naturally made of gold and was placed in a silver tray. We learn about twenty-four throws in playing with dice. The story ends

Figure 2.1. Representation of *Liṭṭa Jātaka* in Bharhut, Indian Museum, Kolkata

Courtesy: Charlotte Gorant.

on a happy note as Vidhura is back to the Kuru king. Vidhurapaṇḍita was Buddha himself. Thus, in this *jātaka* story, too, the game of dice was used as an instrument to gain something which otherwise was impossible to obtain.

The artists at the site of Kanaganahalli[3] have come up with a slab depicting the Vidhurapaṇḍita *Jātaka* story with a label inscription saying *jātakam Vidura Puṇakiyam [/] Tomḍa gahapatino deya dhama sava (Vidura-Pūrṇaka Jātaka,* Meritorious gift of the agricultural landlord Toṇḍa) (Zin 2018). Thus, this inscription not only gives us the title of the narrative but also the name of the donor who was a rich agricultural landlord. The game of dice is represented in the lower part of the panel. According to the description of Monika Zin, 'the players are seated on both sides of the board. It is the *aṣtapada*, eight by eight square fields. Dice with an elongated shape are visible in the hand of the right player.' The hand of another player is broken. At least four persons are depicted seated behind the players. From the various representations of the story of Vidhurapaṇḍita, in the visual worlds of Bharhut, Kanaganahalli (Fig. 2.2) and Ajanta (cave no. 2),

Figure 2.2. Representation of the game of dice from Vidhurapaṇḍita *Jātaka* at Kanaganahalli, Karnataka, ASI

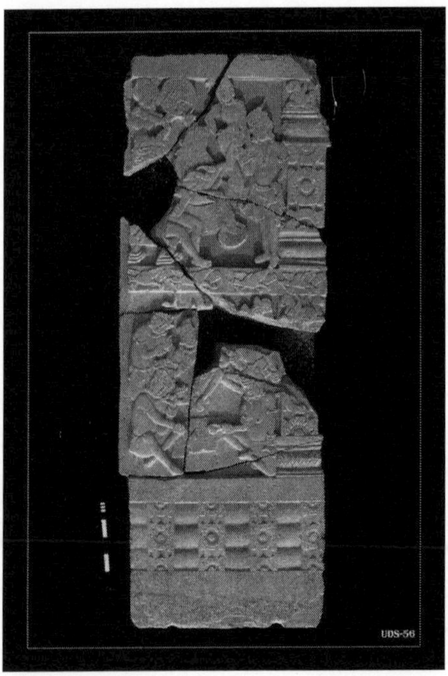

Courtesy: Dayalan Duraiswamy.

its popularity can be recognised. This narrative was also popular in Thailand and we find the episode of dice painted in a mural of Wat Yai Intharam in Chonburi province.

The site of Chandraketugarh,[4] an important node in the riverine network of Bengal, offers a huge concentration of narrative plaques in baked clay, depicting aspects of everyday life where leisure activities formed an important genre (Ghosh and Pal 2018). Among the many plaques recovered from the site, our attention is drawn to one, now in private collection, where a game of dice is displayed. From the ambience depicted, we can make out that it is a scene of leisure and enjoyment and set outdoor. We find here a royal person/an elite having a parasol above the head seated in a leisurely posture. He is accompanied by chowrie-bearing females and women attendants with plates of food. There are two other men seated, accompanied by ladies but without parasol. They could be members of nobility. All of them are depicted holding a sort of wine glass. The central place is occupied by the two players with the dice board and two oblong and three roundish dices. There are spectators, both men and women, a couple in a conjugal pose and people selling sweets and some kind of drink (wine?), as a pitcher-like spouted vessel is shown and people are holding tumblers. One can recognise the difference in the class hierarchy of the people by observing their head gear (Fig. 2.3). This plaque from Chandraketugarh dated probably in the early centuries of the common era undoubtedly

Figure 2.3. Dicing scene in terracotta from Chandraketugarh, West Bengal. Private collection in USA

Courtesy: Internet. Swayamkatha. (I have no other source for this. Personal communication from Vidya Dehejia confirms that according to the owner it is tested original.)

indicates the amusement aspect of the game of dice. Excavations from Chandraketugarh have also revealed pieces of dice (Fig. 2.4).

From the visual world when we again move to the textual world, we have texts like the *Mrcchakaṭika*, which gives us a picture of the gambling houses. Gambling houses had become a part of urban ways of life by the post-Mauryan period. These houses were sanctioned by the ruler. A person called Sabhika was appointed for keeping records of a *sabhā*, that is, an assembly of gamblers. The state earned revenue through these gambling houses, *Sabhika* received 5 per cent from the winner's deposit and 10 per cent from the loser's and paid a fixed amount to the state. Collecting money from the losing gambler was one of his primary duties. According to Yajnavalkya (II) (Olivelle 2020), the onlookers of the game were to be treated as witnesses and, if any foul play or false dice were detected against any gambler, he was to be branded and banished from the kingdom. In Act II of *Mrcchakaṭika*, we learn about the charm of the rattle of dice which could be compared to the song of cuckoo (Ryder 1905). In *Mrcchakaṭika*, the Sabhika Mathurā is seen to be exercising his power to collect ten gold coins from the loser Saṁvāhaka on behalf of the winning gambler. Another character in *Mrcchakaṭika*, Durdaraka, sums up the agonies and ecstasies of

Figure 2.4. Dice pieces, personal collection of Asadujjaman

Courtesy: Rajat Sanyal.

gambling like 'you earn your coin by gambling, your friends and wife by gambling, your gifts and food by gambling and your last cent goes by gambling' (Ryder 1905). The *Kāmasūtra* gives a vivid picture of the outer bedroom of the man about town, the *nāgaraka*, where along with other things a board for dice adorns the bedroom as an ingredient of recreation (Doniger and Kakkar 2002). It is accompanied by a gambling board too. It will be worthy to note that it is kept in the outer bedroom which is a recreational space of the *nāgaraka* often visited by the *gaṇikā*. Auboyer states that 'dice also played a part in affairs of love, for the elegant *nāgaraka* used them to decide which young woman should be his companion for the night' (Auboyer 1994). Picnics are described in the *Kāmasūtra* where, among other things, gambling is also a mode of enjoyment. Thus, the game of dice was a favourite pursuit of the urban male and the lure of money could convert an ordinary player enjoying the game into a gambler.

From a game of skill and chance when we shift our gaze to ancient Indian wrestling practices, we are directed to questions related to the purpose of wrestling as a sport or as an activity of pure entertainment. Unlike the Grecian world, India did not have a tradition of a space like gymnasium which catered to the physical and mental requirement. The male beauty could be enhanced by regular visits to gymnasium which was integral to the Greek way of life and was also considered a pastime. The gymnasium actually provided an entrance into public life. We are fortunate only in case of the Greek city of Ai Khanoum in northern Afghanistan where a gymnasium was uncovered. The gymnasium (100 by 100 m), one of the largest of antiquity, had spaces for physical training and large lecture halls built around an impressive inner courtyard devoted to intellectual activities (Veuve 1987; Ghosh 2017). Though we did not have gymnasiums per se, practice of physical exercise in the form of sports was present in early India. From Bharhut we have a wrestling scene in a carved medallion which shows two men grappling each other, each trying to make the other retreat (Auboyer 1994). The clinching evidence, however, comes from the art of Gandhara[5] (Ghosh 2019) which provides us a few interesting images of wrestlers engaging in their sport and, in some cases, spectators enjoying the wrestling bouts in their leisure. The exercise of leisure in the quotidian life of Gandhara was partially laced by refined Greek environment characterised by musical performances, visit to the theatre, gymnasium, wine drinking and merry making and so on. Wrestling, as a sport, received much patronage from the royal court and elites. It seems to be a recurrent theme in the Gandharan art. The Peshawar museum is a repository of a few stone slabs which were recovered from Gandhara along with representation of wrestling on them, mostly belonging to 2nd and 3rd centuries CE (Ali and Kazi 2008). I shall discuss a few of them now. The first one is a stone slab that comes from Lalpura (Afghanistan) (Acc. no. PM-02738) (Fig. 2.5). It depicts two wrestlers in high relief, with muscular bodies, wearing wrestling costumes. Facing each other, they are grappling hand-to-hand. The left foot of one is on top of the right foot of the other, probably representing a traditional wrestling pose. On top of the weight is written 'Minamdrasa', meaning 'of Menandros' in Kharosthi which was probably the name of the donor (Bernard and Jullien 1982). This suggests that they could also have functioned as votive objects. The ripples of the muscle of the wrestlers remind one of Hellenistic art style of Lysippos. From Mardan comes another panel (Acc. no. PM-02739) where two wrestlers are engaged in the combat in a similar fashion, grappling each other and wearing the same kind of attire. The figure on the left is probably holding a thunderbolt in his upstretched right hand. His left-hand rests on his hip while his head is missing. The figure on the right is touching his lips with his right hand to show astonishment. He too is having his left hand on his hip. Similar depiction of wrestlers is found from another panel in Peshawar museum (Acc. no. PM-02740), whose provenance is not known. In this case too the two wrestlers are shown grappling with each other and clad in short wrestling costumes. There are two other figures; the figure on the right appears to be holding a drumstick in his slightly upstretched right hand and a drum in his left. He wears the same type of dress as the wrestlers and, based on this, it has been assumed here that he is the referee, beating the drum to get the wrestlers' attention. The figure to the left of the scene is clad in monastic dress. He watches the contest with similar amazement as in earlier cases, with his right hand touching his lips.

Figure 2.5. Stone slabs with two wrestlers, Peshawar Museum

Courtesy: Late Paul Bernard.

His head is defaced. The panel is severely damaged. Significantly, the narrative is depicted against the backdrop of a house and the bout is taking place as if in the verandah which is flanked by framed Corinthian pilaster. The Hellenistic influence is unmistakable here.

In some cases, the wrestling scenes were represented in a kind of rectangular stone known as the weight-lifting stone. The back of the stone had sockets for lifting the stone. It is possible that these were weights used for exercises prior to wrestling competitions. Sometimes, scenes were engraved on the one or both the surfaces of the objects. In the collection of the Metropolitan Museum of Art, New York, there is an interesting weight-lifting stone which depicts a wrestling match in front of the spectators (Behrendt 2007). One wrestler lifts the other off the ground and proudly looks at the spectators. The moment of win is portrayed here as another man, perhaps a referee, raises his hand in acknowledgement of the wrestler winning the bout. Someone who is holding a flag looks at the wrestlers in awe (Fig. 2.6). The first labour of Herakles, killing the Nemean lion (Pinsent 1988) is portrayed on the other side of the stone (Fig. 2.7). The idea is to highlight the strength and athletic ability of Herakles. One cannot forget that Herakles is associated with the gymnasium as its protector.

Wrestling scenes and archery formed a part of the narrative of Prince Siddhārtha, trying to qualify as a worthy Kshatriya and a perfect suitor of Yaśodharā. These could be seen from sculptures from Sikri and Jamalgarhi, published by Ingholt (1957). A stone slab from a private collection in Japan shows a similar composition with Siddhārtha and a competitor wrestling at the centre, each grabbing the other's robes, the future Buddha backed by a nimbus and surmounted by blossoming foliage, flanked on either side by spectators in varying garb, including

Figure 2.6. One side of a weight-lifting stone with depiction of wrestling bout, MET Museum

Courtesy: Author.

Figure 2.7. The other side depicting the first labour of Herakles, killing the Nemean lion, MET Museum

Courtesy: Author.

a man on the right in princely robes and turban. The different types of people mirrored the heterogeneous character of the society.

Balcony seems to be an essential part of architecture in Gandhara as well as Mathurā. Figures of onlooker couples are integral to the depiction of balconies either in a domestic setting or in a public building where people gather to watch performances. That wrestling performances were watched by the people in a public space is evident from a relief from the sacred area of Chatpat which is presently housed in the Dir museum, Pakistan (Galli 2011). While the upper register depicts balconies, the lower register of the scene shows two pairs of men gripping each other in a pose typical of wrestlers, whilst the upper part shows people—couples—watching the event below from structures that look like 'balconies' or 'boxes'. The decorations of the balustrades of the boxes confirm that this is a festive occasion. This important relief indicates that sporting performances took place which could be watched by public and that these may have occurred during festivals and religious celebrations in the sacred area.

Various texts draw our attention to a variety of entertainers like drummers, acrobats, conjurers, etc. and wrestling too finds a room in the list. In the Vidhurapaṇḍita *Jātaka*, a detailed list of entertainers is given which includes *naṭa* (actors), *nartaka* (dancer), *gāyaka* (singer), *panissar* (expert in handmusic), *kumbhathunikam* (one who plays on earthen drum), *langhika* (one who is skilled at jumping), *malla* (wrestlers), *mayakāra* (magician), *sobhiya* (*sobhanika*, a kind of *naṭa*, possibly one who plays in cave theatres) *muṭṭhika* (boxer), *vaitālika* (bard). Competitions could be for entertainment which was quite popular among all social classes or could be serious combats like that of Bhima and Jarāsandha in the *Mahābhārata*. A 5th-century terracotta sculpture from Uttar Pradesh shows a traditional form of combat wrestling, attesting the regular practice of wrestling as a sport in early India (Fig. 2.8).[6] There must have been a sporting arena where these wrestling bouts would take place; a *vyāmasālā* (a form of gymnasium) could very well be one of those.[7] It will not be out of context if I refer here to a donative record (second-half of 2nd century CE) from Bandhogarh (Madhyapradesh) which talks about the donation of a *vyāmasālā* along with a tank and cave dwelling (Chakravarti and Dutta Majumder 1992). The gift of *vyāmasālā* is unique as till now we have not come across any gift of gymnasium in India. We know that a gymnasium is relevant to Hellenic and Hellenistic cultural contexts but it is hardly to be expected in a forest area in central India. There is no doubt that this *vyāmasālā* was used for recreation for the travelling merchants. Ranabir Chakravarti drew our attention to the fact that the Bandhogarh caves were halting stations for merchants travelling on a long overland route, perhaps the Pratisthana–Sravasti route. (Chakravarti 1995) The dating system of the Bandhogarh records was inspired by the Mathurān system during the Kushaṇa period. There must have been a cultural penetration from Mathurā into this area. The idea of a gymnasium could be the result of such cultural contacts as Mathurā was alive to the practices of the Hellenistic world as suggested from the weight-lifting stones from Mathurā. In fact, Mathurā played a pivotal role as a centre of cultural radiation of wrestler's weight. It has been suggested that the Sikri weight-lifting stone found from Gandhara, mentioned earlier, was perhaps brought from Mathurā by the Gandharan athletes returning from Mathurā or by the Mathurān athletes who carried them to Gandhara when they

Figure 2.8. Terracotta wrestling scene from Uttar Pradesh, Los Angeles County Museum of Art, public domain, gift of Neil Kreitman, South and South-east Asian art

went for competition (Di Castro 2007). Literary traditions foreground Mathurā's lineage in the art of wrestling.

The Ghaṭa *Jātaka* (no. 454) (Cowell 1901) paints a graphic picture of the wrestling arena in the context of a wrestling competition. It will be in order to briefly narrate the circumstances leading to the wrestling competition. There was king Mahākaṁsa who ruled in Uttarāpatha in the city of Asitañjanā. He had two sons and a daughter. It was predicted that the son born to Princess Devagabbhā would be the killer of his uncles Kaṁsa and Upakaṁsa. So, the brothers of Devagabbhā resolved to keep her a spinster and imprisoned her in a single pillared tower where she would be far off from any male companion. But, eventually, a young man, Upasāgara, the son of King Mahāsāgara gained access to her. As the story goes, both Devagabbhā and Upasāgara heard of each other and fell in love. With the help of her maid Nandagopa, a meeting was arranged inside the tower. In course of time, ten sons were born to them. These ten sons were wrestlers and were creating disturbances in the kingdom. On learning that they were his sister's sons, King Kaṁsa, as per the advice of his courtiers, organised a wrestling competition where they would be killed by two legendary wrestlers Canura and Muṭṭhika. Proclamations were made ahead of the event allowing people from far and wide to join the match. Thus, a tambourine player went around the town a week before and announced the match, thereby, tempting people to join. The wrestling ring (*yuddha maṇḍala*) was prepared in front of the gate of the palace; there was an enclosure for the ring. Along the round arena, the seats were raised tier above tier in a circular fashion. The pavilion was colourfully decorated with flags, *patākās* and people gathered in huge number looking for entertainment. It was an occasion which were enjoyed both by the elite and the common folks. The story ends, of course, with the death of the king and his brother, the uncles, of these wrestlers. A similar description appears in Chapter 42 of the *Bhāgavata Purāṇa* which is dated much later than the *Jātakas*. It describes how Kṛṣṇa and Balarāma fought the evil king Kaṁsa's wrestlers Canura and Muṣṭika and introduces us to the wrestling arena where the viewing gallery is decorated with garlands, flags, ornamental arches and ribbons. Sounds of drums and other musical instruments permeated the wrestling arena. The tradition of organising wrestling matches with gala decorations thus continued (10.42.33 and 36) (Shastri and Tagare 1950).

While wrestling was a leisurely sport in general, its character often changed and wrestlers were used by the kings for their protection and carrying forth their undue power-lust. The Dhonasākha *Jātaka* (Cowell

1897)[8] informs us about the king of Baranasi who, at the advice of his wicked priest, engaged his wrestlers to brutally kill the captive rulers in order to perform a gruesome ritual with the body parts of those killed. Thus, the might and strength of the wrestlers were misused in this context.

The Jaina literature also gives us some idea about wrestling as a favourite pastime of the upper echelons of the society. The kings were in possession of their own wrestlers. It is said that king Sihagiri who belonged to Soparaya, which would be identified with the famous port of Sopara (ancient Surpāraka), was happy to award money to the victorious wrestlers. In the *Uttaradhyana*, it is mentioned that a wrestler called Aṭṭaṇa of Ujjeni (Ujjayini) participated in the wrestling tournament (*juddhamahā*) every year and won the flag of honour. This wrestler travelled as far as Kaushambi on the banks of the Ganges and defeated the royal wrestler. For this feat he was honoured by the state (Jain 1984).

From the foregoing discussions it is quite evident that both dicing and wrestling cannot be taken as simple games of enjoyment and pleasure. These were much more complex and have multiple layers located within an urban milieu which gave them a certain kind of fluidity. At one level it can be said that the game of dice, largely an elite affair, entered the everyday world of men and at times turned them into gamblers whose changing emotions are narrated in the texts. This can be said to be a transition from youthful pleasure to an act of acquiring the mentality of a gambler. At another level for a *nāgaraka* or a *gaṇikā* or, for that matter, the folks seen watching and enjoying the game in the plaque from Chandraketugarh, this was indeed an act of leisure. Yet a text like *jātaka,* while handling narratives related to dicing, oscillated between enjoyment and greed. The intervention of the Bodhisattva saved people from ruin. Morality obviously is at play here. From the point of view of the state, this game was profitable and so should be encouraged. The spurt in gambling naturally brought revenue to the state and gaming houses were strictly under control and surveillance.

As for wrestling, the image that we get is that these were sources of entertainment as well as arenas to settle scores among competing persons. Here we are negotiating with two sets of people—one, the actual players, the other, the spectators/patrons. For the wrestlers themselves, the question would be whether the purpose of wrestling was sport or a profession or both; for the spectators, it was naturally moments of enjoyment, pure entertainment. The sculpture from Chatpat reveals that real performances of wrestling were watched by the members of the Gandharan society, which was reworking with a local culture and a culture which was deeply Hellenised. The wrestling stones from

Gandhara suggest interplay of influences, both from the Hellenistic world and from regions to the east of the Indus. Wrestling was a popular sport in India too, which is evidenced by textual and archaeological sources. The stories related to wrestling, surrounding Krişņa, gained popularity and the motif of the defeat of Kaṁsa's wrestlers Canura and Muṣṭika gained preeminence in a variety of texts. As it appears, individual wrestlers were appointed by rulers both for entertainment and protection. Thus, the aspect of entertainment, '*vinodan*', should not be lost sight of. I am tempted to close the essay by mentioning a later text *Mānasollāsa* of Someśvara III (1124–1138 CE), the renowned Cālukya king. It is a well-known text of sociocultural history and there the chapter on wrestling is called 'Malla Vinod' (Shrigondekar 1939).

Notes

1 Post-Mauryan period can be identified with a spurt in the growth of urban centres in the north of India, specially demonstrated by field archaeological and visual materials.

2 As an example, an ivory dice from Mohenjodaro is at display at the Asia Department of the British museum, no. being 1939,0619.336, acquisition date, 1939.

3 At Kanaganahalli (district Gulbarga, Karnataka) an important Buddhist site was excavated. Excavations were carried on by ASI between 1994–1998 and 2002–04. A massive stupa was found here with sculptured panels depicting various *jātaka* stories and life of Buddha.

4 The site of Chandraketugarh, located on the banks of the river Bidyadhari, about 35 km north-east of Kolkata in the district of north 24-Parganas, flourished as a riverport of the early historic period. The *Periplus of the Erythraean Sea* and Ptolemy's *Geography* speak of the port of Ganges located in the country of Ganges through which the river Ganges flowed to the sea. The port of Ganges is generally, though not unanimously, identified with Chandraketugarh.

5 Situated in today's northern Pakistan and eastern Afghanistan, Gandhara comprised mainly the fertile valleys of the lower Kabul and Swat rivers and the lower part of the upper Indus river, and was centred around the ancient cities of Pushkalavati (modern Peshawar) and Takshasila (modern Taxila). The boundaries of Gandhara shifted throughout history, and at different times the entire Swat valley was also included. The heart of Gandhara, however, was always the Peshawar valley. Gandhara cannot be isolated from the neighbouring regions that modern historians define as the Greater Gandhara: the upper Swat valley, Dir and the Bajaur agencies in the North-West Frontier Province and Begram-Kapisi and Hadda in Afghanistan

6 It is housed at the Los Angeles County Museum of Art, Public domain, gift of Neil Kreitman, South and South-east Asian art.

7 The term *vyāmasālā* is distinct from a *rangasālā* or sporting arena for entertainment as shown in the *Mahābhārata*.

8 I am thankful to my student Ujjwal Yadav for drawing my attention to this *jātaka* story.

References

Ali, Ihsan and Muhammad Naeem Kazi. 2008. *Gandharan Sculptures in the Peshawar Museum, Life Story of Buddha*. Peshawar: Hazara University, pp. 72–73.

Auboyer, Jeannine. 1955. 'Some Games in Ancient India'. *East and West,* 6 (2): 123–37.

———. 1994 (reprint). *Daily life in Ancient India, from approximately 200 BC to AD 700,* 243. New Delhi: Munshiram Manoharlal Publishers.

Behrendt, K.A. 2007. *The Art of Gandhara in the Metropolitan Museum of Art,* 14. New Heaven, London: Yale University Press.

Bernard, P. and Ch Jullien. 1982. 'Haltères votives de lutteurs dans le Gandhara'. *Studia Iranica,* 11: 33–47. Mélanges offerts à Raoul Curiel.

Chakravarti, Ranabir. 1995. 'Merchants and Other Donors at Ancient Bandhogarh.' *South Asian Studies*, Vol. 11: 33–42.

Chakravarti, Ranabir and Suchandra Dutta Majumder. 1992. 'An Ancient Gymnasium at Bandhogarh'. *Monthly Bulletin of the Asiatic Society,* July: 1–7.

Cowell, E.B. (ed.). 1895–1907. *The Jataka or The Stories of the Buddha's Former Births*. Cambridge: Cambridge University Press.

———. (545) Vol. 6: 126–55.

———. (91) Vol. 1: 221–22.

———. (91) Vol. 1: 151–55.

———. (454) Vol. IV: 50–56.

———. (353) Vol. III: 105–7.

Di Castro, Angelo Andrea. 2007. 'Of Handles and Names: Remarks on Wrestlers' Weights'. *East and West*, December, Vol. 57(¼): 367–76.

Fausboll, V. 1877. Liṭṭa Vol. 1. *The Jātaka Together with Its Commentary*. London: Trubner & Company, p. 379.

Galli, Marco. 2011. 'Hellenistic Court Imagery in the Early Buddhist Art of Gandhara'. *Ancient Civilizations from Scythia to Siberia,* Vol. 17(2): 279–329. Leiden: Brill.

Ghosh, Suchandra. 2017. *From the Oxus to the Indus, A Political and Cultural Study, c.300 BCE to c.100 BCE*. New Delhi: Primus Books.

———. 2019. *The Quotidian pursuit of leisure: Hellenistic Way of Life and the North-Western Borderlands of India (3rd century BCE to 3rd century CE),* Presidential Address, Ancient India, Indian History Congress, 80th Session, Kannur.

Ghosh, Suchandra and Sayantani Pal. 2018. 'Everyday Life in Early Bengal'. In *History of Bangladesh, Early Bengal in Regional Perspectives (up to c.1200 CE),*

Vol. II, Society, Economy and Culture, edited by Abdul Momin Chowdhury and Ranabir Chakravarti. Dhaka: Asiatic Society of Bangladesh, pp. 3–42.

Griffith, Ralph T.H. (trans.). 1999. *Hymns of the Ṛig Veda* (Vol. II). New Delhi: Munshiram Manoharlal, X.34.

Heesterman, J.C. 1985. *The Inner Conflict of Tradition: Essays in Indian Ritual, Kinship and Society*. New Delhi: Oxford University Press.

Ingholt, H. 1957. *Gandharan Art in Pakistan*, 56. New York: Pantheon Books.

Jain, J.C. 1984. *Life in Ancient India as Depicted in Jaina Canon and Commentaries,* 280. New Delhi: Munshiram Manoharlal Publishers.

Olivelle, Patrick. 2020. *Yājñavalkya Dharmaśāstra, The Textual History of a Hindu Legal Code*. New Delhi: Primus Books.

Pinsent, John. 1988. *Greek Mythology*, 87. London: Hamlyn.

Ryder, W. 1905. *The Little Clay Cart, Mrcchakatika, A Hindu Drama Attributed to King Sudraka,* 31. Cambridge Massachusetts: Harvard University Press.

Shastri, J.L. and G.V. Tagare. 1950 (eds). *The Bhāgavata Purāṇa, Part 4, Ancient Indian Tradition and Mythology, vol. 10, 1510–1513*. New Delhi: Motilal Banarsidas.

Shrigondekar, G.K. (ed.). 1939. *Mānasollāsa of King Somesvara III,* vol. II. Baroda: Oriental Institute.

Vatsayana's Kāmasūtra. 2002. A new translation by Wendy Doniger and Sudhir Kakkar, 17–19. Oxford: Oxford University Press.

Veuve, S. 1987. *Fouilles D'Aikhanoum, Le Gymnase*, vol. VI, Paris: Mémoires de la délégation archéologique française en Afghanistan, De Boccard.

Zin, Monika. 2018. *The Kanaganahalli Stūpa, An Analysis of 60 Massive Slabs Covering the Dome*. 35–36. New Delhi: Aryan Books International.

3

HUNTING AND DICING: WHERE LEISURE INTERSECTED WITH MASCULINE ASPIRATION IN EARLY INDIA

Smita Sahgal

Introduction

How would one define leisure? 'Freedom of choice' seems to be the most crucial attribute of the phenomenon of leisure. It conjures up the image of change in routine, of fun and frolic and of an activity that recharges one's flagging spirit. At times it is associated with absence of obligations while at other times with a mood of contemplation. However, one is tempted to ask whether the choice of any leisure activity is innocent and free of intervention of social (and perhaps psychological) factors. Social research has untiringly endeavoured to recognise factors that shape up the choices and historical research provides us with an opportunity to explore the intersectionality of choices made by historical actors within specific temporal, spatial and social locations.

Issues of Concern

Some basic questions emerge from the research process. What is the relation between leisure and work? What are the determinants in deciding leisure choices? Did such choices actually ever exist? When, in the ancient past, was recreation or leisure acknowledged as a social phenomenon? Did leisure in the past, especially in early India, have a class/caste angle to it? Could recreation and leisure for one class be a survival manoeuvre for another? Did leisure activities need a collective to be performed or were individual-isolated activities also recognised as recreational? The issue of collective brings within its ambit the concept of 'sports' with the participants and onlookers becoming a part of a social whole. Further, we may ask whether the choice of fun activities of the past was gendered? Is it possible that what is construed as leisure was actually designed to propel a certain kind of gender-image? In the process, could certain types of sports or activities be understood as masculine, against some that came to be associated with women or with the third gender?

The purpose of the chapter is to understand the phenomenon of leisure in the context of early India and how it distinguished itself from what may be understood as duty, *dharma* or work. Additionally, an attempt would be made to reflect on the ways by which some leisure activities, largely understood as idle pastime or recreation, come to simultaneously define manhood, advertently or inadvertently. The intent is to study the process from a gender vantage and mull over its social contours.

The Canvas and Its Tools

The interconnections between leisure and masculinity are best explored through textual studies. The texts have to be located on a temporal and spatial canvas to get a sense of how the concepts and their interlinkages evolved. We start by tapping the earliest; the *Ṛksamhitā*, which does throw light on the relevance of hunting and forest and gives us an insight into perceived gender relations between 'feminised' forest and the hunter. Chronologically, it is placed between 1500 and 1000 BCE and possibly compiled in the north-western part of the subcontinent. Among the other texts of the Vedic corpus, we cannot miss out on the relevance the *Āraṇyakas*, the forest books, along with the *Upanishads*, that were composed in the forest and give us a clue as to how the forest could become a site for activities other than hunting, meditation and spiritual ascension that offered its inmates serious alternative dimensions to hegemonic masculinity. These texts have been given a broad frame of period between 1000 and 500 BCE in the mid-Ganges belt. The epics, the *Mahābhārata* and the *Rāmāyaṇa*, are very rich in their narratives on all the aspects of leisure—hunting and dice game and on the correlates with masculine images. These have a long compilation time, from about 4th century BCE to 4th century CE that also gives us an idea of their transition from oral popular traditions to written Sanskritised ones. The texts on duties (*dharma*) and politics (*nītī*), including *Arthaśāstra* and *Manusmṛiti*, are especially useful in their elucidation of prescriptions and proscriptions, directed to the manliest individual, the king. Aspects that we understand as falling within the ambit of leisure are listed under proscriptive instructions in the text. Even a text like *Pañcatantra* gives an insight into how the acts of hunting and dice game were viewed by custodians of political treatises. All these texts have a broad frame of what we refer to as post-Mauryan time, from 200 BCE to 300 CE, in the northern part of the subcontinent. Kalidāsa's *Raghuvanśa* and *Abhjñanamśakuntalam* also have references of import for our theme and the texts can be approximately ascribed to early centuries of Common Era. Strabo's *Geographica* is also useful in assessing hunting as a sport for the ruler.

Purāṇa are a rich source of historical material as these abound in myths, ritual formulae, genealogy, reference to geography, climate, etc. However, these need to be handled cautiously as the information provided may not be very distinct and straightforward. Both *Skanda Purāṇa* and *Śiva Purāṇa* have instances or references of dice-game which indicate the existence of such leisure activities. These have also been dealt with by the authors of the texts in metaphorical ways to reflect on issues of *dharma* and consciousness. The texts would fall within what we refer to as early medieval or medieval period: *Śiva Purāṇa* around 800–1100 CE and *Skanda Purāṇa* between 1000 and 1300 CE, in and around southern India.[1]

Aśokan inscription of the 3rd century BCE, found across the subcontinent, are an effective source for becoming conversant with the views of the ruler who chose to espouse nonviolence and attempted to contain hunting for leisure or livelihood. Sculptural depictions of games as those of dice or chess matches give further confirmation of their recognition with the populace as activities of leisure. Śiva's game of dice with Pārvatī has been immortalised in stone at the Kailash Temple in Ellora and Elephanta caves.

Linguistic Conception of the Masculine and the Leisure in Early Indian Texts

Construction of the Masculine

On the historical trajectory of gender studies, masculinity is a recent entrant. Within India, especially early India, it is yet to make a niche for itself. In common parlance, masculinity almost appears as an essence or commodity that can be measured, possessed or lost and where anatomy comprises its bedrock. It is juxtaposed to femininity or to sexuality of the third gender to build its own attributes. The possibility of something like 'failed masculinity' or 'emasculation' reinforces the idea that masculinity is supposed to be a characteristic of men. We do borrow Western models for reconstructing Indian masculinities but we need to do that carefully. R.W. Connell's (1985) work has given us idea about varied masculinities. Borrowing terms from Gramsci, Connell classifies masculinities as hegemonic, complicit, marginalised and subordinate (ibid.) and we need to sift through our material to see if we can create analogous images in the context of early India. 'Hegemonic masculinity' is constructed in relation to women and 'subordinated' masculinity and rotates around the issue of how particular groups of men occupy loci of power and wealth and how they attempt to appropriate and reproduce the social relationships that generate their dominance (Carrigan et al. 1985). A connection between men and power and authority appears natural within this frame, whether in public or in private domains. Often, the tool of violence is used to consolidate this association.

There are men who may subscribe to the hegemonic project but do not exemplify hegemonic masculinity. Masculinities constructed in ways that realise the 'patriarchal dividend' without the tension or risk of 'being the frontline troops of patriarchy' are complicit in this sense (Connell 1985). Connell calls them a slacker version of hegemonic masculinity (those who embody complicit masculinity). Subordinate masculinity is generally construed as dominance of heterosexual men over homosexual men and this is much more than cultural stigmatisation. The heterosexuals subordinate homosexuals through what Connell calls 'an array of material practices and power display'. Marginalised masculinity is constructed outside the gender order, within the social milieu where men are marginalised because of their caste, class, colour or ethnic type. They, too, have to negotiate their aspirations and existence vis-à-vis hegemonic and complicit type who either wield power or support those who wield it.

Looking at early India, we find that even as there is no discourse on masculinity per se in early Indian literature, the idea of masculinity does run through various texts. We come across numerous words in the early Indian literature, related to man, manliness, masculine, masculinity such as *puruṣa, vīra* (man), *paurushah, viryogyah, mahaviryah, narah* (for manly), *parakrama, sahasam, manuṣyatvam* for manliness. Additionally, manhood is understood as *pumstva, puruṣtva* and 'masculine gender' is referred to as *pulingam* and *puman* while 'manly duty' is *naradharma* (M. Williams). There are two other words that are associated with manhood: *surâ*, the hero or a champion, and *śavas*, which imply might, strength and power. Both these words are common in the Vedic literature.[2] There are also words such as *kiṃpuruṣa* (evil man or a monkey-like man) (M. Williams), *klība* (Doniger–Smith), *panḍaka* (passive homosexual) (Staal) and *napuṃsaka* (non-man) (Doniger–Smith) that may be construed in opposition to what has been understood as 'manliness' within a larger question on masculinity. Interestingly, a masculine woman is called *ṛṣabhī* (M. Williams).

A study of these words and the contexts in which these emerge help us dwell on some of the attributes a man who has to be brave and virile too. Heterosexuality is the prescribed norm. The term vīra', which clearly denoted manliness, power and energy in texts such as the *Ṛgveda*, and the *Mahābhārata*, has at its root the reference to semen, *vīrya*. Body is often the site on which the term expands and hence each individual who is shown to be a repository of manliness also gets a delineation of his physical attributes and of his body as a whole. Therefore, we can tentatively suggest that masculinity entails within its ambit attributes of virility, fertility, a good physical frame, immense courage and ability to subordinate or rule. Hegemonic masculinity certainly reiterates claims to power. But, along with these attributes, especially in the context of early India, performance of duty (*dharma*), acquisition of wealth (*artha*) through intelligence or cunning strategies (apart from use of brute force and or creation of fear, *mahābhayah*) and effort towards spiritual well-being for salvation (*mokshạ*), all become the theoretical goals of manhood.

Understanding Leisure

Leisure is described in different ways in the early Indian texts. Sometimes as rest, *avakāśa*,[3] while at other times a pastime or recreation. 'Leisurely' then becomes *sāvakāśam* and *nirvakāśaḥ* implies 'having no leisure'. Leisure is also associated with *vinodaḥ*, amusement, as well as with a sport or *krīdā*. *Vinodaḥ* implies recreation and pastime as in *Hitopdeśa*. In the *Pañcatantra*, in the story on 'The Bull and the Lion', we come across a reference to *vinodasthāna*, the place of pleasure or amusement (hertel). Similarly, *viṣrāmah* is understood as rest or relaxation and reflects in the works of Kālidāsa and in the *Mahābhārata* (M. Williams). *Krīdā* is used in numerous contexts. Within the *Ṛksamhitā*, Marurts are often associated with it; especially in the passages I.37, 1 and 5 and in I.66.2. They are often referred to as 'sporting, resplendent on their car' (Griffith),[4] implying the velocity of the wind. *Krīdāketan* is a reference to a pleasure house (*Kathāsairtsagar* CXIV.57) (M. Williams) and *Krīdā-ratha* to a chariot of amusement as opposed to a war chariot. *Krīdā-mṛga* is a reference to an animal kept for pleasure (like a pet) not to be killed or hunted. *Kundaka Krīdā* (ball game) and *Jala Krīdā* (swimming) are sports recommended for women in the earlier times (Shah 2019). Within the *Kāmasūtra* too an ideal *nāgaraka* (city-man) is supposed to indulge in a number of games (*krīdā*) and one of that is gambling (*Kāmasūtra*). Gambling is one of the most famous games of the early times and is called *dyūta krīdā*—the game of dice. A gambler is known as *kitawa*. In the *Śiva Purāṇa*, Śiva is eulogised for playing the cosmic game (*krīdā*) with his own manifestation, the Śivaśakti (*Śiva Purāṇa*).

We also come across the term *vihāra*, which can also be expressed in the sense of a sport or amusement, wandering or roaming or a place of amusement. In the *Mahābhārata*, it clearly appears to be in the sense of a picnic. In *Raguvaṁśa*, Kālidāsa refers to a *mṛga-vana* as a *vihāra*, almost like an amusement park for the king. A *vihārin* is an individual who wanders around for pleasure.

We would have to dwell upon issues, whether amusement in ancient period could actually be distinguished from duty or *dharma*? Or still, can the two could be interconnected as one makes an easy transition to the other. The Khāṇḍava forest incident was preceded by Arjuna and kṛṣṇa's going for a *vihāra* (picnic) on the bank of Yamunā. The burning down of the forest is shown to be a part of their duty, seamlessly following an episode of their merry-making with their family and servants. Similarly, we wonder how Śiva–Pārvatī's fun game of dice converted into Śiva's duty related to creation–dissolution of the universe. Possibly, work and leisure are not neatly segregated in the ancient context. We would discuss these instances in some detail a little later.

Hunting and Forest: Site of Masculine Objectives

The forest was a site of conflict and violence on one side and that of reinforcement of masculine aspirations on the other. Empires and kingdoms of early India coexisted with vast forest tracts on which the state could not always exercise an absolute control. As a historical process, the forest landscape could never remain steady; its boundaries would change, particularly with the expansion of frontiers of local complex societies and emergence of new kingdoms. Upinder Singh (2017, 400) notes that the forest was not just 'an antithesis of the kingdom; its violent dissemination forms the kingdom's foundation'. It provided both the king, as a representative of new complex set up, and the inhabitants of the forest an occasion to test their masculine might. The reserves of forests constituted potential resources for both the state as well as its inhabitants. The state might have wanted to run its writ on the forest-space but its habitants would have felt a greater claim on it due to their continued relation with its flora and fauna over centuries. This would often materialise in a threat of violence for the forest tribes. Who had the right on the hunt, the state or the forest men? Hunting animals for food would have been a natural occupation for many tribes but for the king this would have constituted something else. Can we assume that hunting was a leisure activity for the ruler? Strabo in *Geographica* (Singh 2017) notes that, apart from war, 'the king moves out of his palace for three different reasons: to hear cases in courts, to perform sacrifices and to hunt' (ibid.). So was this hunt a matter of leisure for the king? The interesting part is the explanation of a type of hunt where women crowd around him in a circle, with spear bearers outside, and the king would shoot an arrow from inside the enclosure from a platform. The act appeared to be stage-created for the benefit of the ruler even as the entire shooting scene mimicked an expedition. Women here assisted him from horses and elephants to ensure his success. Clearly, it's a description of a royal hunt that fascinated Greek observers and appeared more of a sport with a purpose.

Hunts could be of different types. As just noted, some could be for recreation while others were seemingly intended for the purpose of manifesting king's valour and masculinity. That becomes evident when we read theoretical classifications of distinct types of forests within the *Arthaśāstra*. The game-forest was a place for royal sport where hunting (*mṛgaya*) was alluded to as an exercise which led to 'elimination of phlegm, bile, fat and perspiration' and where 'practice in hitting, moving and stationary targets' necessitated 'the understanding the mind of animals, when they are angry, afraid, and at ease …' A similar idea about hunting as a practice in consolidating masculine traits in the forest can be gauged from the reading of *Raghuvanśa*. When Daśaratha desired to hunt, Kālidāsa informs us that his counsellors approved of it as there were many advantages of hunting. 'It imparts skill in hunting, it gives outward signs of their (animals') fears and anger; it improves stamina by conquering fatigue' (Devadhar). Clearly, hunting here was not a leisure activity; it amounted to the sharpening of the king's skills and called for a show of strength. The forest here also appears to be a real place of action. However, a second type of forest was like an animal park, *mṛga-vana*, established for the king's pleasure. It is referred to as a *vihāra*, which has 'a single entrance, is protected by a moat, contains shrubs and bushes bearing sweet fruits', with shallow pools of water and stocked with tamed and wild animals, including deer and elephants with their claws and teeth removed, that could be hunted (Kangle). Otherwise Kautilya also makes an effort to distinguish between forests where deer could be hunted and elephant sanctuaries (*hastivanas*) which were almost like state reserves as elephants of these forests constituted an important wing of their armed force.[5]

A hunting expedition (*ākheṭa*) could also hold metaphorical masculine aspirations for the conqueror, especially if the forest itself was viewed as 'feminine' in terms of its spirit and its resource-generation capacity. There appears to be dichotomy between the forest and the settled agrarian/urban areas which can also be understood in terms of nature–culture debate. We wonder if the forest could be equated to *prakṛti*, the feminine natural force of Indian philosophical tradition. Incidentally, *prakṛti*, despite being the active force, is also projected as subservient to *Puruṣa*, the innate pure consciousness. Can the masculine king be representative of '*Puruṣa*' both in the subtle and material forms? If this line of argument is tenable, then the king's 'control' over the forest is more than a leisure activity.

Within the *Ṛksamhitā,* the forest spirit, *araṇyānī* is feminine (*Ṛksamhitā*). The picture etched out is that of a powerful but a benign and generous deity who devours only those who have a 'murderous enemy approach' (*Ṛksamhitā*). The sense of conflict is there. The enemy could be a tiger or a robber but it could also be a reference to any other man, intent on bringing the forest under control through his indiscriminate hunts. The hunt could also represent an exercise where the king, epitomising the masculine of the settled society, 'marches out to subdue an uncontrollable and dangerous female who is also resourceful and charming' (Sinha 2016). The royal hunt could then be a litmus test of a ruler's strength, stamina and presence of mind in the face of danger. The 'taming of forest' might not always be a successful enterprise but could at times translate into the union of the woman of the forest with the royal hunter. This could well be understood as a union between two elements of nature and culture that results in a progeny that would control both.

Was the subduing of forest, through royal hunts, an easy task for the ruler? Often hunting that simulated a raid would go awry and it seemed that the forest struck back to challenge the king's masculine prowess. Minkowski (2016) points out that several occurrences from the *Mahābhārata* and the *Rāmāyaṇa*, especially the former, where the royal hunt led to hazardous concerns for the king. In the legendary hunt of King Duṣyanta in the *Mahābhārata,* Duṣyanta's armed men reached a pitiable state as they became subjected to an elephant stamped. We have a graphic account of their despair:

> The river they sought out was dry; and thin with despair for water, their hearts exhausted with exertion, they dropped down, unconscious. Overcome by hunger and thirst, they fell prostrate on the ground, exhausted. There were some that were eaten alive by starving tiger men; other woodsmen built a fire, lit it, cut their meat in proper pieces,

> and ate it. There were mighty elephants that were wounded by swords and ran mad; turning up their trunks, they panicked and stampeded frantically. Dropping dung and urine and streaming with blood, the wild tuskers stampeded many men (1.63.21-26). (Sukthankar)

The reprisal by the forest can also be understood in terms of curse of emasculation that it could extend to men involved in reckless hunting. King Pāṇḍu mistakenly killed the sage Kidama, who was making love in the guise of a deer with a doe, while hunting. The sage cursed Pāṇḍu that sexual copulation would bring his end, which effectively ruined the prospect of his having a biological progeny. The text is explicit that it was the curse that came because of hunting that led to Pāṇḍu's sexual invalidity and eventual demise (Sukthankar). King Daśaratha in the *Rāmāyaṇa* was also cursed due to his act of hunting, something that might have been a part of his leisure activity. The king recalled the incident to his chief queen Kuśalyā. As a young, impetuous king, on a hunting expedition, he accidentally killed a young man, Śravaṇa Kumāra, who was drawing water from the river for his old, blind parents. Daśaratha had gained reputation as an expert archer and was fond of hunting buffaloes, elephants and other wild elephants. This leisure activity, that his counsellors had thought would make him a stronger man, had erroneously killed a young man who berated the prince for his folly of killing an innocent ascetic. He confessed the sin to Śravaṇa Kumāra's father, who was an ascetic too, and who told him that one day Daśaratha too would grieve for his son the way he was grieving for his own (*Rāmāyaṇa*). Similarly, the *Raghuvanśa* informs us of Dhruvasamadhi, one of the later kings of the Raghu lineage, was killed by a lion while attempting to hunt it (Singh 2017). The forest had fought back. Do we take this incident as a growing disapproval of leisurely/manly act of hunting by the mythmakers of the day?

Could this have been the reason for looking upon hunting as a vice (*Vyasana*) by the *śāstric* authors? Manu warns the ruler of the ten vices and hunting is one of them (Buhler). The *Arthaśātra* also lists royal vices but here hunting appears to be the least problematic (Kangle). Hunting also figures in as one of the seven royal vices listed within the *Pañcatantra* (26.19). We have already noted how hunting was regarded as a disastrous enterprise within the *Rāmāyaṇa* and *Raghuvṁśa* and brought tremendous grief to King Daśaratha. This may have been a way by which the norm-setters of the day sought to bring down the practice of hunting as a leisure activity. Within *Abhjñanamśakuntalam* too we get a critique of hunting from the character of the *vidūṣaka*, who was tired of Duṣyanta's mindless hunt of deer, tiger and other animals and pretended to be too exhausted to join the routine

(*Abhjnanamśakuntalam*). He even gets into an argument with the senāpati over the validity of the hunting enterprise. Senāpati asserts that hunting was wrongly dubbed as a vice (*doṣa*); in fact, it was a virtuous quality (*guṇa*) for the king as it endowed him with strength and endurance. Kamanaḍaka, elsewhere, is critical of citing hunting as an enterprise that brings physical health and deftness to the ruler. The benefits can be obtained by other means, it is stated *Nītisāstra*. Within the *Abhjnanamśakuntalam*, however, the king decides to give up his hunt after his encounter with Śakuntala and the critique she presented of it. A query that would haunt us is whether hunting was confined to men or was it pursued by women too. Examples from Greek accounts and from *Abhjnanamśakuntalam* inform us that the king had trained *yavana* women archers helping him, but from the same text the critique of hunting also comes from the women. It is safe to assume that among the hunter-gathers, women would also participate in the hunt though Sanskrit literature generally shows it as a male preserve.

From the edicts of the Mauryan king, Aśoka, we get concrete evidences of the royal effort to control it as a leisure/pleasure exercise for the royals, elites and populace in general. In rock edict VIII, he informs us that, 'In earlier times, kings used to go on pleasure royal hunts (*vihāra-yattas*). In these they engaged in hunting and other such pleasures'. In another minor rock edict at Panguraria in central India, Aśoka recalls his younger days when he would go for games such as tigers and leopard while enjoying his stay in the forest area with his consort. Subsequently, Aśoka did not just stop hunting as a leisure activity but expected his subjects also to do so. The Shar-i-Kuna Graeco-Aramaic inscription, located near Kandahar in Afghanistan states, '... and the king abstains from [killing] living beings, and other men and those who [are] huntsmen and fishermen of the king ... have desisted from hunting'. Could it be entirely true? What about the livelihood of *aṭāvīs*, the 'men of forest', who lived by hunting for their survival and also exercised a possessive control over its produce? Their rationale of existence would have brought them in direct conflict with the state which would assert a superior right on the forest. The threat held out to the *āṭavīs* by Aśoka, thus, becomes comprehensible in the same edict (XIII) where he preached the importance of ahimsa. The forest-dwellers, being demographically an important part of any state's population, needed to be made to conform to what the state required. It was not just the forest and its produce that appeared to be of interest to the king. It was the services of men of the forest or those living on its fringes and labelled as *niṣāda, śabaras, kiraṭas, canḍālas*, etc. that was sought by the state and populace of upper castes. Therefore, it's most likely that the king looked at the forest and hunting exercise as something more than just a leisurely act. In fact, the normative tradition of the day considered hunting as one of the vices that he should avoid. As a head of a kingdom or a full-fledged state, he would strategise control over both men and resources of the forest on the one hand while sending the message of his hegemonic strength to the subjects at large on the other.

There may have been times when the rulers were pushed in working out alliances with the men of forest. This would have been for strategic reasons. Only with their supports Brahman and Kshatriya hermits would have felt safe in the forest. The *Mahābhārata* has a story of a *niṣāda* ruler called Kāpavya who, despite being a *dasyu*, was a moral man, pursuing the Kshatriya's code (*dharma*). The tale of Kāpavya tells the story of men on the margins who rigorously upheld Brahmanical-dharmic norms. Kāpavya is described in terms of what ought to be two polarities. On the one hand he knows all the 'forest lore' proper to his status as a forest-roaming man and on the other he knows 'the *dharma* of all beings' and practices the *dharma* appropriate of a Kshatriya, properly looking after his 'blind parents' and 'protecting the Brahman and forest dwelling ascetics (XII.133.6-7)' (Sukthankar).

This is a fascinating intervention because here the *dasyus*, who may have become bandits or forest tribes, were actually motivated to move away from what might have been construed as their *dharma* and adopted practices considered to be moral, bringing about their upliftment as well. Interaction with them was now not quite the problem it might have been at one time. And this incorporation had real benefits for the *niṣādas* too, as perfection (*siddhi*) due to devotion to *dharma* was conferred on the virtuous *dasyu* and this must have facilitated their easier assimilation within the Brahmanical order (ibid.). In this story, changes in livelihood, which are otherwise condoned only under distress, *Āpaddharma*, were encouraged otherwise too. This is a clear attempt by the mythographers of the *Mahābhārata* to Brahmanise forest men, giving them an illusion of upward mobility if they synced in with their notions of masculinity and *dharma*.

The *Rāmāyaṇa* also portrayed some forest tribes in a positive light. The *niṣāda* king, Guhā, is depicted as a strong, brave and loyal forest king and a good friend (*priya-sakhā*) of Rāma. Rāma graced Guhā's forest territory at Śringaverapura by his presence in the early phase of his exile. The text informs us how Rāma asked Guhā about his kingdom (*raṣtra*), allies (*mitra*) and treasury (*dhana*) as well as about the well-being of his people who lived by hunting and boat-making (*Rāmāyaṇa*). When Bharata headed towards the forest to entreat Rama to come back to Ayodhyā, Guhā took care of him and his retinue. Similarly, the character of Śabarī, of the Śabra forest tribe, would grow in the later traditions as an ideal devotee, waiting in the forest for the arrival of

Rāma to attain her spiritual emancipation. Śabarī, in some traditions, is shown to be the daughter of a hunter who renounced the world after being appalled by the sight of slaughtered animals being prepared for her wedding feast. This does appear a little odd as he was a hunter himself and living by animal meat would have been natural. We detect an endeavour to sanitise the aspirations of forest men (and women) through association with other 'evolved men' who could motivate them to renounce their profession of hunting that involved indiscriminate violence. Notions of bhakti and ahimsa became the vehicles of this change. The increasing influence of the heterodox sects could have been a reason for this. Within Jainism, occupations such as hunting and fishing are to be shunned. In the Jain *Rāmāyaṇa*, *Paumacāriyam*, Lakṣmaṇa, who kills Rāvaṇa, goes to the same hell as the latter does (Jaini 1977).

But the assimilative process might not have been a smooth one. The *Rāmāyaṇa* also sheds light on Rāma's disquiet with some men of the forest who seemed to have challenged his caste, status and masculinity on certain occasions. His tussle and eventual killing of Vali has puzzled many historians. Romila Thapar (1978) acknowledges in her work that, 'The killing of Valin remains without adequate explanation.' Rama transgressed the Kshatriya code when he shot at the *vānara*, Vali, in the back when the latter was fighting Sugriva. Was that acceptable of a man whose masculinity would be otherwise branded as hegemonic due to his leadership attributes? In fact, Vali reprimanded Rama for violating the norms of fighting and Rāma gave him a litany of reasons in his own defence, underlying the move as legitimate. One of the explanations given by Rāma was that 'as a representative of the Ikṣavāku king ... he must punish anyone who commits incest'. Vali's act of sleeping with younger brother's wife was nothing short of adultery. Besides, Rāma had made a promise to Sugriva to help him out and kill his wife's abductor. This has often been understood as a strategic move on Rāma's part as he needed help of Sugriva and his tribe in finding his abducted wife, Sīta. And, finally, he said that Vali was a mere animal, ignorant of matters related to *dharma*. Humans, including sage and kings, hunted captured and killed animals even while their backs were turned. Somehow, the issue came to be centred on complexity of *dharma* which Rāma asserted was beyond Vali's comprehension. From our perspective, it is interesting to note that Rāma equated killing of Vali to hunting an animal. However, it was not done as a matter of leisure but as a matter of *dharma*/political duty. In the estimate of the authors of the *Rāmāyaṇa*, this could not have hurt his masculinity at all.

The forest allowed some to become men of superior esoteric knowledge. It was the mystique of forest that must have formed the reason for the compilation of *Āraṇyaka* texts and the transmission of its esoteric knowledge therein. Both the *Āraṇyaka* and the *Upanishads* indicate a diversification of views on masculine aspirations. We encounter discourses on renunciation and eventual attainment of spiritual ascension within the frame of the forest. *Chhāndogya Upanishad* states that those who know the doctrine of the Five Fires and live in the forest, follow faith and austerities go on to the path of the gods. In fact, *Vanaprastha*, the third of the āśarams (life-stage) a man needs to ideally follow in his lifetime, is intricately linked up with renunciation and asceticism, to be achieved within the frame of the forest. The *Bhagvad Gīta* (*Maitri-Upanishad*) also encourages the seeker to go to the 'unpeopled' forest where one would be able to 'restrain the group of senses from noises and meditate on the ultimate reality' (*Bhagavad Gītā*). It is interesting to note that during this stage of one's life the forest is not to be seen as a venue of any hunt/sport but of arriving at the ultimate truth. The forest becomes the site of the individual's salvation, giving a twist to the notion of what is to be a 'real man'. The renouncer is still a man, a conqueror of sorts, but the conquest is one of senses and worldly desires. Could asceticism of forest be motivated by as much a desire to break away from the uncertainties of a changing society as by the conviction that spiritual reflection was an effective way of acquiring the knowledge that furthers self-realisation? That cannot be totally negated as, many a times, inability to discharge 'manly' duties might also prompt many to take a refuge in the forest. For many Brahman men associated with ritual performances, the forest would have become a ground to practise their control over magic and perfect the sacrificial ritual performances.

While on the theme of hunting and forest, we need to reflect on the issue of forest-burning, especially if it appears to be an act done on purpose. We have some instances of incidental forest fire in epics but some forest-burning acts are touted as deliberate. We cannot surely call them 'acts of leisure' but wonder how, at times, leisure activities preface them as was the case within the Ādiparva of the *Mahābhārata*. The Ādiparva concludes with the episode of burning of a forest: *Khāṇḍavadāha* (I.214-25) (Sukthankar). Yudhiṣṭhīra and his brothers had set up their rule over a forested tract of land to the west of Hastinapura, the seat of their cousins, the Kauravas. As the episode begins, the reign is described as peaceful and prosperous, with new heirs born to Draupadī and Subhadra. It was, in fact, the birth of this sixth prince, Abhimanyu, who would be the link to the eventual sole heir, that brought Kṛṣṇa Vāsudeva to Indraprastha to perform the child's birth rites (ibid.). On a hot summer day, Arjuna proposed to Kṛṣṇa that they all go for a picnic, to overcome the heat.

Kṛṣṇa gladly agreed. Together with their womenfolk they went to the bank of Yamunā and enjoyed themselves. We get a sense of their revelry and leisure. Both Draupadī and Subhadra got intoxicated (ibid.) and distributed their priceless clothes and ornaments to the women around. Some women danced rapturously, some shouted, some quarrelled while others laughed aloud. While talking to each other, Arjuna and Kṛṣṇa retreated to the nearby forest. It was then that they were approached by a Brahman who demanded food from them. When the two decided to satiate him, he revealed his true nature as Agni and declared that ordinary food would not gratify him. He sought to devour the whole forest, but each time he had made an effort earlier, his attempt was foiled by Indra who was bent on protecting his friend, Takṣaka, who lived in that forest. The duo agreed to assist him but needed superior weapons. In order to help them Agni requested Varuna to do the needful. Varuṇa provided Arjuna with a powerful bow and inexhaustible quivers along with a very fast chariot. Kṛṣṇa was given an infallible discus. Fortified with weapons, Arjuna and Kṛṣṇa began to burn the forest down. Indra tried to protect the forest and poured rain but was stalled by Arjuna and Kṛṣṇa. Further, the two stopped all the creatures that strained to escape the misery. It was a grisly site and only Maya, a demon, Aśvasena, the son of Taksaka, four little birds and their mother could escape. Agni was extremely happy with this cruel feast that lasted six days, and eventually dismissed his two helpers after thanking them.

How does one rationalise the scene? It was an act of hunting of sorts, pushed to an irreversible point that rendered the entire forest waste, extinguishing its flora and fauna. It, however, ensured Arjuna and Kṛṣṇa much appreciation from Agni. The duo was also made aware of their identity as Nara and Nārāyaṇa and their duty of cleansing the earth of the evil. But it leaves the readers disconcerted. Interestingly, the scene was prefaced by an act that could be called a 'picnic', '*krīdā*', full of joyfulness and abandon, giving the audience/readers a feel of a lull before the storm. They are flummoxed at the apparent casualness of the event. Arjuna and Kṛṣṇa were out on a fun-filled picnic and ended up becoming inducers of a massacre, all in the name of *dharma* or duty. Scholars, too, are mystified by the introduction of this theme and attempt to reason it out in different ways. Was it a reference to clearing of the forest for agrarian purposes? C.V. Vaidya (1966) notes a slash and burn form of land cultivation here, and Agni being used for the purpose of clearing the land. For Holtzmann, the forest was probably a retreat for natives (*asuras*) in their resistance to '*die anruckenden Arier*' (the approaching Aryans) (Hiltebeitel 1976). Irawati Karve (1969, 141) concurs in the Aryan conquest theory and endeavours to explain the notion of a mythologised conquest further: the Nāgas and the birds were a reference to the forest clans whom the Aryan 'conquering settlers' and Arjuna and Kṛṣṇa deliberately liquidated. Rajagopalachari (1958, 65). and van Buitenen (1973, 8), too, hold the same position. There is little doubt that, subsequently, the tracts of erstwhile forest would convert into areas of rural and urban settlements of Indraprastha. From the perspective of masculine projections, however, we wonder how heroic was the act? We clearly see strains of hegemonic masculinity, fuelled in by doses of unbridled violence that reflect both intra-Aryan rivalry as well as one with the indigenous settlers. We wonder if it behoved well on superior men and gods. It appears as if the authors of the epic themselves felt perturbed and tweaked the story in later *parvas* to bring about a moralistic retribution.

The acts of plunder by the Pāṇḍavas and Kṛṣṇa did not go completely unchallenged. The hunted are shown to have a way of responding in the long run. The price had to be paid. Kuntī, the mother of the Pāṇḍavas, eventually, died of burns in the forest and Kṛṣṇa was also killed by a hunter named Jara who mistook him for a sleeping deer in the forest. Earlier, in anger and grief over the death of her sons and the Kaurava soldiers, Gāndhārī blamed Kṛṣṇa for the destruction in the war and cursed that Yadavas would meet the end in a manner similar to the demise of her sons. Kṛṣṇa accepted the curse. His eventual death by the hunter was almost like poetic justice rendered to one responsible for the death of so many innocent inmates of the forest. The hunted could retaliate. We are tempted to believe that a detailed description of *Khāṇḍavadāhā* was done intentionally by the authors/compilers of the epic as a matter of warning to the readers/listeners. Even as it spelt out momentary victory for men and gods involved therein, the price had to be paid. Mind-numbing display of aggressive masculinity was eventually circumscribed within long drawn frame of morality.

We are inclined here to make a comparison with another leisure sport, wrestling, which also allowed intersectionality of aggressive masculinity with leisure and power. Kṛṣṇa, who could bring down the forest in *Khāṇḍavadāhā* episode of the *Mahābhārata*, is shown as a very young but adept wrestler in yet another text, the *Bhāgvatpurāṇa*. In Chapter X, cantos 44 of the text, we get a detailed version of the wrestling episode where Kṛṣṇa and Balarāma were pitted against accomplished wresters of Kaṁsa, Canura and Musthika. The match was well attended by a crowd hooting initially in favour the king of Mathurā, Kaṁsa. The details of the match between very young boys and mature wrestlers are intended to highlight the divine might of young brothers, especially that of Kṛṣṇa, who defied age to first bring down the wrestlers and then eventually pull Kaṁsa off from his throne and kill him in wide public view. Throughout the text the tenor is in favour of Kṛṣṇa.

He performed a masculine feat that many mature men could not. The display of masculinity here is touted as something very essential in performance of *dharma*/duty. The scale had to be enormous as it challenged the might of a ruler and the message had to be clear too—that the power could not rest with one representing the vice. It was a show of brute dominance, just as would happen in hunting or burning down the forest. The medium chosen to convey this, however, was a leisure sport that many among the populace could identify with. The crowd got drawn to the sport by watching, cheering at times or getting mesmerised by the feat of young Kṛṣṇa. They could not remain a mute audience as a leisure sport became a hegemonic display of strength and power.

Reflections on Hunting as Leisure

We start by attempting to understand the true rationale of hunting by the elite, especially the king. Was it a mere act of leisure or a part of a larger hegemonic project of the ruling class? Without a doubt, hunting could be a leisure sport for the king/elites but it appears to be more than that. Hunting was an integral part of the king's existence and duty as he had to exercise control over all regions and resources within his kingdom and this might require repeated reiteration of his authority. There was a fear that forest resources could deplete through indiscriminate consumption or rivals staking a claim. Hence, the king with his retinue returned time and again to the forest, either to hunt for leisure or to establish hegemony through conquest. In addition, hunting promised the king a chance to show off his masculine self to his subjects. Even though many spectators may not be present, stories of the king's hunting strength would spread fast to consolidate his popular image. At the same time, excesses in hunting could trigger calls to exercise caution and abandon the idea of indiscriminate killing. Slaughter in the forest by a virtuous king could, at times, create a dilemma about his manhood; Rāma's killing of Vali being the case in point.

The proscription on casual exploitation of forest resources, so beautifully expressed in Aśokan inscriptions or normative texts' classification of hunting as a vice, becomes intelligible in the context of the need to conserve forest assets. It may have also been propelled by the fact that mindless exploitation of its resources could beckon a retaliation from the forest. Animals could kill the hunters; nature could turn hostile. Daśaratha was cursed for accidentally killing Śravaṇa Kumāra and lost his beloved son to forest exile. Pandu became unproductive because of his love for hunting and Kuntī took the curse of her son's/brother's burning down the forest by dying from a forest fire herself. What was reiterated was a cautious pursuit of hunting by the outsiders (to the forest).

But what of the forest inmates, the *aṭāvīs*? Can hunting be assumed as a leisure sport for them too? And could they be refrained from hunting when the ruler deemed it so? Our research shows that hunting was an essential activity for forest-dwellers, essential for their own survival. It was not really a recreational sport or a chosen occasion to prove one's manhood; hunting was fundamentally a way to subsist.[6] We have already noted that both the forest resources and forest dwellers were indispensable for the state and its arms: the king and the norm-setters. Forest inhabitants were recognised as necessary evils by those who manned the state. Even as they were not much liked by them, the state and norm setters had to accommodate them. The norm-setters (usually Brahmans) of the day finally found a key to deal with this complex issue; they put the forest dwellers low in social hierarchy but gave them the hope of upward mobilisation, if they followed the upper-caste codes. The story of Kāpavya can be interpreted as one which indicates an attempted Brahmanisation of the forest men to the advantage of the state, king and Brahmans. This must have become necessary as the ascetics would not have survived in the forest to pursue their esoteric goals without an alliance with the people of the forest.

The Game of Dice: Dyūta krīḍā; *Chance to Prove Manhood*

Amongst all leisure games in early India, dicing or gambling receives maximum literary attention. We have references of it right from the Vedic texts. It is believed that in the 'Vedic times' people gambled using the *vibhītaka* fruits as dice (*Ṛksamhitā*). Within the *Śatapatha Brāhmaṇa* (Eggeling) and *Taittirīya Samhitā* (Weber), however, there is mention of golden dice (*akṣa*). It appears that these were used by the rulers, perhaps during the performance of a sacrifice. This cannot be proved archaeologically but we know that the popularity of some dice games since the Harappan period which has thrown up proofs of quadrangular ivory bars or cubical dice. In the *Ṛksamhitā,* we can infer that generally four dices were used in the dice game, possibly as a part of a ritual (Weber). The passage also indicates that Varuṇa holds the dice in his hand. Can we relate the hymn of Varuṇa holding the dice as a clue to his upholding the moral order (*ṛta*)? Throwing the dice in a ritual context could be taken as symptomatic of tribal practices where resources were not contained by an individual but shared with the populace. It is interesting to note that there is a hymn in the text that is dedicated to the dice, that is, where the dice is deified (*Ṛksamhitā*). Dice-throwing or gambling was so pervasive during the time that we get references to its social outcome too, which we would address a little later. Even within the linguistic frames, we get the references to it in a metaphorical form. Sometime when one is losing in battle, he invokes Aśvins and requests them to help him in a 'a luckless game'.

We get a sense of the details of the ritual game from the commentary of *Śatapatha Brāhmaṇa* (Eggeling). No board was used then, the Satyāgni priests would spread a piece of ox-hide at the north side of the sacrificial fire and, thereafter, put a brass pot upside down which would then be used to throw dice on. The vessel which contained the *akṣa* was called *aksāvapana* and the individual in charge of it was called *akṣāvāpa*; *glah* or *grabh* was the throw of the dice. Points gained were called *aya* while stake was known as *vija*. The four sides of the *akṣa* had different names: the side marked with one point was kali, that with two points was dvāpara, that with three points was tretā and that with four points was called kṛta. Other *ṛcas*[7] give us an idea about what happens to the family when a man loses the game. The *Atharvaveda* also makes references to some details of the game. The hymn XXXVIII alludes to 'a charm for success in gambling' and summoning the *apsāras* to obtain the stake and gain the victory with skill. We also sense the anger of the loser, which we will discuss later.

Within the *Mahābhārata*, the game of dice holds a very central position. We do come across terms such as *dyūta* and *dūrodara* (misfortune) a couple of times. A past master in dice game, Śakuni, used hollow dice plugged with lead with which he could easily cheat. *Salakā*, a four-sided bar made of ivory, was also often used in the game. The issue of dice game and its consequences are brought out time and again. What is evident is that the dice game by then had evolved into a board game. A bas-relief, ascribable to second century, on the Bahrut rail depicts an act of gambling where two men are sitting face-to-face. There appears to be a board in front of them which has squares and cubes with marks on the sides lying outside the board.

Jātakas are also replete with references to gambling with dice. In *Liṭṭa Jātaka* (Book I.91), there is mention of poisoned dice while the *Vidurapandita Jātaka* (Book XXII.545) informs us of a magic dice. Reference to the throwing of dice in air to indicate descent of nymphs comes in the *Guttila Jataka* (Book II.243). The pervasiveness of the practice becomes obvious in other post-Mauryan texts such as the *Arthśāstra* and *Manusmṛti*, where gambling is not just listed as one of the *vyāsanas* (vices) to be avoided by the rulers but has become a state concern when it comes to its popularity amongst the people. *Manusmṛti* states 'Gambling and betting; let the king exclude from his realm; those two vices cause the destruction of the kingdoms of princes (Doniger–Smith)'. Gambling and betting amount to open robbery; the king shall always exert himself in suppressing both (Doniger–Smith). Other *smritikaras* were more pragmatic about this practice and noted that if the practice cannot be completely proscribed, it needs to be regulated by the state. The *Kātyāyanasmṛiti* of the post-Gupta times (around 6th century) states, 'If gambling cannot be stopped in the kingdom, it shall be regulated. Gambling should be allowed to be carried on openly in the gambling hall (the hall licensed for the purpose).' The suggestion is to have a designated space such as a gambling hall which should be provided with an ornamental arch to indicate its distinction, and the king should impose tax on gambling and make it a source of income. In this way, gambling became a legitimised source of income for the state and practice for the men around.

In fact, within the *Kāmasūtra*, its social acceptance stands out. Vātsyāyana in his list of sixty-four forms of art or *kalās* has named the art of playing *Dyūta-viśeṣa* and *Ākarṣa-krīdā* as two different *kalās* (Roy 1939). Vātsyāyana has mentioned *dyūtaphalaka* and *ākarṣa-phalaka*, that is, boards for playing dice and *ākarṣa*. *Dyūta* here meant dice and *ākarṣa* possibly meant staves. What is significant is that, within the *Kāmasūtra*, Vātsyāyana mentions a list of festivals which have been termed as '*samasyā-krīdā*'—the play in which some citizens assemble together and amuse themselves. Some of these had dice games as an integral part of celebration such as the *Yakṣarātrī*, which would be performed during the night of the new moon of Kārttika. People generally gambled during this night. This is usually known the night of Diwali. The next is the *Kaumudī-jāgara*. This was a reference to the clearest moonlit night of the year when people engaged in gambling and *dolā-krīdā*, that is, swinging in hammocks, etc. This night was mostly celebrated for the worship of Goddess Laksmī. The belief was that whoever gambled that night became rich. No wonder this night was also called *Dyūta-pūrṇimārātrī*.

The intent here is not to trace the historical trajectory of the practice of gambling in early India but to understand it within the contexts of leisure and masculinity. We had raised the issue earlier; whether leisure could actually be qualified by a sense of freedom from work and redemption from a set of prescribed social norms. If one is thinking of leisure simply as taking a break or resting and not indulging in any activity then it may be possible to assume leisure as freedom of sorts but if the leisure time was used for a sport, then leisure did not remain a simple act; rules were bound to emerge. *Dyūta krīdā* was also a game of gambling where rules did evolve. We get to know that, from being just a ritual act, it gradually became a board game. We see that numerous kinds of dice and staves were used and how these were placed on ground or on the board. We also get a sense from texts such as *Nāradasmṛiti*[8] that, when a person had lost money and remained in debt, he was not allowed to enter the premises till he paid off his debts. But, at the same time, we also get a sense that many a times within the game norms were flouted. The idea was to win and all kinds of strategies were employed. If that was the case, then can dice game really be understood as a leisure activity? Is there a sense of abandonment, recreation and innocent fun involved in order to rejuvenate sagging spirit? Or does it get associated with cerebral activity and professional deftness? A study of its long course pushes us to believe that dicing seemed to have seen many phases: from ritual act it graduated into a sport that required a degree of training and use of intelligence, to a kind of profession; a profession linked with identity, resource acquisition and larger social matrix. From our perspective, it was an occasion to manifest one's cunning/cleverness that could translate into masculine pride. For a man it was a shortcut to gain wealth and identity. Defeat in the game was not taken well.

In the *Atharvaveda* (Lanman), we come across references that indicate either victory or defeat of the dice players and the verses seem to be invested with emotional intensity. One passage (Lanman) has been interpreted by some scholars as 'I shall crush your *kṛta* (victory throw) as a wolf tear to pieces a sheep'. We can sense acute anger and helplessness at what awaits the loser as he faces loss of wealth and crashing of dreams. According to Mehendale (1992, 153) here, one of gamesters seems to challenge the opponent who has won the game by making a *kṛta.* The intent is to invalidate the opponent's accomplishment. How does one comprehend this defiance? Mehendale explains further. He takes the cue from Luders' interpretation that a game comes to an end when the two players in turn have thrown the dice on the ground. In such a game, the loser has no chance to undo what the winner has achieved. He suggests, this *Atharvaveda* line meant that the speaker wanted to prevent his opponent from making the *kṛta aya* by reciting some magic formulae. In the same passage, the victor teased his opponent by claiming that he has confined him and would not let him go till the due is paid.[9] There is a possibility that, at the time of the game, the players were enclosed through a draw of circle and here the victor rejoiced at 'confining' the loser.

Without a doubt, *dyūta krīdā* was linked to manly aggression. In the above passage, the one losing the game envisaged crushing the victor brutally even as he was clear who the true victor was, while the winner provoked the loser with assumption of circumscribing his manhood. The game truly proxied a battle scene. Within the *Mahābhārata* (*Mahābhārata* II.51.3), Śakuni drew parallels between the dice game and archery. He said, 'know the *glahas* to be my bows, dice the arrows, the *akṣahṛdaya* (heart of the dice) my bow-string, and *āstara* (dicing-rug) my chariot'. For Śakuni, the dice game, especially with the Pāṇḍavas, was not really a leisure exercise, nor was it a form of art; it was an act of pulverising the opponent, an instrument of vengeance both of which constitute powerful attributes of hegemonic masculinity. While on the issue of the *Mahābhārata*, let us also discuss what the game meant to the eldest Pāṇḍava, Yudhiṣṭhīra.

Yudhiṣṭhīra was an epitome of *dharma*, virtue, truth and duty but had a fatal flaw—passion for the dice game. In the Sabhāparva of the *Mahābhārata*, we get to know that the Pāṇḍavas had built a magnificent capital for themselves at Indraprastha and invited Kauravas at the inauguration of the new palace. The eldest Kaurava, Duryodhana, was smitten with envy at the accomplishment of the Pāṇḍavas, which was further aggravated when he was mocked at by the Pāṇḍava brothers and Draupadī because of his clumsiness in the hall of illusions within the palace. He opened up to his uncle Śakuni and both worked out a way to settle scores with the Pāṇḍavas. The plan was to invite the Pāṇḍavas to the Kaurava capital of Hastinapura, supposedly to participate in a grand game of dice which they knew Yudhiṣṭhīra would not be able to decline, especially if the invite came from King Dhṛtrāṣtra. Yudhiṣṭhīra had gauged the dangers of such an enterprise when he got to know who all would be present. He was sure that 'dangerous gamblers' would play 'with dangerous tricks' and that if he were to decline, he would be challenged by Śakuni (*Mahābhārata* I.214-25). This is exactly what happened. Yudhiṣṭhīra initially desisted from playing as he suspected foul play but was challenged by a mocking Śakuni. So, he finally gave in despite subtle and overt warnings from Vidura.

Bit by bit, Yudhiṣṭhīra put at stake valued ornaments from his treasury, livestock, horses, armies, slaves, servants and courtesans; then his lands, his capital and his cherished palace. This was what shrewd Śakuni, playing on behalf of Duryodhna, was waiting for and kept rolling his dice with winning strokes. Despite Vidura's protests to Dhṛtrāṣtra, the game was not stopped and Yudhiṣṭhīra, desperate to win, subsequently gambled away each of his four younger brothers and finally himself. The cunning Śakuni finally proposed that he put at stake his feisty and beautiful wife Draupadī and Yudhiṣṭhīra fell for the trick and lost her too. Draupadī was put through unparalleled disgrace before the full assembly. Her bitter words finally awakened Dhṛtrāṣtra to his son's evil doings. He returned to Yudhiṣṭhīra all that he had lost in the gambling, attempted to console Draupadī burning with anger at her humiliation and sent back the Pāṇḍavas to their city with honour. But the Pāṇḍavas were tempted again to play and Yudhiṣṭhīra lost again and they were all sent to thirteen years of exile.

How do we assess masculinities of all involved in this gambling episode? It held mirror to personalities of many men. This game became intertwined with the issue of Kshatriya *dharma*, the duty code of Kshatriyas. Challenge hurled in the direction of a Kshatriya had to be accepted—this was the norm. Yudhiṣṭhīra was *dharma* incarnate, the most virtuous of all the Pāṇḍavas and yet easily lured into gambling. He was aware that his opponents would flout all norms of the game and he still agreed to enter it. Was it really because of the call of his station duty? We are sceptical about that. After all, he could be very critical of other Kshatriya values. More than any other Pāṇḍava, Yudhiṣṭhīra abhorred violence and staunchly supported ahimsa and *ānṛṣanya* (non-cruelty), and provided a subtle critique to the Kshatriya *dharma*. However, he accepted the challenge to play the dice game in the name of Kshatriya-*dharma*, despite Vidura's recurrent caution. We are tempted to question if he was ensnared by the game, just as an addict, or that there was some external intervention. He had paid no heed to his duty as a king, patriarch and most important as a husband. By and large, within the text, it is shown to be his own compromise and a reflection of his masculine aspiration gone awry. However, there appears to be an interpolation in South Indian Kumbakonam edition of the *Mahābhārata* that states that Yudhiṣṭhīra was penetrated by fate, *daivabalāviṣṭa*, and 'for a moment Kali entered, and being entered by kali, he said "so be it", and played' (II.98.24 f).[10] He later lamented that he was cheated by the Kauravas but at no point did he acknowledge that acceptance of the challenge, in the first place, was the most foolish act. This was clearly the moment when his masculinity stood punctured and his kingdom and family faced ruin. Draupadī is often blamed for bringing on the great war but, was it not the game of dice and an addiction to it that were the foundational reasons? Vidura had warned,

> The root of all quarrels, the dicing game, Leads to mutual breach and a great war Dhṛtrāṣtra's son undertakes it, Duryodhana starts and awesome feud. (*Mahābhārata* II.56.1)

The dicing match is an occasion for readers of the epic to anatomise masculinities of men in the *sabhā*. What about stalwarts like Bhīṣma? Draupadī's repeated pleas for succour to him fell on deaf ears. Bhīṣma was more concerned about the legality of the issue than her plight. If we go by Connell's description of masculinities, this was the moment when a giant of a man chose to comply to norms set by others and so his masculinity would fall in the frame of 'complicit masculinity'. Karṇa chose the moment to settle old records with Draupadī and humiliated her by calling her a wanton woman. His aggression was most apparent. He mocked at all the Pāṇḍavas, especially Arjuna, and told him that now that he had become a slave, 'what use is his gallantry and manliness'? (*Mahābhārata* II.63.1-5). Later, he teased the Pāṇḍavas that Draupadī had saved them from the disaster when she chose to free her husbands from slavery in return for the boon given by Dhṛtrāṣtra. Karṇa called her the 'boat' that saved the Pāṇḍavas from sinking (*Mahābhārata* II). Except for Vidura and Vikarṇa, Draupadī found no supporters in the *sabhā*. It is true that Bhīma was ready to attack the Kauravas with his raw animal-like energy but was contained by his elder brother. Bhīma was one Pāṇḍava who was expressive about his bruised masculinity. He was aghast at Yudhiṣṭhīra's inaction and later accused him of acting like a eunuch and vowed to avenge Draupadī's humiliation himself.

The game of dice brought out skewed up gender relations within the Pāṇḍava household. Draupadī was shown her place in the social and familial hierarchy and she in turn showed the world what this game could do to both the household and to women in the family. Not only did Yudhiṣṭhīra lose wealth and material assets, he lost self-respect, social prestige and peace of mind as well. But, most importantly, he lost the respect of his wife, something that she continued to remind him for life and something for which he could never forgive her personally.[11] There is a 14th century Telugu variant of the epic, where Draupadī asks for a chance to play with Duryodhan as one of the boons granted, playing behind the screen and moving the dice with her toes. She opposes Duryodhana directly and wins back husbands' kingdom rather than their freedom from slavery. This they then refuse to accept, preferring to win it back justly in a battle (Hiltebeitel 1988). Within the frame of gender relations, the intervention is interesting. It not only critiques asymmetrical gender relations, but it actually balances those as well. Somehow, women seem to be absent from the scene of dicing games, especially as participants. Here Draupadī not only plays the game but settles the scores with Kauravas. Her intelligence comes through and the unhurried playing of dice with foot can also be seen as trivialising the game. For once, dicing appears to be like a leisure activity, at least for Draupadī. But, most importantly, in this version, Draupadī comes out of victim mould. She does not have to turn to her husbands or to god for rescue; she holds it out on her own. She reminds us of Pārvatī, who, too, excelled in the game of dice.

It was not that Yudhiṣṭhīra was not filled with the sense of remorse at the dicing game. In the Vanaparva, he opened up his heart to sage Bṛhadaśva and lamented how he lost his prestige, kingdom at the hands of gamblers to cheats who also humiliated his wife. 'There is no man,

I think, unhappier than me,' he bemoaned (*Mahābhārata* III.49.34). It was then that sage Bṛhadaśva narrated to him the story of Niṣādha king, Nala who, too, had lost the kingdom at the hands of his brother Puṣakara, again in the dice game, and faced a fate more disastrous. Nala had married Damayantī, the beautiful princess of Vidharbha. As the story goes, a number of years later, his brother Puṣakara challenged him to the game of dice and, like Yudhiṣṭhīra he desisted it initially but then Kāli entered his body and made him accept the offer. After that he continued to play with his brother, losing one thing after another. His wife and countrymen tried to dissuade him but to no avail. He lost everything and even abandoned Damayantī. Deserted by her husband in the forest, ruined by his neglect she cried aloud, 'Gambler where are you … leaving behind your loving wife, asleep in a void? Where you directed her, she is sitting, waiting for you, burning with grief, covered with half a skirt. She constantly weeps with the same sorrow. Please show your Grace and award her an answer' (*Mahābhārata* III.67.5-10). Through many twists and turns, the two were reunited and Nala won his kingdom back from his brother through victory in another dice game' (*Mahābhārata* III.77.15-20).

The retribution here came from another game of dice. Yet the story is explicit about the devastation the game caused to so many people, especially to the virtuous wife. She remained faithful to him but had to ward off lustful glances and moves of many men, crying so many times in distress. The parallels with Draupadī are hard to miss out. In a subtle way the sage was reprimanding Yudhiṣṭhīra but also telling him that he was better off as he was there in the forest with his family. What was reiterated was the ruin that accompanies the game. Could this be the reason that the *śāstric* writers called it a *vyasana*, a vice to be avoided by the king and others? The knowledge about the desolation caused by the dice game is recorded as early as the *Ṛgvedic* times. In the hymn X.34, the gambler begs the dice to spare him as he has been losing game one after another. This has led to the ruin of his family life as his wife 'held him aloof and his mother-in-law hated him' (*Ṛksamhitā*) and other men teased the 'wife of a man who has lost all to gambling'. Is this a reference to pawning of the wife by the gambler? However, even with his masculinity compromised, he continued to frequent the gaming house, hoping to win the game. The hymn concludes with a clear warning to the gambler. 'Play not with the dice: Till well your own field: Rejoice in your portion and value it highly: See there, O Gambler, your cattle, your wife. This is the counsel of the noble Savitar' (*Ṛksamhitā* X.34.13). Dice game was not understood as a recreation activity for sure here; it was the opposite of that—an addiction that compilers of the text sought to warn the populace about.

The *Pañcatantra* reflects on the importance of self-control. The seven vices of kingship are enumerated as: women, gambling, hunting, drinking, harsh speech, severe punishment and undue seizure of wealth (Ollivell). The king is told that the power of king is inherently unstable and that he must not indulge in the aforesaid vices. Interestingly, gambling comes second from the top. The *Arthaśātra* (Kangle) also discusses the seriousness of royal vices and places gambling as one of them. In fact, Kautilya, at a place, mentions that gambling is worse than wine (drinking). Among oligarchies and royal families, having character of oligarchies, gambling could result in dissensions and destruction. Clearly it was associated with evil men and their masculine intentions. A king is asked to control his senses (Kangle). Kamanḍaka too recognises hunting, womanising, drinking and gambling as vices the king should avoid and states that gambling and hunting should be shunned as far as possible (Singh 2017, 438). That the king should be self-controlled (*atmavān*) is something reasserted within the *Manusmṛti* as well. A list of seven vices is mentioned and gambling is one of them (*Manusmṛti*, VII, 47). Even within Buddhist literature, we get warnings against dabbling in gambling. Buddhist scholar, Buddhaghosa, in his commentary *Sumangala vilāsinī* of Dighanikäya, has explained *Attapada* (we understand it as chess today) as one of the games monks should avoid associating with (Roy 1939, 253).

One wonders if despite repeated warnings and desolate descriptions, people, especially the kings, learnt their lesson. Yudhiṣṭhīra surely did not. Even after all the tragic outcome of his weakness for gambling, Yudhiṣṭhīra was inclined to take pointless risk at the end of the war too. He staked the entire empire on the outcome of a duel between Duryodhana and Bhīma. He was lucky this time as Bhīma settled the score in favour of the Pāṇḍavas and Duryodhana met his end. But did Yudhiṣṭhīra really learn from the past experiences, the endless turmoil caused by his predilection for putting things on the stake? We are not sure that he really did.

There is one instance in Puranic mythology where the game of dice is actually played as a fun sport to start with but, as it progresses, it challenges gender equations and has serious consequences for those involved in it. We are referring to the game of dice played between Śiva and Pārvatī (also referred to as Śivaśaktī), explained in detail in the *Skanda Purāṇa* (*Skanda Purāṇa* 1.1.34). The game is interesting as it has multiple layers of implications. We are informed that Nārada visits Śiva and Pārvatī to disrupt their long lasting love-making, and incites them to play a game of dice as he and others join in as spectators. Pārvatī is as deft as her husband in the game and both consent to it. In the first round, we are told that, despite Pārvatī's playing the game fraudulently

(*Skanda Purāṇa* 1.1.34.69), Śiva wins the round, much to applause of Nārada and others. Pārvatī became angry, but was shown her place by Bringi who unabashedly showed his reverence for his master, Śiva, and exhibited confidence at his victory. In the next round both pledge their ornaments and all they have, as a wager. Pārvatī won the round and insisted that Śiva removed all that adorns his body. Bringi was nonplussed and Śiva amused, at least initially. He was ready to give up everything but was puzzled at Pārvatī's insistence on his removal of the loin cloth too. She reiterated that she had won the game of dice and proceeded to remove the loincloth with force, much to his horror and shame of all the onlookers. She appeared brutal in asserting her superiority to her husband. She appeared to have no regrets about the game as she was playing for fun and with the intent to observe 'the causes of his emerging into activity'. The emergence did happen. The god, previously inert, got activated; angry at her as she had made him the laughing stock of men and gods alike. His masculinity hurt, Śiva, finally, drove away to the forest and chose this moment for meditation as an ascetic to invoke the *ātman*.

Pārvatī was soon tormented by his going away and longed for him. Her attendant, Vijayā, then remarked that that she had won Śiva by self-mortification; it was wrong to play dice with him. 'Haven't you heard that dicing is full of flaws?' She asked Pārvatī to forgive Śiva and advised her to look for him before it was too late. Pārvatī then took the form of beautiful Śabri woman to ensnare him. Śiva was duped: he showed his desire for her but the reality was eventually revealed to him. Nārada laughingly said, 'Contact with women always makes men ridiculous' (1.1.35). Śiva was, however, persuaded to return to Pārvatī.

The episode is interesting from a couple of vantages: (a) it clearly shows that women could also play the dice game well and resort to cheating as and when required, (b) Pārvatī could stand up to incitement and insults coming her way from Śiva supporters, (c) she could be as ruthless to her opponent as any player is in a normal game. And yet, in conclusion, she is shown to be a woman who resorted to charming guile to fool her husband. Nārada came up with a misogynist conclusion that contact with women was the doom of a man. Mythographers were intent on showing Pārvatī her place, despite the fact that she was the winner in the dice game. Here was an occasion for the compilers of *Skanda Purāṇa* to give women a space of equality, rather, of superiority; Śiva had been duped twice over. However, the conclusion favoured the man who was shown to be losing the game/or an act not because of his flaws but because of a woman's fickleness. This appears to be a case of assuaging bruised masculinity. Otherwise Nārada could have easily responded in a different way. For instance, he could have asked his master how could a woman (that too not his wife) break his intense *tapas* and how did he let his self-control dwindle. Or why did his master get annoyed when Pārvatī disrobed him. After all, she did what a winning gambler does. Why should the sense of propriety and a wife's duty become rationale for upsetting an ascetic/master as tall as Śiva? From our perspective, the episode also becomes significant as it showed that the dice game was sure to bring in fissures; this time in the context of a divine household.

However, the episode has also been interpreted in a different way by scholars. Handelman and Shulman (1997) argue that this notion of the god at play, and that too at dice has metaphysical dimensions and has remained integral to the description of episodes around Śiva in popular discourse. But there is a litany of questions that bother the readers/ listeners. If one is God, why does he play dice game in the first place or worse still lose the game? What does it mean for him to sacrifice his attributes? Why could he not stop Pārvatī or reverse the decision? It is true that sometimes he was more than a little reluctant to play.

According to this perspective, the *dhyūta krīdha* was not just a fun sport; it was indicative of something profound. It was a projection of an inner division within Śiva (as androgynous *ardhnarisvara*) who was pushed into playing the game and then separate into masculine and feminine parts that temporarily moved away from each other (Richard 2009). It was Pārvatī (*Prakṛti*) who forced Śiva (*Puruṣa*) into the process of bifurcation and, as Handelman and Shulman say, she also identified herself with the power of playing and with the implicit devolution. Śiva was reluctant to undergo the process that the game entailed. He was tentative, at times he took it lightly at other times became obstructive and angry, but was mostly unwilling to subscribe to the possibility of a loss. Was he, in effect, rejecting the necessity of his inner division and responding to the possibility of a deeper destructive cycle that he was being dragged into? The dice throws could correlate with the four *yugas*, the cosmic ages in their 'recursive, devolutionary sequence'. So, was he trying to stop the impending destruction? As the principal actor in the scene/game of the cosmos, Śiva agonised over the fate of any player who was helplessly caught up in this innately disruptive game.

His unwillingness to play the game had a cosmic-gender angle too, explained well within Sāṁkhya philosophy. Within the Sāṁkhya, the whole process of spiritual liberation is *kaivalya* is understood as the detachment of *Puruṣa*, or primordial mind, from its experience (Handelman and Shulman 1997). Śiva is the *Puruṣa*, that is, the non-moving pure consciousness and Pārvatī is *Prakṛti*, the unconscious active materiality, with the function of creation and propelling devolution. *Puruṣa* has no attributes; they all belong to *Prakṛti*; that is why *Puruṣa* always loses the game. Śiva's loss in dice game and giving up of his attributes to Pārvatī, then, becomes explicable. However, for liberation, *Puruṣa* had to distance himself from *Prakṛti* and when *Puruṣa* (Śiva) goes off (to the forest), there is bliss but *Prakṛti* gets him back. However, the union this time does not overpower *Puruṣa*. He has understood that reality of *Prakṛti*. Interestingly, this philosophy also reiterates in a refined theological way what Nārada had said jokingly that contact with women amounted to self-loss and self-diminution. Moreover, the dice game in this context moves away from its leisure implications and gets intertwined with the idea of *dharma* or duty, but this time that of the god.

Conclusion

We return to some of the queries that we started with. Did leisure choices really exist in our period of study? Looking at ancient India, through our short survey, we can safely say that it did exist for some, especially for the upper castes like that of the Kshatriyas. We have already seen how, in the *Mahābhārata*, Draupadī, Subhadrā, Arjuna and Kṛṣṇa enjoyed a picnic with their retinue that cannot be explained in any way other than seeking leisure, fun and relaxation. We also noted that, many a times, rulers were inclined to dabble in hunting for fun or as a passion. Within the *Rāmāyaṇa*, Daśratha clearly stated that he revelled in hunting. But more often than not there was a pressure to pursue the sports either due to the class location of the aspirant or from expectations to prove his masculine prowess. Hunting was understood in diverse ways; sometimes it was cited as one of the vices to be avoided by ruler, while at other times as a celebrated sport. Ultimately, it defined a ruler's personality as it opened up forays for eventual taming of the forest and control of its resources. In this sense, this leisure activity or a 'sport' got intertwined with a king's '*dharma*' or duty. A king was expected to harness more resources and keep forest under his control for the benefit of many others.

As referred to earlier, hunting, however, was extremely essential for the class of hunter-gatherers or forest tribes whose livelihood depended on it. In this case, hunting might not have been a fun activity but a sustenance act. In both the cases, the link with masculine strength was unmistakable. Yet, the Brahmanical perception of the male valour of the hunters, put the latter lower in hierarchy as they lived by hunting and consumed hunted animal meat without consecrating it. Strategic necessity at times pushed men of higher classes to forge alliances with these tribes as happened in the case of the *Rāmāyaṇa*, but largely these men of forest remained marginalised and were treated with a sense of hostility. The difference between the king and nobility on the one side and the forest-men on the other could lie in the way in which the act of hunting was perceived by the two. For the Kshatriya caste, it was a sport (though at times necessary), while for the forest men it was a survival tactic. This also partially answers our question whether leisure could be a matter of choice.

Where did these leisure choices emerge from? We have understood the relevance of hunting. Dice game was at some point in time institutionalised as a part of ritual performance. But it must have become pervasive, cut across classes and castes, as it appealed to masculine aspiration of memetic victory in a battle and a plausible source of quick cornering of resources. It also involved deployment of strategy and cleverness, teasing of intelligence and must have given the participants the satisfaction of putting the opponent in the dock. The recognition from the onlookers must have been a boost to their manliness.[12] Its popularity can be gauged from the fact that state had to intervene to regulate it within gaming-houses.

Yet the flip side of both these leisure activities cannot be overlooked. There were not just the participants getting affected by the outcome of these sports, but the entire household and at times the kingdoms too, if the participants happened to be the rulers. Moreover, the play of gender relations also cannot be overlooked. A hunting expedition gone awry meant loss of human lives, animal and other resources as can be seen from Duṣyanta episode or receiving of a curse as in the case of Daśratha accidentally killing Śravaṇa Kumar. We have already seen how the control of forest and its resources often implied that the forest (or its feminine spirit) did fight back.

The interplay of gender relations comes out strongly with the outcome of gambling. This was one sport that had disastrous impact on the entire household. The females of the family were the worst affected, something that we can gauge from the earliest of the texts, *Ṛksamhitā*. Other texts such as the *Mahābhārata* in Draupadī and Damayantī episodes gave a large space to *dyūta krīdā* in order to caution the posterity of its ill consequences. Draupadī was wagered in the dice game while Damayantī suffered endlessly as her husband lost everything. The household equations changed drastically and women suffered for no fault of their own. They were angry, humiliated and saddened by their fate; Draupadī even questioned patriarchal mores and critiqued masculine values of her Kshatriya husbands but both could not disturb the frames of patriarchy. Interestingly, they still remained faithful to their husbands. It was Pārvatī, in the game of dice with Śiva, who openly mocked Śiva on his defeat, threatened his masculinity and turned upside down the set frames of patriarchal expectations. Ironically, she was blamed by Nārada for precisely that as the mythographers of the day made her plead Śiva for his return to their home. Pārvatī had altered the gendered nature of this game. It did not appear to be a male reserve alone.[13] The leisure game had wobbled the divine household. The philosophers, however, consider that this episode of *dyūta krīdā* an important intervention to awaken the *puruṣa* traits of Śiva and reinitiate his cosmic duties. Can we say that, in this case at least, the leisure game was bait to provoke the god towards his dharmic duty?

Notes

1 Approximate dates of the *Purāṇas* are taken from Hazra (1940).

2 *The Hymns of Rigveda* (*Ṛksamhitā*). VII. 27.1.

3 Monier-Williams, M. (1999). *A Dictionary English and Sanskrit*. Delhi: Motilal Banarsidass, p. 447. (reprint)

4 Translation by Griffith (1991, 5).

5 The importance of elephants can also be assessed from the name of the Kuru capital, Hastinapur, the 'city of elephants'.

6 We can, however, not deny that many a times hunting could also become a mix of fun activity and masculine exhibition along with primary need to secure food.

7 *Ṛksamhitā*. X.34.8.

8 *Nāradasmrt*i 17.5 *ašuddhah kitavo nänyad äsrayed dyütamandalam* can very well mean: 'a gambler who has not cleared himself of the dues should not go to another *dyūtasabhā*'.

9 A circle was drawn round the players and the one who lost the game could not come out of the circle unless he paid his dues, Mehendale (1992, 153).

10 II.98.24 f. This is probably copied from the episode of Nala. Cf. Hopkins (1974, 77).

11 In the Svaragārohaṇaparvạ, when Draupadī fell and Bhīma shrieked to save her, Yudhiṣṭhīra remained nonchalant about it.

12 This comes out strongly in yet another sport, wrestling, which too can be taken a s a dummy battle, where crowds cheered the victors.

13 Just as Draupadī had done so in the Telegu version of the epic.

References

Abhjñanamśakuntalam in *Works of Kalidāsa*. 1966/2005. Translated by C.R. Devadhar. Delhi: Motilal Banarasidass.

Bhatt, G.H. (trans.). 1960. *Rāmāyaṇa* (critical edition). Baroda: Oriental Institute.

Carrigan, T., B. Connell and J. Lee. 1985. 'Towards a New Sociology of Masculinity'. *Theory and Society*, Vol. 14 (5): 551–603.

Chhāndogyopanisad. 1969. Translated by F. Max Muller, *Sacred Books of East*, Vol.1, reprint New Delhi: Motilal Banarsidass Publications.

Connell, R.W. 1985. *Masculinities*. Cambridge: Polity.

Cowell, E.B. (ed.). 1990. *Jātakas*. 6 Vols, Indian reprint. New Delhi: Motilal Banarsidass Publications.

Devadhar, C.R. (ed. and trans.). 1985. *Raghuvaṁśa of Kalidāsa*. New Delhi: Motilal Banarasidass Publications.

———. (trans.). 2005. *Abhjñanamśakuntalam* in *Works of Kalidāsa*. New Delhi: Motilal Banarasidass Publications.

Doniger, Wendy and Sudhir Kakar (trans). 2002. *Kāmasūtra*. Oxford: Oxford University Press.

Gharpure, J.R. and Tim Lubin (trans). 1936. *Yajñvalkyasmṛti*. Bombay: S.N. Bombay

Griffith, R.T.H. 1991 (reprint). *The Hymns of Rigveda*. New Delhi: Motilal Banarsidass Publications.

Handelman, Don and David Shulman. 1997. *God Inside Out: Shiva's Game of Dice*. New York: Oxford University Press.

Hazra, R.C. 1940. *Studies in Puranic Records on Hindu Rites and Customs*. New Delhi: Motilal Banarsidass Publications.

Hiltebeitel, Alf. 1976. 'The Burning of the Forest Myth'. In *Hinduism: New Essays in the History of Religions,Studies in History of Religions XXXII*, edited by B.L. Smith. Leiden: Brill.

———. 1988. *The Cult of Draupadī Mythologies; From Gingee to Kurekṣetra*. Chicago: University of Chicago Press.

Hopkins, E.W. 1974 (reprint). *Epic Mythology*. Delhi: Motilal Banarasidass.

Jaini, Padmanabh. 1977. *The Jaina Path of Purification*. New Delhi: Motilal Banarsidass Publications.

Kane, P.V. (edited with reconstructed text, translation notes and introduction). 1993. *Kātyāyanasmṛti on Vyavahara*. Bombay: Digital Library of India.

Karve, Iravati 1969 (reprint 2006). *Yuganta: The End of an Epoch*. Hyderabad: Orient Blackswan.

Kautilya. 1960–65. *Arthaśāstra*, by Kautilya, edited and translated and studied by R.P. Kangle, 3 pts., Bombay.

Lanman, C.R. 1905. *Atharvaveda*, translated by W.D. Whitney, Hos, New Delhi, India; 1962, 1971[reprint]; translated in parts by M. Bloomfield, *SBE*, XLII, Oxford, 1897.

Manusmṛti. Trans. G. Buhler, *Sacred Book of the East*, XXV, Oxford, 1886; translated by Wendy Doniger with Brian Smith (1991). New Delhi: Penguin.

Mehendale, M.A. 1992. 'The Game of Dice in Ancient India'. *Bulletin of the Deccan College Post-Graduate and Research Institute*, 1991–92, Vol. 51/52, Professor S.M. Katre Felicitation Volume (1991–92), p. 153.

Minkowski, Christopher. 2016. 'Epic Kings in the Wilderness' presented as the 2nd C.R. Parekh Memorial Lecture organised by the Institute of Indian Thought, CSDS on 16 September.

Mitra, Rajendralala (ed.). 1890. *Taittirīya Brahmana*. Calcutta: Asiatic Society of Bengal.

Mitra, Raja Rajendra Lala (ed.). 2008. *Nītisāra*. Kolkata: The Asiatic Society.

Nāradasmṛti. 1889. Translated by J. Jolly SBE, XXXIII, Oxford.

Ollivelle, Patrick (trans.). 1997. *The Pañctantra: The Book of Indian Folk Wisdom*. Oxford: Oxford University Press.

Rajgopalachari, C. 1958. *Mahabharata*. Delhi: Bhartiya Vidya Bhavan.

Richard, Smoley. 2009. *The Game of Dice: How Consciousness Creates the Universe*. California: New World Library (online).

Roy, Tridipt Nath. 1939. 'The Indoor and Outdoor Games in Ancient India'. *Proceedings of the Indian History Congress*, Vol. 3.

Śatapatha Brāhmaṇa, Translated J. Eggeling (1882–1900), *Sacred Book of the East*. Oxford: Oxford University Press.

Shastri, J.L. (ed.). 1992. *Śiva Purāṇa, Ancient Indian Tradition and Mythology*. New Delhi: Motilal Banarasidass Publications, Vols 1–4 (reprint).

Shah, Shalini. 2019. 'Engendering the Body: A Study of Sanskrit Literature'. *Social Scientist*, Vol. 47.7–8. July–August.

Singh, Upinder. 2017. *Political Violence in Ancient India*. Cambridge, Massachusetts: Harvard University Press.

Sinha, Kanad. 2016. 'The Hunter, the Hunted and the Hunt: Reading the Royal Hunting Episodes in the *Mahābhārata*'. *Proceedings of Indian History Congress*, Vol. 77: 41–44.

Sukthankar, V.K. 1933–66. *Mahabharata*, critical edition. Poona: Bhandarkar Oriental Research Institute, 19 Vols.

Staal, Frit. 2008. *Discovering the Vedas, Origins, Mantras, Rituals, Insights*. New Delhi: Penguin Books.

Tagare, G.V. (trans.). 1976. *Bhāgavata Purāṇa. Ancient Indian Tradition and Mythology*. New Delhi: Motilal Banarasidass Publications (reprint).

———. (trans.). 1993. *Skanda Purāṇa, Ancient Indian Tradition and Mythology*, New Delhi: Motilal Banarasidass Publications, Vol. 49–66 (reprint).

Telang, K.T. (trans.). 1882. *Bhagavad Gītā*. *Sacred Books of the East*. Oxford: Oxford University Press.

Thapar, Romila. 1978. *Exile and the Kingdom: Some Thoughts on the Ramayana*. Mythic Society: Bangalore.

Vaidya, C.V. 1966. *The Mahābhārata: A Criticism*. Franklin Classics Trade Press.

van Buitenen, J.A.B. (tr). 1973. *The Mahabharata: The Book of the Beginning*, Vol. 1. Chicago: University of Chicago Press.

Weber, A. (ed.). 2018 (reprint). *Taittirīya Samhita*. Sagwan Press (open library).

Williams, M. 1991. *A Dictionary English and Sanskrit*. New Delhi: Motilal Banarasidass Publications (reprint).

Wilson, H.H. (ed. and trans.). 1977. *Ṛgveda Saṁhitā*. New Delhi: Nag Publishers.

4

A ROYAL HUNTSMAN: THE AMBIGUITY OF THE HUNT AS ARISTOCRATIC PASTIME IN SOUTH ASIA AND ITS REPRESENTATION IN REVANTA IMAGERY

Marion Frenger

Introduction

In many cultures, hunting, apart from being an occupation of professionals, was seen as one of the suitable leisure occupations for a ruler and his court. Premodern South Asia is no exception and many narratives are set against the background of the ruler hunting in the wilderness. Literary sources for these narratives include the stories about the former births of the Buddha (*jātakas*) as well as the great epics, plays and poetry. Depictions of hunters—both professionals and leisure seekers—can be found in the earliest representations of these stories in reliefs at archaeological sites. The attitude towards hunting as reflected in literature is, however, ambivalent. While its positive effects on the ruler's physical and strategic abilities and as a display of his virility and military competence are generally appreciated, hunting, together with drinking, gambling and womanising, is also counted as one of the essential vices that are able to distract the attention from the core tasks of governance and can potentially have devastating consequences both for the ruler and his realm. Against this background it seems unusual that the hunt became an integral part of the iconography of a deity particularly associated and probably venerated by rulers, the god Revanta, who according to myth was the son of the sun god Sūrya. It is, therefore, worth exploring how—taking into account the ambivalence of the hunt—this activity is included in the representations of this particular deity that appeared all over North India shortly after the middle of the 1st millennium CE.

Perspectives on Hunting in Ancient India[1]

The attitude towards those groups of society that were engaged in hunting on a professional level—which usually meant that they hunted to provide food for their family and community—was determined by the fact that they had to employ tricks to hunt down animals and raw force to kill them. Therefore, members of tribes and other groups involved in hunting like *caṇḍālas*, *niṣādas* or *śabaras* were regarded as inferior and are often characterised as sly, greedy, ruthless and willing to abandon the fundamental rules of human decency in pursuit of their advantage (Krottenthaler 1996: 92–93). For example, in a number of Buddhist *jātakas* such as the Ṣaḍdanta, hunters are portrayed as treacherous figures who approach their quarry using traps or unfair means and denounce their benefactors, often an animal or a human that saved them from a precarious situation, on the promise of short-lived material advantages. The following considerations are not—or at least only marginally—concerned with hunting as a profession or as an indispensable means of providing food and earn one's living but rather with hunting as an activity of the social elite who neither depended on it for food nor as a for-profit undertaking. Though these leisure hunters are not judged along the lines of their professional counterparts, their involvement in the hunt is still fraught with problems that in part are also related to the fact that the killing of animals puts the hunter into a position potentially contradictory to the moral principles of society and religion.

Leisure activities of the ruling elites in ancient India, as almost everywhere else, were generally perceived as ambiguous. While on the one hand they were instrumental to express the exalted position of the person pursuing them, on the other hand, the fact that they at first glance do not serve any superior purpose invariably invokes critical comments. This also holds true for hunting (Wojtilla 2009) which is frequently described as one of the private pastimes of the ruling class and the rich but is also considered by many authors a vice, making a ruler unfit or unable to govern his territory, at least if practised excessively. Legal texts as well as literary sources devoted to religious and doctrinal instruction held a depreciating view and expressed their anxiety that a ruler might forget his duty over his pursuit of pleasures like hunting, gambling, drinking and womanising. Exemplary for this sceptical attitude towards hunting is the stance taken by Kautilya in his *Arthaśāstra*; he, as many other authors, refers to hunting as one of the four essential vices that affect a man's ability to lead a proper life (*Arthaśāstra* 8.3.38). However, in his evaluation of the relative dangers of all four of these leisure activities, he concludes that hunting is the least problematic of all four (*Arthaśāstra* 8.3.44–64) and even finds some positive aspects in hunting when he points out that '[...] in hunting, there is exercise, getting rid of phlegm, bile, fat and (a tendency to) perspiration, practice in hitting the targets of moving and stationary bodies, knowledge of the minds of animals in anger, fear and condition of ease, and (only) occasional marching' (*Arthaśāstra* 8.3.46; Kangle 1972, 395).

A number of educational stories illustrate the negative aspects of the hunt. In them the hunting king causes, though sometimes unwittingly, a sequence of bad or tragic events or exposes himself and his subjects to attacks by adversaries that end in him losing his kingdom—sometimes even his life—unless he realises his wrongdoing in time to turn the events in his favour. The Buddhist Syama *jātaka* (Fig. 4.1) is exemplary in its description of the hunting expedition of king Brahmadatta. Here, the hunt kicks off a tragic plot turn as the king on his horse shoots an arrow into a thicket on a river bank. Instead of the boar or deer he expected, the arrow hits Syama, the son of his former house priest who just took a bath in the river. The depiction of this *jātaka* in the ceiling of cave 114 in Kizil in the modern Chinese province Xinjiang shows this key moment

Figure 4.1. Syama *jātaka*. Kizil Cave 114. One of a series of *jātaka* scenes from the right half of the vaulted ceiling. Museum für Asiatische Kunst Berlin. Acc. no. III 9103

in a composition that is reduced to the moment immediately before the fatal shot—the king on his horse points his arrow at the innocent Syama. The different versions of this story emphasise the misery caused by the king's hunt not just for Syama himself but also for his aged parents who depend on their son's support and care. The underlying negative perception of the hunt as such is in this case clearly expressed when the king himself says, 'There is no worse vice among men then the passion for the hunt since it is the reason even such righteous people are harmed by a frivolous person out of carelessness.'[2]

The vanity of a king and his ambition to prove himself towards his courtiers as a successful hunter and best among all men caused him to pursue a deer (who was, of course, the Bodhisattva in one of his former lives) in another *jātaka*, the Śarabha-mṛga *jātaka*. In his blind ambition, the king did not notice (or, according to other versions, overrated his horse's capability to jump over) a deep, overgrown pit and fell into it. Unable to free himself, the king was finally rescued by the compassionate deer.

In the Sutasoma-Saudāsa *jātaka*, it is again a hunting expedition that provides opportunity for what later turns out to be a disastrous liaison between King Sudāsa and a lioness in heat. The king who is separated from his entourage while pursuing a deer falls asleep near a pond and is roused by the ruttish lioness. Either out of fear or out of desire the king responds to her advances and the lioness later gives birth to a son whom she brings to the king's palace. Sudāsa accepts the boy as his son and in time he becomes the next king. The predilection for human flesh, inherited from his mother, then kicks off the further events that lead to him being banned from his kingdom, ending up as a man-eater in the mountains who captures other kings and princes to regain his realm.[3] Again, the hunt is described as a potentially dangerous activity not so much because it may cause immediate physical harm to the ruler but because the hunt may provide an environment in which unforeseeable and uncontrollable things can happen.

The intent of the Buddhist *jātaka* stories is of course to inspire in their audience the desire for asceticism and renunciation and certainly an attitude of indifference, if not rejection towards all forms of idle worldly pleasures, particularly if harmful to other beings. It, therefore, is not surprising that the attitude towards hunting is not an encouraging one. Literary genres closer associated to the courts of worldly rulers can be expected to draw a more positive picture of these pleasures. Yet the epics also treat hunting as a potentially dangerous undertaking; the *Mahābhārata*, for example, contains several episodes relating how a hunting expedition into the forest can result in devastating results for the king and his subjects—the episode of king Saṃvaraṇa who married a daughter of Sūrya, Tapatī, during a hunting expedition, and spent years with her in the forest while his kingdom suffered mismanagement, loss of wealth and death due to his absence, is but one example of how hunting could be the gateway to other vices and the neglect of duty.[4]

Plays and the ornate poetry of the *kāvyas* took a positive or at least more lenient view at the hunt and the other leisure occupations of the king despite them being employed as a topos to start off a storyline full of dramatic turns by their authors, too. Kālidāsa, in the *Raghuvanśa* (IX.7), thus, refers to all four, emphasising that neither has hampered King Daśaratha's strive for his kingdom's prosperity (Wojtilla 2009, 200); a remark that may be read as an indication that these occupations are unproblematic as long as they are kept under control. Afterwards, however, King Daśaratha after preparing himself by putting on a suitable garment including mail, securing his hair with a forest garland and equipping himself with his bow (IX.50–51), sets out to hunt. Kālidāsa describes the forest the king enters as:

> [...] a forest [...] already occupied by persons who carried with them nets and packs of dogs, which was cleared of forest-conflagrations and robbers, in which the ground was made solid for horses, which had many pools of water and which was full of antelopes, birds and the Gayals. (*Raghuvanśa* IX.53; Nandargikar 1897, 281)

The environment thus described is a park or a hunting enclosure rather than an actually untouched piece of wilderness; here, the king successfully pursues deer, wild boars, buffalos, rhinoceroses, tigers, lions, elephants, yaks and only spares a peacock because his plumage reminded him of his queen's braided hair. Kālidāsa then expresses the problematic aspect of the hunt very precisely when he writes:

> Hunting, like an artful damsel, thus captivated the Lord of the earth, forgetful of his other regal duties, who had entrusted the burden of administration of his kingdom to his ministers and whose love (or passion for hunting) had increased by its constant application. (*Raghuvanśa* IX.69; Nandargikar 1897, 288)

It is this overboarding passion and the loss of control that induce the king to finally overstep the rules of hunting and shoot an arrow into the direction of what sounded like an elephant. Instead, he mistakenly shoots and kills a hermit with his arrow. In this narrative, resembling the plot of the Syama *jātaka*, the boy's father in turn curses the king to die of grief over his own son (IX.74–79). Not only is this curse fulfilled but the son in question, Rāma, also falls under the spell of 'the artful damsel'. In fact, Rāvaṇa takes advantage of his passion when he sends Mārīca in the guise of the notorious golden deer and tempts Rāma into pursuing it; again, the uncontrolled passion for hunting clears the way for the core event of the *Rāmāyaṇa*, the abduction of Sīta and all the disastrous events following this fatal moment. It is, therefore, not surprising that even those authors supportive of hunting demand that it should be practised by the ruler in a measured way.

The fact that hunting involves the killing of animals seems to have become a problem only over time (Wojtilla 2009, 209). In Kālidāsa's *Abhijñānaśakuntalam*, the confrontation of interests and the limitations customary law sets to the king's hunting ambition are alluded to; here, Duṣyanta is prevented from killing a deer with his arrows by the simple statement that this deer lives at the hermitage of Kaṇva and is thus beyond reach for the king. This short scene is but one of the many cases where another inherent problem of the hunt becomes obvious—as the notion gained popularity that the killing of animals was not acceptable for someone striving to follow the proper religious path and every living being deserved protection, it obviously became more and more difficult to console the role of the ruler as a model of behaviour for his subjects with the idea of hunting and killing animals as a pastime. Numerous narratives make it plain that the ruler has the right to hunt and kill animals, particularly deer (Krottenthaler 1996, 13–16), and in certain cases it even is his duty to kill animals that pose a danger to the inhabitants of his kingdom or threaten to destroy the fields and the agricultural produce grown on them. The fact that such statements exist, and that legal texts and other sources repeatedly discuss them, explicitly exempting the kill brought back from a hunt by the king, stressing the right of a king to hunt and even claiming it as part of the royal *dharma* (ibid., 14–15), may be taken as indicators of the growing doubts about this leisure activity of the ruling elites.

Finally, apart from the different ethical considerations, the safety of the ruler was another, probably equally important, aspect that is repeatedly discussed in literary sources, usually as an argument against hunting (ibid., 24–26). The dangers considered in these sources encompass hunting accidents leading to injuries or death as well as murderous attacks initiated by internal rivals or competing kings after luring the ruler into a hunting expedition. According to the *Arthaśāstra* (XIII.2.39–41), the killing or taking hostage of a king during a hunt is an acceptable means of politics. This may also explain why Kautilya, like several other authors, demands that a special animal park for the king's recreation should be created on land not usable for agricultural purposes and that it should be prepared to be 'hazard-free' in every regard:

> He should cause an animal park for the king's recreation to be laid out, [...], with a single entrance, protected by a moat, containing shrubs and bushes bearing sweet fruits, having trees without thorns, with shallow pools of water and stocked with tamed deer and (other) animals, containing wild animals with their claws and teeth removed (and) having male and female elephants and cubs useful for hunting. And he should establish on its border or in conformity with the (suitability of the) land, another animal park where all animals are (welcomed) as guests (and given full protection). (*Arthaśāstra* II.2.3–4)

This seems to be in strange contrast to the idea that hunting is a means of preparing the king for the mental and physical demands of warfare and the dangers of moving in unknown and uncivilised areas. However, the fact that royal hunts often took place in specially established hunting enclosures—reminiscent of the walled paradise (*pairidaeza*) gardens of ancient Persia—or areas of forest prepared by the king's entourage to minimise the risks for the ruler is well documented; the passage from the *Raghuvanśa* quoted above (IX.53) is but one other instance where an author refers to the preparations taken to ascertain the ruler's safety.

As we have seen, hunting has been part of many narratives, in worldly as well as in religious contexts spanning across all major South Asian religious traditions. Yet, actual representations of hunting as a leisure activity of an aristocratic elite are not very common; it is only in Mughal miniature paintings of the 16th century that hunting scenes becomes a frequent and one of the most stunning, dynamic motifs. There are, however, occasional representations of hunting parties with a narrative character, for example, a relief in the upper storey of the Rani Gumpha at Udayagiri/Odisha depicting a king hunting deer (Fig. 4.2). While most of them are rather abbreviated like the representation of the Syama *jātaka* from Kizil already mentioned (Fig. 4.1), others provide a more complete image of what the ruler and his hunting party may have looked like. Among these rather rare depictions is a wall painting in cave seventeen in Ajanta. The first two of altogether thirty individual scenes illustrating the Sutasoma-Saudāsa *jātaka* mentioned above show king Sudāsa leaving the city (Fig. 4.3). The king is depicted on horseback, accompanied by a parasol bearer and a number of males equipped with spears and shields reminiscent of a military exercise rather than a hunting excursion. This may be a reflection of the fears for life and health of the ruler entertained according to the literary sources. Behind the king a second horse rider leaves the city gate; in front and between the soldier-like figures a group of hounds are running; some of them seem to be kept on a leash by

Figure 4.2. Deer hunt. Udayagiri/Odisha, Rani Gumpha. Upper storey

Courtesy: A.L. Basham, ANU Archive; Reference No. ANUA 682-340.

Figure 4.3. Sutasoma-Saudāsa *jātaka*. Detail: Sudāsa's hunting party. Ajanta cave 17

Drawing: M. Zin.

one of the men. The second scene, immediately to the left of the first, shows the king again, this time alone in a landscape that is characterised as rocky wooded wilderness by the layers of geometric rock patterns inhabited by different animals placed between the scattered trees and shrubs. The visual representation of this hunting party shows remarkable similarities to more detailed descriptions of the royal hunt that can be found in Indian literary sources as well as in the early report by Megasthenes which unfortunately is only known from quotations and references in other works. In one of the known fragments of his *Indika*, he mentions the hunt as one of the few occasions when the ruler leaves his palace and his city at all—the others being to dispense justice and to take his place in sacrifices. According to Megasthenes the king goes:

> [...] to the chase, for which he departs in Bacchanalian fashion. Crowds of women surround him and outside of this circle spearmen are ranged. The road is marked off with ropes, and it is death, for man and woman alike, to pass within the ropes. Men with drums and gongs lead the procession. The king hunts in the enclosures [...]. (McCrindle 1877: 72)

This description further mentions that the king either shoots his arrows from a specially erected platform or hunts in the open ground from the back of an elephant. The description altogether seems to reflect the worries also expressed in Indian sources regarding the potential dangers for the king's life and safety during a hunting expedition; strict measures like the demarcation of the road and the mention of a guard bearing spears can hardly be interpreted otherwise. On the other hand, the participation of women and musicians as well as the label 'Bacchanalian' that Megasthenes used to characterise the nature of the undertaking add another dimension to it that may make the reservations against hunting and its inclusion in the list of vices slightly more understandable.

Revanta—A Hunter Par Excellence?

Representations of the hunt discussed until now were limited to narrative contexts also laid down in literary sources, which means the hunt was depicted as part of a larger storyline. It is only in the 5th or 6th century CE that hunting as a topic is for the first time not represented in such a narrative context but becomes part of a cult-related image. Around this time, a deity appears in literary sources as well as visual representations that is characterised to a large extent by his engagement in hunting and similar sport. The deity in question is Revanta.[5] The origins of this deity are by no means certain; most scholars consider him a rather late addition to the family of the sun god Sūrya (Sharma 1975, 26; Suneson 1984, 237–38; Mevissen 2010, 30). The connection of his representation to that of other divine horse riders from Central and West Asia and the Mediterranean has been discussed by several scholars (Schmidt 1977; Carter 1988), yet it has not been able to firmly determine if and how Revanta is related to the divine entities represented in these other images.

The first mention of Revanta in a literary source is probably a half-verse from Varāhamihira's *Bṛhat Saṁhitā*: 'Revanta [...] should be shown seated on horse-back, with his attendants in hunting, sports etc.' (*Bṛhat Saṁhitā* 58.56; Bhat 1987, 561).[6] This first brief description already portrays him as riding a horse and enjoying a hunt with his entourage. Following Puranic descriptions as well as inscriptions continue to refer to Revanta's engagement in hunting as a major feature; it is further mentioned in some *Purāṇas* (for example, the *Mārkandeya Purāṇa*) that his father Sūrya made him the leader of the Gūhyakas, a category of superhuman beings said to live in caves and be part of either Kubera's entourage or of Gaṇeśa's host of mountain-dwelling spirits (Raven 1988).

As mentioned above, the earliest representations of Revanta date back to ca. the 5th or early 6th century. At this point in time, they seem to appear more or less simultaneously along the Ganges and the Yamunā in findspots in modern-day Uttar Pradesh and Bihar. The probably earliest, unfortunately severely damaged example is said to have come from Mathurā.[7] The earliest images of Revanta,[8] among them, besides the aforementioned relief in the collection of the Burdwan University Museum, a relief on the boulder that supports the Ajgaivinath Temple in Sultanganj/Bihar (Fig. 4.4) and a sculpture from Pācār/Bihar (Patna Museum, Acc. no. 10648; Fig. 4.5) do show the god on his horse accompanied only by a few other figures; in the most minimalist representation, the god is joined only by an attendant who follows the horse carrying a high parasol and another figure leading the way in front of the horse. While the parasol and

Figure 4.4. Revanta. Relief on a boulder supporting the Ajgaivinath Temple, Sultanganj/Bihar

Drawing: M. Zin.

Figure 4.5. Revanta. Pācār. Patna Museum Acc. no. 10648

Courtesy: American Institute of Indian Studies, Neg. no. 287.21.

its bearer are invariably present, the figure in front of the horse shows a greater variability and may either carry a sword with a bent blade or, as in the Pācār sculpture, an object held in front of the figure's chest with both hands, possibly representing a wind instrument, either a type of shawm or—more likely—a shell trumpet. Another element of the composition present in almost all images is a dog; he either runs between the legs of the horse or follows it closely. In fact, in the basic composition reflected by the Pācār sculpture, the dog is the only element that may allude to the activity of hunting. Neither the two attendants nor the god himself who, in the case of the Pācār image, with his tight-fitting garment, boots, a quiver suspended from an additional strap of his belt, a flower raised to the chest in his right hand, the opulent coiffure and an elaborate crown with long fluttering ribbons reflects an amalgam of Indian and Irano–Central Asian characteristics,[9] are immediately related to the act of hunting. The image presented is that of a ruler on an outing of some kind, accompanied by attendants who are indicative of his status, not of a particular activity.

It is, therefore, of particular interest to observe how the hunt, which literary sources describe as Revanta's foremost occupation, is actually represented over the course of time, and which elements receive particular attention since this does reflect how hunting as a leisure activity was perceived—or rather ideally imagined—by those creating, sponsoring and venerating these images. This is even more interesting because in later Revanta images, though the complexity of the representation increases and the number and activities of the accompanying figures develop and vary, the figure of the god himself remains almost unaltered as do the attendant with the parasol and, to a lesser extent, the one leading the way. Revanta continues to be shown two-armed, an unusual feature he only shares with the sun god, Sūrya, whom most literary sources refer to as Revanta's father.[10] A connection to the sun god is not explicitly visualised in the early images unless we take the dress of Revanta, which essentially is the dress of nomadic Central Asian horsemen, to be indicative of his relation to Sūrya. The first of the characteristics ascribed to Revanta, which is more elaborately visualised in his images, is thus not his genealogical tie to the sun god but his connection with hunting. In the relief from Sultanganj (Fig. 4.4), several figures and other elements are already added to the core figural repertoire of the image. The god himself is shown on his horse, holding what seems to be a flat bowl with a flower in his left hand and an almost indiscernible object, maybe a single flower, in his raised right hand. Behind the attendant carrying a tall parasol with long ribbons stands another male servant; he carries a dead animal on his shoulders and is followed by a hound watching him expectantly. In front of the horse, there is, in this larger composition, not just one figure leading the way but a group of four males. The two immediately in front of the horse's head hold up long objects; its lower end is held close to their respective face. These objects most probably are a particular type of trumpet with an angular mouthpiece similar to those shown centuries earlier in a relief at Sanci. A third figure plays an hourglass-shaped drum while the object in the left hand of a fourth figure remains unidentified. Above this group of four musicians a pair of birds indicates that Revanta and his entourage are moving in nature, not in an urban environment. Several elements in this relief such as the conical caps and the tunics and boots worn by most figures refer back to the visual patterns connected with the Irano–Central Asian sphere; a larger study that included a re-evaluation of the theories about a connection between Revanta and the concept of Mithras on horseback hunting the bull (Schmidt 1977, 140–42) would therefore be highly desirable.

The hunting aspect, though more pronounced than in the image discussed above, still is not very obvious but steps back behind the event of the royal entourage being a visible and audible spectacle. This is very much in tune with the early description of a hunting party by Megasthenes and the depiction of Sudāsa's entourage in Ajanta discussed above. The same focus on the practices surrounding the actual hunt can be observed in more elaborate and complex representations of Revanta such as a relief from Tumain/Madhya Pradesh (Fig. 4.6), datable to ca. the 8th–9th century, that was built into the porch wall of the local Vindhyavasini temple at some point in time, or a ca. 10th century stela from Telhana, Patna district /Bihar, today in the collection of the Indian Museum Kolkata (Fig. 4.7). Despite the larger number of

Figure 4.6. Revanta and his hunting party. Tumain, Distr. Guna. Built into the (porch?) wall of the Vindhyavasini Temple

Courtesy: American Institute of Indian Studies, Neg. no. 81.85.

Figure 4.7. Telhara, Patna/Bihar IM Kolkata

Courtesy: Regents of the University of Michigan, Department of the History of Art, Visual Resources Collections.

figures accompanying the god, the actual hunt—if depicted at all—is usually restricted to the front of the pedestal and often has to share this space with a group of small musicians. In some cases, a hunter on foot is shown shooting arrows at a fleeing animal or confronting it directly; other representations show hounds attacking boars or deer. The presence of these dogs in almost all representations of Revanta and his hunting party—either closely following the horse and its rider or actually attacking wild animals like deer or, more often, wild boars, usually by sinking their teeth into the hind quarters of the animal—deserves a brief remark. Despite the predominant modern perception that dogs are and always were regarded as impure animals to which any contact should be avoided, there are several indications that, in ancient India, dogs were bred especially for hunting. These breeds obviously were very much appreciated for their stamina, speed and courage when confronting wild boars, lions and tigers. Several Greek sources praise the qualities of these dogs and it seems that at times they were highly desirable commodities as far to the West as Mesopotamia (Krottenthaler 1996, 88–89; a more general overview in van der Geer 2008, 160–66).

The larger part of the image continues to represent the god and his entourage; however, additional elements and figures provide a more detailed environment for Revanta's hunting party. The relief from Tumain, like a number of other Revanta images, shows a large mango tree as a dominant element in the composition. Be it as a rather naturalistic representation of the branches, leaves and fruit or in a far more stylised manner as in a sculpture from North India now in the collection of the Linden-Museum Stuttgart (Fig. 4.8), this tree is indicative of the particular environment the hunt takes place in. The mango tree (*Mangifera Indica*), being one of the oldest cultivated fruit-bearing trees of South Asia (Mukherjee 1953, 130–31), is frequently cultivated in orchards and parks as is documented amongst many other mentions by the large number of mango groves mentioned in Buddhist contexts, for example, as donations by lay people (Nugteren 2005, 159). Its close association to amorous adventures and to the love god Kama (ibid., 106–7) suggests that by choosing this particular tree as the only means to represent the environment of the hunt the artists alluded to the fact that entertainment and dalliance were as much of a focus of the expedition as the hunt itself. The presence of women in different representations of Revanta should be noted, most obvious in an image now in Ajmer Museum (Fig. 4.9). Despite the remarkably large number of wild boars and hounds pursuing and attacking each other between the legs of the horse, apart from the parasol bearer and the armed male in front of Revanta's horse, there are just two female figures depicted.

Figure 4.8. Revanta. Central India. Sandstone. Linden-Museum Stuttgart, Acc. no. SA 32607

Courtesy: T.S. Maxwell.

Figure 4.9. Revanta. Ajmer Museum. Acc. no. 375

Courtesy: M. Frenger.

One, usually female, figure included in many Revanta images is shown holding a jar or pitcher and is positioned just within reach to pour a drink into the shallow drinking bowl held by the deity in one of his hands (Figs 4.7, 4.9, 4.10; Mevissen 2013, 63). These women further add to the general impression of leisure and relaxation that prevails in almost all Revanta images.

Revanta—More Than Just a Hunter; Leader of the Gūhyakas and Protector from Dangers

Another aspect of Revanta connected to and derived from hunting is his position as the king or leader of the Gūhyakas. The Gūhyakas were one of the many classes of spirit deities known to inhabit the land and particularly forests and other lonely or deserted places. Traditionally, they were among the hosts of nature spirits (*yakṣas*) lead by Kubera, the god of wealth and inhabitant of the northern mountains. Their name, derived from the root √*guh* 'to cover, conceal, hid, keep secret' (Monier-Williams 1899, 360.2) and thus connected to the noun *guhā*—'hiding place, cave, cavern' (ibd., 360.3)—is indicative not only of their secretive nature but also of their connection to the mountainous regions that are the pathless, wild and intrinsically dangerous home of Kubera.

The fact that Revanta in some literary sources seems to replace Kubera as the leader of the Gūhyakas has not been fully studied; in the current context it is of interest in several respects. On the one hand, it may add another level of meaning to the mango tree depicted in some of the Revanta sculptures since it could be regarded as an allusion to Kubera's famed garden Caitraratha. On the other hand, the claim that Revanta is the leader of the Gūhyakas may be read as a way to express his knowledge and mastery of the wilderness and the mountainous regions inhabited by these semi-demonic, latently dangerous beings usually associated with Kubera. This in turn refers back to him as a hunter since the pursuit of the quarry can easily lead the hunter deep into the unknown and uncontrolled regions beyond the borders of civilisation. Literary sources like the 8th-century Jain novel *Kuvalayamālā* mention occasionally that Revanta was venerated as a protector from the dangers of wilderness at the roads leading out of a town. The existence of several small stone images from ca. 10th–12th century Bihar seems to indicate that Revanta also saw veneration by individuals or was worshipped to gain his protection when undertaking a journey though regions deemed dangerous. These small, rather simple, often broken or very worn images may well have served as transportable objects of devotion for the travellers who deposited them as votives after the successful completion of the journey.[11] The complete, though severely

Figure 4.10. Revanta. Bengalen. Black Stone. 12 cm high. Museum Rietberg, Zürich. Acc. no. RVI 216. Gift Eduard von der Heydt

Courtesy: © Museum Rietberg Zürich/Photographer Rainer Wolfsberger.

rubbed, example kept in the Museum Rietberg, Zürich (Fig. 4.10) is representative of these small images in displaying the deity in profile on his horse, accompanied by his core group of attendants: the parasol-bearer, an armed attendant leading the way, a small figure holding a water (?) vessel and a fourth figure who may be carrying an animal on his shoulders. Under Revanta's booted foot a prancing dog is depicted in a rather unusual cubic block that cannot easily be explained; on the shallow base there were at least three more figures which unfortunately are too worn off to be properly described or identified. Despite Revanta usually being portrayed enjoying himself while hunting in a well-kept enclosure or park rather than in the absolute wilderness, it may be assumed that his engagement in hunting qualified him for his position as the master of the Gūhyakas and, in a second step, to be venerated as a protector from dangerous situations in forests, conflagrations, enemies and robbers. Both the leadership over the Gūhyakas and the function as a protector from dangers are connected already in the *Mārkaṇḍeya Purāṇa* (105. 20–22).

Solar Relations—Revanta and the Sun God

Revanta is generally best known as the son of Sūrya begotten by him to his wife Nikṣubhā when the two reunited in Uttarakhanda after she fled his brightness and heat and the sun god consequently had his radiance pared down by his father-in-law, Viśvakarman. From a rather early stage Revanta was also regarded as one of the Manus. The chapter on the Manus in book three of the *Viṣṇudharmottarapurāṇa* (70.5) argues that 'the past Manus should be endowed with the signs of royalty. And hence the lord Revanta should be depicted, like Sūrya, as riding on the back of a horse' (Bhattacharyya 1991, 139); a statement rather remarkable since the sun god Sūrya is hardly ever represented riding a horse.

Although the relation of Revanta to the sun god runs through the literary sources and almost the entire, unfortunately very fragmented, mythology of Revanta has been transmitted in conjunction with bits and pieces of solar mythology, it has become clear by now that Revanta's early representations do contain hardly any indication of this relation apart from Revanta being depicted on horseback. Since Sūrya does not have any obvious connection to hunting—if we do not take his being represented as a regal figure, equipped with the regalia of the time and driving the royal vehicle par excellence, a chariot, already in the earliest images to imply that he also enjoys royal pastimes like hunting—he cannot be the model for Revanta being depicted as a hunter.

It should also be noted that it is only in reliefs from ca. the 7th or early 8th century that this family connection gradually becomes more obvious. A few of the reliefs with the single rider Revanta, like one belonging to the Harshad Mata temple complex,[12] may show the sun god's attendants on foot among his entourage, before finally Revanta is accompanied by the sun god's own attendants, Daṇḍin and Piṅgala, both on horseback like Revanta himself, and even Sūrya is occasionally included in larger, more complex reliefs like the one from Bhita in the collection of the Allahabad Museum (Acc. no. 402; Fig. 4.11).[13] Their strongly structured shape with the central vertical projection and the added upper registers with group deities like the *navagrahas* or the *dikpālas* suggests that at least some of these reliefs were integrated into the outer walls of sun temples. In these far more formalised representations with their obviously much stronger visual emphasis on the solar aspect of Revanta, the underlying element of the 'hunting deity' is shifted even more towards the leisure aspect of the hunt, contrary to the earlier images the hunter pursuing and killing animals is not depicted in these elaborate compositions, while all the other visual elements, musicians, armed guards, male and female attendants catering for the needs of the main figures, etc. all still find space in these representations.

Figure 4.11. Revanta and the attendants Dandin and Piṅgala. Bhita. Allahabad Museum

Courtesy: M. Frenger.

Conclusion

The representations of Revanta seem to reflect the ambiguous attitude towards hunting expressed in the literary sources in several regards. Although already the earliest mentions of the deity connect him with hunting, the actual pursuit and killing of the quarry at no point in time becomes the centre of the composition; the depictions of an archer shooting his arrows at a deer or boar as well as the hounds attacking such animals are usually limited to the margins of the image, be it the front of the pedestal or the small space between or behind the horse of Revanta or one of his attendants. It may be assumed that this marginalisation of the actual hunt in the representation is due to the ambivalence attached to the killing of animals and the consumption of meat as well as the general scepticism regarding the hunt as a royal pastime.

The composition instead focusses on the events before and after the actual hunt, with armed attendants securing the royal hunting party while others provide music, food and drink or follow the party carrying the animals killed by the hunters. The impression created is, thus, that of a pleasurable expedition devoted to light-hearted dalliance and all kinds of physical enjoyment that even includes activities like drinking and the enjoyment of female company—both equally held in contempt as severe vices potentially compromising a king's ability to govern his realm according to the literary sources. While adapting to the general notions on the one hand—by limiting the depiction of the act of killing to small, often unobtrusive areas of the composition or leaving this part out altogether—the representation on the other hand manages, thus, to convey the feeling of a leisurely conducted expedition into an idyllic part of nature that incorporates all those other leisure activities which were deemed potentially dangerous for a ruler and may have been particularly tempting for that reason.

Notes

1 Scholarly literature dealing with hunting in ancient India is comparatively scarce; apart from a limited number of articles, the PhD dissertation by Robert Krottenthaler (Krottenthaler 1996) seems to be the most concise compilation of literary and visual sources. According to Wojtilla (2009, 209) there is also only one, probably rather late, Sanskrit manual devoted exclusively to hunting. The substantial chapter on hunting in the *Mānasollāsa*, which Krottenthaler included in his work (Krottenthaler 1996, 125–66), also seems to be rather unique in length and detail.

2 'Es gibt kein schlimmeres Laster unter den Menschen als diese Jagdleidenschaft, die es mit sich bringt, dass sogar solch guten Menschen von Leichtfertigen aus Achtlosigkeit Leid zugefügt wird.' See Demoto and Hahn (2010, 229–30).

3 For an overview of the different versions of this popular Buddhist narrative see Schlingloff (2013, I.261–266).

4 See Sinha (2016) for a discussion of other *Mahābhārata* episodes where the hunt initiates a sequence of negative events; see also Wojtilla (2009, 202– 3) on the Pāṇḍu narrative. It is beyond the scope of this paper to explore the additional layers of meaning potentially underlying the metaphor of 'the king hunting in the forest' that Sinha touches upon in the second half of the article, which is a valid contribution towards a more general understanding of the complex notions connected to the topic.

5 Revanta has been the topic of several studies since an image in the Indian Museum Kolkata was first identified by Bidyabinod (1909); see, for example, Sharma (1973), Sharma (1975), Schmidt (1977), Carter (1988), and shorter discussions with a regional or local focus like Jash (1978), Handa (1982), Sarkar (2003), Mevissen (2010), Mevissen (2013) and Gupta (2013)

6 In the *Viṣṇudharmottarapurāṇa* (Vdh III.87.5) Revanta is described in the context of the brief chapter on the Manus and their representation; it says:

> Attītāḥ manavaḥ kāryā rājalakṣaṇalakṣitāḥ /
> pṛṣthe'śve sūryavatkāryo revantaśca tathā prabhuḥ //
>
> 'The past Manus should be endowed with the signs of royalty.
> And hence, the lord Revanta should be depicted, like Sūrya, as riding on the back of a horse.' (Bhattacharyya 1991: 139)

Hunting as Revanta's pastime is not mentioned in this context; it does, however, contain the first indication that Revanta should be represented like

Sūrya, as whose son he is mentioned in the chapter on Āditya (Vdh III.67). It has to be emphasised, though, that at least the *Viṣṇudharmottarapurāṇa* (ca. 7th–8th century) is considerably younger than the earliest Revanta sculptures.

7 The relief was documented by the American Institute of Indian Studies as part of the collection of the Burdwan University Museum (Photo: AIIS Neg. No. 226.85; https://dsal.uchicago.edu/cgi-bin/aiis/aiis_query.py?image_id=ar_032804&get_large=yes); unfortunately, it has not been possible to verify the circumstances of its discovery and exact findspot; see also Mevissen (2013, 64, pl.5.2B).

8 It has to be emphasised that the development of Revanta iconography and images, like that of every other divine entity in South Asia and beyond, has not been a linear one. While more complex versions of his representation developed, simpler compositions continued to be produced, be it to comply to restrictions in the space available, to indicate lesser importance of an image or for other reasons. The large number of images without any documentation of provenance or with severe damages as well as the relative scarcity of literary sources further hamper a proper understanding of how Revanta developed as a deity.

9 The strong presence of non-Indian features in the earlier representations of Revanta was already observed and discussed by Schmidt (1977) and Carter (1988); an in-depth study of this aspect, particularly in the light of new finds from Central Asia and the growing corpus of studies devoted to horse-riding deities and heroes venerated in different parts of the Eurasian steppes, has still to be undertaken.

10 It should be noted that the *Bṛhat Saṁhitā* does not mention that relation and that the half-verse quoted above is not immediately connected to the long passage dealing with the image of Sūrya (58.46–52) but follows the discussion of the shape of the *liṅga* and, in the first half of verse 56, the *mātṛkās*.

11 A remarkable number of these small sculptures was discovered at Nalanda and Gaya; whether there was any affiliation of Revanta and a Buddhist cult is not clear. However, it is conceivable that Revanta was venerated by travellers of all affiliations, including Buddhist pilgrims, to ascertain their safe journey from one site to the next.

12 See https://www.jstor.org/stable/community.15419921 for an image; in several other cases the degree of damage does not allow for a reliable identification of the smaller surrounding figures.

13 Other examples of Revanta accompanied by Daṇḍin and Piṅgala on horseback include a c. 9th century example from Keravi in the Mathurā Museum, 10th century pieces in the Bharatpur Museum (Acc. No. 104) and from Durgaganj/UP in the Allahabad Museum, as well as a relief in the Brooklyn Museum (Acc. no. 77.260.1; see https://www.brooklynmuseum.org/opencollection/objects/103896); also see Mevissen (2013, pl. 5.5.B and 5.6.A) for two relief panels sold by art dealers; ibid. pl. 5.6.B and 5.7 for fragments of several other Revanta images with Daṇḍin and Piṅgala on horseback. One of the most striking

examples (Bhattacharya 2005; Mevissen 2013, pl. 5.5.A) gained notoriety when it was withdrawn from an auction in New York in 2016 because of a suspected connection to the criminal case of art dealer Subhash Kapoor (Hufnagel and Chappell 2019, 445–46).

References

Arthaśāstra. 1972. *The Kauṭilya Arthaśāstra*. Part II. An English Translation by R.P. Kangle. Bombay: University of Bombay.

Askari, S.H. 1968. 'Hunting in India under the Early Turks'. *Annals of the Bhandarkar Oriental Research Institute 48/49 (Golden Jubilee Volume 1917–1967)*: 33–43.

Bhat, M. Ramakrishna. 1987. *Varāhamihira's Bṛhat Saṁhitā with English Translation, Exhaustive Notes and Literary Comments*. 2 vols. (Second revised edition). Delhi: Motilal Banarsidass.

Bhattacharyya, D.C. 1991. *Pratimālakṣaṇa of the Viṣṇudharmottara*. New Delhi: Harman.

Bidyabinoda, Binoda Bihari. 1909. 'An Illustrated Note on an Indian Deity Called Rēvanta'. *Journal and Proceedings of the Asiatic Society of Bengal*, 5 (N.S.): 391–392.

Carter, Martha L. 1988. 'Revanta, an Indian Cavalier God'. *Annali*, 48: 127–37.

Demoto, Mitsuya and Michael Hahn. 2010. 'Ergänzungen zur Überlieferung des Śyāmajātaka'. In *From Turfan to Ajanta. Festschrift for Dieter Schlingloff on the Occasion of His Eightiest Birthday*, edited by Eli Franco and Monika Zin, 2 vols, pp. 217–50. Bhairahawa, Rupandehi: Lumbini International Research Institute.

Gupta, Vinay Kumar. 2013. 'Revanta Images from Mathura Region'. *Indo-Asiatische Zeitschrift. Mitteilungen der Gesellschaft für indo-asiatische Kunst*, 17: 50–56.

Handa, Devendra. 1982. 'Icons of Revanta from Osian'. *Vishveshvaranand Indological Journal*, 20: 197–200.

Hufnagel, Saskia and Duncan Chappell (eds). 2019. *The Palgrave Handbook of Art Crime*. London: Palgrave Macmillan.

Jash, Pranabhananda. 1978. 'The Cult of Revanta in Eastern India'. *Proceedings of the Indian History Congress*, 39.2: 990–99.

Krottenthaler, Robert. 1996. *Die Jagd im alten Indien unter Berücksichtigung des mṛgayāvinoda-Kapitels im Mānasollāsa*. Frankfurt am Main: Lang.

McCrindle, J.W. 1877. *Ancient India as Described by Megasthenes and Arrian Being a Translation of the Indika of Megasthenes Collected by Dr Schwanbeck, and of the First Part of the Indika of Arrian*. London: Trübner.

Mevissen, Gerd. 2010. 'Gods on Horseback: Images of Revanta and Kalkin. Predominantly from Bengal'. In *The Glorious Heritage of India (In Memory of Prof. R.C. Sharma)*, edited by S.D. Trivedi, pp. 29–52. Delhi: Agam Kala Prakashan.

———. 2013. 'Revanta Images Mainly from Bihar and a Special Type of Three Equestrian Deities from North Bengal'. *Journal of Bengal Art*, 18: 61–86.

Migron, Saul. 1980. 'Ṛgvedic van: an old hunting term?' *Indo-Iranian Journal*, 22: 269–82.

Mukherjee, S.K. 1953. 'The Mango: It's Botany, Cultivation, Uses and Future Improvement, Especially as Observed in India'. *Economic Botany*, 7.2: 130–62.

Nandargikar, Gopal Raghunath. 1897. *The Raghuvaṃśa of Kālidāsa with the Commentary of Mallinātha.* Edited with a Litteral English Translation. Bombay: Gopal Narayan.

Nugteren, Albertina. 2005. *Belief, Bounty and Beauty. Rituals around Sacred Trees in India.* Leiden/Boston: Brill.

Pandey, Lalta Prasad. 1969. 'The Worship of Revanta in Ancient India'. *Vishveshvaranand Indological Journal*, 7: 134–36.

Rajendran, Chettiarthodi. 2006. 'Encountering the Forest: Kālidāsa's Perception on Hunting'. In *Pandanus '06: nature in literature and ritual*, edited by Jaroslav Vacek, pp. 131–42. Prague: Signeta.

Raven, Ellen. 1988. 'The Secret Servants of Kubera: The Naras or Guhyakas'. In *Studies in South and Southeast Asian Archaeology No. 2. Essays offered to Dr R. Soekmono on the occasion of his retirement as the first occupant of the 'Wisseleerstoel' for Indonesian Studies in Leiden*, edited by H.I.R. Hinzler, pp. 105–45. Leiden: Koentji Press.

Samaddar, J.N. 1928. 'A Note on Revanta'. *Journal of the Bihar and Orissa Research Society*, 14: 132–34.

Sanyal, Niradbandhu. 1927. 'A New Type of Revanta from the Dinajpur District'. *Indian Historical Quarterly*, 3: 469–72.

Sarkar, Bijoy Kumar. 2003. 'The Worship of Revanta in Early Bengal'. *Proceedings of the Indian History Congress*, 64: 286–94.

Schlingloff, Dieter. 2013. *Ajanta. Handbook of the Paintings. 1. Narrative Wall-Paintings*, 3 vols. New Delhi: IGNCA/Aryan Books.

Schmidt, Hanns-Peter. 1977. 'Mithras the Horseman and Revanta the Lord of Horses'. In *Some Aspects of Indo-Iranian Literary and Cultural Traditions. Commemoration Volume of Dr V.G. Paranjipe*, edited by Suniti Kumar Chaterji, V. Raghavan, H.-P. Schmidt, T.G. Mainkar and S.N. Gajendragadkar, pp. 132–57. New Delhi: Ajanta.

Sharma, Brijendra Nath. 1973. 'Revanta in Literature, Art and Epigraphs'. *East and West*, 23.1–2: 155–68.

Sinha, Kanad. 2016. 'The Hunter, the Hunted and the Hunt: Reading the Royal Hunting Episodes in the Mahābhārata'. *Proceedings of the Indian History Congress*, 77: 41–44.

Suneson, Carl. 1984. 'From God to Horse: A Mythological and Semasiological Study of Revanta in Sanskrit and Gujarātī/Rājasthānī'. *Indologica Taurinensia*, 12: 233–62.

van der Geer, Alexandra. 2008. *Animals in Stone. Indian Mammals Sculpted through Time.* Leiden, Boston: Brill.

Wojtilla, Gyula. 2009. 'The King Is Hunting: Is It Good or Bad?' In *Kings and Ascetics in Indian Classical Literature: International Seminar 21–22 September 2007. Proceedings*, edited by Paola M. Rossi and Cinzia Pieruccini, pp. 199–212. Milano: Cisalpino.

5

LEISURE IN ANCIENT INDIAN DRAMA: AN ACT OF PROXIMITY WITH NATURE AND SELF

Mrityunjay Prabhakar

Leisure, recreation and *pleasure* are not just interrelated and just don't coexist but grow with the help of each other as well. According to me, they are interdependent terms, as *recreation* can't happen without *leisure* and, thus, *pleasure* can't be obtained without *recreational* activities. And if there is no recreation or pleasure obtained through leisure, that might be anything but leisure. Because leisure is not just free time or no work, as per definition, but it also has element of free will to engage or engross into something which you like doing personally. And, particularly for this reason, in its paper on recreation titled 'Recreation Working Paper', Australian Council for Health, Education and Recreation has meticulously established:

> Leisure is a state of mind which ordinarily is characterised by un-obligated time and willing optimism. It can involve extensive activity or no activity. The key ingredient is an attitude which fosters a peaceful and productive co-existence with the elements in one's environment. (Australian Council for Health)

Thus, leisure is not just about being free or doing nothing or no work hour or free time in life, as I said earlier. It is a kind of psychological and physiological condition or state of mind in which a person can engage with themselves or people or the society or world around according to their own free will which might lead to a fruitful discussion or cherish the moment through discussing memory or present or gain some pleasure through some recreational activities. One can see their dependency on each other through the analogy given. That's why Max Kaplan has noted in his book *Leisure: Theory and Practice*:

> Leisure consists of relatively self-determined activity-experience that falls into one's economically free-time roles, that is seen as leisure by participants, that is psychologically pleasant in anticipation and

> recollection, that potentially covers the whole range of commitment and intensity, that contains characteristic norms and constraints, and that provides opportunities for recreation, personal growth and service to others. (Kaplan 1975)

The main thing is that he is not only engaged and engrossed but also feels for it and for himself. His own self is very much part of the process. As scholar David E. Gray has mentioned in his paper 'This Alien Thing Called Leisure':

> … an activity which involves pursuit of truth and self-understanding. It is an act of aesthetic, psychological, religious and philosophical contemplation. (Gray 1971)

Though many scholars have tried to establish leisure and recreation as synonyms, scholarship on this area is a divided house in itself. There are scholars who have established through their ideas and deliberations that both the terms may be similar in nature but hint for different meaning, exposer and understanding. Recreation is mostly activity based. It demands different sense of engagement rather than leisure. This is why Robert A. Stebbins has argued in his chapter titled 'Nature of Leisure' in his book on leisure:

> The idea of recreation is most distinctive when referring to activity done in free time, which, after work, refreshes and restores a person to return to work again (Godbey, 1999, pp. 12–13). Of course, some leisure can accomplish the same thing, though that term fails to underscore this function as clearly as the term recreation. (Stebbins 2017)

And, as I have mentioned in the beginning of the paper, pleasure is a thing to obtain out of this work or no-work situation or activities one undergoes in his free time in the name of leisure or recreation while engaging with his self. Pleasure can be felt or obtained through such activities. It is not a given thing as it demands one's engagement at a very deep level. It demands mental and emotional investment of a person to feel for it. The exposition of the term pleasure and its connection or dependency on leisure or recreation reminds me of the very process of cultivation of Rasa based on *bhava* in ancient Indian drama. How? What could be better beginning than discussing Rasa and *bhava* while talking about ancient Indian drama, as this is its foremost and upfront contribution to the world?

This is the established fact that the basic framework of ancient Indian drama is different from the rest of the world. While plays in the rest of the world are specifically plot and dialogue driven, play texts of ancient Indian drama are mostly driven by mood of the character. If we compare the play texts of Indian and Western countries, we will come to know the level of contrasts at which they unfold. Western drama is based on the trinity of action, space and time as pleaded by Horace in his work *Ars Poetica.* The union of these three is very much important for their play texts. The narrative of the western plays are mostly event, action and conflict based. While, on the other hand, Indian drama is based on settlement and depiction of mood of the characters. In ancient Indian drama, events and actions mostly happen in the background of the narrative. The repercussion of these events and actions are being showcased on stage through the changing moods of the characters and their reflection on the events. As H.H. Ingalls has written:

> The Sanskrit play is not a drama, for the word drama means action and can only refer to a piece where action and the conflict (agonia) of character and principle are essential factors of the piece. The Sanskrit plays has been described by those who best knew it, as a drishyakavya, a spectacle poem. Its text is lyric rather than dramatic and this text functions as an accompaniment to pantomime, dance and music. The object of this combination of arts is the unfolding of mood [rasa]. Always it is mood rather than plot which determines the content and selection of a Sanskrit play. (Goodwin 1998)

Henceforth, the concept of *rasa* and *bhava* becomes utmost important for *ancient Indian drama*. It is in the very basis of it. Saint Bharata, the first exponent of Drama in India according to scriptures, has discussed and elaborated the concept of *rasa* and *bhava* in detail in chapter six and seven of his treatise named *Nāṭyaśāstra*, which is one of the ancient scriptures on Drama in the world. According to him, the main purpose of drama is to produce *rasa* for savouring of the audience. And *rasa* happens because of the permutations and combinations of different *bhavas*, which exist in characters. According to him, human beings are always possessed by one or other *bhava*, which are *sthayi bhavas* and are eight in numbers. However, they keep fluctuating according to the situations. And those *bhavas* itself convert into *Rasas* in certain situations. That is what suggested by the *rasa sutra,* that Bharata had developed in chapter six of *Nāṭyaśāstra*, which goes like this:

> *Tatra Vibhavanubhavvyabhicarisanyogad rasnishpatih* (Tripathi 2009)

According to this sutra, *rasa* could be achieved or savoured through the union of *vibhava, anubhava* and *vyabhicari bhavas.* Here, *vibhava* stands for the external factors which affects the emotions, *anubhava* stands for physical attributes or changes one goes through in particular emotive condition and *vyabhicari* stands for the transitory moments or emotions between *sthayi bhavas* (permanent emotions). This *vyabhicari bhava* is, thus, also known as *sancari bhava.* I am not delving into details of what they are and what they really mean, as it will lead us onto a different path, but I'll certainly use the analogy to establish the relationship of leisure or recreation and pleasure with *rasa* and *bhava.*

As, we can see that, according to the *rasa sutra, vibhava* is one important factor in savouring of *rasa. Vibhava*s, as discussed above, are the external factors which heightens the settings, mental conditions or emotions of the characters. First, let us understand how it works. *Vibhavas* could be human beings, events or natural settings. It is of two types: *alambana vibhava* (main cause) and *uddipana vibhava* (external cause). Let's take a popular example from the epic, the *Rāmāyaṇa*, to understand it clearly. Here, Rama first meets Sīta before *swayamvar* (marriage competition) in the garden where Sīta has come to worship her family goddess (*kul devi*). Rama sees her and gets attracted towards her. Here, Sīta's beauty, her features and characteristics are the main factors behind Rama's attraction towards her, as he falls for her instantly by just seeing her, so here Sīta becomes the *alambana vibhava* (base cause). But, the beautiful garden as the setting of the scene also works here as *uddipana vibhava* (cause of excitement) which inspires and provokes the *srngara* element within Rama. Thus, the setting of the scene also becomes an important factor to arouse particular emotion in a human being.

And there is no dearth of these kinds of settings utilised to arouse the emotions of the characters of play texts in ancient Indian drama. In fact, they are best known for them as most of the play texts utilise this motif to arouse particular emotion in their protagonist character according to the need of the narrative. Thus, we see a lot of portrayal of the natural backdrops in play texts of ancient Indian drama, whether it is the palace garden or other natural places like ashrama (hermitage), *vanvihar* (forest) and *udyan* (garden). As they are the best catalyst for triggering the emotions of *srngara*, that is, ashrama in the play *Abhjnanamśakuntalam, palace garden* in *Malvikaagnimitram* and *Vikrmourvashiyam, palace garden* and *samudra griha* (ocean room) in the *Swapnavasavdatta*, the Dandaka forest in *Uttarramcharita* and many others.

Here, *vibhava*, as discussed, works as a trigger to arouse particular emotion in characters. The setting helps the characters in getting into particular emotions as external cause and factor. In the similar fashion, leisure and recreation functions as trigger to obtain pleasure. As

I have established earlier in the beginning of the paper, they are not just interdependent but they flourish with the help of each other and, to relish pleasure, one needs to have leisure and recreation by their side. Thus, leisure and recreation are the external factors upon which pleasure thrives as *rasa* thrives on *bhava*. Now, after establishing the relation between *rasa* and *bhava* and the terms leisure, recreation and pleasure, let me directly jump into the main territory of my paper and establish a connection between the concept of leisure and drama or leisure and ancient Indian drama before delving deeper into its aesthetic and philosophical issues like *dharma* and *siddhi*.

For the sake of grooming the idea of the paper, let's establish first the connection between leisure and drama. As we all know that, like other art forms, practice of *drama* is also not in the essential activity list of the state or the society. It is not something which is in the essential category for the human society without which humans or humankind can't survive. Humans have survived hundreds of years before venturing into the domain of art and culture, which is a later development in the life of human civilisation. Though, signs of practice of art goes back to the ancient times and are visible in the rock settlement age too, but, even then, it was not the essential commodity for life.

This has been also approved by Marxian philosophy as it divides the resources of the society in two categories: base (substructure) and superstructure. Anything which produces materials or products and which has a utilitarian value is part of the base and rest of others are part of superstructure. This is how it has been defined by great egalitarian philosophers and ideologue like Karl Marx, first in his book *German Ideology* and later in other writings. According to their understanding, art and culture is also part of superstructure rather than base or substructure. Nicki Lisa Cole has elaborated their concept in her paper 'Definition of Base and Superstructure':

> Base and superstructure are two linked theoretical concepts developed by Karl Marx, one of sociology's founders. Base refers to the production forces, or the materials and resources, that generate the goods society needs. Superstructure describes all other aspects of society.[1]

What better way to establish it than just reminding us of the Covid-19 regulations laid upon by governments of the world in their respective states and countries in recent times! We all have seen that how performances have been banned overnight all over the world and were in the least priority to reopen again with so many restrictions to follow. It makes it clear that drama, or in that sense practice of any other form of art, is not an essential commodity or object either for the society or state. It directly then refers it to the other category which is nonessential or non-work category which is, of course, leisure, as discussed above in the paper. Because, if it could have been considered as work, though it provides livelihood to many, the governments world over might not have acted heavily against it, as we all have seen in recent past. While the whole paradigm of work/livelihood versus leisure is established on the binary of the two itself, as defined by Robert A. Stebbins in his book *Leisure Legacy: Challenging the Common Sense View of Free Time*:

> Efforts to define leisure and hence to describe its nature date to ancient Greece and the philosophizing of Plato and Aristotle. Then as now these efforts often resulted in a comparison with work, which was and still is seen as necessary, as the way of making one's livelihood. (Stebbins 2017)

This is applicable to the art practitioners, performers and artists of *drama*. But the issue is that art can't happen in isolation. It might be practised in isolation but it's incomplete without audience as existence of art and its practise primarily depends on the audience. What about them? What art practice in general and a play performance in particular means for the audience, who has come over to watch it on a designated place or space after travelling for an hour or so? Monetary expanses might also be involved for him to be part of the audience. Many a times, the audience is not only investing his time and money but also investing heavily mentally and emotionally (*bhava*) according to the nature of the performance. And after investing so much in a performance, what he is his achievement. *Rasa*? Pleasure? Entertainment? It might be all of it but after all these are just experiences, nothing in material and, thus, it should be considered as a part of recreation activity itself, as understood by George Torkildsen in his book *Leisure and Recreation Management*:

> … recreation can be viewed as personal experience (what it does to a person), as activities (the forms it takes) or as an institution (the structure in which it is made available to the community). Taken yet another way recreation can be viewed as a process (what happens to an individual) and as a structure (the framework in which recreation is practised). (Torkildsen 1986)

And, as we have established earlier in the paper, pleasure or any such experience is a bona fide culmination of leisure and recreational activities. Therefore, I am bound to say that not only any art practice in general or performance of a drama in particular but also its savouring as an audience is part of leisure and recreation itself. Here, we are seeing a clear link or connection between leisure, recreation and drama or any other form of art practice. It has been clearly established through the idea propagated and references or examples provided. After validating the art activities in general and drama in particular (as it is the subject matter of enquiry) as part of leisure and recreation activities, let's try to figure out whether ancient Indian drama has to offer anything substantial and meaningful regarding it.

In my understanding based on the texts and treatises of ancient Indian drama, and even on the basis of general understanding about the field, I must say that leisure, recreation and pleasure are the guiding forces of ancient Indian drama, which is also known as Sanskrit drama.[2] It is the very basis upon which the foundation of dramaturgical narratives of ancient Indian drama has been laid and built upon. Though the scholars and theoreticians claim that ancient Indian drama achieve higher theological ground through its narrative, that is, achieving *dharma* and *siddhi*, and they rightly claim so, I will come upon this later in my paper. But, on the basis of the available play texts, it could be said safely that most of the narratives and themes of ancient Indian drama revolves around leisure and pleasure. And, even though the highest goal of a drama is to achieve *dharma* and siddhi, it goes through the canal of leisure and pleasure itself.

It's a well-known and established fact that most of the ancient Indian dramas follow the narratives of the royalty, courtesan, businessmen, ministers of states and other high-class people or people who belong to the ruling class of the society. There is hardly any drama where people from lower strata of society or the marginalised sections had been projected or presented as leading or protagonist figure of the narrative being told by these play texts. It's not that, they are not there in the narrative or they are not part of the drama as such. They are very much present there with their language, dialect and behavioural patterns but they follow the roles assigned to them similar as they follow it in their real life. Their roles and activities are not only limited but also not that substantial in respect with people from the abovementioned categories, who are not only ruling the society and life but also the representation of it in drama, as the role of drama is to represent the real life situations and people living into it.

This is what is prescribed by Bharata in *Nāṭyaśāstra* in the very first chapter while discussing the origin and first performance of drama with saint Atreya and his associates, who happened to visit him one day. While discussing the first ever performance, Bharata mentions the episode where Virupaksa, the leader of the demons, questions their representation in bad light in the drama, *Tripurdah,* the first play staged. To pacify them, Brahma says that the *Natyaveda* I have created is the true representation of the world around and, thus, it is the duty of the drama practitioners to represent the life as it, in shloka 111–112 of chapter one of *Nāṭyaśāstra*:

> The Drama as I have devised, is a mimicry of actions and conducts of people, which is rich in various emotions, and which depicts different situations. This will relate to actions of men good, bad and indifferent, and will give courage, amusement and happiness as well as counsel to them all.[3]

So, the representation of the life of that society can be seen in the plays written at that point of time and are part of the ancient Indian drama. We certainly know that the one obvious divide apart from money, power and pride between the high class and low class is leisure, as people of the high class gets leisure in life, which has been created by ordinary or mundane daily works done for them by marginalised sections of the society. Thus, they have enough free time to enjoy this leisure according to their own free will. This is also because they have gathered enough resources to enjoy it by various lawful or unlawful means. People coming from higher class or from higher strata of the society have various ways to utilise this time called leisure after finishing their jobs or works. About which Joffre Dumazedier has mentioned in his paper:

> Leisure consists of a number of occupations in which the individual may indulge of his own free will—either to rest, to amuse himself, to add to his knowledge or improve his skills disinterestedly or to increase his voluntary participation in the life of the community after discharging his professional, family and social duties. (Dumazedier 1960)

Supporting staffs keep the high-class people free from the mundane physical works, for the sake of their survival, as they get their bread and butter through it. So, the first category people, that is, people of upper class or high strata has a lot of leisure in their life and have their ways to enjoy it through *recreational* activities like gaming, hunting, debating or socialising with same order of people in general, while they enjoy dancing, singing, savouring art and drama and other recreational activities at personal or private level to amuse or entertain themselves. About the same scholar T.S. Yukic has written:

> Recreation is an act or experience, selected by the individual during his leisure time, to meet a personal want or desire, primarily for his own satisfaction. (Yukic 1970)

This leisure availed and enjoyed by the protagonist characters of the texts of ancient Indian drama is visibly similar in these plays. Most of these characters coming from royalty or aristocratic families are seen doing nothing at the forefront while enjoying their leisure and life through recreational activities. In most of the cases, they are looking for love or their love interest while they are already married and sometimes their harem is already full of queens, as they keep getting smitten by new beauties. And once they get attracted to anybody, by all means they try to get the girl through various courtly gestures and promises made to woo her. Whether those promises were kept or not in later phases is not so hard to guess (*Abhjnanamśakuntalam*). The narratives of such plays have been built upon the lovelorn kings, their new love interests and the queens who have got jealous because of king's new extravaganza. Though, at the end, the protagonist will achieve what he wanted and, thus, a sense of fulfilment happens. But, even without going into the crux of the narratives of the plays, we can very well assume that these narratives themselves demand leisure and recreation as the core element and sentiment of the ancient Indian drama.

Ancient Indian drama or the mainstream plays and playwrights truly follows this pattern and are, thus, true representative of leisure, recreation and pleasure in drama. However, this is not the end of the tunnel. Apart from it, it is exciting to note that our age-old dramatists have much more to offer through our ancient Indian drama in this respect. Playwrights like Bhasa, Kālidāsa, Harṣa's, Shudraka, Bhavabhuti and others have devised whole new acts of leisure and recreation, which has been portrayed in most of their plays—*Swapanavasavdatta, Abhjnanamśakuntalam, Malvikaagnimtra, Vikrmourvashiya, Priyadarśikā, Ratnāvalī, Uttarramcharita* and many others.

And as the saying goes in the field of art practice, the content of the art piece decides its form. So, not only the content of the plays we are talking about moves around seeking pleasure through leisure and recreation but even the setting of the plays were developed accordingly by the playwrights. It was like a sure thing in the plays that an act has been kept to be performed in the background of natural setting, which is there to help the protagonists to emote their real feelings and thus meet their true self, as we have discussed above in the paper. Many a times, number of such acts used to be more than one in some of the plays. This can be seen also in the popular epics and other literary narratives.

And for the matters of heart what could be better than the natural settings and backdrops, as we all know that they are the best available catalyst in the world! The natural backdrop of the courtly garden or other natural places like *ashram, vanvihar, udyan, samudra griha* are the best catalyst for *srngara* or mood of love; what Robert E. Goodwin terms as '*pleasure garden*' as discussed above in his book *The Playworld of Sanskrit Drama*. These natural places help the characters in emoting their true feelings to themselves or to their love interest or the loved ones. It works both ways whether in *sambhoga* (union) or *viyoga/vipralambha* (separation), and in the process they are being aware of the self and their true feelings simultaneously. This has been well established by Goodwin, in his book *The Playworld of Sanskrit Drama*:

> The mood of love (Sringara), for example must be furnished in both major varieties, love-in-engagement (Sambhoga) and love-in-seperation (Vipralambha, Viraha). (Goodwin 1998)

The best example of this is *Abhjnanamśakuntalam* by Kālidāsa. Here the backdrop of the ashrama provides the necessary setting to fall in love with each other for both the protagonists Dusyanta and Sakuntala from the first to the third act of the play. The chance meeting of the two in saint Kanva's ashrama sprouts into a full-blown love affair which results into *gandharva vivaha* (love marriage without any ritual). In the play, the desperation for love of the lovelorn couple was shown in the natural setting, which functions as *uddipana vibhava* for them. Whereas, in the fourth act, the whole setting becomes filled with *shoka bhava* or *karuna* rasa as Sakuntala is leaving the ashrama. Kālidāsa shows everybody grieving and lamenting because Sakuntala is getting separated from her roots where she was raised and where she nurtured several living creatures—animals or the trees—while being raised. Thus, they all were in grief when Sakuntala was being sent to Dusyanta palace by saint Kanva, the head priest of the ashrama, who comes to know about their *gandharva vivaha* and Sakuntala's pregnancy out of this affair once he gets back.

In a similar fashion, Rama emotes his true feelings in the play *Uttarramcarita*, written by Bhavabhuti, while he revisits the Dandaka forest for a special purpose. There he remembers all the beautiful moments spent with Sīta in act two of the play. Memories keep coming and haunting him while going through the forest and recognising the places and trees and animals around. Those days, before his beloved Sīta got abducted by Ravana, are still fresh in his mind. He keeps on weeping and lamenting for a long period while hugging the trees around and asking for the well-being of Sīta from different creatures, whom he himself has thrown away to mother earth after winning her back from the clutch of Ravana after a fierce battle, to set an example as a ruler.

Udayana too emotes in *Swapnavasavdatta* in the natural setting of the palace garden of Rajgriha, where he accepts to his friend *vidūṣaka* (Vasantaka) that though his new wife, Padmāvatī, the princess of

Magadha, is young, beautiful, passionate, well-behaved and charming in all manners but still his heart goes for Vasavdatta, whom he has lost in fire. The same lamentation carries on in the fifth act of the play which is the iconic *samudra griha* (ocean room) scene of the play, where he comes to terms with reality while dreaming and talking about Vasavdatta. In this particular scene, the binary of presence and absence of a person has been depicted or synchronised in a great theatrical manner which can't be compared with any other scene of any other play written in the world.

These are popular examples of *nataka*s (plays) written in ancient Indian drama. As we all know, drama is considered to be of ten types (*dasrupaka*)—*nataka, prakarna, prahasna, samvakara, vyayoga, bhana, vitthi, ihamriga, dima* and *anka* in *Nāṭyaśāstra*. Other varieties of plays have also been built up on similar foundations as such *prakarna* like *Mrichchhkatika* and *Prahasna* like *Bhagvadjjukam* and *Dhurtasamagam*. In all these forms of drama, apart from nataka, prakarna and prahasna, *bhana* deals with the concepts of leisure and pleasure in explicit manner. Most of the themes of *bhana* plays revolve around subject matters related to courtesans. And, by all means, leisure and pleasure are the primary concerns in their narratives. Whether it is Shudraka's work, *Padmaprabhritak*, Ishwardatta's *Dhurtavitsamvad*, Varruchi's *Ubhayābhisārikā* or Shyamilak's work *Padtaditak*. All of these are solo plays where an actor, who is *viṭa*, talks and describes the situations and conditions of the streets and houses of the courtesans and people who used to visit them.

There are numerous such scenes, acts and plays in ancient Indian drama which could be utilised or cited to give examples here, as I have mentioned earlier that it is in the very basic intent of the playwrights to showcase the emotions and moods of the characters through these plays. These scenes are best known as ashram/garden/palace garden/ *samudra griha* (ocean room) scenes or with a setting in other private spaces where the protagonists can afford to be on his own. These acts were symbolised as surrendering to mother earth (nature) to fulfil one's goal that could be *artha* (political ambitions), *kāma* (*srngara*) or *moksha* (spiritual). These leisure scenes carry the plutonic romances, chance meetings of the lovebirds, coming closer of the loved ones through suggestive means, opening of one's heart to a close friend and through that to the lover and even getting to know about each other's feelings.

Thus, it has been established that the natural settings help the play texts of ancient Indian drama to achieve what they were meant for. And it achieves so through the union of protagonist characters with their self and the loved ones, with the help of the natural settings working as catalyst forces. Now the question arises whether this union with self and the loved ones lead us anywhere else or this is it.

As far as the understanding of ancient Indian drama is concerned, as originated and developed by many experts and exponents of the field, the main aim of drama is to make the audience aware about four supreme human goals (*dharma, artha, kāma* and *moksha*) through the performance and help them achieve it by realising their duties. These four supreme human goals are known as four *purusarthas*—the ultimate realisations of human beings—according to Hindu scriptures. Seeing the importance of these in Indian culture and life, Robert E. Goodwin has also emphasised on this while writing on ancient Indian drama and its primary objective.

> This is the place to introduce the scheme of the four human goals (*purusartha*) without which no discussion of classical Indian culture can proceed. Three pertain to life in the world and are, in order to importance, *dharma* ('law, duty'), *artha* ('material success, profit') and *kāma* ('desire, pleasure'). The last is *moksha* ('liberation' from the cycle of rebirth). (Goodwin 1998)

Here *dharma* is not about religious following or filled with ritualistic overtones, as we see nowadays around us. *Dharma* here stands for owning the duties as per the social order. As a human being one has to follow his own *dharma* with certain righteousness and sense of duty according to his own position in the society. This is how Robert E. Goodwin elaborates about the same:

> *Dharma* can be conceived objectively as the socio-religious order which extends throughout the cosmos. One's duty is determined by one's place in the social hierarchy and by one's stage of life (student, householder, forest dweller, renouncer). (ibid.)

As, I have mentioned earlier in the chapter, the plays of ancient Indian drama follow this *dharma* quite passionately. I have talked about it through the roles assigned to different characters in the plays and how they religiously follow their *dharma*. Characters like Udayana (*Pratigyayougandhrayan, Swapnavasavdatta*), Dushyanta (*Abhijnānaśakuntalam*), Agnimitra (*Malvikaagnimitra*) and others, who come from royalty, enjoy their majestic powers bestowed upon them by the virtue of being born into a royal family and being inheritor of the throne. The character mostly named as *vidūṣaka* in these plays are kind of close friends of the *nayakas* (protagonists) and mostly help them in managing their private life and affairs. They try their best to fulfil their master's wishes like Maitreya (*Mrichchhakatika*), Vasantaka (*Swapnavasavdatta*) and others. Meanwhile, ministers like Yougandhrayan, Rumnavan

(*Pratigyayougandhrayan, Swapnavasavdatta*), Rakshas and Chanakya (*Mudrarakshas*) perform their duty to help running and securing the states from the clutch of miscreants or enemies. In a similar fashion, women like Sakuntala, Hamsapadika (*Abhjnanamśakuntalam*) Malavika, Dharani, Iravati (*Malvikaagnimitram*), Vasavdatta, Padmāvatī (*Swapnavasavdatta*) and others are there to please their men or make sacrifices for the betterment of their masters. On the other hand, small characters like fisherman (*Abhjnanamśakuntalam*), Sthavarka, Mathurā, Darduraka, Chandanaka (*Mrichchhakatika*) and others in different plays—mostly the servants of palaces, kings and queens—are there to make their life easy by being on their toes. The misery of them were rightly iterated by the character Kanchuki (head servant of the palace) in the third act of the play *Mudrarakshas* written by Vishakhdatta.

One of the prominent examples of it could be shown through analysing the linguistic pattern of these characters. The common notion about ancient Indian drama is that all the plays are written in Sanskrit language but that is not true. As Bharata himself, in *Nāṭyaśāstra*, has prescribed that only characters coming from royal lineage and the Brahmans can speak Sanskrit. Even the woman folk of royal lineage—queens and princesses—were not allowed to speak in Sanskrit. They were allowed to speak *Prakrit* languages according to their regions. So is the case with Brahmans who are devoid of qualities of a Brahman, as prescribed in scriptures. For example, the *vidūṣakas* like Maitreya and Vasantaka of ancient Indian drama were barred from speaking Sanskrit. Rest of other characters were prescribed to speak their own regional variations of *Prakrit* languages according to their habitus.

And this is what we get through various play texts. Thus, we can safely say that ancient Indian drama closely follow *dharma*, one of the four *purusarthas,* to instill it in the general public, since it is the audience who should understand their position in the society and own their *dharma* and act accordingly. So is the case with other worldly affairs like *artha* and *kāma*. These are duties prescribed to human beings and it could be achieved by following one's own *dharma,* as mentioned by Goodwin in the same text:

> Artha has special significance for a ruler, since his success theoretically maintains the dharmic order for all others ... Kama is of value—according to the scheme, which inherently reflects the dharmic perspective—only in the householder stage, when it accounts for offspring. (ibid.)

In the light of ancient Indian drama, it seems that *kāma* takes the centre stage and rest of the *purusarthas* follow accordingly. It is very well established by Robert E. Goodwin through the example of union of Sri and Viṣṇu, *purusha* and *prakriti*, in his book. Here, Sri figure is a concept of pre-Vedic era in which fertility, wealth and happiness is personified. According to him, it is the main duty (*dharma*) of the protagonist (particularly the royal entities) to achieve the conjugation with Sri, which will be followed by *artha* and *moksha* for him as well as his people:

> The monarchy therefore becomes a conduit of divine radiance, representing or embodying the paradisal playworld of divinity on earth. Notions of magical correspondence between the person of the king and the state of the kingdomoften remarked on in studies of Indian kingshipmake it possible for the king's dalliance with beautiful women, all auspicious representative of the Sri-principle, to be taken as a magical inducement to social prosperity. (ibid.)

Attaining *moksha* from human birth and the circle of life is the ultimate goal of the human beings according to certain scriptures. And *moksha* could be achieved once your soul and mind is without any desire. It could be achieved only if there are no distractions in the soul and mind, no attachment with the worldly affairs, subjects and objects. This is again very well established by Goodwin in following lines:

> In other stages it is the distraction which keeps us from *mokṣa*, the supreme good. Without desire and its concomitant ignorance there could be no world to have to escape. (ibid.)

Here the drama performance comes in handy for the audience to achieve such mental condition where one becomes devoid of their own desires. Attaining this kind of mental state is the main requisite to relish *rasa* for the audience and it is possible only if the audience is a *sahrdaya*, a term denoted for those audiences who are well versed in the matters of drama, literature, emotions and knowledge of various things related to life, as deliberated in Chapter 27 of *Nāṭyaśāstra* by Bharata.

And, at this point, let me introduce the concept of *siddhi*, which the audience attains after a dramatic performance. Bharata recommends it as the measuring tool of success of a performance. In chapter twenty-seven of *Nāṭyaśāstra*, he writes that there are two kinds of *siddhis* which the audience achieve through a dramatic performance. One is *Manusi siddhi* and other one is *Daiviki siddhi*. Then he adds that only those who have qualities of a *Sahrdaya* audience can achieve *Daiviki Siddhi*. And for the audience to achieve that, the protagonists have to take the shelter of a natural settings to create a *pleasure garden* (Goowin 1998), so that they can have proximity with nature and self, which helps realise the union with Sri. Thus, *ancient Indian drama*, through its text and practice (leisure and recreation) help its audience attaining a kind of *rasa* and *siddhi* (pleasure) which is not just earthly but heavenly too.

Notes

1 Available at https://www.thoughtco.com/definition-of-base-and-superstructure-3026372#:~:text=Base%20and%20superstructure%20are%20two,all%20other%20aspects%20of%20society (accessed on 2 February 2022).

2 Though many scholars love to use the term 'Sanskrit Drama' rather than ancient Indian Drama, since play texts and performances had been written and performed, but I have certain reservations regarding use of this term. I do believe that most of the play texts written in ancient India are multilingual and, thus, labelling them upon a particular language is like snatching its very characteristic and foundation. So, I will be using the term Ancient Indian Drama or Classical Indian Drama while discussing the very topic.

3 Available at https://www.wisdomlib.org/hinduism/book/the-natyasastra/d/doc202329.html (accessed on 4 February 2022).

References

Australian Council for Health, Physical Education and Recreation/Royal Australian Institute of Parks and Recreation. 1980. Recreation Working Paper, Adelaide: ACHPER Publications, p. 3.

Dumazedier, Joffre. 1960. 'Current Problems of the Sociology of Leisure'. *International Social Science Journal*, 4 (4): 522–31.

Goodwin, Robert E. 1998. *The Playworld of Sanskrit Drama*. New Delhi: Motilal Banarasidass, p. x.

Gray, David E. 1971. 'This Alien Thing Called Leisure'. Paper presented at Oregon State University, Corvallis, Oregon, 8 July, quoted in J.F. Murphy (ed.), *Concepts of Leisure*. Englewood Cliffs, NJ: Prentice-Hall, p. 42.

Kaplan, Max. 1975. *Leisure: Theory and Practice*. New York: John Wiley, p. 26.

Stebbins, Robert A. 2017. *Leisure Legacy: Challenging the Common Sense View of Free Time*. London: Palgrave Macmillan.

Torkildsen, George. 1986. *Leisure and Recreation Management*. 2nd edn, London: E.&F.N. Spon, p. 164.

Tripathi, Radhaballabh. 2009. *Sankshipt Natyasastra*. New Delhi: Vani Prakashan, p. 82.

Yukic, T.S. 1970. *Fundamentals of Recreation*. 2nd edn, New York: Harper & Row, p. 5.

6

FROM SERVICE TO ENTERTAINMENT: MUSIC IN EARLY TAMIL INDIA

T.K. Venkatasubramanian

Perception on 'Leisure'

For many of us, free time is the interval when we are not engaged in putting in labour as work. Karl Marx has pointed out that labour becomes a commodity that is exchangeable with capitalism and is not considered an outcome of collaborative social relations. The interesting paradox of free time lies in the fact that it does not regard itself as possessing an exchange value or 'reification' (Bernstein 1991). Theodor Adorno has explained this contradiction differently as 'profit-oriented social life'. This paradox is the result of industrialisation, which is behind the creation of the distinct categories of 'work' and its opposite—'leisure'. Capitalism's invention of leisure has resulted in its commodification and manufacturing by markets for profits. Adorno and Horkheimer, in their analysis of the culture industry and entertainment, highlight the mindless immersion of the masses into entertainment:

> Amusement under late capitalism is … sought after as an escape from the mechanized work process, and to recruit strength in order to cope with it again. But ... mechanization has such power over leisure and happiness ... no independent thinking must be expected from the audience, the product prescribes every reaction.... (Adorno and Max 1992)

Robert A. Stebbins defines 'serious leisure' as the systematic pursuit of an amateur, hobbyist or volunteer activity that participants find substantial and launch themselves on a career. Stebbins goes on to list six distinctive traits or qualities of serious leisure (Stebbins 1992).

In the rapidly changing social, economic and political context due to factors such as urbanisation, industrialisation, modernisation, globalisation, privatisation, colonial heritage, large-scale migration and others, traditional leisure practices have undergone changes. Impact of these developments have been studied by sociologists (Modi 1985). Amanda Weidman, writing on a particular historical moment, studies the emergence of upper-caste women as performers of classical music on the concert stage in early 20th-century South India and has addressed the issue of 'Gender and the Politics of Voice' (Weidman 2003). In engaging with this specific historical and ethnographic moment, she has addressed broader questions about the relationship among voice, subjectivity and agency, and to ask how a consideration of music might enrich our thoughts on these issues. The revival of Carnatic music is a notion that this music could take its place as a sign of tradition and Indianness alongside the trappings of an emergent middle-class modernity. It is common knowledge that particular notions of female respectability and ideal womanhood are central to the project of defining middle-class identity, modernity and the aims of colonial nationalism (Banerjee 1989). Weidman has successfully interiorised the conceptions of voice to explain new notions of public and private in colonial modernity, and concludes that the roles of artist and respectable women reinforce each other, and to 'come into voice' on the musical stage involves engaging with not just the conventions of musical art but the conventions of female respectability as well.

The indissoluble link between history and sociology is not new to the social sciences. Max Weber saw relationships between history and sociology as based on mutual and essential support and logical priority. Alessandro Cavalli said, 'Sociology without history is blind, and history without sociology is mute.' Sociology is nomothetic while history is idiographic and offers a better explanation to the relationship between the two. The historians describe unique events, while the sociologist derives generalisations from the social world. In other words, history uses generalisations to examine particular sequences of events while sociology often analyses events through biographical (epistemological) and hermeneutical lens. History is mainly concerned with the past or past-human society, and social processes represent the principal objects of study. Sociology is more concerned with the investigation of the present and complex social phenomena like 'leisure'. The historian's focus is always 'how it was' in a long-term perspective. We wish to look at Tamil music in this perspective and show singing as an activity that began as a social service and finally ended up as 'entertainment' when it became part of court culture.

Tamil Literature Provides the Clue

Music is linked with the life of the people. Devotion to music is a part of Tamil culture. Tamil society nurtured music that had its genesis and growth in the soil of Tamil Nadu, through the ages in diverse ways and forms. The origin of such music is largely speculative, but its evolution has a systematic chronological history (Kuppuswami 1992).

It has crossed different stages of development, taken shape as cognisable system of science and art with an individual identity. It is also possible to construct a music tradition of Tamil Nadu by following shifts in the literary tradition. Singing the praise of a patron is an important activity in the Sangam classics. Various types of Kingship like Heroic, Moral, Ritual, Divine and Dharmic are recoverable from historical sources. Singing as an activity, combined with patronage, enables historians of music to construct the musical tradition of Tamil Nadu, and also demonstrates how a social activity becomes entertainment when it enters 'court culture' (Shulman 2001). In David Shulman's opinion, and that of George L. Hart III, 'poetry at the Sangam stage is a bardic corpus created and maintained through the relationship of patrons and wandering poets' (Kailasapathy 1968). This relationship is in many ways reminiscent of patron–bard relations in other 'heroic' cultures like Homeric Greece. Bardic patronage subsists on superlatives because of the bard's total dependency on the patron for survival, poetry is full of pathetic descriptions (Hart-III 1979). Hero to become a hero needs the bard and the bard depends on the patron, and the hero has a duty towards the minstrel in the form of *Paan Kadan*.

Readiness of the hero to accept his duty and the poet to sing his praise (*Pugal*) or eulogy came out clearly in Sangam poetry. Bards also had a monopoly of sorts over the major values of society. An asymmetrical relationship exists between poet/patron/*paanan* (actual singer) (Venkatasubramanian, 2010). In the next stage, the Sangam poet at times compared his patron to a god (or several gods), where the deities mentioned are in no way active partners in the relationship of the poet and the lord. This is known as *Puvainilai* in medieval grammar (Kailasapathy 1968). This situation further changes in the 6th and 7th centuries (Pallava–Pandya). F. Hardy notes that this shift is part of a much wider process of transformation in South Indian civilisation in this period. Many of the basic institutional features of Tamil Nadu take shape for the first time in these centuries (*c.* 4th to early 9th centuries) (Hardy 1983). Amidst these, a new form of kingship comes into being as one can see from its classic expressions in works like *Cilappatikaram* and *Manimekalai*.

This new form of kingship entailed greater accountability than in the heroic kingship of earlier times and problematised king's authority and legitimacy. Simultaneously, it found expression in institutionalised patterns of royal endowments in *dana* of many kinds including to Brahmans, temples and poets. The king needs his poets and other recipients of gifts. The poet becomes the kingmaker and dealer in images of authority and propriety and has an increasingly powerful role. It is during this period that the *Arruppadai* genre gets transformed into a *Bhakti* format. Poets now guide the devotees not to a patron of flesh and blood but rather to a god. For example, Sundarar (*Tevaram* 34.1) follows *Arruppadai* pattern of praising patron over others, but his choice is now built into the opposition between temple and king, god and human donor. Now one can notice the change from complaints to shopping list also. Poet's human patrons to the god, or to the temple, within this framework, is a perpetuation and extension of the earlier contours of the poet–patron relationships. Shulman observes:

> Even if we leave that Chola period hagiography aside and remain within the confines of *Tevaram* poems themselves, we can easily see how the older patron-poet relation of the bardic period survives, somewhat transformed in the relation of the bhakti poet to his deity. The same intimate connection that we noted with respect to Sangam period patronage recurs in the Bhakti context; only now the *puram* (exterior) frame and panegyric is mixed with the contents of *akam* (interior/love) poetry. The poet is in love with the deity he extols, the latter is no longer wholly outside him—like the Sangam hero—but has penetrated the poet and taken up residence within him. Still, poets like Sundaramurtti treats this partly internalized patron as someone, who like the Sangam patron, can be manipulated by emotional means. Indeed, the bhakti poets' power in this respect seems by far to outweigh his Sangam period predecessor. (Shulman 2001)

One notices a conspicuous displacement of the poet's focus from human patrons to god, or to the temple where he is established. In singing the praise activity, perpetuation and extension of the earlier contours of the poet–patron relationship, and a concomitant emergence of poetry abusing and deriding the old pattern of interdependence between human patrons and poets are noticed. According to Shulman, this feature remains a standard theme in South Indian poetry, in Tamil, Telugu and Sanskrit, right up to modern times (Peterson 1992).[1]

The king needs his poet's encomia; the Court poets, at least, need the king's support. And yet a rival centre has emerged, the temple, with its own resources for patronage (many of them of course of royal origin) and with a poetic ideology that is largely hostile to the traditional heroic or courtly panegyric. Now the king needs the authority of the temple deity and the latter's servants in order to maintain his own tenuous claims. At this stage, older type of poetic praise becomes subordinated to a new end. For example, Kamban dedicated his opening verses to Lord Rama, and then celebrated his patron, Sadaiyappan of Vennainallur. Somewhat similar is the case of Villiputturar, the poet of the Tamil *Mahābhārata*, who praises his patron Varapati Atkondan Varapatiyathantan for his virtues and also his loyalty to the Chola overlord. There are other forms of indirect or subtly complicated panegyric in the *Kovai* genre where the patron–king, hero or deity appear in conjunction with each other as fictive hero and erotic exemplar.

The collapse of the distinction in later works is taken as an indication of culture change. However, as far as Chola courts are concerned, and in the context of the historical rivalry between king and temple deity over Tamil poet, two patterns are discernible. First runs the king himself into the humblest of god's devotees, and the second explores and plays with the king's own proximity to the divine. The Chola kings are portrayed as ardent worshippers of Siva, Sundaramurtti heaps scorn on Brahma and Vishnu, Cekkilar's portrayal of Ceraman Perumal prostrated himself at the feet of washerman. By now, the king's largesse is seen as a function of devotion. We wish to quote Shulman in this context for the sake of clarity:

> The pattern we are observing is, at this stage, strongly suggestive of harmony and resolution of tension: king, poet and god have sorted out their relative positions, and the human patron has found a perfectly acceptable place in this devotional scheme of things. The poet has no difficulty in praising him in this manner. The second pattern appears by way of contrast, to perpetuate an existing tension between king and deity by exploring their actual or potential similarities, to the option of implying an identity between them. (Shulman 2001)

The Sangam poet was capable of comparing his patrons to god or gods (although it was heroic kingship). By Chola times the court poets extend this practice to establish the king's basic affinity with one god (Hardy 1983). Kulottunga I united the Eastern Chalukya and Chola dynasties (claiming descent from the lunar and solar kingly genealogies). His birth is seen as a new avatar, hence, Kamban's *Ramavataram* (and not Ramayanam) of the God Vishnu (Cox 2016).[2] Following the demise of Chola court, we notice the hypertrophy of the satirical powers vested in the Tamil poet and triumphant statement of the poet's absolute superiority over his patron.

Singing for the Legitimacy of the Order

Now let us focus our attention on actual singers and singing in early Tamil India. *Panar* are the actual practitioners of music in the Sangam age who sing. *Pan Isaippavar, Senniyar, Vairiyar, Mathankar* and *Innisaikkarar* were males, while *Padini, Virali, Patti, Madangi* and *Padalmagalir* were females. Naccinarkkiniyar, a famous commentator, classified *Panar* into *Isaippanar* and *Yalppanar*.[3] The *Pulavar* and *Panar* were two separate social groups. *Pulavar* was a mere composer of learned verses and included Brahmanas also in their ranks (Pillay 1966). Poem number 335 of the anthology *Purananuru* informs that the *Panan, Paraiyan, Tudiyan* and *Kadamban* are the earliest inhabitants of Tamilagam. Many writers emphasise the ambiguity of *Panar* also. K.A. Nilakanta Sastri affirms, 'There are only four castes namely *Tudiyan, Panan, Paraiyan, Kadamban* ... perhaps survivals from pre-Aryan times' (ibid.). 'A bard speaks of the *Panar* as one of the noble clans. In passing, it is interesting to note that another ambient clan—the *Paraiyar* (Drummers) enumerated under the category in the same poem was also degraded in the caste-hierarchy of later time' (Kailasapathy 1968). The *Panar* as a group is rarely heard after Sangam era, although Cekkilar, the author of *Periyapuranam*, mentions the name of Tiruppanalvar and *Tirunilakanda Yalppanar* at a later date. *Panar* concerned themselves with the activities of the Sangam society. They were message-carriers between lovers. There were mendicants among them. Different sections of *Panar* were experts in handling varieties of instruments like Kinai (percussion), *Sanku* (couch), stringed instruments, *Parai* and *Kombu*, etc. *Yal*, the musical instrument with the Yalppanar played, is associated with *Kurunji*, while *Kulal* (Flute) is accounted with *Mullai*. It is obvious that the *Panar* performed various social services of the Sangam society. The link between the *Panar* and others in Tamil society could be recognised only in terms of services rendered. Though not in the sphere of agriculture, the services have been 'socially necessary and useful'. There is primary need to assess the extent to which the value system based on social equality to understand the role of *Panar* (singers) in the Sangam society.

R. Champakalakshmi writes that, in the early medieval context, ritual singing of bhakti hymns had more than a religious function (Champakalakshmi 2011). The institution of ritual singing by functionaries called *Padigam Vinnappam Ceyvar* appears in late 9th-century Pallava inscriptions, and later becomes a regular part of temple worship under early Cholas in the 10th century and becomes a preeminent socioreligious activity under the splendid sovereigns Raja Raja I and Rajendra. The word *Padigam* is derived from Sanskrit

Padya or verse and those who sing the hymns and verses are known in inscriptions are *Padigam Vinnappam Ceyvar* (Nagaswamy 1959), that is, those who offer hymns in worship. Later on, in traditional parlance, they came to be called *Padigam Paduvar* or *Oduvar* (chanters of hymns) (Sridevi 1999). The role of the early medieval *Padigam* singer needs to be understood in the changing socio-political context at the end of Pallava and beginning of Chola periods. 'Patikam singing represents a regional cultural form in the evolution of the temple as the channel of communication and the chief mechanisms of ideological consolidation for the emerging Chola State' (Champakalakshmi 2011). As David Shulman says, 'The Southern Bhakti movements were oriented towards life in this world, with its conventional social categories; far from being revolutionary in a social sense, bhakti, religion, in its most extreme manifestations tends towards the preservation of social order through the sanctification of the present' (Shulman 1980). R. Champakalakshmi is categorical about the arrangements made at Tanjavur for ritual singing when considered in conjunction with the legend of the recovery of the *Tevaram* hymns that is narrated in the 14th century *Tirumurai Kanda Puranam*. It strengthens the view that the ideological needs of Chola royalty were fulfilled by the text and its continuing importance in the temple movement (Champakalakshmi 2011). We have tried to explore the historical dimensions of the musical part elsewhere (Venkatasubramanian 2011).

Music as an instrument of power makes people forget the general fear of jungle life, makes them believe in the harmony of civilised life and silences their misgivings. Music is a ritual power, it is a question of making people forget the fear of violence, it is representative power when it is a question of making them believe and bureaucratic power when it is a question of silencing those who oppose it. Music, thus, localises and specifies power. The primary function of music depends on its mysterious oppositeness to a code of power in the way in which it participates in the crystallisation of social organisation in an order. Music creates political order because it is a minor form of sacrifice. Music of the Sangam era stimulated the accepted norms of social transformation. Confucius said, 'To speak and carry into execution what you have spoken is ceremony, to act without effort or violence is music' (Lagge 1967). At the Sangam stage, economic and social changes directly affected several components of the political structure (Chiefdom). Poets who praised themselves by composing eulogies were held in high esteem, and we identified a patron poet–bard relationship also (Venkatasubramanian 1998). Music served as a regulating tool in the society. In rituals, music was a locus of subversion or transcendence of the body. Society attempted to integrate into an official religion. As a quintessential mass activity, it functioned as a necessary factor for legitimacy. Support from *Vendu* (king) was necessary to channelise it as a system of power.[4] Since the *Panan* invariably sang and *Pulavan* composed eulogies, it was deemed as 'court music' and not necessarily an entertainment for a leisurely 'courtly culture'. The consumers of such music belonged to every social class. The *Panar* moved from place to place, offering service. They organised circulation of music (propaganda) within society (Venkatasubramanian 2003). During the Sangam days, music and dance were loci of subversion, transcendence of the body, and society did not make a special attempt to integrate them into official religion. *Veriyadal*, for instance, was a quintessential mass activity. In that next stage of Tamil history, the Pallavas attempted to integrate music with religion by linking it with temples and forging the fine arts as tools for ensuring cultural and political unity. It is pertinent to note that temples did not condemn artists. Ritualistic routines based on *Agamas* helped to shape religion as an instrument of order, a prop for political power and a legitimiser of royal succession. Artists rendering temple service were domesticated by royal favours. Music created ritual order, then represented a simulacrum of order and served as a stake in the game of power. Forms, sources and roles have changed along with, and by means of, changes in the support of power. Its code and original usage have undergone transformation. The birth of a new genre of music, a renewed syntax, witnessed a new system throwing open the field for new exploration of the possible expressions of music.

With the rise of the Vijayalaya Chola power, there ensued a broadening of the channels of literature and a more copious flow of literary effrontery, an expression of fresh energy released by the realisation of an imperial state in Tamilagam. The *Prasasthis* of the Chola kings, with a few exceptions, maybe classed among the best specimens of the literature of the age marked by stately diction, easy flow of verse and animated narration of historical incidents. These *Prasasthi* compositions must have been the works of court poets of a high calibre. The steady demand for their services furnished great impetus to the cultivation of a secular literature. The chola king was an ardent worshipper and his disposition received ample recognition at the hands of Court poets.[5] The king's largesse was seen as an inherent factor and this largesse was different from that of the Sangam kings, chieftains or *Muvendar*. The panegyric now was different from the bardic style. The king was only a second hero, after the deity. The poet determined the king's rank within a devotional context. The patron and the poet which saw deity as their ultimate refuge. The Chola court poet established a suggested graded link between king and god. A patent change in the balance of relations between patron and poet could be noticed in post-Chola times. The king who denied honour to the poet ended up sharing his throne with him. We may surmise that, during Chola epoch, the king, artists and god seemed to have sorted out their relative positions and the human patron focused a perfectly acceptable place in the devotional scheme.[6]

Historical evidence from the Sangam age suggests that music originated in ritual undertakings. In course of time, music became an attribute of religious and political power. The practice of remunerating artistes indicates the entry of music into a relation of commodity exchange. All these provide a rough sketch of a society under construction, a society in which music and dance were mass-produced and consumed. Music and dance became prophetic and the social organisation echoed this. Since the dawn of the Bhakti Movement, music and dance have served as tools for the consolidation of society in Tamilagam. They linked the power centre to the subjects and, thus, become an attribute of power in various forms. The Chola state was always fascinated by the performing arts. The economic and political dynamics of Chola society led the 'state' to invest in art. Music and dance became objects of consumption, like everything else. Their distribution was organised through the temple and they became activities essential for knowledge and social relations, to be inscribed with precision to the economic hierarchy of the Chola state. The artistes became economically bound to a machine of power. The state paid the artistes for creating what needed to affirm legitimacy. The livelihood of the artistes depended on the goodwill of the ruler. When official power used arts to make people forget their woes, they became ritual sacrifice (scapegoats). When the state desired to enlist the faith of the ruled, music became an 'enactment' (representation).

Two Contrasting Treatises

Daud Ali writes:

> Though sources from the fourth to seventh centuries provide only partial descriptions of the procedures within the assembly hall, later texts like the Chalukya king Somesvara III's political and, sumptuary manual, 'The Delight of the Mind' (*Mānasollāsa*) composed in 1129–30 CE contains more detailed accounts which were clearly based on earlier precedents (see Figure 3.1). The *Mānasollāsa* includes the holding of Court among the twenty 'enjoyments' (*Upabhogas*)

> recommended for a king. According to Somesvara, the King was to sit on a lion-throne in the assembly hall, flanked by his whisk bearers and instruct his Chamberlain to issue a general invitation to Court (*Sarvavahana*). (Ali 2004)

Scholars opine that *Mānasollāsa* or *Abhilashitarta Chintamani* as a mixed genre of part encyclopedia and part 'mirror of princes' was probably by a court scholar under Kalyana Chalukya Someśvara III in 113 CE. It was also known as Jagadacharya Pustaka containing five principal sections: *Rajyapraptikarana* (acquisition of political power), *Rajyasthirikarana*, (consolidation of power), *Rajyopabhoga* (physical enjoyment of power), *Apayakavinoda* (entertainments of intellectual delight) and *Sukhopapadikakinoda* (pleasures of sort); the fourth section Kavya comes under *Sastra Vinoda* (entertainment of learned discourse) and *Katha Vinoda* (entertainment of storytelling) also. Reciters were known as *pathaka*s and singers as *gayaka*s, while the epic reciters were *sutas* and the genealogists were *Magadha Bandin*s (8.2). There is specific mention about Gita Vinoda which included Melody, rhythm, prosody, etc.

There were some elements of song in storytelling, not as *Gita/Giti* but as music. The expression *Desabhasha Visaradha* in the text devotes the consciousness about sounds (*svara*) from *Samaveda*, notes (*grāma*), scales (*jati*) and determination of melody (raganirnaya) from different languages. Dialects (*Vibhasa*) and codes (*Antarabhashika*) are also known. *Manasollosa* is a clear proof of music as an entertainment for the court under Kalyana Chalukyas by 12th century AD.

In India, *Sastra*s and *Purāṇas* were produced in Sanskrit, *Sthola Purāṇas* and Kavyas in Prakrit and regional languages. These received patronage as well. The text (treatise) *Silappatikaram* at the Dharamic level reiterates through Kannagi, the profound narrative of the devoted wives, the *pativrata*s like Sīta, Anusuya, Draupadī, Tara, Savitri, Damayanti, Shakuntala and many others. At the social level, the text establishes the spiritual, aesthetic and commercial value of plastic and performing arts, of the *shilpa*s, of dance, music and poetry. Kovalan, the hero, with his wife Kannagi is bound in a householder's vows, and with Madhavi the courtesan was an aesthete or *rasika* of the Tamil ideal of *iyal, isai* and *nadagam* (poetry, music and drama). The term *Cilappatikaram* is made up of two words—*Silambu* and *Adigaram*—or literally the story that centres round the anklet. One among the *Perun-kappiyam*s (*Mahakavya*s in Sanskrit), it will come under *Todarnilacceyyul* in which drama (*nadagam*) is the chief characteristic. The commentators Adiyarkkunallar and Arumpadavurai Aciriyar have written commentaries which are helpful to researchers. This work speaks about the grammar and theory of Tamil music in sections like 'Aycciyar Kuravai', 'Arangerruk Kadai', 'Venir Kadai' and 'Nadukan Kadai' which provide enormous information on Tamil music. The fundamental scale is given as '*Sempatai*' which is equated with present day Harikambhodi. Twelve zodiac names frame a circle for placing notes. This is known as '*Vattappalai*' scales, derived from the modal shift of toxic—the *Palai* or seven-note scales and pentatonic or five-note scales. Musical instruments are also mentioned like *yal*, etc. Few musical forms are also mentioned in 'Kanalvari'. UKU, *vari, padal, pattu, pan* are synonyms meaning song in the Tamil language. Rhythms for the song were *cir*, *orru* and *pani*. With such developed musical grammar and theory, obviously from the singing of *Panar* and *Padigam Paduvar*, the music did not become an entertainment in court culture even during the time of the Cholas. It definitely entered the Vijayanagar court as entertainment for the court and its elite.

Ergo

Certain ideas in modern societies correspond well with Cicero's classical insight; what is most outstanding and chiefly to be defined by all healthy, good and well-off persons is leisure with honour.[7] What is 'honourable leisure' is a question that haunts the minds of contemporary sociologists like Harrison White (1993) and Charles Taylor (1989). In other words, how does the descriptive sociology understand the astonishing commitment of men and women to activities outside their work? There is no conceptual agreement and much phenomenological uncertainty associated with understanding the adventures of climbers, roamers of the seven seas, collectors, role-players, backpackers, bird watchers, participants in extreme sports and many others. Although several depictions exist, all share the notion that individuals somehow shape their identity by carrying out opportunities outside work. Leisure in contemporary world come in distinct forms when, (a) participants make an effort to fill their freedom with systematic experiences that ends in themselves, (b) Willingness to invest considerable effort and assess for emotional and intellectual engagements, (c) keep work and 'leisure' separate and (d) reach a degree of accomplishment in any activities other than work.

We wish to point out one of the perceptions mentioned earlier on Amanda Weidman's poser that revival of Carnatic music is a notion that this music could take its place as a sign of tradition and Indianness alongside the happenings of an emergent middle-class modernity to explain the issue of gender and politics of voice. We took it back to its roots, and focused on singing as an activity which was not for entertainment of the court and it's elite up to Vijayanagara rule in early Tamil India. Singing as an activity legitimatised the socio-political order during Sangam, Pallava and Chola periods of Tamil history. Musical activities began as a societal need and became an entertainment for the leisurely class of elite at a particular historical stage.

Notes

1 Example, Dhurjati, Kalahastisvarastakamu, or Tyagaraja.
2 This book is an essay on Chola history, taking the emergence of Kulottunga I (1070–1120) as its focus.
3 Tolkappiyam, Porulatikaram (commentary) Nurpa 91.
4 Charlemagne had to force Cultural and political Unity of his Kingdom by imposing the Universal Practice of the 'Gregorian Chant'.
5 Raja Raja I is described as 'Sivapada Sekara' (worshipper of the feet of Śiva).
6 We have already seen that the *Panar* of Sangam age also compares his patron to a god or few gods. This does not mean that the *Panar* make Sangam kingship either sacred or divine.
7 Classical scholars seem to agree that the guiding principle throughout Cicero's political career was to advocate some sort of individual freedom as a necessary condition worthy of existence, as opposed to slave's idea of a good master.

References

Adorno, Theodore W. and Horkheimer Max. 1992. *Dialectic of Enlightenment*. London: Stanford University Press, p. 137.

Ali, Daud. 2004. *Courtly Culture and Political Life in Early Medieval India*, Cambridge. Cambridge University Press, pp. 112–13.

Banerjee, S. 1989. *The Parlour and the Streets Elite and Popular Culture in Nineteenth Century Calcutta*. Kolkata: Seagull Books.

Bernstein, J.M. (ed.). 1991. *The Culture Industry*. Theodor Adorno. London: Stanford University Press, p. 189.

Champakalakshmi, R. 2011. 'Patikam Patuvar, Ritual singing as a Means of Communication in Early Medieval South India'. In *Religion, Tradition, and Ideology: Pre-Colonial South India*. New Delhi: Oxford University Press, pp. 215–34.

Cox, Whitney. 2016. *Politics, Kingship and Poetry in Medieval South India, Moonset on Sunrise Mountain*, South Asia Edition. Cambridge Univeristy Press.

Hancook, M. 2000. *Womanhood in the Making: Domestic Ritual and Public Culture in Urban South*. India: Berkley Avalon Publishing.

Hardy, Friedheim. 1983. *Viraha Bhakti*. New Delhi: Oxford University Press, p. 225.

Hart-III, George L. 1979. *Poetry of the Tamil Anthologies*. Princeton: Princeton University Press.

Kailasapathy, K. 1968. *Tamil Heroic Poetry*. Oxford University Press, pp. 55–93.

Kuppuswami, T.V. 1992. *Carnatic Music and the Tamils*. New Delhi: Kalinga.

Lagge, James (trans.). 1967. *Book of Rites*, Vol. II. New York: New York University Books, p. 276.

Manbekar, Purnima. 1991. *Screening Culture, Viewing Politics: An Ethnography of Television, Womanhood, and Notion in Post-Colonial India*. Durham, NC: Duke University Press.

Modi, Ishwar. 1985. 'Leisure, Mass Media and Social Structure'. *Leisure and Social Transformation Sociological Bulletin*, Vol. I (3): 386–403.

Nagaswamy, R. 1959. *Tanjaripperuvudiyar Koyil Kalvettugal* (in Tal9911), Part-I, State Department of Archaeology, Tamil Nadu, Ins. No. 6.

Peterson, Indira V. 1992. 'In Praise of Their Lord: The Image of the Royal Patron in the Songs of Samit Sundaramurti and the Composer Tyagaraja'. In *The Powers of Art: Patronage in Indian Culture*, edited by Miller B. Stoller. New Delhi: Oxford University Press, pp. 120–41.

Pillay, K.K. 1966. 'Aryan Influences in Tamilakam, during Sangam Epoch'. *Tamil Culture*, XII (2–3): 164.

Sastri, K.A. Nilakanta. 1968. *A History of South India: From Prehistoric Times to the Fall of Vijayanagar* (3rd Edition). New Delhi: Oxford University Press, p. 24.

Shulman, D. 1980. *Tamil temple Myths: Sacrifice and Divine Marriage in the South Indians Saiva Tradition*. Princeton: Princeton University Press, p. 21.

———. 2001. *The Wisdom of Poets*. New Delhi. Oxford University Press, pp. 4, 82

———. 2001. *'Poets and Patrons in Tamil Literature and Literary Legend'. The Wisdom of Poets, Studies in Tamil, Telugu and Sanskrit* Oxford: Oxford University Press, pp. 63–102.

Sridevi, P. 1999. *A Study of the Oduvar Tradition with Reference to Select Temples in Tamilnadu*. Unpublished PhD. Thesis, Department of Indian Music, University of Madras.

Srinivasan, A. 1985. 'Reform and Revival of the Devadasi and Her Dance'. *Economic and Political Weekly*, 20 (44): 1869–76.

Stebbins, R.A. 1992. 'Amateurs, Professionals and Serious Leisure'. In *Work, Leisure and Well Being*, edited by J.T. Haworth. London: Routledge.

———. 1997. 'Serious Leisure and Well Being'. In *Work Leisure and Well Being*, edited by J.T. Haworth. London: Routledge, p. 119.

Taylor, C. 1989. *Sources of the Self*. Cambridge: Massachusetts Harvard University Press.

Venkatasubramanian, T.K. 1998. 'Rational and Social Foundations of Music and Dance of Early Tamils First to Fourth C.' *Proceedings of the Indian History Congress*, 59: 186–99.

Venkatasubramanian, T.K. 2003. 'The Legitimacy of Order, Music as Ideology in Ancient and Medieval Tamilakam'. In *Negotiating India's Past: Essays in Memory of Partha Sarathi Gupta*, edited by Biswamoy Pati et al. New Delhi: Tulika Books, pp. 67–86.
———. 2010. *Music as History in Tamil Nadu*. New Delhi: Primus.
———. 2011. 'Historical Dimensions of Thevara Isai'. *Sangeet Natak: Journal of Music and Dance*, Vol. XLV (1). New Delhi: Sangeet-Natak Akademi.
Weidman, A. 2003. 'Gender and the Politics of Voice: Colonial Modernity and Classical Music in South India'. *Cultural Anthropology*, Vol. 18 (2): 194–232.
White, H.C. 1993. *Careers and Creativity Social Forces in the Arts*. Colorado: Westview Press, Boulder.

7

VISUALISING LEISURE IN JAIN MANUSCRIPT PAINTINGS FROM WESTERN INDIA

Patrick Krüger

The Jina Legend

Jainism is generally regarded as a religion determined by renunciation and abstinence. Its roots go back to the ascetic reform movements which formed around the middle of the 1st millennium BCE as an opposition to the socially and spiritually dominant Brahmanism. The supposed founder of Jainism, Vardhāmana Mahāvīra, according to Jain tradition belonged to a royal family, but renounced rulership and riches in order to attain salvation as a mendicant. He became omniscient and was given the honorary title *Jina* (conqueror) because, by achieving salvation, he broke the cycle of perpetual rebirths. To his followers he preached a doctrine based on rigorous renunciation and nonviolence. He is, thus, regarded as the ideal ascetic by his followers, and his way of life is seen as exemplary. The life story of Jina Mahāvīra and his mythical precursors is mentioned in numerous works of Jain literature. The version most widely known, the *Jinacaritra* (life story of the Jina), which is one of the earliest narrations on the topic, is part of the Kalpasūtra.

At least since the 11th century, increasing numbers of illustrated manuscripts were created in western India, first on palm leaves, later on paper; they were donations to Jain libraries (*bhaṇḍāra*), usually associated to a Jain temple, by wealthy merchants and other citizens. During the 15th and 16th centuries, manuscript production reached its peak; a large number of them were copies of the Kalpasūtra.

Jain manuscript painting of the 15th and 16th century is dominated by formulaic repetitions and the constant return of the same motifs. This means that the iconography must have been precisely determined and that artists followed these prescriptions exactly when preparing their illustrations. The miniatures in the paper manuscripts are narrative and occasionally follow a 'completing' style of composition. In many cases, however, the narrative component of the representation has been drastically reduced to only a rather generalised content which is then used transmitting different meanings in different texts. Miniatures generally serve as illustrations to the texts they are included in. It is a particularity of the Kalpasūtra manuscripts that many of the motifs depicted do not have an obvious connection to the content of the text. The cycle of illustrations rather narrates a slightly different story compared to that in the text. While some important episodes from the text are missing in the illustrations, others not told in it are included.

For the Jina legend, this means that besides the literary version there must have existed another narrative that spread orally among the lay worshippers and finally became the basis for the selection of the illustrations. However, since this narrative is hardly comprehensible, the text passages on which the individual motifs are based must always be consulted when looking at the miniatures. Of course, the events illustrated are primarily based on the Jina legend handed down in the Kalpasūtra, but they also include episodes from Hemacandra's 'Biographies of 63 Important Men' (*Triṣaṣṭiśalākāpuruṣacaritra*; abbreviated hereafter as *Tr*), which were very popular among the Śvetāmbaras during the Middle Ages. The production of miniatures were probably preferred over the commentaries of the Kalpasūtra. Overall, the miniatures were less of an illustration than rather an adornment of the manuscript; the number and quality of miniatures determined the value of the donation and hence the amount of religious merit to the donor. In addition, the illustrated manuscripts also fulfilled a ritual function, being shown to the congregation during the recitation of the Kalpasūtra during the Paryuṣaṇā festival.[1]

Up to Mahāvīra's renunciation of the world, the textual tradition of the Kalpasūtra at several points reports on the life and wealth of the noble upper class at the time the text was written. The early modern illustrations take up this theme and also focus on the leisure activities of the elite, whose representatives had the manuscripts made and donated them to religious institutions. The text and especially the illustrations, thus, reflect a tension between leisure and ascetic renunciation that still characterises the Jain communities of ascetics and laypeople today. Some of the motifs from manuscripts in the Berlin collections, in which amusements and leisure at the court of the future Jina's parents are shown, will be discussed with regard to their pictorial content and their function within the cycle of illustrations.

The Royal Household

Princes and kings are among the most common figures in Jain legends, and scenes of courtly life are, therefore, returning motifs in miniature painting. When a ruler is introduced into the narrative or the action shifts to his environment, the miniatures often make use of iconographic formulas that stand for court life in general and that are either integrated into a complex scenery as a pictorial element or are the subject of a complete miniature. These motifs include those of 'king with entourage' and of 'king and queen'; both can be placed in different positions in the Kalpasūtra's pictorial narratives and, therefore, often illustrate different episodes of the narrative despite being identical in composition and representation. As individual scenes, these two motifs cannot be attributed to any particular episode within Jain literature.[2] They appear to be interchangeable and their content can only be determined in connection with the other miniatures in a manuscript.

The picture cycle of the Mahāvīra legend contains a series of scenes of courtly life, which are situated in the plot of the Kalpasūtra between the conception and the birth of Jina. Some of these scenes are related to episodes from the Jina legend, while others depict life at the royal court without any direct reference to the text, using common pictorial formulas that were also used in a similar way in other manuscripts. The first half of the illustration cycle is devoted to the parents of the future Jina and shows their life of wealth and luxuries at the royal court. Only when Mahāvīra decided to renounce the world does the future Jina become the focus of the illustrations. Thus, the path of salvation, characterised by the strictest asceticism, is contrasted with the comforts of courtly life. The Jina's parents, who are hardly mentioned outside the Jina legend, are given a special role here. In the canonical writings of the Śvetāmbaras, the Jina's parents are of little or no importance. Nevertheless, at the latest since the Middle Ages, a worship cult developed among Jain lay followers seems to have included the parents of the Tīrthaṃkaras. Thus, the parents of the Tīrthaṃkaras are addressed in various rites, especially in the *pratiṣṭhavidhi* (Shah 1955–57, 23), where greater importance is assigned to the mothers than to the fathers. Maybe those cult images that show a—usually seated—couple accompanied by the Tīrthaṃkara (cf. ibid., Figs 11, 13) and that are interpreted as depicting the parents of the Jina are a concession to the rise in popularity of this worship. The couple is seated under a tree in whose crown the Tīrthaṃkara, shown in reduced size, is placed. However, since in some illustrations (Shah 1955–57, Fig. 13; Shah 1987, Fig. 80) the couple is accompanied by children, one of whom is sitting on the woman's knee, it is equally possible that such portraits represent a *yākṣa* couple (Shah 1987, 49). However, that the parents of the Jinas were also occasionally depicted with a child is attested by a ceiling relief on the west side of the *raṅgamaṇḍapa* in the Mahāvīra temple of Kumbhariya, Gujarat (12th/13th century, illustrated in Dhaky and Moorti 2001, Fig. 57).

Here the Pārśva legend is arranged around the twenty-four pairs of parents, each with the respective newborn Tīrthaṃkara.

The pictorial motifs that particularly highlight Mahāvīra's parents are, therefore, also to be understood from this point of view. In addition to the 'mythical' world of the Jina legend, these motifs also reflect the lives of the wealthy lay followers who, as donors of Jain manuscripts, commissioned the production of the miniatures. Through the endowment of temples, libraries and the reproduction of manuscripts, the laity provided the necessary structures that ensured the continuity of medieval Jainism through the education of disciples and the instruction of the faithful in right conduct. In addition to the right way of life and the ritual worship of the Tīrthaṃkaras, the task of the laity was, thus, also to provide for the ascetics and to provide the necessary conditions for the practice of the religion. In this way, the Jain laity, within their respective means, in a sense fulfil the role of responsible 'parents' who ensure the continuity of the communities. The elevation of the parents of the Tīrthaṃkaras may be understood as an ideological explanation of this function and, thus, also stands for the self-image of a lay class whose members were well aware of their importance for the continuity of the religion and expressed this in their endowments by choosing appropriate motifs to place their world on an equal footing with the world of the ascetics. This becomes visible, for example, in the decoration of the depicted fabrics, whose patterns and ornaments were oriented towards the common fashions of the time, as well as in the custom of chewing betel (*tāṃbulā*), which was an integral part of the courtly scenery and was constantly practised in everyday life.

The King with Entourage

The motif of the king with entourage usually follows a defined iconography. The left half of the picture is filled with the figure of the king sitting on a throne under an honorary parasol; he is usually depicted with a beard. Opposite him, in the right half of the picture, three vertically arranged followers sit on cushions or carpets (Figs 7.1 and 7.2). To situate the scene in a courtly environment, either the king himself or his retainers carry a sword as a sign of worldly rule.

In the depiction of the royal throne, the painter was apparently given a certain degree of artistic freedom. The illustrations show the ruler either seated on a lion's throne (*siṃhāsana*) (Fig. 7.2) or on a plain throne chair without backrest, which corresponds in form and decoration to the *bhadrāsana* (Fig. 7.1). The position of the miniatures within the manuscripts clearly identifies the king as Siddhārtha in both

Figure 7.1. King with entourage

Source: Folio from an undated Kalpasūtra manuscript (*c.* 15th century). Staatsbibliothek zu Berlin - Preußischer Kulturbesitz, Orientabteilung, HS or. 10745, Folio 57 (b).

Figure 7.2. King with entourage

Source: Folio from an undated Kalpasūtra manuscript (*c.* 15th century). Staatliche Museen zu Berlin, Museum für Asiatische Kunst, Inv.-Nr. I 5040, Folio 20.

the miniatures, although different episodes of the Mahāvīra legend are illustrated.

One miniature (Fig. 7.1) follows the dedication ceremony of the newborn prince in the manuscript's picture cycle and, thus, shows Siddhārtha's command to prepare for the birth festivities:

> After the deities of the [four categories, namely the] Bhavanapati, Vyantara, Jyotiṣka and Vaimānika had performed the solemn consecration ceremony on the occasion of the birth of the Tīrthaṃkara, the Kṣatriya Siddhārtha summoned the city guard before daybreak [...].[3]

In this case, looking at the narrative, the retainers can be identified as armed city guards[4] of Kuṇḍagrāma, who are ordered by the king to decorate the city and release all prisoners (Kalpasūtra § 99f.). Hemacandra (*Tr* X.2.91f.) explains the king's order to release the prisoners with the birth of the Jina, which provides people the opportunity to gain liberation from rebirth. The release of the captives was actually the first act of government of every newly appointed king and goes back mythologically to an episode in the Aitareya-Brahmana, where the release of Śunaḥśepa is reported. The latter was to be sacrificed to Varuṇa, but was saved by Uṣas (Widengren 1965, 57). The Ācārāṅga (740) does not contain this episode; here, the consecration ceremony is followed by a detailed description of all the royal riches that had been steadily increasing since Triśalā's pregnancy.

While this illustration can be attributed relatively easily to Siddhārtha's command to his city guard, the second miniature (Fig. 7.2) is somewhat more difficult to assign. In the manuscript, the illustration follows the dream images of Triśalā, which is why it is conceivable that one of the persons depicted could be identified as Siddhārtha's wife, who reports her dream to her husband (Kalpasūtra §§47–49). The Ācārāṅga does not include this episode and Hemacandra (*Tr* X.2.27ff.), who apparently attached less importance to this event, only mentions in passing the joy the queen felt at the unexpected pregnancy.

Since male and female figures are sometimes indistinguishable in the depiction, it would be obvious here to address the central figure, who is distinguished from the others with a decorated nimbus and crown, as Queen Triśalā; but this is contradicted by the fact that she also carries a sword. So here, too, the figures depicted most probably are the king's retainers or householders (*koḍuṃbiya-purisā*) whom he summoned after the consultation with his wife to prepare the audience hall for the dream interpreters:

> At daybreak, the Kṣatriya Siddhārtha summoned the people of his household [...]. (Kalpasūtra)

Whether Siddhārtha's entourage consisted of noble relatives and members of the royal family (Chandra 1949, 143) or whether they are the commanders of his army, who are shown here with their arms, remains unclear. It is possible, however, that the miniature painter was simply not familiar with the content of the episode he was illustrating, and that this accounts for the inconsistencies in the design of the motif.

The motif of the 'king with entourage' bears a striking resemblance to 'Śakra's court' in the heaven of the gods in terms of figurative decoration and composition (Fig. 7.3). In both cases, the king, be it the one ruling the earthly village of Kuṇḍagrāma, or the one ruling the *Saudharma* heaven, occupies the left half of the picture, while the members of his court are depicted smaller and are arranged one above the other in the remaining half of the picture. The two rulers and their courtiers are similar in their dresses and jewellery. Only the number of arms and the attributes held in his hands distinguish Śakra from the king, with the divine retinue consisting of two-armed figures that are not recognisable as gods individually. By using these closely related representations, the artists established a visual connection between ruler in the human world and the king of the gods, which cannot be derived directly from the Kalpasūtra, but which clarifies Jainism's own conception of the world of the gods.

In both the cases, although the place of action is a kind of assembly hall, neither the description of the scenery nor the naming of the room indicates any correspondence. The divine assembly hall is transmitted in the text (Kalpasūtra §14) as *sabhā* (Pkt./Skt. '[royal] assembly hall'), which can also be translated as the 'royal court', while Siddhārtha's audience hall is more generally described as Pkt. *uvaṭṭhāṇa-sālā* (Skt. *upasthāna-sālā* 'assembly hall'; Kalpasūtra §57). In the Kalpasūtra, Siddhārtha is reported to order the preparation of the assembly hall, which in this version, however, he only enters later to sit down on his throne. The depiction of the throne in both miniatures, on the other hand, relocates the events in the pictorial narrative to the assembly hall from the beginning.

According to this, the world of the gods is a kind of reflection of the world of men (Schubring 1935, 155), and this ultimately also includes courtly life. This equation of the courtly worlds of humans and gods is also referred to in the captions of the illustrations, which in some cases are placed next to the respective miniature. The illustration of the king with retinue (Fig. 7.1) is labelled as '*rājasabhā*' (Skt. 'retinue of the king'), while Śakra's court is named '*iṃdrasabhā*' (Skt. 'retinue of [king of the gods] Indra', Fig. 7.3). The equation in the manuscript paintings of the royal assembly with that of the ruler over the gods also alludes to the ancient Indian concept of the king as *deva*, who in this function represents the gods in the world of men. This form of divine kingship is based, among other things, on the idea that the ruler as a superhuman being was originally created from divine particles.[5] After all, the introduction of the particular royal court from which Prince Vardhamāna comes into the imagery narrative in a similar way to the court of Śakra, the king of the gods, may, however, also be inspired by the elevation of the Tīrthaṃkara to the rank of a divine being—an idea which prevailed in lay circles.

We can conclude that the pictorial formula of a king accompanied by his retinue developed in west Indian miniature painting of the 15th/16th century into a pictogram with the fixed meaning 'royal court' or 'courtly life'.[6]

The King of the Gods with Entourage

In most 15th and 16th centuries manuscripts, the depiction of the king of the gods with his court follows a relatively uniform iconography (Fig. 7.3). The scene in the heaven of the gods is described in the Kalpasūtra as follows:

> At that time, at that moment, Śakra, the supreme and king of the gods [...], clothed in spotless (actually: dustless) robes, garlanded and crowned [...] [was] in the *Saudharma* heaven, in the heavenly palace [called] *Saudharma* Avataṃsaka, in the assembly hall [called] *Sudharman*, on his lion throne called Śakra. (Kalpasūtra)

In addition to the crown (Pkt. mauḍa < Skt. mukuṭa) and garland (Pkt. māla < Skt. mālā), Śakra wears other ornaments, viz.,

> [...] splendidly radiant, trembling ear ornaments [made] of fresh gold, that touched his cheeks [as well as] a forest [flower] garland hanging down from his radiant body [...]. (Kalpasūtra)

The description of the god's ornaments is already contained in the Sūtrakṛtāṅga, the second aṅga of the Śvetāmbara canon, and was presumably adopted from there by the authors of the Kalpasūtra (Jacobi 1895, 381, note 1). In medieval miniature painting, however, this decoration no longer seems to be reserved for the gods alone; rather, its description was used by the miniature painters as a model

Figure 7.3. King of the Gods with entourage

Source: Folio from an undated Kalpasūtra manuscript (*c.* 15th century). Staatsbibliothek zu Berlin - Preußischer Kulturbesitz, Orientabteilung, HS or. 10745, Folio 8(b).

for the decoration of the Jina and all the other figures too. If we regard the gods as a model for the laity, the way the gods' jewellery is used here, on the one hand, underlines the cultic function of all the *dramatis personae* depicted in the miniatures as adorants who accompany the Tīrthaṃkara on his path to salvation. On the other hand, it serves as an indication that the concept is alive not only in the artistic representation but also in the temple ritual; in its course, the temple priest is equipped with regalia that appear to be modelled on the medieval concept of the divine adornments. The fact that the depiction of these ornaments was not determined by the original meaning but that its contemporary conception and fashion served as a model is most clearly shown in the design of the crown. It appears in the miniatures as a kind of diadem (*koṭīra*) and, thus, clearly differs from the common ancient Indian crown (*mukuṭa*), which is called *mauḍe* in the text. The artists follow a similar approach in the clothing as well, where the patterns of the depicted fabrics and the cut of the garments draw on contemporary fashion.

In the textual tradition, the description of the figure of the king of the gods is followed by a list of the heavenly hosts who are under his command. The ruler himself, it is reported, was enjoying games and music at this time. The event as a whole is not included in either the Ācārāṅga or in Hemacandra's narration of the Jina legend.

Śakra is always depicted with four arms and holds an elephant hook *(aṅkuśa)* in his upper left hand, which refers to his mount, the white elephant Airāvata, and, thus, emphasises his position as king and leader of the Indras. As such, he is also equipped with a thunderbolt *(vajra)*, the sceptre of the king of the gods,[7] which in miniature painting is usually depicted with three points at each end. As a third attribute, Śakra usually holds a fruit[8] in his lower left hand, while with his right hand he indicates a threatening gesture *(tarjanīhasta)*, which is presumably to be understood here as an expression of imperious power. Śakra and his retinue are all adorned with crown, necklaces and nimbus *(bhāmaṇḍala)*; unlike the king of the gods, however, his retainers are usually depicted with only two arms. Deviating from the tradition of the Kalpasūtra, where the gods enjoy music and dance in a boisterous mood, the painters of the medieval manuscripts used a pictorial formula that seems to depict a courtly audience rather than heavenly pleasure. The king of the gods on his lion throne and the honorary parasol occupies the entire left half of the picture, while opposite him sit two or three Indras of his retinue, each of whom is depicted in reduced size and arranged one above the other, filling the right half of the picture.

Neither Śakra nor the other gods of the celestial spheres received special veneration in Jainism. In fact, the figure of the king of the gods, Śakra, who is the first to submit to the Jinas and worship them, and who afterwards protects their path to salvation and pays homage to them on several occasions, serves as a model for laity; his devotion also seems to be a means to explain the lay tradition of image worship. Since the practice of any kind of asceticism is impossible for the gods, and their desires are already fulfilled the moment they come into being, all that remains for them is the worship of the Tīrthaṃkaras. Thus, while monks and nuns follow the example of the founder of the religion and wander about as itinerant ascetics, the lay people instead follow the mythical model of the gods by submitting to and worshipping the Tīrthaṃkara and his teachings.[9] In this sense, the worship ceremony (*pūjā*) is to be understood as a symbolic act where the temple priests (*pujārī*) as representatives of the lay community assume the function of the gods.[10] Whether this idea already existed in ancient India or only emerged in the Middle Ages to strengthen the importance of Jain laity is unclear. However, the preference of the donors of medieval manuscripts for the depiction of the *Saudharma* heaven probably reflects the desire of many lay people to become a god in Śakra's wake after their own death in order to enjoy a share of heavenly pleasures. It is not least for this reason that the events in the heaven of the gods are included in almost every illustrated Kalpasūtra manuscript.

King and Queen

The royal couple is a frequently recurring pictorial formula in Jain book illumination of the 15th century. In the Kalpasūtra manuscripts, it usually illustrates the conversation between the parents of the future Jina (Figs 7.4 and 7.5) that follows the dream images. The motif is used to illustrate different episodes. The couple can represent, for example, Mahāvīra's parents (Fig. 7.4) as well as Ṛṣabhas (Fig. 7.5). In other texts, such as the Uttarādhyayana Sūtra[11] or the Kālakācāryakathā,[12] the same motif is used in almost identical execution to illustrate entirely different episodes.

Figure 7.4. King and queen

Source: Folio from an undated Kalpasūtra manuscript (*c.* 15th century). Staatsbibliothek zu Berlin - Preußischer Kulturbesitz, Orientabteilung, HS or. 10745, Folio 35(a).

Figure 7.5. King and queen

Source: Folio from an undated Kalpasūtra manuscript (*c.* 15th century). Staatsbibliothek zu Berlin - Preußischer Kulturbesitz, Orientabteilung, HS or. 10745, Folio 102(a).

In the manuscript's cycle of images, the conversation between Mahāvīra's parents usually follows the dream images envisioned by Triśalā, thus, illustrating the moment after the queen came to her husband's bedside and roused him to relate her dreams:

> Then, with Siddhārtha's permission, the Kṣatriyāṇī Triśalā settled down on a throne chair with ornaments of gems and jewels [...]. (Kalpasūtra)

The image of Triśalā and Siddhārtha can, thus, be assigned to a specific episode in the Kalpasūtra. Despite minor variations, the inventory of images seems to be largely fixed and is repeated formulaically in most manuscripts: the king on his lion throne (*siṃhāsana*) is always positioned on the left; opposite him sits his consort on a simple throne chair (*bhadrāsana*), the shape of which corresponds to the auspicious throne symbol of the *aṣṭamaṅgala*; the placement of the queen on a *bhadrāsana* corresponds to the narrative in the Kalpasūtra, but the text does not provide any information about Siddhārtha's seating; above the king the parasol is visible while the queen sits under a splendidly decorated canopy; in addition to the beard, the king's defined iconography includes, above all, a sword that the ruler holds in front of his right shoulder; this element, however, is missing in this case. Yet, the ruler's hand position alludes to him holding a sword, and it, thus, seems likely that the absence of the weapon itself is due to an error or omission on the part of the artist.

King and queen, moreover, both hold betel leaves (*tāṃbulā*) in their hands. The custom of betel chewing, which is still common today, dates back to ancient India and primarily served to deepen interpersonal relationships (Moser-Schmitt 1982, 941). In this sense, the chewing of betel by the depicted couple is an everyday act that has no close connection with the episode illustrated here by the king and queen. Its inclusion was probably primarily a tribute to the habits of the bourgeois elite in medieval Gujarat, who, as donors of the manuscripts and patrons of the miniatures, also wanted to find their world reflected in the picture cycles. The fact that betel was also considered distinctly aphrodisiac in ancient India (Meyer 1937, II, 109) is likely to have been incorporated into the pictorial formula rather incidentally and as additional symbolic content, although the placement of king and queen on separate pieces of furniture actually distinguishes the motif from the lovers who usually sit together on a couch or bench. The giving and taking of betel leaves also play an important role in certain rites such as the wedding ceremony (Moser-Schmitt 1982, 947).

Idleness and Mundane Enjoyments

To illustrate the pleasurable life of women at court, the Kalpasūtra manuscripts use their own pictorial formula, which can be described as a 'lady at rest'. This motif is a common pictorial formula within west-Indian miniature painting and symbolically depicts the everyday life of the upper class, which is focused on pleasurable activities or idleness without physical exertion. In this sense, the motif is included in various illustrations of the Jina legend; for example, the auspicious dreams of Devānandā and Triśalā, the relocation of the embryo and finally the birth of the Jina, each of which is created by adding further fixed pictorial elements to the established core motif. Essentially, the motif of the 'resting lady' shows a sumptuously robed woman in side view on a couch, occasionally accompanied by a servant who fans her with a cloth or fly wisk. Supporting herself with one arm, her upper body appears slightly raised, one leg is stretched out, the other drawn up and she holds a betel leaf in her hand (Fig. 7.6).

Figure 7.6. Auspicious dreams of Devānandā

Source: Folio from an undated Kalpasūtra manuscript (*c.* 15th century). Staatliche Museen zu Berlin, Museum für Asiatische Kunst, Inv.-Nr. I 5040, Folio 3.

The consumption of betel leaves was, as already mentioned, widespread among the early modern upper classes in western India. In the hand of the reclining woman, the betel leaf has an additional symbolic meaning. In ancient India, betel generally stood for fertility, it inflamed desire and was said to promote amourous joy (Meyer 1937, I, 25). In the *Pariśiṣṭaparvan* (VIII, 205), Hemacandra mentions the wearing of betel leaves as an adornment of bridal guests at a wedding and places this in a symbolic context with the Goddess Śrī (Hertel 1908, 187). The fertility symbolism of the betel leaf is probably connected with its shape, which is reminiscent of the female sexual organ. Betel leaf and fruit (areca nut) symbolise the fertilised womb, with the leaf enclosing the betel nut, which stands for the fruit of the womb (Moser-Schmitt 1982, 951). The red pigment (areca red) contained in the areca nut symbolises the woman's menstruation. It is, therefore, hardly surprising that the resting lady, who in the miniatures of the Kalpasūtra is representing episodes of conception and birth in particular, is depicted with a betel leaf in her hand. The depiction of a betel leaf in connection with the birth, however, also demonstrates the frozen pictorial formula of the resting lady. In the birth scene, the woman in labour would otherwise be expected to hold a 'male' fruit (grammatical gender) in her hands[13] as this promotes, according to ancient Indian belief, the birth of sons.

In the illustration cycles to the Kalpasūtra, the pictorial formula of the 'resting lady' is applied in a uniform manner to various persons who are outwardly indistinguishable. Thus, the dreaming Devānandā is shown in the same way as the dreaming Triśalā. Devānandā (Fig. 7.6) is lying on a couch with her upper body raised by pillows, her right leg raised, dressed in precious robes and adorned with a crown and nimbus as well as necklaces, earrings and bracelets; her eyes are open while she is half asleep.[14] In her left hand she holds a betel bag (*tāmbūla*) and under her bed are other utensils associated with the custom of chewing betel: a water bottle, a box with other betel bags and a spittoon. Triśalā is depicted in the same way (Fig. 7.7), although here the dream images are usually placed on a separate miniature.

In general, however, the 'resting queen' cannot be assigned exclusively to any particular subject area within west-Indian miniature painting; outside the sphere of Jain manuscripts, the same composition

Figure 7.7. Auspicious dreams of Triśalā

Source: Folio from an undated Kalpasūtra manuscript (*c.* 15th century). Staatliche Museen zu Berlin, Museum für Asiatische Kunst, Inv.-Nr. I 5040, Folio 15.

is used to illustrate a wide range of subjects, such as the lonely lover in a manuscript of Vasanta Vilāsa (Brown 1962, Pl. 21, Fig. 37) or the birth of Samudrapāla (here with child) in the Uttarādhyayana sūtra (Brown 1941, Fig. 80). In rare cases, the pictorial formula even serves to depict a male figure, who in the Kalpasūtra may be interpreted as King Siddhārtha (Fig. 7.8).

Apart from idleness, the amenities of court life also include physical exercise. While the women at court are usually shown in relaxed pleasure, the men's activity includes sport and personal hygiene. Thus, the dream interpretation ceremony in the Mahāvīra legend of the Kalpasūtra is preceded by a description of the king's physical exercises and a subsequent bath. This episode, illustrated in most manuscripts by one or two miniatures, is of rather secondary importance to the actual course of the Jina legend and instead highlights the splendour and wealth at the court of the future Tīrthaṃkaras' parents.

In the Kalpasūtra, it is reported that after learning of his consort's auspicious dreams, the king first exercised his body through several

Figure 7.8. King Siddhārtha (?)

Source: Folio from an undated Kalpasūtra manuscript (*c.* 16th century). Staatsbibliothek zu Berlin - Preußischer Kulturbesitz, Orientabteilung, HS or. 14662, Folio 31(b).

suitable sports such as jumping, wrestling and boxing,[15] and then underwent a massage. Afterwards he visited the bathhouse,[16] went to the bathing pavilion[17] and sat down on a bathing chair decorated with ornaments of precious stones and jewels,[18] where he bathed himself.[19]

In most manuscripts, this episode is depicted in a single miniature showing the king's bath or massage. Here the ruler is seated on a stool (Fig. 7.9) and is accompanied by a servant who is treating the king's open hair. The scene shows both persons in a building that may be interpreted as a bathing pavilion. It is unusual in this illustration that not only the king but also his servant is shown bearded, since a full beard in west-Indian miniature painting is usually reserved for the ruler or the master of the house. In some manuscripts, the episode is divided into two registers (Fig. 7.10): the lower one corresponding to the pictorial formula already described, while above it apparently the king is shown being massaged. On the other hand, an unusual variant of the motif showing the king beardless and with a mirror in his hand (Fig. 7.11) is probably due to an error on the part of the artist, who in this case painted the king with a mirror in his hand. Kings being

Figure 7.9. King Siddhārtha's bath

Source: Folio from an undated Kalpasūtra manuscript (*c.* 15th century). Staatliche Museen zu Berlin, Museum für Asiatische Kunst, Inv.-Nr. I 5040, Folio 27.

Figure 7.10. King Siddhārtha's bath (lower register) and massage (upper register)

Source: Staatliche Museen zu Berlin, Museum für Asiatische Kunst, Inv.-Nr. I 5042, not numbered.

Figure 7.11. King Siddhārtha's bath (lower register) and physical exercises (upper register)

Source: Folio from an undated Kalpasūtra manuscript (*c.* 15th century). Staatsbibliothek zu Berlin - Preußischer Kulturbesitz, Orientabteilung, HS or. 10745, Folio 40(b).

Figure 7.12. King Siddhārtha's physical exercises

Source: Folio from an undated Kalpasūtra manuscript (*c.* 16th century). Staatsbibliothek zu Berlin - Preußischer Kulturbesitz, Orientabteilung, HS or. 14662, Folio 37(b).

depicted beardless is not that unusual, but the mirror in west-Indian miniature painting is exclusively the attribute of women. Apparently, the artist was aware of the gender of the persons depicted when he created the miniature.

In some manuscripts, the image of Siddhārtha's bath is preceded by an illustration of the king's physical exercises (Fig. 7.12); in these compositions the artists used a pictorial formula generally employed to illustrate wrestling or duelling (Fig. 7.13).[20] The image space is divided into two registers and shows both in the upper and lower register a group of three men wrestling with each other.

Children's Games

In the early versions, the Jina legend is largely limited to the description of the five beneficial events (*pañcakalyāṇa*) in the life of the Tīrthaṃkaras, whereas, nothing is reported about their childhood and youth. Although individual episodes are included in the Āvaśyaka literature and are later recounted by Hemacandra in his Jain world history, on the whole, the years before the renunciation were probably regarded as rather marginal,

Figure 7.13. Children's games

Source: Folio from an undated Kalpasūtra manuscript (*c.* 15th century). Staatsbibliothek zu Berlin - Preußischer Kulturbesitz, Orientabteilung, HS or. 10745, Folio 62(b).

and a brief hint that the prince was married off and led a virtuous life in the parental palace until he escaped the world (Ācārāṅga 742) was deemed sufficient. However, by the Middle Ages, the childhood stories about the special qualities or powers of the youthful prince gained more prominence, and although these tales are not included in the Kalpasūtra, illustrations of them can be found in numerous manuscripts.

In the Mahāvīra legend of the Kalpasūtra itself, the childhood experiences of Jina are largely omitted. The ten days of ceremonies associated with the prince's birth are reported in some detail, including the birth feast, the presentation of the newborn to the sun and moon, the ritual vigil on the sixth day and the subsequent festivities with relatives and members of the royal court (Kalpasūtra §§ 104–108). This is followed by an account of Mahāvīra's family relations, which reveals that the prince married and became the father of a daughter before renouncing the world after the death of his parents (Kalpasūtra §§ 109–110). In the Ācārāṅga, on the other hand, it is only briefly reported that five wet nurses looked after the future Tīrthaṃkara and that, having left his childhood behind, he lived virtuously by indulging only in the five permissible pleasures (Ācārāṅga 741–742). These permissible pleasures are associated with the five senses, namely, hearing, touch, taste and the senses of colour and smell. According to ancient Indian tradition, childhood ends in the eighth year after conception through admission to the teacher (Hillebrandt 1897, 50). According to Brahmanic law, this marks the beginning of the first of the four stages of life (student, householder, forest hermit and mendicant monk). This division is binding for all four classes (Jolly 1896, 148) and seems to have been adapted by the followers of Jainism as well.

Thus, while the Jina legend transmitted in the Kalpasūtra only briefly mentions that the future Jina led a virtuous life in his youth, the illustrations in the manuscripts show some episodes from this period of Mahāvīra's life. More detailed accounts of the events of Mahāvīra's childhood are scattered over the Āvaśyaka literature; parts of them are also told by Hemacandra (*Tr* X.2.88–124). The corresponding episodes in the Kalpasūtra illustrations were taken from Hemacandra's narration of the Jina legend.

There are predominantly two motifs illustrating Mahāvīra's childhood in the manuscripts, namely, the birth festival and an event that describes the young prince's courage and strength during the Āmalakī game. It should be noted, however, that these episodes from the prince's life before his renunciation are by no means included in all illustration cycles. This episode primarily illustrates the courage of the prince and future Jina, while at the same time providing an insight into the pleasures at the court.

The childhood experiences of the Jina Mahāvīra also include a test of the future Jina by an unnamed god who challenges the prince twice in different guises. This event was taken up in miniature painting and became another particularly popular motif since it referred to an episode bearing witness to the courage and strength of the prince, who was not yet eight years old. This episode has been handed down in the Āvaśyakavṛtti of Malayagiri (Mette 2010, 272f.), in the narrations of Hemacandra (*Tr* X.2.103–118) and Śīlānka (Bruhn 1954, 96f.) as well as in the commentaries on the Āvaśyakasūtra.[21]

The legend tells of a god from Hari's retinue,[22] who doubts the bravery of Prince Vardhamāna and wants to challenge him. To this end, he transforms himself into a poisonous snake and waits under a tree near which the prince was enjoying a game of Āmalakī with the other sons of the king. When the children notice the snake, they run in all directions in fear. In Hemacandra (*Tr* X.2.207), it is reported that Vardhamāna seizes the snake and hurls it to the ground. In the Malayagiri version, the future Tīrthaṃkara hurls the snake up into the seventh plane of heaven (Mette 2010, 39) and in the Digambara tradition Vardhamāna additionally performs a victory dance on the head of the snake

(Shah 1987, 188 with reference to *Uttarapurāṇa* 74.287ff.); this element may have been borrowed from the Kṛṣṇa legend.

Having failed to frighten the future Jina in the form of a snake, the god takes the form of a prince and mingles with the children who compete to climb a tree. Vardhamāna reaches the top first and as the victor he was allowed to ride like a horseman on the back of the other children. But when he climbs onto the god's back,[23] the god turns into a demon and grows until he reaches the size of a mountain. Vardhamāna remains fearless even now and strikes the demon with his fist, so that it becomes a dwarf. The motif of a demon growing into the size of a giant before being thrown down or defeated by a blow of his fist is also found in the Kṛṣṇa legend (Ruben 1941, 97 and 120). Finally, the god assumes his true form, bows to the future Tīrthaṃkara and goes home.

In miniature painting, these events are usually illustrated following an established routine, depicting the prince first meeting the snake under the tree and then riding on the back of the supposed playmate. In terms of composition and iconography, this pictorial motif is also depicted in a fairly similar way in most manuscripts, as a miniature from a 15th-century manuscript shows. The image area is divided into two relatively equal zones by the centrally placed tree around whose trunk the snake winds (Fig. 7.13). The right part is filled by the figure of the prince approaching the snake, while the left half shows the prince sitting on the shoulders of the god. In keeping with the traditions of western India, the figures are not distinguishable by their shape; they all have a nimbus, are uniformly dressed and have identical jewellery. In an illustration from a somewhat later manuscript (16th century), the prince competing to climb the crown of the tree and some of his playmates are added to the pictorial programme (Fig. 7.14). In this miniature, too, the figures are of uniform shape, but the god who tests the young prince's bravery lacks the nimbus, thus, being iconographically identified as 'negative' or 'evil'. The right-hand zone of the picture is divided into two registers by a narrow strip that repeats the decoration of the frame. By doing this, the artist has created a separate space for the beginning of the episode, namely, the encounter between the prince and the snake shown in the right half of the picture. The figure depicted in the upper register can, thus, be assigned to the events around the crown of the tree, where the story continues with the competition between the playmates.

Vardhamāna, who was the first to climb the tree, is depicted in the crown, with two other princes flanking the action. That both of them are Vardhamāna's playmates can be seen from the slightly curved sticks all three are holding in their hands; these were presumably used in the Āmalakī game. What this Āmalakī game[24] may originally have been about can only be conjectured due to the lack of relevant sources.

Figure 7.14. Children's games

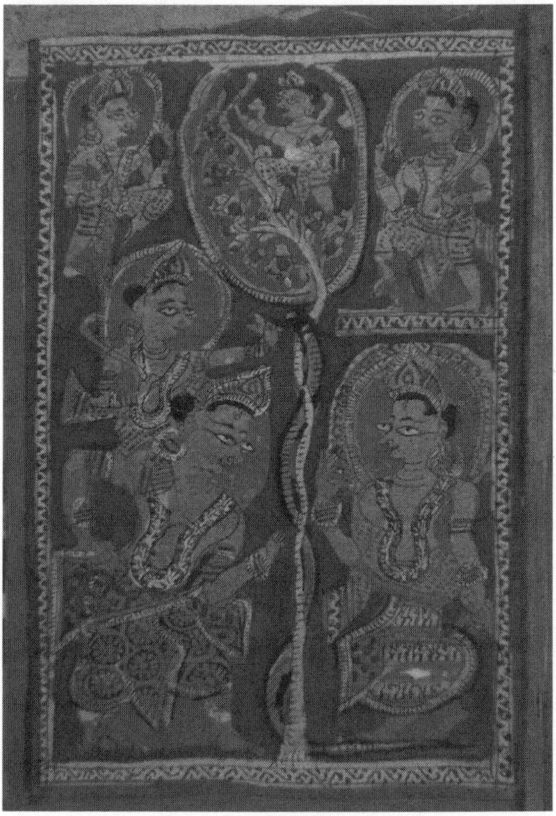

Source: Folio from an undated Kalpasūtra manuscript (*c.* 16th century). Staatsbibliothek zu Berlin - Preußischer Kulturbesitz, Orientabteilung, HS or. 14662, Folio 59(b).

It seems to have been a kind of competition, with a special reward for the winner.

According to Hemacandra's account, the one who reached the finish line first was allowed to ride on the losers' backs as if on a horse. In Malayagiri's description of the episode, the children's game is called *suṃkali*. Although this term is not documented anywhere else (Mette 2010, 273), the game seems to have been competitive in character as well. However, the exact rules and procedure of this game are unclear. Stevenson (1915, 29) uses the term āmbalī-pīpaḷī in her summary of the episode and assumes that it is a variant of the tag-game (also known as 'tick' or 'tig') that is still widespread today. In this connection, Johnson (1931–62, vi, 33 [note 67]) mentions that a 'touch-and-go' game popular among boys under the name āmalā-pippalī was known in Gujarat until the recent past. However, while according to Hemacandra the princes climb a treetop, Malayagiri relates that they have to reach the trunk of a particular tree in the park. In the end, here too the winner rides on the shoulders of the losers (Mette 2010, 38).

The apparent naming of this game after one or more trees is remarkable, namely, first of all after the Indian gooseberry.[25] Perhaps the curved sticks carried by the players in the illustration, which undoubtedly served to practise the game, were made from the wood of one of the trees mentioned. The purpose of the sticks and their use in the game is unclear; however, it is striking that these sticks are held in front of the shoulder in the miniatures in a gesture and position similar to the way the king's sword is presented elsewhere (Krüger 2020, 167ff., Fig. 91). Both the sticks and the game associated with them seem to have had a certain meaning and significance for the medieval artists, which is why these objects became an established part of the pictorial programme of those miniatures illustrating the young prince's tests of courage during the game.

Conclusion

The selected episodes show how the descriptions in the text of the Kalpasūtra reflect the lifestyle of the royal upper class at the time this text was composed. The manuscript illustrations refer to these topics and elaborate on the courtly life at the time of the Jina while at the same time representing the leisure activities of the elites who sponsored the creation of the manuscripts and donated them to religious institutions. The text, but particularly the miniatures, reflect a certain tension between leisure and the ideal of ascestic renunciation—a tension that persists until today in the Jain communities as they consist of ascetics and laity. The analysis of the illustrations shows how motifs related to leisure and pleasure, which seem to contradict the intention of the text, were employed as means to describe the ascetic path to salvation of Jina Mahāvīra and his predecessors. The Jain path to salvation is characterised by renunciation and rigorous asceticism. The Jina as the remembered founder or renovator of the doctrine is, therefore, regarded as the ideal ascetic. Though the Kalpasūtra itself focusses on the description of the life of this ascetic, a considerable share of the illustrations rather deals with the leisure activities at the court that was home to the future Jina prior to his renunciation. By doing so, they illustrate the riches and amenities the Jina left behind when he decided to renounce and search for salvation; at the same time, they provide a platform to include the wealth-oriented world of the Jain laity in the Jina legend. The cycles of illustrations which contain elements of acceptance of life as well as rejection of worldly matters bring together the world of the ascetic and that of the laity and are, thus, instrumental in constructing and reconfirming the unity of both constituents of the Jain community. All the figures represented in the miniatures are associates of the Jina; they accompany him on his way to salvation. For the laity, the figures shown in these miniatures are protagonists of a sacred act; (re)presenting them is a means for the laity to get closer to their own salvation. This is the reason for the opulent representation of all the *dramatis personae*; they are equipped almost like cult images and indeed they are at this occasion venerated in a fashion similar to the veneration of the Jina himself.

Notes

1 The display of images was a frequently used means of religious instruction in ancient India. A description of such an event can be found in the Jain story *Kuvalayamālā,* datable to ca. 778 CE (Zin and Schlingloff 2007, 13f.).

2 Thus, the motif *'king with entourage'* is also present in a manuscript of the Kālaka legend (Kālakācāryakathā) from 15th to 16th century, where it serves to illustrate the court of king Gardabhilla, a mythical ruler of Ujjayinī (Brown 1933, Fig. 25); the number of courtiers, however, is much higher in this miniature. The motif *'king and queen'* frequently occurs in manuscripts of the Uttarādhyayana; here, it illustrates different ruling couples (ibid., Fig. 27 [Nami und Śakra]).

3 *tae ṇaṃ se siddhatthe khattie bhavaṇavai-vāṇamaṃtara-joisa-vemāṇiehiṃ devehiṃ titthayara-jammaṇa-abhiseya-mahimāe kayāe samāṇīe paccūsa-kāla-samayaṃsi nagara-guttie saddāvei* [...] (Kalpasūtra § 99).

4 At a later point in the text (Kalpasūtra § 101) the city guards are called house-people (*koḍuṃbiya-purisā*).

5 Literary evidence for this concept can be found in the legal literature as well as in the Indian epics (Gonda 1969, 24f.).

6 Eastman (1938, 139) interprets the king's beard as a visual formula for the representation of a particular group of people that encompasses not just the king himself but also his soldiers and other attendants; they are by this means distinguished from monks, gods and Jinas. It has to be noted, however, that this formula was not applied consistently for the entourage and that Śakra in his function as king of the gods is occasionally shown with a beard as well.

7 In the Kalpasūtra, Śakra is also called vajra bearer (*vajja-pāṇī,* literally: '[the one who carries a] Vajra [in his] hand') (Kalpasūtra § 14).

8 Nawab (1956, 32) interprets it as a Bijorā fruit, though without any further explanation.

9 Babb (1996, 79) remarks:

> We see, therefore, that in the redemptive economy of the Jain cosmos the deities' role is not to serve as objects of worship, but

to serve as the traditions's archetypal worshipers. They are not ascetics, and (as we know) ascetics alone are true objects of worship to the Jains. Instead, they are lay Jains who protect an ideal image of what lay Jains must do as ones who worship ascetics.

10 In order to emphasise this position, the temple priests, during particular festivals, are equipped with 'divine' jewels and a crown; their shapes closely resemble that of the ornaments shown in medieval miniatures (Babb 1996, 79 and Fig. 8). The rite itself usually symbolizes the consecration ceremony after the birth of the future Tīrthaṃkara (Cort 2010, 92), which is performed by the god on Mount Meru.

11 See Brown (1941, Figs 50 and 68). In an Uttarādhyayana manuscript dated to 1583 CE (V.S. 1639) the royal couple is interpreted as a representation of king Iṣukāra and his queen Kamalavatī (ibid., Fig. 50). A similar representation of king and queen in an Uttarādhyayana-sūtra dated to 1591 CE (V.S. 1647) shows king Balabhadra and queen Mṛgā (ibid., Fig. 68).

12 For example, the representation of king Vairisinhas and queen Surasundari (Nawab 1959, Figs 29 [=27] and 56), and that of king Sātvāhana in conversation with two queens (ibid., Fig. 22). Another variant of the motif is the scene of Kālaka asking his parents for permission to enter the monastic order (Brown 1933, Fig. 14). The tiny Kālaka is standing between his parents; apart from this element, the scene is identical with the motif of king and queen.

13 *hastasthapuṃnāmaphalāṃ*, Aṣṭāṅgahṛdayasaṃhita Śarirasthāna 1.77; *punnāmaphalahastāṃ*, Suśrutasaṃhitā Śarirasthāna 10.8 (see Shrikantha Murthy 1991).

14 The depiction of sleeping figures with closed eyes was an idea embraced by the artists of the West Indian schools of painting. Open eyes therefore do not do not provide information about the actual state of the person depicted who, in this case, is shown between sleep and awakening.

15 [...] *ttā aṇega-vāyāma-jogga-vaggaṇa-vāmaddaṇa-malla-juddha-karaṇehiṃ* [...] (Kalpasūtra § 60).

16 [...] *ttā jeṇ'eva majjaṇa-ghare* [...] (Kalpasūtra § 61).

17 [...] *ṇhāṇa-maṃḍavaṃsi* [...] (Kalpasūtra § 61).

18 [...] *nāna-maṇi-rayaṇa-bhatti-cittaṃsi-nhāṇa-pīḍhaṃsi* [...] (Kalpasūtra § 61).

19 This episode which is not part of the Ācārāṅga was probably transferred from Aupapātika Sūtra into the Mahāvīra legend of the Kalpasūtra. There (§ 48) the king's preparations for a pilgrimage are described using almost exactly the same wording (Mette 2010, 260).

20 See for example some image cycles of the Uttarādhyayana; here the motif illustrates an episode from the Aṭṭana narrative (Brown 1941, Figs 12 and 13).

21 This indicates a joint transmission of Āvaśyakacūrṇi and -ṭīkā (see Bruhn 1954, 34).

22 Johnson (1931–62, vi, 32) identifies him with Śakra, the king of gods.

23 The joint tradition of Āvaśyakacūrṇi and -ṭīkā deviates and reports that the prince had to beat the god in a ball game before that (Bruhn 1954, 34).

24 [...] *āmalakī-krīḍā* [...] *Tr* X.2.106.

25 *Phyllanthus emblica*, Skt. āmalakī (see Monier-Williams 1883, 339). In addition, Brown (1934, 32, Anm. 12) in this context mentions another miniature of the same motif that bears the title *tindūsavṛkśakrīḍā* ('Tindūsa [?]-tree-game'). Which tree is denominated by Skt. *tindūsa* remains unclear since the word is not attested anywhere else. It is possible, however, that it is an erroneous spelling for Skt. *tinduka* 'persimmon' or 'ebony' (*Diospyros embryopteris*). The final part of the—probably modern—names āmbalī-pīpaḷī and āmalā-pippalī may also allude to the names of different trees, namely, Indian Long Pepper (*Piper longum*, Skt. *pippalī*) or the Sacred Fig Tree (*Ficus religiosa*, Skt. *pippala*).

References

Ācārāṅga Sūtra (Pkt. *Āyārańga-suttaṃ*). 1976. Edited by Muni Jambūvijaya, *Āyārańga-suttam*, translated by Jacobi. Bombay: Shrī Mahāvīra Jaina Vidyālaya, Transl. Jacobi 1884.

Aupapātika Sūtra (Pkt. *Uvavāiya-suttaṃ*). 1883. Edited by Ernst Leumann, *Das Aupapātika Sūtra, erstes Upānga der Jaina. I. Theil. Einleitung, Text und Glossar*. Leipzig: Brockhaus.

Babb, Lawrence. 1996. *Absent Lord. Ascetics and Kings in a Jain Ritual Culture*. Berkeley: University of California Press.

Brown, Norman. 1933. *The Story of Kālaka. Texts, History, Legends, and Miniature Paintings of the Śvetāmbara Jain Hagiographical Work the Kālakācāryakathā*. Washington: Smithsonian Institution.

———. 1934. *A Descriptive and Illustrated Catalogue of Miniature Paintings of the Jaina Kalpasūtra as Executed in the Early Western Indian Style*. Washington: Smithsonian Institution.

———. 1941. *Manuscript Illustrations of the Uttarādhyayana Sūtra*. New Haven: American Oriental Society.

———. 1962. *The Vasanta Vilāsa. A Poem of the Spring Festival in Old Gujarāti* (Accompanied by Sanskrit and Prakrit Stanzas and Illustrated with Miniature Paintings. Critically Edited and Translated, with an Introduction and a Description of the Paintings). New Haven: American Oriental Society.

Bruhn, Klaus. 1954. *Śīlānkas Cauppaṇṇamahāpurisacariya. Ein Beitrag zur Kenntnis der Jaina-Universalgeschichte*. Hamburg: Cram.

Chandra, Moti. 1949. *Jain Miniature Paintings*. Ahmedabad: Sarabhai Manilal Nawab.

Cort, John. 2010. *Framing the Jina. Narratives of Icons and Idols in Jain History*. New York: Oxford University Press.

Dhaky, Madhusudan and Udayaravi Moorti. 2001. *The Temples in Kumbhāriyā*. New Delhi: American Institute of Indian Studies.

Eastman, Alvan. 1938. 'A Survey of Formulae in the Miniature Painting of Western India'. *The Art Bulletin*, Vol. 20 (2): 133–44.

Gonda, Jan. 1969. *Ancient Indian Kingship from the Religious Point of View* (Reprinted from 'Numen' III and IV with Addenda and an Index). Leiden: Brill.

Hertel, Johannes. 1908. *Ausgewählte Erzählungen aus Hemacandras Pariśiṣṭaparvan. Deutsch mit Einleitung und Anmerkungen*. Leipzig: Heims.

Hillebrandt, Alfred. 1897. *Ritual-Litteratur. Vedische Opfer und Zauber*. Strassburg: Trübner.

Jacobi, Hermann. 1884. *Jaina Sūtras, Part I: The Ācārāṅga Sūtra, the Kalpa Sūtra*. Oxford: Clarendon Press.

———. 1895. *Jaina Sūtras, Part II: The Uttarādhyayana Sūtra, the Sūtrakṛtāṅga Sūtra*. Oxford: Clarendon Press.

Johnson, Helen. 1931–62. *Triṣaṣṭiśalākāpuruṣacaritra, or The Lives of the Sixty-Three Illustrious Persons*, by Acarya Shri Hemacandra, translated into English by Helen M. Johnson, Vols 1–6. Baroda: Oriental Institute.

Jolly, Julius. 1896. *Recht und Sitte. Einschliesslich der einheimischen Litteratur*. Strassburg: Trübner.

Kalpasūtra (Pkt. *Kappa-suttaṃ*). 1879. Edited by Hermann Jacobi, *The Kalpasūtra of Bhadrabāhu, edited with an Introduction, Notes and a Prākṛit-Saṃskṛit Glossary*, translated by Jacobi. Leipzig: Brockhaus.

Krüger, Patrick. 2020. *Miniaturen mittelalterlicher Kalpasūtra-Handschriften. Eine ikonographische Betrachtung mit kultur- und religionsgeschichtlichen Anmerkungen*. Wiesbaden: Reichert.

Mette, Adelheid. 2010. *Die Erlösungslehre der Jaina. Legenden, Parabeln, Erzählungen aus dem Sanskrit und Prakrit übersetzt und herausgegeben von A. Mette*. Berlin: Verlag der Weltreligionen im Insel Verlag.

Meyer, Johann Jakob. 1937. *Trilogie altindischer Mächte und Feste der Vegetation. Ein Beitrag zur vergleichenden Religions- und Kulturgeschichte, Fest- und Volkskunde*, Vols 1–3. Zürich: Niehans.

Monier-Williams, Monier. 1883. *Religious Thought and Life in India. An account of the religions of the Indian peoples, based on a life's study of their literature and on personal investigations in their own country, Pt. 1: Vedism, Brāhmanism, and Hindūism*, London: Murray.

Moser-Schmitt, Erika. 1982. Sozioritueller Gebrauch von Cannabis in Indien'. *In Rausch und Realität. Drogen im Kulturvergleich. 2. Drogen in den frühen Hochkulturen*, edited by Gisela Völger and Karin von Welck. Reinbek: Rowolt.

Nawab, Sarabhai. 1956. *Masterpieces of the Kalpasutra Paintings*. Ahmedabad: Sarabhai Manilal Nawab.

———. 1959. *The Oldest Rajasthani Paintings from Jain Bhandars*. Ahmedabad: Sarabhai Manilal Nawab.

Ruben, Walter. 1941. *Krishna. Konkordanz und Kommentar der Motive seines Heldenlebens*. Wien: Holzhausen.

Schubring, Walther. 1935. *Die Lehre der Jainas, nach den alten Quellen dargestellt*. Berlin: Walter de Gruyter.

Shah, Umakant. 1955–57. 'Parents of the Tīrthaṃkaras'. *Bulletin of the Prince of Wales Museum of Western India*, Vol. 5: 24–32.

———. 1987. *Jaina-rūpa-maṇḍana (Jaina iconography)*. New Delhi: Abhinav.

Shrikantha Murthy, K.R. 1991. *Vāgbhaṭa's Aṣṭāñga hṛdayam. Text, English translation, Notes, Appendix and Indices). 1. Sūtrasthāna and Śārīrasthāna. Aṣṭāṅgahṛdaya*, Varanasi: Krishnadas Acadademy.

Stevenson, Mrs S. [Alice Margaret]. 1915. *The Heart of Jainism*. Oxford: University Press.

Triṣaṣṭiśalākāpuruṣacaritra. 1936. Edited by Muni Charanavijaya, *The Triṣaṣṭiśalākāpuruṣacaritra-Mahā-kavyam by Śrī-Hemacandra-Ācārya*, Vols 1–5, translated by Johnson. Bhavnagar: Śrī-Jaina-Ātmānanda-Sabhā, Transl. Johnson 1931–62.

Widengren, Geo. 1965. *Die Religionen Irans*. Stuttgart: Kohlhammer.

Zin, Monika and Dieter Schlingloff. 2007. *Saṃsāracakra. Das Rad der Wiedergeburten in der indischen Überlieferung*. Düsseldorf: Ekō-Haus der japanischen Kultur.

8

TRANSITIONS IN LEISURE: GARDENS, HUNTING AND PUBLIC ENTERTAINMENT[1]

Vipul Singh

Introduction

The chronicles, vernaculars and travel writings of early modern period from across the globe are full of description of beautiful gardens and represented as hallmark of sophistication. Although an artificially constructed natural environment, they were well integrated with the surroundings. By using 12th-century Chalukyan Sanskrit text, *Mansollassa* (delight of the mind), Daud Ali has shown how royal garden was used as an aristocratic enjoyment (Daud Ali). In India, the Lodis and the Mughals constructed beautiful gardens for leisure around their monuments. The gardens were looked at as 'paradise of earth' (Ronald Inden). Gardens were developed in distant locations and began to be seen as a place connected to the leisure of the elites. They also enjoyed musical performance in the midst of the garden. The local communities were away from the walled areas but they had a huge area of dense forest in the surroundings and riverfronts of rivers to enjoy the cool evening breeze. Rituals, prayers, dance, community feasting, plays and *melas* often accompanied their daily work and, thus, were major components of commoners' leisure activities. Hunting was also an important leisure activity of the rulers in early modern times. They would go for hunting with all their paraphernalia looking for wild animals in the dense forest.

Controlling Mughal Baghs

Mughal Baghs, the gardens of Mughals, were originally pleasure retreats. When the Europeans came to India as traders, they developed an opinion about the native Indians as 'cold-hearted, dull, and frigid people'. Such overgeneraligation of the Indians done by Horatio Smith in *Calcutta Review* in 1851 based on business interaction could be misleading (Horatio Smith). Rather, their recreation and leisure evident in the design of palaces of the kings, festivals, sports and evening talk give a completely different picture. The garden craft was already very developed even when the Europeans had not arrived in India.

The earliest form of a garden in India was the sacred groves. It has a very long tradition. Many villages all across India used to have community-owned green landscapes. The planting of trees was considered a pious act in Indian tradition. Many rulers planted trees on trade routes to shade the wayfarers. This love for trees no doubt has a very long history as many of the ancient texts mention its benefits and prohibition against cutting trees. This is, however, a garden in a horticultural sense. The art of building monuments in harmony with trees for leisure came in the 16th century. We may call it the garden craft. Water supply was also an important consideration when the gardens were developed. In almost all the gardens across India, 'water architecture' was integral to recreation and leisure (Rötzer and Sohoni).

The garden-craft tradition got a new fillip when rulers from Central Asia and Persia came up with a whole new concept of gardens that were aligned with royal buildings. The Lodi Afghans were the pioneers to introduce this new concept of gardens around their monuments. This was later carried forward by the Mughals and the monuments and palaces, that were constructed by early Mughal rulers such as Babar, Humayun, Akbar, Jahangir and Shah Jahan, were always featured with gardens. Jahangir and Shah Jahan in particular were very fond of leisure. While they constructed many beautiful monuments, they also ensured that these were adorned with equally beautiful gardens. Babur mentions in his memoir that he got a char-bagh garden called Bagh-i-Wafa made in Kabul, which he used to visit for rest during his long campaign (Beveridge 2014).[2] It overlooked a river that flowed between the fort and the palace. Jahangir and Shah Jahan also constructed solitary royal baghs (gardens) in naturally bounteous locations. Two best examples are Shalimar and Nishat Bagh on the shorelines of Dal Lake in Srinagar. During the summers, Mughal emperor Jahangir used to move to Srinagar with his full retinue and court and live in the midst of Shalimar Bagh (Stuart 1913). He visited the Kashmir valley many times despite difficulties of transport and dangers involved in crossing mountain passes.

The Mughal baghs were invariably rectangular in shape and were divided into a series of smaller square parts. They were adorned by an imposing entrance. For keeping the garden lush green, a canal was run through the entire enclosure. The water rushing through these canals also supplied water to *baradari* and numerous fountains (Stuart). The misty sprays provided a cool and airy atmosphere to the Mughal family. The Mughals loved to recline at ease on a hot summer day in *baradari*, which was open from all sides for free flow of air. There used to be musical parties, dance performances and recitations by rulers' favourite Persian and Turki poets during cool evenings. There was always a harmony of buildings and gardens in all the Mughal palaces. The Mughal emperors could afford to take adventurous journeys from Agra to Kashmir, crossing the snowy passes on elephants. For the nobles, such adventures were not possible and, therefore, most of them developed gardens with running water and fountains close to their homes to overcome the heat. Bernier, during his stay at the court of Aurangzeb in 1660, observed the significance of gardens in Delhi. He wrote that most of the houses of the nobles were situated on the banks of the River Yamunā and in the suburbs and had, in its courtyards, gardens, trees, basins of water and fountains. Recent studies have also established how garden-making along the riverfronts began under Babur, taken forward under Akbar and Jahangir, and the tradition culminated in its most grandeur form under Shah Jahan with the construction of the Taj Mahal. The garden inside the new capital of the Mughals, Shahjahanbad, was the culmination of the leisure baghs. A. Deane, who travelled through these significant leisurely locations in early 19th century, wrote the following about the garden inside the Red Fort:

> A number of wide paved walks crossed each other at right angles, and in the centre of them was a bason containing gold and silver fish; besides which were fountains playing upon beds of flowers, laid out in the Dutch style of tiresome uniformity. Small circular buildings, supported by pillars and faced with marble, terminated the principal walks. (Deane 1823)

Apart from being a garden for leisure, the Mughal baghs also evolved as demonstrations of imperial power. At least in the initial years, as James Wescoat has argued, gardens were symbols of 'Mughal territorial presence' and through it the Mughals tried to reinforce a 'cultural identity' of a sort (Wescoat). For the modern art historians, the Mughal gardens exemplified an aesthetic association and a 'visual metaphor' to control a foreign landscape (Asher 1992). They argued that these gardens had political significance and were intended to add to the image of the Mughal emperor. Historians have also explained the Mughal gardens as 'intensely political spaces' (Koch). Its designs, in particular, defined the Mughal 'sovereignty and authority' (Ruggles 1997).

The Mughals also maintained a menagerie. Menagerie are similar to modern zoo where wild animals were kept for the entertainment of royalty and their guests. Lucknow royals in 19th century kept tiger, leopards, wild cats, deer, fighting rams and hill pheasants along with white sparrows (Archer 1883). The courts organised elephant and tiger fights for entertainment (ibid.). Hyena chased by dogs, wolf chasing partridges, deer chased by cheetahs and leopards were some other common scenes. The royal palace inside Delhi's Red Fort had an aviary; it contained 'singing birds'. There was also an aviary in Zenana Garden but access to it was limited (Deane). In the menagerie at Delhi, the animals included tigers, lynxes, leopards, hyenas, monkeys, but surprisingly no lions (ibid.). The animals were kept 'under colonnades of marble' and were chained through iron frames (ibid.).

The banks of Yamunā provided game animals and game birds. The Mughals often went hunting with all their paraphernalia looking for wild animals in the dense forest. They also had various courtly performances in Agra and later in Delhi. Bharatpur located not far from Delhi served as an important site for entertainment for British officials in the first half of the 19th century. It was here, where local nobility organised hunting exercises. One of the activities in hunting involved hawking. British officials have recorded locals using twenty types of raptor birds for hunting (Archer). One of the most eye-catching raptors was Bhyree (peregrine falcon). A typical hawking involved a heron bird, which was released first and, after a brief pause, the Bhyree was unleashed on the hapless bird (ibid.). Hawking and falconry was an important sport as it was a symbol of sovereignty among Mughals and falcons were tamed for sports. These hawking exercises also involved military drills of the royals.

> During the time of hawking, the prince with his suite passed by on an elephant; the lancers went before him, the whole party surrounded by skirmishes on horseback; there were glancing in the sunbeams of as delicious a morning as ever appeared; the superb dresses of the men and caparisons of the horses threw a lustre upon the cavalcade. The effect was peculiarly striking and conveyed to a stranger like myself, the most pleasurable sensations from its novelty and style. (Archer)

The entertainment of Mughal elites in the 19th century included water sports and dance performances.

> The building that most interested me was the royal zenana ghar. At certain times of the year, the emperor of Delhi used to retire to this spot with all his ladies; the place is prettily situated amidst rocks and trees: there seated at ease on his cushions of state, his amusement was to watch the sports of the ladies of the zenana, as they jumped from the roof of a verandah into the water below, and they came up

> to jump again … During these sports guards were stationed around to prevent the intrusion of any profane eye on the sacredness of the zenana. (Fanny Parks Parbly)

One of the ways to entertain guests by royals and nobles in Delhi was by organising dancing and singing performances in their gardens. It generally involved women and their dance performance called 'nautch' (*naach*) (Mundy). Their dance portrayed stories and many of their dance movements were inspired by animal forms. 'Nautch' women were trained dancers and sometimes had a troupe. Their nautch women were assisted by Kulamets who were male singers and played musical instruments (Archer). Sometimes buffoons or clowns also accompanied them. The buffoons performed comic roles but they didn't hesitate to critique royal guests and royalty through satire.

Under the British, the Mughal gardens became their new centres of pleasure and entertainment, especially after the incidence of 1857. The British administration took control of all gardens in Delhi. The British officials started these gardens as space for entertainment and leisure. To make garden more appealing, various steps were taken, which included introducing exotic bird species. Their 'graceful forms' were quite an attraction (*The Times of India*). In one such public garden, a missionary named J. Smith introduced three black swans which he had carried all the way from Australia (*The Times of India*).[3] Gardens started becoming the partying spot for British soldiers in the decade of 1860s in Delhi:

> [T]he under ten thousands assisted by the non-commissioned officers of the Rifle brigade are going to have a 'grand hep' in the public garden tomorrow evening the upper tea, having set them the example a few days ago. These are pleasant brakes to chronicle, but I fear very slow affairs after all. (*The Times of India*)

In 1862, British officials posted in Delhi described the city as 'Dull Delhi' without its European inhabitants, but the 'weather and crops' gave a beautiful setting (*The Times of India*). Trips from Delhi to Meerut were considered exciting because they provided scenic beauty of 'many green countrysides with fields full of pods maturing to be harvested' (*The Times of India).* Meerut was called a peculiar city in the plains because it provided something very unique to British residents staying in Delhi that few other cities offered in the plains; this was exclusive zones free from locals. These zones were called Malls. Malls were referred to as the 'Anglicised portion of Meerut' that were free from 'native hackeries as much as possible from foot passengers who do not wear Christian clothing' (*The Times of India*). The British also converted these green places of leisure, earlier exclusive to the royal family, into picnic spots and public parks (Sharma).

Garden reclamation projects became a common practice in the decades following the 1860s. Many garden projects were in progress in many colonial cities such as Lucknow, Delhi and Lahore (Sharma). In March 1863, the British officers posted in the Sagour region in central India restored Sagour's public garden (*The Times of India*). The project was supervised by a British officer named Campbell. The Sagour public garden was located adjoining the Sagour Lake; the lake was around five miles wide, and was surrounded by sandstone and basaltic hills. The garden provided imagery of an amphitheater. The amphitheatre was supposed to make the stay of the British officers in Sagour enjoyable. The amphitheatre was to serve as a resting ground for the British officials; it was envisaged that the garden amphitheatre would allow the British officials to enjoy the vista of the lake and the hills. The area of the garden was reclaimed from a swamp in the vicinity of a lake. Poppy flowers and pendant vines added a picturesque view to the garden. A terrace was also set up; it gave a 'commanding lake view' and began to be used as a perfect site for picnic by the British officers.

Hunting for Leisure

The Mughals were very fond of hunting. They would often travel to jungle locations with all their paraphernalia looking for wild animals in the dense forest. Hunting of the deer and antelope was common (Divyabhanusinh 2006). The Mughals used cheetah for deer hunting. Akbar, the Mughal ruler, as many know, was dyslexic. But he developed a fondness for cheetahs in his childhood. When he was just thirteen years old, he was presented a cheetah as a gift by an old courtier Wali Beg. Akbar used to call him Fatehbaz. As Akbar acquired adulthood, he developed a keen interest in hunting and would take Fatehbaz along. He would keep Fatehbaz leashed in the court. Later, he tamed many more cheetahs and gave them different names. One of his cheetahs was so awe-inspiring and drop-dead gorgeous in appearance that Akbar declared it the head of all the cheetahs. He named it Madan Kali. Madan Kali would sit alongside Akbar's throne. There were many other robust cheetahs that were tied around Akbar's court, which were captured from various locations of central and western India. *Akbarnama* is replete with many episodes of his capture of cheetahs from different locations. It is mentioned that Akbar had around 9,000 cheetahs in his menagerie.

The Persian chronicles of the 16th century would tell us that there were at least 10,000 Asiatic cheetahs at that time in India. The cheetahs were dangerous indeed, but normally did not attack the humans. Therefore, humans found this wild cat relatively easier to tame for hunting. Ever since medieval times, they were tamed like dogs and were tied to a leash. Prithviraj Chauhan is also said to have tamed cheetahs. The wild cheetah was trained by individual keepers and it normally took three to four months before being used for royal hunts. The Mughals used wild cheetahs routinely to hunt other animals which was called coursing. The painters of the Mughal court have often depicted the royal hunt with cheetah accompanying the badshah. It rather became very common during the reign of Emperor Akbar and Jahangir. Jahangir was a great lover of nature. Like his father, he too was very fond of animals and used the cheetahs for hunting. He has mentioned in his autobiography, *Tuzuk-e-Jahangiri*, that he had engaged in cheetah coursing for capturing more than 400 antelopes near Delhi. Jahangir not only tamed cheetahs, but also hunted the wild cheetahs.

Abul Fazl mentions in *Akbarnama* that Akbar attempted to breed the cheetahs. He did not realise that cheetah's ability to breed in captivity is limited. They do not really mate in captivity and need a wild environment. The result was that gradually the population of the cheetahs began to decline and the Mughals did not realise this. During the time of Emperor Jahangir, however, the first cheetah was successfully bred in captivity. This was possibly one-off incident. The practice of hunting and taming of cheetah continued even under the regional kingdoms of Rajasthan and central India.

After the arrival of the British, the fate of the wild cats, particularly cheetah, was sealed completely. There was a tremendous increase in the hunting of wild cats and cheetahs were no exception. The British also cleared many forest habitats initially to make way for tea and coffee plantations and then for the logs they required for railways. The habitat of many of the wild animals such as the cheetahs were threatened. The colonial documents also suggest that the British government considered the cheetah as a vermin harmful for humans and even placed bounties on its killing. The British officers hunted many of the wild cats and got themselves photographed with it. These bounty hunting accelerated the pace of decline of cheetah population in India.

In Delhi, banks of Yamunā provided an excellent space for game animals and game birds. Hogs, partridges, hog deer, hares. While cheetah was used by the Mughals, the British officers and soldiers used greyhound dogs to hunt deer, antelope, hare and foxes from the surroundings along the Yamuna (Archer). They were particularly interested in hare hunting. Few of the documents mention that that the

British found the Indian hare difficult to kill as they were small and agile and ran quickly as compared to the European hare.

Censoring Public Entertainment

In 1862, when the new viceroy of India, James Bruce, of 8th Elgin arrived in India with his wife Lady Elgin, they were given a military guard of honour at Meerut. A military parade was organised to welcome them. Lady Elgin was much delighted by the sight of siege guns being drawn by elephants. A ball was also hosted by the 'civil' and 'militarily' inhabitants of Meerut in the honour of James Bruce and Lady Elgin. A *durbar* was also organised in Meerut and certain rich people from *bunneah* and banker communities were invited to the event. These local representatives were, however, not seen as a welcome addition to the *durbar* and balls organised by the British officials. The British officers looked at the local *bunneah* and bankers as spoiling the pleasure of the British officials in their hours of leisure (*The Times of India*). Such invitations to the locals became rare.

The locals of Delhi had their own conception of leisure and festivals. Festivals like Holi was perceived as times of inversion when societal norms were not adhered to. The occasion was marked by practice of women beating their husbands with sticks, throwing coloured water on strangers and smearing each other with mud, coloured powder. Similarly, Muharram was seen as an occasion when rumours of bloodsheds loomed large and the *bunneahs* would take advantage of this. They would store all the grain and raise the price (*The Times of India*). The colonial officials, therefore, recorded these festivals with utter revulsion. A British official in Delhi 1864 records:

> The Holee obscenities have just passed away and I can safely say that not on any other occasion since the rebellion, have I witnessed so much drunken riots and disgusting brutality. It was bad enough to know that ladies could not avoid the disgusting scene enacted; without knowing that her majesty's court of justice were libeled in the Chaudney Chowk and dureeba, by highly coloured imitations of the worshipful administrators of Justice, calculated to create contempt and derisive laughter. In the Dureeba, a set of cowardly bullies threw in road pieces of silver (two and four anna bits) and when an unfortunate ignoramus picked them up, he was immediately set upon and shoe beaten the tomasha creating a scene of riot and confusion impossible to describe, but which the police were calmly contemplating and never lifting a finger of warning. (*The Times of India*)

The festivals and processions were seen as suspicious events capable of inducing the locals to revolt against the British state.

The British officials began controlling the leisure activities of the people. Gambling was described as one of the evils that haunted the 'natives of Delhi' (*The Times of India*). Police organised routine crackdown to curb gambling networks in Delhi in the 1860s. Local customs and festivals continued but under strict supervision of British authorities. Diwali *tamasha*, which was a source of entertainment for locals in Delhi, was although tolerated (*The Times of India*). In the year 1863, Delhi artisans made clay model dolls of British civil and military officers (*The Times of India*). The clay models made fun of the officers in the Diwali *tamasha* but the 'inflection' was tolerated because of its similarity with Guy Fawkes Day festival of England (*The Times of India*).

Dramatic Performance Act of 1876 was one of the legislation which helped colonial state to reform theatre. The British government was 'trying to act as a guardian state' and believed that it was necessary to regulate theatre and other sources of entertainment of its subject in subcontinent (Das Gupta). The rationale for the regulation was that it would restore civility and reform moral depravity in the society. R.K. Das Gupta has argued that the colonial state used to censure political commentary in entertainment by labelling it obscene.

In the decade of the 1870s, the plays performed by theatre troupes in British India started to critique the colonial state. Plays like *Sarojini* (1875), *Purubikram* (1874) and *Surendra-Binodini* (1874) came under the purview of Dramatic Performance Act because their content was seen as problematic by the British state. *Surendra-Binodini*, written in 1874, was a play which depicted court officials as corrupt, dictatorial agents of the state who worked closely in nexus with the zamindars. The zamindars were portrayed as the oppressors of the working class who swindled money from the wages of their tenants and landless labourers. *Surendra-Bindodini* showed that court officials took loans from zamindars and always favoured them in judicial hearings. The play, thus, underlined the the institutionalisation of the oppression. Its director, Upendranath Das, and manager, Amritalal Bose, were initially charged under the Dramatic Performance Act but were later acquitted in the high court (Home Department, GOI).

Rumours of the second revolt were always persistent and colonial officials were always on their heels to curb such rumours. Also, the vernacular newspapers started to emerge in the later decades of the 19th century, which further aggravated colonial anxiety. The colonial state was suspicious about the activities of the vernacular newspapers and blamed them for running a propaganda to malign the British state

(*The Pioneer*). Many of the vernacular newspaper were accused of running seditious stories against the state. Sedition was defined as:

> A seditious intention is an intention to bring into hatred or contempt of or to excite the disaffection against the person of her majesty, her heir or successors, or the government and constitution of the United Kingdom as by law established. (*The Pioneer*)

Seditious literature came under the purview of Section 124A of the penal code, along with it Press Act of 1878 was passed by Lord Lytton to reform the vernacular literature (*The Pioneer*). The British state believed that locals lacked the intellectual rigour to engage with slanderous stories published in vernacular literature 'on which is fed a people docile indeed and easily contended, but credulous superstitious, and liable to unreasoning panics' (*The Pioneer*).

Vernacular newspapers and national theatre based in Bengal province had started critiquing British state and its oppressive exploitation of the working class (Home Department, GOI). Gradually, this tendency of critiquing state started to gain momentum in the other states too. The critique of state in pleasure literature was not always direct and it was often subtle. A literature piece published in the year 1897 called 'Kalir Rajsuya' described the imperial assemblage of Delhi *durbar* of 1877 (Home Department, GOI). The literature was aimed towards the Queen and wanted her to end the racial boundaries between the Indians and the English (ibid.). It also requested Queen to stop sending evil men to rule over India and suppress innocent people and, lastly, it wanted Queen to reflect upon the atrocities committed by British officials on locals. But not all literature published in the 19th century were mild in their criticism. Close to Delhi in Awadh Province, a text, *Hakikat-ul-Islam*, was published in the year 1874 and sold more than 1,000 copies (ibid.). The text was written by Muhammad Abdullah, but it seems like it was a pen name; the real name was kept hidden in order to avoid legal situation (ibid.). The work accused the British state of running an unholy rule over India. The book also derided locals enlisting in the British Indian army and called them '*Gora sipahi*' who will suffer for their misgivings (ibid.).

The British were very well aware that the reach of vernacular literature was limited as very few people were literate and rich enough to afford such reading materials. There was tremendous influence of dramatic works or adaptations to the old legends on the mass of the people (Home Department, GOI). Legends of Rama, Usha, Sarangadhra along with classical Sansksrit works like *Sakuntala* and *Mālavikāgnimitra* and their theatrical adaptations were popular among masses. Indian tradition had a vibrant culture of storytelling tradition which involved puppets, pictures, shadow theatres, mask performances and, in Delhi, the tradition of Dastaan (Sharma and Singh). These popular performative traditions had a wider reach among the audience as compared to written literature.

In 1913–14, close to Delhi, Lieutenant Governor of the United province Agra and Awadh region got a copy of a postcard printed in Hindi. The postcard contained Kṛṣṇa Leela (stories and miracles of God Kṛṣṇa). The content of the postcard translated as follows:

> How the merchants of an Unknown place become rulers. They came for trade and giving their sister took the whole house. They ate all my cows and calves. How. Hundreds of thousands of poor widows are in distress and there is no one to relieve their distress how … whenever our Krishna Chand comes, he will give us all husbands. We will then have nose rings and neck Jewels.

The British state continued it with its role of 'guardian state' in the 20th century and the anxiety of saving gullible locals from the slandering maligning content of theatre remained. One of the challenges that the British state had to confront in first decades of 20th century was the emergence of film projectors and bioscopes (Home Department, GOI).

The States patronising attitude towards locals is evident in these lines:

> It is doubtful whether the public can be relied upon to prevent the presentation of undesirable films if their theme is only sufficiently sensational and the situation is complicated in India by religious susceptibilities and the ignorance of the producers of such films of the effect upon Indian spectators of Incidents and situations.... (Home Department, GOI)

In July 1913, a question regarding pre-censorship of content in films was raised in the parliament. Many officials in Delhi were of the view that police acts were enough to curb such nuisance, however, other officials disagreed, as they wanted to reform the Dramatic Performance Act in order to combat the menace of unregulated films (Home Department, GOI). It seems that the main distinction between the Indian Penal Code and Dramatic Performance Act was that Indian Penal Code convicted criminals after they committed a crime while, on the other hand, Dramatic Performance Act was put forward to 'prevent' theatre managers from showcasing 'undesirable content in front of public' (Home Department, GOI). British authorities saw theatre managers as profit mongers who wanted to 'please' the audience and didn't care about offensive content (Home Department, GOI). It was also said that the Dramatic Performance Act of 1876 was found wanting with the emergence of bioscope and films (Home Department, GOI). It was stressed that the magistrates must be emboldened by giving them special powers in order to curb chaos and lawlessness: 'A magistrate should have power to prohibit the performance if the performance is likely to injure religious feelings of any sect, or if the performance is likely to lead to a breach of the peace' (Home Department, GOI).

Certain provisions in Police Act in Bombay and Calcutta presidency had already empowered the magistrate for 'licensing and controlling theatres' (Home Department, GOI). The other public places of public amusement, entertainment or assembly were also brought under control and such arrangement was recommended for Delhi and other provinces as well. Some of the films that came under the purview of Dramatic Performances Act were *The Relief of Lucknow* and *Azeem* (Home Department, GOI). *The Relief of Lucknow* showed locals slaughtering British women and their children in the Revolt of 1857. Film *Azeem*, it was argued, showed Prophet Muhammad in negative light. Muslim community members filed a court case against *Azeem*. The Muslim community also had problems with portrayal of the friends of Prophet in the film. Meanwhile, the Hindus in Delhi were offended by bullfights (Home Department, GOI).

Officials also realised that it was not possible to censure 'small dramatic performances given by strolling players' (Home Department, GOI), but larger gatherings were to restricted and regulated. A curious case of Miss Maud Allen's visit to India shows the British authorities' zeal to regulate and censor entertainment performances (ibid.). It also gives us some inkling about racial segregation in 20th century. Miss Maud Allen, a famous American dancer, was to tour India in 1925–26 (ibid.). Her troupe was to perform in Bombay, Poona, Bangalore, Madras, Calcutta, Allahabad, Lucknow, Agra, Lahore, Cawnpore, Delhi, Karachi and Rangoon. Authorities at Delhi were quite anxious about her public performances. The British Indian state was not happy with the kind of dances Miss Allen performed in Europe. British Indian state labelled her dances as immoral that had the possibility to disrupt peace and order in the Indian cities (Home Department, GOI). The authorities wanted Miss Maud Allen to cancel her dance performances in India. It is said that the British government had sent a notice to Miss Maud Allen, explaining to her that her dance performance was 'objectionable' and it infringed upon the law. If she continued with her performance despite the warnings, then she was to be apprehended under the Dramatic Performances Act and Police Act (Home Department, GOI).

The authorities believed that her performances 'could deprave and corrupt the persons witnessing them'. The persons here referred to are locals whom authorities believed lacked the intellectual wherewithal to engage with mature content. Officials also stressed that Miss Allen dances had the potential to 'outrage morality and decency' (Home Department, GOI).

Miss Allen, in her response to notice, refused to cancel the trip. But she relented to certain directions given by the administration. She agreed to not perform her Salome dance which was labelled objectionable by British authorities. She also agreed to avoid putting a mass advertisement campaign to promote her performances except on newspapers. The tickets of her shows were to be sold 'privately' and were 'nontransferable' (Home Department, GOI). Also, the prices of the tickets were to be kept high so as to restrict 'lower classes' from coming to the shows. A regulation was placed to restrict entry of locals and only Europeans were allowed in her shows.

'There would be no absolute limitation of the audience to Europeans nor would that purport to be the object of the plan, but practically the arrangement would tend in that direction, as also towards making the performances more of a semi-private than a public nature admission to which would be by subscription list rather than by payment at the door' (Home Department, GOI).

Conclusion

The gardens in precolonial times were conceived as a hallmark of sophistication and were developed by the rulers and elites purely as a leisure space. They were depicted as 'cultural space' in paintings, vernacular poetry and chronicles and, thus, began to be used as a metaphor for scenic beauty. That is why they were represented along with various Indian seasons both in the paintings and the vernaculars. After the coming of the British, gardens became a sphere of leisure with European conception. The British took away the control of the existing royal gardens for leisure. Most of these gardens were located near the urban settlements that the British developed. They were restricted as a space for European leisure for health. They did not want the appreciation for local gardens and vistas to extend to local people. The Mughal gardens were brought under British control proclaiming a healthy environment. There was a marked shift in the way gardens and monuments were seen in the 19th century. In some cases, such as Delhi's Nawab Safdarjung's Tomb garden, there was dramatic transformation in the way the private pleasure retreats were converted into public spaces after the Revolt of 1857 (Sharma). In many cases, the sites of historic interest were not converted into public spaces. Rather, they became private spaces of leisure for the British officials, and were kept away from the mass. The British officers continued the Mughal practice of hunting and hawking for their leisure but the intensity increased. The Dramatic Performance Act of 1876 censored public space performances that expressed the oppression of colonial rule. They censored commoners' leisure such as festivities and performances in the name of conspiracy against the state.

Notes

1 This chapter is part of a larger study on Delhi, which I plan to incorporate in a forthcoming book. I would like to acknowledge the financial support given by Institution of Eminence, University of Delhi. I am thankful to Vineet K. Giri for his research assistance.

2 *The Times of India*, 9 February 1864. Unfortunately, the swans were shot dead by a British soldier of Rifle brigade, who confused them with wild birds. But the blame of the killing of the birds was pushed on locals, it was said that the locals insinuated the soldiers because they didn't like the swans eating *singadha* (water chestnut) which the locals wanted for themselves and wanted the swans dead.

References

Ali, Daud. 2012. 'Garden Culture in *Mānasollasa*.' In *Garden and Landscape Practices in Pre-Colonial India: Histories from the Deccan,* edited by D. Ali and Emma J. Flatt, pp. 39–53. New Delhi: Routledge.

Archer, M. 1833. *Tours in Upper India: And in Parts of the Himalayan Mountains with Accounts of the Courts of the Native Princes.* London: Richard Bentley, Vol. 1 and 2.

Asher, C.B. 1992. *Architecture of Mughal India.* Cambridge: Cambridge University Press.

Babur, Z.M. 2014. *Baburnama* (*Memoirs of* Babur), translated by A.S. Beveridge. New Delhi: Low Price.

Deane, A. 1823. *A Tour through the Upper Provinces of Hindustan Comparing a Period between the Years 1804 and 1814, with Remarks and Authentic Anecdotes to which is Annexed a Guide up the River Ganges with a Map from the Source to the Mouth*. London: C&J Rivington.

Deputy Commissioner files (Delhi State Archives), *File no. 26*, 1913.

Deputy Commissioner files (DSA), *File no. 26*, 1913.

Divyabhanusinh. 2006. *The End of a Trail: The Cheetah in India.* New Delhi: Oxford University Press.

Gupta, R.K.D. 1958. 'The Political Background of the Dramatic Performances Control Act of 1876.' *Proceedings of the Indian History Congress*, 21: 510–14.

Home Department (DSA), *Chief commissioner confidential. File no. 3*, 1915.

Home Department (DSA), *Chief commissioner confidential. File no. 18*. 1925.

Home Department (Government of India). 1877. Report on Publication Issued and registered in the several provinces of British India, during the year 1875 (Selections from the Records of the Government of India, Home Department). Calcutta: The Superintendent of Government Printing.

———. 1895. Report on Publication issued and registered in the several Provinces of British India, during the year 1894. Delhi: The Superintendent of Government Printing.

Koch, E. 1997. 'Mughal Palace Gardens from Babur to Shah Jahan (1526–1648).' *Muqarnas*, 14: 143–65.

Mundy. 1832. *Pen and Pencil Sketches: Being the Journal of a Tour in India*. London: John Murray.

Ronald, I. 2012. 'Paradise on Earth: The Deccan Sultanates.' In *Garden and Landscape Practices in Pre-Colonial India: Histories from the Deccan*, edited by Daud Ali and Emma J. Flatt, pp. 74–88. New Delhi: Routledge.

Rötzer, K. and Pushkar Sohoni. 2012. 'Nature, Dams, Wells, and Gardens: The Route of Water in and around Bidar.' In *Garden and Landscape Practices in Pre-Colonial India: Histories from the Deccan*, edited by Daud Ali and Emma J. Flatt, pp. 54–73. New Delhi: Routledge.

Rötzer, K. 1994. 'Mughal Gardens in Benares and Its Neighbourhood in the Eighteenth and Nineteenth Centuries.' In *Confluence of Cultures: French Contributions to Indo-Persian Studies*, edited by Françoise 'Nalini' Delvoye, pp. 131–70. New Delhi: Manohar Publishers and Distributors.

Ruggles, D.F. 1997. 'Humayun's Tomb and Garden: Typologies and Visual Order.' In *Gardens in the Time of the Great Muslim Empires: Theory and Design*, edited by in Attilio Petruccioli, pp. 173–86. Leiden: E.J. Brill.

Sarma, D. and A.H. Singh. 2010. 'Storytelling and Puppet Traditions of India.' *Akhyan: Celebration of Masks, Puppets and Picture Showmen Traditions of India*, 3: 34–41.

Sharma, J.P. 2007. 'The British Treatment of Historic Gardens in the Indian Subcontinent: The Transformation of Delhi's Nawab Safdarjung's Tomb Complex from a Funerary Garden into a Public Park.' *Gender History*, 35 (2): 210–28.

———. 2014. 'Spatialising Leisure: Colonial Punjab's Public Parks as a Paradigm of Modernity.' *Tekton*, 1 (1): 14–30.

Smith, H. 1851. 'Festivals, Games and Amusements; Ancient and Modern.' *Calcutta Review*, XV: 334.

Stuart, C.M.V. 1913. *Gardens of the Great Mughals*. London: Adam and Charles Black Soho Square.

The Pioneer, 1894, 1897.

The Times of India, 1863, 1864.

Wescoat, J.L. 1991. 'Landscapes of Conquest and Transformation: Lessons from the Earliest Mughal gardens in India, 1526–1530.' *Landscape Journal*, 10 (2): 105–14.

———. 1992. 'Gardens versus Citadels: The Territorial Context of Early Mughal Gardens.' In *Garden History: Issues, Approaches, Methods*, edited by John Dixon Hunt, pp. 331–58. Washington DC: Dumbarton Oaks Research Library and Collection.

9

GARDENS AS URBAN LEISURE LANDSCAPE IN EARLY INDIA

Prem Kumar

Introduction

Leisure and pleasure were integral parts of the social and cultural life in early Indian cities. Early Indian literature provides a meaningful representation of leisure and leisure spaces even though it has not been a popular topic of study in early Indian history. Literature offers various words for leisure such as *vinoda*, *pramoda*, *kṣaṇa*, *prakrama*, *avakāśa*, *vitāna*, *vīci*, *sāvakāśatā*, *labdhāvaāśa* and *kṣemya*. Like *kāma* for pleasure, literature does not provide a specific word for leisure. Early Indian literature, both normative and non-normative, deals with various types of gardens and means of leisure—how people spent their leisure time and amused themselves in gardens. Gardens, parks and other leisure spaces were intertwined with the growth of cities in early India. Association of leisure and gardens is discernible in plenty of literary sources, offering evidence for embedded historical contexts.

The primary source for reconstructing garden as an urban leisure landscape are the plays *(nāṭya)*, such as Bhāsa's *Svapnavāsavadatta*, *Pratijñāyaugandharāyaṇa*, *Avimāraka* and *Daridracārudatta* (1st–3rd century CE), Śūdraka's *Mrcchakaṭika* (3rd–5th century CE), Kālidāsa's *Mālavikāgnimitra* (5th century CE); the four monologue plays (*Caturbhāṇī*) wiz. Vararuci's *Ubhayābhisārikā*, Īśvaradatta's *Dhūrta-viṭa-saṁvāda*, Śūdraka's *Padmaprābhṛtaka* and Śyāmilaka's *Pādatāḍitaka* (The Klick) (5th–6th century CE); Viśākhadatta's *Mudrārākṣasa* (6th–7th century CE); Harṣa's *Ratnāvalī* and *Priyadarśikā*; Bhavabhūti's *Mālatiimādhava* (6th–7th century CE); Mahendravarman's *Mattavilāsa-Prahasana* and *Bhagavadajjuka* (7th century CE); Vijayā's *Kaumudī-mahotsva* (8th century CE) and Rājaśekhara's *Karpūramañjarī* and *Viddhaśālabhañjikā* (12th century CE). The *nāṭyas* are immensely useful as they carry actual historical connections; they are less eulogistic and biased. The normative or prescriptive texts referred to here are the *Arthaśāstra*, the *Kāmasūtra* (4th–5th century CE), the *Manusmṛti* and the *Nāṭyaśāstra* (500 BCE–500 CE). The study of normative literature, along with that of creative literature, can help unravel the nuances of the complex and dynamic relationship between code and practice.

Different Types of Leisure Activities

Before the coming of social media (Facebook, YouTube, Twitter, Instagram), watching Bollywood films and talking about celebrities was a leisure pastime and cultural export of the millions of Indians in modern times (Spracklen 2011, 115). We can anticipate the changing patterns of work and leisure in our times. Likewise, the perspectives and patterns of leisure of early urbanites depicted in the literary sources are different. The *Kāmasūtra* sees leisure from the standpoint of the *nāgaraka*, while the *Arthaśāstra* discusses leisure from the perspective of the state. However, the *kavyas* and *nāṭyas* focus more on the practical aspects of leisure. The *Kāmasūtra* mentions various leisure activities such as singing, playing musical instruments, dancing, painting, cutting leaves into shapes, making lines on the floor with rice powder and flowers (today's *Rangoli*), arranging flowers, the colouring of teeth, clothes and limbs, making jewelled floor, making music on the rims of a glass of water, playing water sports, visiting gardens, making garlands and singing. The life of pleasure and amusement was one of the most important aspects of early Indian city life, including cultural, intellectual, artistic, social and erotic activities, as Kanad Sinha argues (Sinha 2013, 7). However, according to Kumkum Bhattacharya, the description of leisure activities, as found in the epics and the accounts of *Kāmasūtra*, Kālidāsa's *Abhijñānaśākuntalam* and *Meghadūtam*, and Bāṇabhaṭṭa's *Kādambarī*, often distinguishes between the 'mundane' and the 'high', taking 'mundane' as folk and the 'high' as classical (Bhattacharya 2006: 75). Bhattacharya also points to the distinctions between the rural and urban leisure practices (ibid.). With the advent of cities and states in early India, the settlement–wilderness (*grāma-araṇya*) dichotomy expanded into a tripartite relationship between the city, village and forest (Singh 2017, 375). The *nāṭyas* recognise the city as a preeminent urban landscape over village and forest.

Detailed studies about gardens as the 'leisure landscape' of early India are still a desideratum. Scholars like Daud Ali (2003 and 2016),[1] Patrick Bowe (2016, 272–78), Tara Sheemar (2008, 187–95)[2] and Nupur Dasgupta (2016, 133–52)[3] have produced some meaningful articles on the gardens of ancient India. However, these works are by and large confined to pleasure gardens or monastic gardens or gardens in general, not to gardens as leisure landscapes. On the other hand, a lot has been written on pleasure.[4] Kanad Sinha's article 'Sporting with Kama: Amusements, Games, Sports and Festivities in Early Indian Urban Culture' focuses on the theme of interchangeability with pleasure (Sinha 2013, 73–120).[5] He thinks that eroticism was the most critical aspect of urban amusement (ibid., 10).

Urban Leisure Spaces

Like anything, leisure also requires physical space to indulge in. Regarding a leisure space, three components matter according to Sam Elington and Sean Gammon—first, the physical setting of the space; second, leisure activities; and, third, the meaning (Elington and Gammon 2015: 1–4).

The interaction between leisure spaces and people's experiences is the primary focus of this chapter. Along with highways, roads and streets, gardens and city parks were the public or social spaces of the city. Landscape (space and places) determined the pattern of relaxation and leisure experiences. The places where early leisure took place were still functional spaces of the city. It is the aim of this chapter to highlight the early urban experiences of leisure in spatial terms. These leisure landscapes or 'leisurescapes' were the significant sites of the city.

The Garden

Descriptions of cities are replete with thoes of the gardens. Gardens have a strong presence in Indian literary tradition. Because of their late origin, the *nāṭya* literature talks about fully developed cities and gardens. *Śāstric* literature also mentions gardens. Some non-*śāstric* literature do so too, but they draw a lot from the *śāstric* traditions. Along with houses, fields, buildings of any kind, lakes, tanks and gardens are called *vāstu* in the *Arthaśāstra* (Rangarajan 1992, 238). The *Arthaśāstra* prescribes a set of regulations for the gardens. The *Arthaśāstra* most often uses gardens associated with fields, not cities. The *Arthaśāstra* gardens are horticultural or 'productive' gardens, not for leisure or pleasure. On the other hand, gardens mentioned in the *Kāmasūtra* are purely leisure or pleasure gardens. Out of all landscape forms, the gardens were the city's most frequented leisure spaces. Various gardens in the city indicate enough space for leisure within the cityscape. City gardens were deeply embedded in the urban culture and intimately related to the urban landforms, architecture, arts, food, dress, festivity, politics, social interaction, leisure, pleasure, and public and private lives. The gardens, thus, dominate the leisure and pleasure landscape of a city. Most of these gardens had architectural forms associated with relaxation. All the sources studied here are fully aware of the paraphernalia of the garden related to leisure, such as rows of plants, trees, pavilions, swings, benches, ponds, artificial hills, birds, animals, etc. All aspects of leisure and pleasure, such as sight, smell, sound, feeling, etc. were considered essential to planning an urban garden. Along with eroticism, the gardens depicted in the *nāṭyas* also invoke a strong association with recreation or leisure. Recreation, leisure, romance, aestheticism and eroticism were common and integral to the garden landscapes.

The *nāṭyas* used Sanskrit terms for garden such as *udyāna, upavana, kānana, vṛkṣavāṭikā, vāṭikā* and their Prakrit equivalents as part of the urban vocabulary of their times. *Ārāma* was also a common tern for garden but was not popular with the playwrights. Gardens served several purposes for the urban folk, such as respite, recreation, pleasure, playfulness, conglomeration, festivity, refuge, etc. All gardens, including the temple gardens, invoke a strong sense of leisure and pleasure. Gardens played a significant role in the lives of the elite and the common folk of early Indian city.

There were two kinds of gardens within the cities was—indoor and outdoor. City parks and temple gardens belonged to the latter category, while domestic and royal gardens belonged to the former.

Bhāsa's *Svapnavāsavadatta* and *Pratijñāyaugandharāyaṇa*, Kālidāsa's *Mālavikāgnimitra*, Harṣa's *Ratnāvalī* and *Priyadarśikā* and Rājaśekhara's *Karpūramañjarī*—all provide a vivid descriptions of pleasure gardens and royal leisure activities associated with them. The *Makaranda* garden was part of the women's quarters or *antaḥpura* of king Udayana of Kauśāmbī in *Ratnāvalī* (Kale 2011, 126). The fountain (*dhārādhara*) of Harṣa's *Priyadarśikā* was such a new and fascinating structure that the royal garden is named after it. The garden is called *dhārādharodyāna* (Nariman et al. 2000, 10).

Gardens were integral to the palace architecture or scheme and reflected the urban context of the city where they were located. Every royal household not only constructed palatial buildings but also gardens and ponds for leisure purposes. In the royal household, there were many gardens. Gardens were not central to palace architecture, but they were placed at various locations in the palace. The primary objective of the royal garden was to provide leisure and pleasure to royal householders. The king, the *vidūṣaka*, queens and their retinue used to visit these pleasure gardens. Queen's leisure activities were confined to the inner pleasure garden. At the same time, the king had greater control and could participate in different leisure activities, such as hunting or shooting arrows outside the royal household. Tara Seemar argues that the upper-class royal household in the urban areas had constructed the gardens as central to their existence. As markers of the elite status, they were accessible only to its members and those closely linked with them (Sheemar 2008, 193).

There were many architectures in the gardens for leisure, such as bowers, stone benches, wood, wooden pavilions, sea houses, swing houses and waterworks. Pleasure gardens contained many small structures, such as painted pavilions, decorated architecture, ornamented pillars, etc. To enhance the view of the garden, in the *Svapnavāsavadatta*, there is a hill house of wood or pavilion full of birds and beasts painted on the walls (Woolner and Sarup 1999, 22). Someśvara's *Mānasollāsa* describes games played in the royal garden, such as board games, water games and swing games (Ali 2011, 40). The royalty allowed their children to play in the garden. For example, in the *Svapnavāsavadatta*, princess Padmāvatī is playing a ball near the jasmine bower in the pleasure garden at Magadhā's palace (Woolner and Sarup 1999, 15). The various bowers of the gardens were used for purposes like sitting, resting, pleasure making, etc. These bowers provided closed space inside the open gardens (Ghosh 1972, 235). In the *Ratnāvalī*, in the plantain bower (*kadalīgṛha*) of the *Makaranda* garden of king Udayana of Kauśāmbī, Sāgarikā is painting *kāma* (Kale 2011, 120). The *Svapnavāsavadatta* refers to a stone bench set in the *Śephālikā* bower and a jasmine bower where princess Padmāvatī is playing (Ayyar 1959, 183). Swings and swing houses were the leisure architecture of the gardens. Swings were placed in both open as well as in closed enclosures. Womenfolk of the royal households primarily used them. The queens also swung along with their husbands or the kings. In the *Mālavikāgnimitra*, queen Irāvatī wishes to enjoy the ride in the swing (*ḍolā*) in the company of her husband (Tawney 1875, 32). The stone benches were simple architectural works primarily used for sitting purposes. The fragrant trees or creepers overhead the stone benches create an aromatic environment. For example, in the pleasure garden of Udayana, there was a stone bench under the *Priyaṅgu* creeper in the palace garden (Woolner and Sarup 1999, 18); stone benches were usually placed in a shady area. For example, in the *Ratnāvalī*, a stone slab placed in the plantain bower is covered with cool plantain leaves (Kale 2011, 138). Like plants and animals, water bodies got installed in the pleasure garden for leisure purposes. Waterworks supported the construction of many water-based architectures, such as lake houses, bowers, etc. Water bodies also provided them with aquatic plants and birds in the gardens. The pond of the pleasure garden of king Udayana is full of female royal swans and lotuses (ibid.). The pleasure gardens' trees, flowers, creepers, bowers, bushes, ponds, etc. attracted large numbers of birds and other creatures. Some birds and animals were intentionally kept in the pleasure gardens for pleasure, amusement, aesthetics, etc., for example, in the pleasure garden in *Mālavikāgnimitra*, a deer (*hariṇa*) is browsing the shoots of the young Aśoka tree (Tawney 1875, 33–59).

House Gardens

Gardens were also attached to almost every big or moderate city house. Compared to royal and city gardens, the house garden of a general household was smaller in dimension with very few paraphernalia, trees and plants. According to Motichandra and Agrawal (1960), ancient urban houses had two types of gardens—outer and inner gardens. The inner gardens were termed variously as *gṛhodyāna* or *bhavanodyāna*. The outer garden (*bāhyodyāna*) was in the open space between the outer boundary wall and the house. The inner gardens were made inside the inner apartments or in inner open spaces (*madhyamuddhesya*). People utilised these open spaces or courtyards (*saṁjavana*). The term *saṁjavana* for courtyard indicates that the central open space was planted with trees and converted into a garden.

The outer gardens were placed at the beginning of the houses at one corner. Householders built a few small structures inside the house gardens because of scarcity of space. Architectural forms like garden-canopy, avenues, stone seats, swings, etc. were placed in the outer garden. In the *Pādatāḍitaka*, in the house garden (*vṛkṣavāṭikā*) of a courtesan named Śūrasenā, there is a *Priyaṅgu* avenue (*priyaṅguvīthī* or *Priyaṅgu bower*) and stone bench (*śilātala*) is placed inside it (*Pādatāḍitaka* 1960, 67). The *Padmaprābhṛtaka* refers to a swing (*ḍolā*) in the outer garden of the courtesan Devasenā on which she had started swinging after listening to the *viṭa* (*Padmaprābhṛtaka* 1960, 42).

In the *Mrcchakaṭika*, there is a garden at the entrance of Cārudatta's house. Most of the courtesan's houses had gardens at their entrances. In the open area of the house garden, male protagonists performed their societal duties. The outsiders were entertained in the house gardens. Thus, in the *Mrcchakaṭika*, when Kumbhilakā visits Cārudatta's house, he is sitting in his house garden (*vṛkṣavāṭikā*), and the gate of the garden is closed (Karmarkar 1950, 149). House garden was used as a reception or living area where visitors were received. The gardens were used as recreational spaces for kids. In the *Padmaprābhṛtaka*, the courtesan's daughter (*gaṇikā-dārikā*) Priyaṅguṣikā is playing ball (*kanduka*) along with her friends in the outer garden of her house (*vṛkṣavāṭikā*) (*Padmaprābhṛtaka* 1960, 29). Corollary to *kulavadhūs*, courtesans used their house gardens to perform personal as well as social actions. In the *Padmaprābhṛtaka*, courtesan Devasenā is enjoying the open air in the company of her maid named Priyavādinikā in her outer garden (*Padmaprābhṛtaka* 1960, 36).

The central courtyards or quadrangles got converted into small inner gardens by planting trees and installing some architecture. It also functioned as gardens with architecture like small ponds, pavilions, basements, bowers, painting houses, etc. There were small ponds (*puṣkariṇī*) with lotus in the middle of the house. The inner courtyard was the most favoured location for waterworks. Water basins or small ponds were made above the ground level. In the house gardens near the pond, architecture like artificial hills, pleasure rocks (*dāruparvata* made of wood) or pavilions were installed for sporting purposes. They also made basements (*bhūmitalagṛha*) and creeper houses (*latāgṛha*) for summer purposes near the ponds. In gardens, painting houses (*citraśālā)* were also made to station special guests. The walls of the *painting houses (citraśālā*) were either painted or decorated with reliefs. They were also decorated with pearls, corals and nets of tiny bells and lotus flowers. In the *Mrcchakaṭika*, the courtesan Vasantasenā's mansion has a garden in her inner quadrangle. The *Mrcchakaṭika* uses the term *saṁjavana* for an enclosed courtyard or a quadrangle surrounded by buildings or rooms on four sides (Kale 2015, 194).

Public Parks or City Gardens

There were gardens or parks in almost every early historic city. They were the logical expansion of house gardens or pleasure gardens. These gardens were equally accessible for everyone—men and women, transgender people, royal and non-royal, elite and commoners, cultured and uncultured or high and low. They were the most accessible public space in the city. City parks exhibit civic, recreational, leisure, erotic and religious associations and played multifunctional roles. Besides markets, roads and streets, gardens were the most shared public space of the city. Within the fixed boundary of the city, the city park was the most vibrant space for urban folk.

In the city, there were many public gardens—old (*jīrṇodyāna)* and new (*bālodyāna*). For example, the *Madanodyāna* of the *Mālatīmādhava* is a new garden (*bālodyāna*), and the *Puṣpakaraṇḍaka* of Ujjayinī (in *Mrcchakaṭika*) is an old garden (*jīrṇodyāna).* The *Mudrārākṣasa* also mentions a *jīrṇodyāna* (weed-grown garden) in the sixth act of the play (Dhruv 1923, 84). Public parks or gardens, primarily old, were located on the outskirt or outside the city while new gardens were placed within the city. Urban folks went to the public gardens to amuse themselves. People used their own vehicles to visit gardens on the outskirts of the city.

City parks also had many architectures associated with leisure and pleasure. Stone slabs are there to sit in the *Puṣpakaraṇḍaka* garden of Ujjayinī. The stone slabs are not decorated but look charming (Kale 2015, 245, 261). There are stone benches on the banks of the ponds (*dīrghikātīraśilātalam*) in the *Kusumākarodyāna*. In the *Kusumākarodyāna*, a *maṇḍapa* is arranged in the garden across the trees near the pond (*dīrghikā*) (Rai 2014, 250). Water is essential for humans, plants, animals and birds; hence, water bodies were installed in the city parks. The gardens contained pools that provided free access to city folk, animals and birds. The water bodies also attracted animals and birds and further enhanced the natural element of the garden. City garden pools were also for aquatic sports. The *Ubhayābhisārikā* mention a pool (*dīrghikā*) in the *Aśokavana* in Pāṭaliputra. The courtesan Ratisenā and her lover Dhanamitra go to the park to bathe. The pool is also gated and guarded. Here, Ratisenā leaves Dhanamitra and flees after closing the gate. Gates being closed, Dhanamitra comes out of the pool through a small door with the help of the park's keepers (*Ubhayābhisārikā* 1960, 24).

Visiting temple gardens and offering flowers to temple deities was another leisure pursuit of urbanites. The *Mālatīmādhava* mentions a garden called Kusumākara garden (*Kusumākarodyāna*) in the vicinity of the temple of Śiva. People used to take flowers from the garden to offer to the temple deities. Thus, in the play, Mālatī plucks flowers from different bowers to worship Śaṃkara (Kale 1928, 26). Temple gardens also copied many architectural elements from the mainstream garden, such as groves, bowers, ponds, etc. In the *Kusumākarodyāna*, there is a grove of red Aśoka (*Raktāśoka*) tree, *Kaṇṭakī, Kurabaka* and other bowers, Kadamba and mango trees, lotus plants, along with cuckoos, bees and caged tigers (ibid., 26–31). In the temple, a tiger is kept in an iron cage that comes out and is killed by Mādhava's friend, Makaranda (Rai 2014, 134–39). Wild animals were kept in the city garden to amuse people.

City gardens served the town in general and those who were deprived of gardens at home in particular. They were used for various purposes, such as pleasure, leisure, respite, organising festivities, picnics, fairs, religious gatherings, marriages, resorts for outsiders, etc. The urbanites exploited the city gardens for what they were; they were made for relaxation, recreation, romance and religious congregations. The city parks were strategically built to support significant events like the festivals where the whole city was supposed to assemble. The garden was also a party place or open banquet. The *Kāmasūtra* also suggests that men should go to the garden on horseback in the noon, accompanied by courtesans and followed by servants. And they should return home in the afternoon, bringing bunches of flowers (*The Kāmasūtra of Vātsyāyana* 1883–1925, 20). However, the city gardens of the *nāṭyas* are not only for the *nāgaraka* (man about the town) and *gaṇikās* (courtesans), but also for all urbanites including the royal. The *nāṭya* sources also support the idea that gardens served as 'respite' for those who do not belong to the city or do not own gardens. However, those having gardens at home also visited city gardens for different purposes. For example, in the *Mrcchakaṭika*, both Cārudatta and courtesan Vasantasenā have gardens in their respective houses but, for *abhisāra* purpose, they choose *Puṣpakaraṇḍaka* garden located at the outskirt of Ujjayinī. Common womenfolk would visit these gardens for religious observations or conglomeration. In the *Avimāraka*, the *naṭī*, the actress of the play, wishes to go to the park (*udyāna*) with her husband (*sūtradhāra*) to attend a religious observance carried out by womenfolk (*strīkaraṇīyaṃ niyamakāryam*, Kunbae 1968, 3). In the *Mrcchakaṭika*, Saṁvāhaka, the Buddhist monk, visits the Puṣpakaraṇḍaka garden of Ujjayinī to wash his clothes.

Royal people also visited city gardens. In the *Avimāraka*, princess Kuraṅgī visits the city garden with her entourage, which is guarded against all sides. City folk avoid the city parks when royalty visits. Thus, in the *Avimāraka*, the *sūtradhāra* says to his wife, 'the princess has gone to the garden. Therefore, the gardens are now guarded on all sides; when the princess returns home, we shall go there at will' (Kunbae 1968, 5). No one wanted to visit the garden at the will of the royal people. The king visited the outer park to practise shooting. In the *Mudrārākṣasa*, Rākśaṣa says that, in the outer garden, his majesty Nanda formerly hit his arrow at moving marks with his horse in full swing, letting loose the reign by stretching the bow. In the field of the garden, he halted and chattered with kings (*Mudrārākṣasa*, VII.9).

Young boys and girls spent their time visiting public parks for *abhisāra* purposes. They visited gardens in their clique or age group. For *abhisāra* with courtesan Vasantasenā, Cārudatta, the protagonist of the play, visit the *Puṣpakaraṇḍaka* garden of Ujjayinī at the outskirt of the city of Ujjayinī in his closed cart to avoid public gaze. Outskirt gardens were also protected. There used to be watchmen to guard the Puṣpakaraṇḍaka garden as per the king's order (Kale 2015, 259). Courtesans also visited city gardens along with their retinue to amuse and relax. In the *Bhagavadajjuka Prahasana*, Ajjuka, the chief courtesan, visits the city park to Kāñcīpuram to enjoy a drinking party (*āsava goṣṭhī*) (Lockwood and Bhat 2005, 60–61). In the *Ubhayābhisārikā*, maid, Kanakalatā, says about her mistress Narayaṇadattā:

> When our mistress's heart was overcome by jealousy, giving up bathing, sleeping, eating, and ornaments, she went to Aśoka park (the city garden) and sat on a rock sheltered by a young Aśoka tree. While the soft words of his friend were consoling her, she saw a man passing, turning the scale of his vina to indistinct notes and singing these vaktra and apavaktra verses. And she got softened by the song. (Venkatacharya and Warder 1967, 79–80)

Beyond the city boundary, there existed some suburbs. Some gardens were placed outside the city orbit associated with religious institutions like Buddhist monasteries or hermitages. These gardens were used for excursions by city people. It is worth noting that city people also patronised the gardens associated with *vihāra* (*ārāma*). For example, in *Mrcchakaṭika*, Cārudatta, the great patron of the city, has founded *vihāras* and a garden (ārāma) outside Ujjayinī (Kale 2015, 340). For Gregory Schopen, *vihāra* was a Buddhist monastery and a place of recreation or pleasure (Schopen 2006, 484).

Other Spaces and Leisure Activities

Besides the gardens, the royal household had places for recreational and leisure activities. The *Mālavikāgnimitra* mentions a cultural complex situated in the middle area, probably between male and female apartments (*antaḥpura*). In the cultural complex area, theatre, music and painting were organised in separate quarters or houses for the inmates of the *antaḥpura*. In the cultural-complex area, there would be a painting hall (*citraśālā*), music hall (*saṃgītaśālā*) and theatre hall (*prekṣāgṛha*). The king, the *vidūṣaka*, queens and their assistants visited the place to enjoy paintings, dances, music and theatre. In the *Mālavikāgnimitra*, the queen has gone to *citraśālā* to look at the picture of the master painter; there is a music hall (*smgītśālā*) where the dance teacher Ganadāsa teaches Mālavikā; there is a theatre hall (*prekṣāgṛha*) where orchestral performance for the royal family takes place (Tawney 1875, 4–18). Royal theatres had fixed audiences. Women of the harems are also enacted in the plays.

The *Ratnāvalī* also refers to a picture hall (*citraśālikā)* in the royal palace of Rājgrha (Shastri 2019, 221). The *Priyadarśikā* mentions a wonderful playhouse or the theatre hall in the palace where the royal household ladies enact new plays. The servants also participate in theatrical enactment. Nariman and Jackson think that *prekṣāgṛha* was not a theatre hall in a sense but a gallery of the palace, usually adjoining the harem, used not only for dramatic presentation but also for instructions in music, singing and dancing (Nariman et al. 1923, 117). *Priyadarśikā* also mentions the presence of a music–dance room (*gandharavaśālā*) as well as a painting hall (*citraśālā*) or pavilion or picture gallery mainly adorned with frescos adjoined by the playhouse (ibid., 20–23). Royal households employed bards (*vaitālikas*) to sing poetry. According to M.R. Kale, these bards were not the paid panegyrist of the court but living on the kings' bounties (Dhruva 1923, 131). They had to sing the morning songs to wake the kings. For example, in the *Viddhaśālabhañjikā*, bards (*mahāmallakas*) dwell around the king's palace to sing morning songs (ibid., 7).

The house of the elites of the town also had recreational spaces. In *Mālatīimādhava*, the minister's house (*amātyabhavana)* has a music room and a sports room (*uparyaliṇdam*) in the upper storey of the palace (Rai 2014, 69). It has pavilions called *valabhī* or *maṇḍapa* with *gavākṣa* on the top of the palaces where Mālatī stand to watch the road outside her house. Houses of the city had porticos where inmates of the house sit at leisure. Sitting at the entrance (*dvārakoṣṭhaka*) was another leisure pursuit of urbanites. In the *Padmaprābhṛtaka*, the poet Sārasvatabhadra is seated in the portico when the *viṭa* encounters him (Motichandra and Agrawal 1960, 9–10). In the *Dhūrta-viṭa-saṁvāda*, Bandhumatikā is sitting and chatting with Caturikā at the entrance of her house (ibid., 79). In the *Padmaprābhṛtaka*, grammarian Dattakalaśi is worshipping in the portico when he gets touched by courtesan Raśanāvatī (ibid., 19). Since porticos were situated outside the houses, it was considered pure and fit for worship in courtesan households.

Unlike courtesans and other women, *kulavadhūs* were home centred. *Kulavadhūs* maintained a strict social ritual and ordered behaviour in contrast to other women. Inside the *kulavadhū's* household, the quadrangular courtyards were used for workplace and leisure activities such as sitting, cooking, keeping domestic animals, dining, talking, meditating and meeting visitors. Household activities utilised most of the leisure time of married women or *Kulavadhūs*. The leisure behaviour patterns differed on gender, age and community lines. The companionship was very limited to *kulavadhūs*. *Kulavadhūs* were on the margins of pursuit of the culture of leisure and pleasure. They had no distinct pattern of leisurely behaviour. Within the boundary of the household, beyond the household chores, their leisure activities were confined to bird watching, painting, looking for pets, playing with children, etc. These activities had no public gaze and, thus, lead to social isolation. The *Kāmasūtra* makes tree planting a manner of living and leisure for virtuous women, mainly when their husbands are absent from the home (*The Kāmasūtra of Vātsyāyana* 1883–1925, 19).[6]

Practising music, singing, dancing and painting inside the household was another favourite pastime of wives and young girls. The *nāṭyas* reveal that the music was practised by general householders of the cities and by royal people. When *Avimāraka* is walking around the city at night, he finds people playing with lutes, women singing with nasal and vocal organs and clapping with bracelet-clad hands (Kunbae 1968, 76). The *Pratijñāyaugandharāyaṇa* mentions that the daughter of Mahāsenā Vāsavadattā started learning the music or lute at her marriageable age. She developed this interest in music after seeing her friend Kañcanamālā playing the instrument (Devadhar 1962, 18).

A courtesan's household had different leisure activities from a general household. Courtesans enjoyed leisure time in their community along with servants, mothers, *bandhulas*, *viṭas* and visitors. In courtesan households, visitors were offered books, games and drinks. The third quadrangle of Vasantasenā's mansion is meant for the leisure or retiring room, where seats are duly arranged for the use of well-born youths. There are gaming tables. There is a half-read volume lying on the gaming table. Chessmen made up of precious stones are placed on another table (Kale 2015, 161). The courtesan's household chores and leisure were seemingly performed in both open and covered areas. Chores like offering oblation to crows, feeding pet animals, gambling, reading books, practising music, cooking, ornament making, dying, drinking wine, gardening and domesticating birds were carried out either in verandahs or in open areas. Keeping pets and birds was the favourite leisure pursuit of courtesans. Vasantasenā house is full of pets and birds such as quills, ram and cocks (Kale 2015).[7] The *Kāmasūtra* of Vatsayayana also prescribes quail fights, ram fights and cock fights for the *nāgaraka*[8] to amuse themselves (*Kāmasūtra* 2002, 1.4.7–9). The presence of these quail, ram and cock indicates that these animals were kept for fighting and amusing the visitors. Kenneth R. Cunningham categorises keeping a house full of birds and pets as an example of idiosyncratic behaviour (Cunningham 1961, 13).

The *Mrcchakaṭika* remarks that exhibitions of new plays are a regular phenomenon in a city like Ujjayinī (Kale 2015, 55). The *nāṭyas* speak of two types of theatres in a city—the public or city theatre and the private theatre. Open performances were carried out in city theatres where most actors were male. Women also contributed to a theatrical production. Female roles were mainly played by women like *naṭī* (wife of *sūtradhāra*) and courtesans. Courtesans were given the written scripts (*patraka*) before they acted in the play. In the *Padmaprābhṛtaka*, *nāṭakācārya* Gandharvadatta asks Dardurka, the *nāṭeraka*, to give the script of Kumudvatī Prākāraṇa to courtesan Devasenā *(Padmaprābhṛtaka* 1960, 35.18–19). Theatrical performances were also carried out privately. In the *Pādatāḍitaka* Pratihāra Droṇilaka, the superintendent of courtesans (*veśyādhyakṣa*) organises *prekṣā* (theatre) at his house where courtesan Mayurasenā is called to perform purposely. In city theatre, males dominated the audience. *Kulavadhūs* did not participate in the audience. In the *Mrcchakaṭika*, only Cārudatta and his friend are returning from attending consort, not his wife and maid. In *nāṭyas*, male protagonists spend more leisure time with others than with own's family For example, in the *Mrcchakaṭika*, Cārudatta is involved more in public leisure than private life. For males, leisure and companionship were expressed in friendship terms than formal companionship of family. The private life for urban males was limited to eating and sleeping in the house.

Participating in theatre (*prekṣā*), dance and music (*saṅgītaka*) and *goṣṭhīs* (poetry recitation) and discussing the performances of the artists were the leisure pastime for most urbanites in early India. The saṅgītaka seems to occupy the most important place in early Indian leisure. It was both indoor and outdoor activity for male householders where married wives were not allowed. Musical concerts (*saṅgītaka*) were organised in the city, mostly at night till midnight. The *Mrcchakaṭika* mentions a late-night music consort of Ujjayinī attended by Cārudatta and his friend Maitreya. In a musical concert, the lute is played and the singer sings beautifully. Cārudatta is very apprehensive about Rebhila's singing (Kale 2015, 105). Urbanites had keen interests and deep knowledge of music. *Ubhayābhisārikā* reveals that, in the city of Pāṭaliputra, a saṇgītaka named the sacrifice of *Madana* gets organised where Nārāyandattā (courtesan) and Kuberadatta (son of a *śreṣṭhī*) quarrel over 'rasa' (*Ubhayābhisārikā* 1960, 3).

City people organised *goṣṭhīs* on different occasions. *Goṣṭhīs* were organised to discuss or conversate on favourite themes of pleasure (romantic liaison) and poetry. The *Dhūrta-viṭa-saṁvāda* mentions some big *goṣṭhīśālās* in the city (*Dhūrta-viṭa-saṁvāda* 1960, 29.20). *Goṣṭhīs* of the city were named after their patrons. The *Dhūrta-viṭa-samvāda* refers to the Rāmīlaka's *goṣṭhī*, where participants like Viṣṇudāsa debated and doubted over the *Kāmatantra* where *dhūrta* Viśvalaka is also a participant (*Dhūrta-viṭa-saṁvāda* 1960, 29.6). Courtesans also organised *goṣṭhīs* in their houses.

Urbanism came with both prosperity and free time and money to cultivate leisure activities. As leisure-time pursuits, drinking, gambling and visiting courtesans all required money. However, these leisure pursuits were not connected with social status. Drinking was an old phenomenon. The *Pratijñāyaugandharāyaṇa*, *Pādatāḍitaka*, *and Mattavilāsa-Prahasana* provide a vivid picture of the taverns and drinking culture of the city. Taverns were situated in various parts of the city, in the market, on the highway, etc. Drinking was common urban leisure pursuit in those days. Drinking parties were also being held where red radish was being served (Kale 2015, 225). Many drinking pubs in the cities served various kinds of wines. Some wines were made as sweet as mulled wine (Devadhar 1962, 26). The *nāṭyas* provide references to a variety of wines in the taverns and households of a city. Typology included *vāruṇī* (*Dhūrta-viṭa-saṁvāda*, 11), *āsava* (*Dhūrta-viṭa-saṁvāda* 1960, 15), *śīdhu* (*Dhūrta-viṭa-saṁvāda*, 1960, 16), *madhu* (*Pādatāḍitaka* 1960, 135) and *madira* (*Pādatāḍitaka* 1960, 82). In the *Mrcchakaṭika*, the *viṭa* says that Vasantasenā's mother has become fat and sick after consuming *śīdhu, surâ* and *āsava* (*Mrcchakaṭika* 2015, IV.30). The *Mālatīimādhava* refers to two kinds of wines—*Maitreya* and *Indramayūkha*. According to M.R. Kale, *Maitreya* was an intoxicating wine, and *Indramayūkha* was a wine drunk after being exposed to moonlight (Kale 2015, 63–72). In the *Pratijñāyaugandharāyaṇa*, the tavern located on the highway in the city of Ujjayinī is run by a woman keeper, serving wines to customers. Women also used to drink liquor. Drinking was not prohibited. In the *Pratijñāyaugandharāyaṇa*, the pageboy (*gātrasevaka*) says, 'when the daughter-in-law is drunk, she gets love-smitten for her father-in-law; but the mother-in-law is there ready with her stick' (Devadhar 1962, 36). Liquor was also served to cash run-down people. The tavern keeper deposited some goods for the liquor. In the *Pratijñāyaugandharāyaṇa*, the page boy pawned the royal elephant's goods such as *aṅkuśa*, necklace (*kṣurapramālā*), the bell (*ghaṇṭā*) and whip (*kaśā*) and the royal elephant itself to tavern keeper for liquor (ibid., 36–37). There are so many taverns in Kāncīpuram that Devasoma (the consort of *kapāli*) compares the city with liquor Goddess *Vāruni* in the *Mattavilāsa-Prahasana* (*Mattavilāsa-Prahasana* 2005, I.44). In the *Mattavilāsa-Prahasana*, in the city of Kāñcipuraṃ, the *kapāli* couples visit many drinking pubs in search of his lost *kapāla* (Giri 1966, 9). Some taverns were magnificent. For example, in the *Mattavilāsa-Prahasana,* the tavern of Kāñcipuraṃ resembles a sacrificial hall in its entire splendour (*Mattavilāsa-Prahasana*, I.45). The *Arthaśāstra* regulates selling alcoholic beverages and drinking in public. The *Arthaśāstra* prescribes that only persons of good character could buy and take away a small quantity of liquor and prohibits moving about drunk (*Arthaśāstra* 1992, 2.25.5). When it comes to drinking, the *nāṭyas*' references indicate that the *Arthaśāstra* prescriptions were not followed.

Gambling was integral to urban leisure. Gambling was carried out in public, and gambling salons were situated in different parts of the city. The pursuit of gambling was open to all. The public gambling house (*dyūtasabhā*) was a prominent place in the city, with gaming laws and regulations operating under state patronage. Gambling appears to have been somewhat institutionalised in the city. Many gambling masters and gamesters inhabited the city as gambling was an important leisure activity in the city. In the *Mrcchakaṭika*, the keeper of the gambling house (*sabhā*) is called *sabhika* and the gamesters are called *dyūtakara* (Kale 2015, 72–73). In the *Mrcchakaṭika*, Mathurā is a keeper of the gambling house (*sabhika*); Saṁvāhaka a gambler (*dyūtakara*) and Darduraka a rake or former gambler. Mathurā is also the head of all gambling masters (*pradhāna-sabhika*) (ibid., 84–85). The *Arthaśāstra* prescribes rules and fines for some leisure activities like gambling, betting, drinking, visiting courtesans, etc. The *Arthaśāstra* prohibits gambling in places other than authorised gambling halls. The fine for gambling elsewhere was twelve *paṇas* (*Arthaśāstra* 1992, 3.20.01–02). The *Arthaśāstra* prescribes severe punishment for cheating by a gambler by cutting off his hands or a penalty of 400 *paṇas* (*Arthaśāstra*, 4.10.09). The Brahmanical normative texts such as the *Manusmṛti* prohibit gambling and consider it a vice of civil society (*Manusmṛti* 2005, 9.221). However, as evident from the *nāṭya* literature, gambling was a well-established profession and a leisure pursuit in the cities.

Visiting a courtesan's quarters was a favourite pastime of urbanites. Courtesan's quarters were located on the highway of the city and well connected with the other parts of the city. The *nāṭya* literature offers long lists of visitors, which include royal people, Buddhist monks, Brahmans, *vidūṣaka*, officials and royal officers. In the *Ubhayābhisārikā*, the king's brother-in-law, Rāmasena, is staying in the Ratilatikā house (maidservant of courtesans) for several days (*Ubhayābhisārikā* 1960, 22). In *Caturbhāṇī*, the *viṭas* provide a tour guide to the courtesan's quarters. In courtesan's quarters, *viṭas* encounter every type of urbanite visiting the veśa, including bankers (*śreṣthīs*), merchants (*sārthavāha*), Buddhist monks and nuns, parivrājikās, lute teachers, poets, drummers, son of *naṭī* (*nāṭeraka*), *Caukṣa bhāgavata*, singers, dancers, high officials, old *viṭas*, physicians, military officials, prices, corrupt officials, third gender, brother-in-law of king, hill men (tribes), *mlecchas*, cobblers and officer-in-charge of courtesan quarters. References of the officer-in-charge of the courtesan's quarters support the *śāstric* prescription of taxing courtesans and regulating leisure and pleasure activities in the city. The *Pādatāḍitaka* refers to an official called veśadhyakśa pratihāra Drauṇalika (*Pādatāḍitaka* 1960, 97.4). Chapter VII and part VI of *Arthaśāstra* is dealing with official controlling leisure activities. Here, Kauṭilya prescribes the head of the department of courtesans to supervise not only courtesans but also other entertainers—actors, dancers, singers, musicians, etc.

The *Arthaśāstra* does not put any special qualifications for the chief controller of leisure activities (Rangarajan 1992, 347).

Some public leisure places were formal and open to all, while some were institutional. Public parks, royal roads, crossroads and streets were formal spaces. Places like courtesan's quarters, gambling houses, *viṭasabhās*, etc. were institutional in characters. The highway was the most crowded space in the city. In the *Mrcchakaṭika*, the highway was used by courtesans, ascetics, elephants, maidservants, officials, etc. The highway was a crowded place in the daytime. In the *Mattavilāsa-Prahasana*, the crowd of the royal road of Kāñcipuraṃ is carefree (*Mattavilāsa-Prahasanam* 2005, 65). The *Kaumudī-mahotsva* describes the beautiful evening of Kuśumpura, which is thronged with thousands of men and women in perpetual glee (*Kaumudī-mahotsva* 1952, 315). The royal road of Kuśumpura is very noisy with the girdles and jingling sounds of the beautiful young ladies who are alone on the royal road to the residences of their lovers (*Kaumudī-mahotsva* 1952, 318). A street is an essential form of connecting landscape. The streets were crowded spaces of towns with their own social life. The streets were immediate transitional spaces between the private (homes) and the public (streets). The streets were used as spaces of sociability as well as crime. In the daytime, they were used for socialisation. Here, people stopped, met, mingled and spent time together. Courtesans sat down at the front of the gate and interacted with the passers by on the streets. Fighting, whoring, patrolling, burgling, marriage processions, victory processions, etc. were carried out in the streets. It was a socially fluid space with fewer restrictions. The street of *veśa* was called *veśāvīthī*. The street leading to *veśa* is also called *Makrarathyā* in the *Pādatāḍitaka* (*Pādatāḍitaka* 1960: 30.2). The streets leading to *veśa* are named *veśagāminī rathyās* in *Dhūrta-viṭa-saṁvāda* (*Dhūrta-viṭa-saṁvāda* 1960, 14.2). Outdoor leisure activities for women generally took place in the daytime; the males, however, enjoyed leisure time throughout the day.

The *sabhās, maṇḍapas* and *pīṭhikās* were community-bond leisure spaces. In the *Avimāraka*, there is an empty *viṭasabhā* in the middle of the crossroad of the city. *Avimāraka* sneaks into the *viṭasabhā* to evade a watchman (Kunbae 1968, 80). In *Pādatāḍitaka*, there were *maṇḍapas* of *viṭas* (*viṭamaṇḍapa*) where bald Śyāmilaka, the herald of the rogues, is suing proclamation while striking upon the gong (*Pādatāḍitaka* 1960, 5.4). The *Pādatāḍitaka* refers to *Brāhmaṇapīṭhikā* in the city of Ujjayinī, where learned Brahmans deliver on the issue of Vīṣṇunāga (*Pādatāḍitaka* 1960, 12.3). It appears that every community had its places for discussion in the city in the forms of *maṇḍapa* and *pīṭhikā*. Since the *nāṭyas* do not provide the organisational structure of its space and architecture, nothing can be called with certainty whether they had any particular architecture. They had their presence in different parts of the city. *Brāhmaṇapīṭhikā* was a community club of learned Brahmans where they discussed and delivered various issues on *dharma*.

City people also welcomed folk artists. The *Mudrārākṣasa* mentions various folk artists present in the city of Pāṭaliputra. Early cities had a special relationship with the outside world of folk culture. Folk artists visited cities from house to house to display their art. They included snake charmers, *Yamapaṭṭika* exhibitioners, *Indrajalika*, etc. The existence of folk artists in the leisurescape indicates that the cultural boundary of the city was porous. City people, as protagonists of the dominant culture, not only gave space to folk arts but also preserved them by patronising them.

Personalisation of leisure led to the creation of a special class of people, salaried or patronised, or entertainers in the society. Through their personal experiences and communications, people like the *pīṭhmarda*, the *vidūṣaka* and *viṭas* mediated leisure pursuits across spaces and people. The *vidūṣaka* for the high class and vita for common urban folk were the true connoisseur of pleasure and leisure. Both appreciated poetry, music, dance, arts, beauty, wine, food and dress. Those in leisure classes in the daytime turn to anti-leisure of the nighttime. The cityscape was entirely different at night. The highway remained deserted at night. Few people, such as courtesans, their parasites, attendants and men who were royal favourites, walked on the royal road of Ujjayinī at night. In *Mrcchakaṭika*, *viduṣaka* refuses to walk on the royal road in the nighttime to prevent himself from becoming prey to courtesans, *viṭas*, *ceṭa* and *rājavallabhāpuruṣās* (Kale 2015, 27). Courtesans and royal favourites such as *viṭa* were considered predators of the royal road.

Conclusion

In conclusion, we assume that, in early India, both men and women, elite and commoners, rich and poor and almost every section of society were attracted to and involved in leisure. Almost every space in the city was used for different kinds of leisure activities. Among all, gardens emerged as excellent leisure spaces in the city. There was a garden for every urbanite. There were gardens in every part of the city—in the royal household, in the common household, in the city, on the outskirts and even outside the city. Urbanites used them for various purposes such as excursions, picnics, religious discourses, respires, etc. Gardens played essential roles in city life. Men occupied more urban leisure space than the woman. Being confined to the household, *kulavadhūs* were at the margin of the urban leisurescape. Among women, the urban leisure landscape was dominated by courtesans, followed by unmarried girls and maidservants. Courtesans were free to visit every space of the city. Compared to *kulavadhūs*, *kulakanyās* were given more special freedom and greater access to outdoor spaces to pursue leisure activities. In the *nāṭyas*, leisure tends to be expressed in some group activities. Group or community leisure was further segregated on the age-sex line. The choice of leisure not only depended upon an individual or community but also on contemporary socioeconomic and cultural settings.

Notes

1 Daud Ali was instrumental in reconstructing essential features of the early Indian garden in association with the rise and growth of cities.

2 In this paper, Tara Sheemar examines how the garden is represented as a spatial category in the *Kathāsaritasāgara*. The *Kathāsaritasāgara* is a courtly narrative from 11th century Kashmir.

3 According to Nupur Dasgupta, all gardens of ancient India were floral gardens.

4 Seema Bawa's edited work, *Locating Pleasure in Indian History* (2021) is the most recent contribution to the topic.

5 The article explores the nature of amusement and pastimes in the cities of the period 400–1300 CE.

6 The *Kāmasūtra* recommends virtuous women to plant beds of green vegetables, bunches of sugarcane, clumps of a fig tree, mustard plants, the parsley plant (*Petroselinum crispum*) and false mangoes (*Xanthochymus pistorius*); clusters of flowers such as the water chestnut (*Trapa bispinosa*), jasmine (*Jasminum genus*), Spanish or royal jasmine (*Jasminum grandiflorum*), yellow amaranth (*Amaranthus tricolour*), wild jasmine (*Jasminum angustifolium*), pinwheel flower (*Tabernaemontana coronaria*), nadyaworta, China rose (*Hibiscus rosa-sinesis*); and fragrant grass (*Andropogon*), camel grass or lemongrass (*Cymbopogon schaenanthus*); and aromatic root of the plant andropogon miricatu.

7 *Mrcchakaṭika* reports that in her seventh quadrangle of Vasantasenā's palatial home, there are a pair of pigeons (*pārāvata*) enjoying sitting comfortably in dovecots (*vihaṅgavātī*), parrot (*śuka*), in its cage, is being fed on curd and rice and is reciting a Vedic hymn; a mynah (*madanasārikā*) is chattering more than a housemaid; a cuckoo (*parapuṣṭā*) is cooing like a procuress; quails (*lāvakā*) are being incited to fight, partridges (kapīañjalā) are being made to talk; caged pigeons (*pañjarakapota*) are sitting over each other, a domestic peacock (*gṛhamayura*) is fanning and dancing; pairs of a royal swan (*rājahaṁsa*) walking behind lovely damsels, tame cranes (*gṛhasārasa*) are moving here and there. Besides birds, her house has rams, horses, elephants and bullocks.

8 *Nāgaraka* is the urban ideal of *Kāmasūtra,* not any other literature. According to Shonaleeka Kaul, the term '*nāgaraka*' is hardly used in

the kavyas (Kaul 2006, 62). The *nāṭyas* also do not idealise the man-about-the-town or *nāgaraka*. The denial highlights the code-practice relationship.

References

Ali, Daud. 2003. 'Gardens in Early Indian Court Life'. *Studies in History* Vol. 19 (2).

———. 2011. 'Rethinking the History of the Kama world in Early India'. *Journal of Indian Philosophy*, Vol. 39 (1).

———. 2016. *Bhoja's Mechanical Garden: Translating Wonder Across the Indian Ocean, circa 800–1100 AD*. Chicago: University of Chicago.

Ayyar, A.S.P. 1959. *Two Plays of Bhāsa*. Madras: Chandrika Press.

Bhattacharya, Kumkum. 2006. 'Non-Western Traditions: Leisure in India'. In *A Handbook of Leisure Studies*, edited by Chris Rojek, Susan M. Shaw and A.J. Veal. New York: Palgrave Macmillan.

Bowe, Patrick. 2016. 'Ancient Hindu Garden Design'. *Garden History*, Vol. 44 (2).

Cunningham, Kenneth R. 1961. 'The Meaning of Leisure: An Analysis of Community Studies'. *The Family Life Coordinator*, Vol. 6 (1).

Dasgupta, Nupur. 2016. 'Gardens in Ancient India: Concepts, Practices and Imaginations'. *Puravritta*, Vol. 1.

Devadhar, C.R. 1962. *Pratijñāyaugandharāyaṇa*. Poona: Oriental Book Agency.

Dhruva, K.H. 1923. *Mudrārākṣasa*. Poona: The Oriental Book Supplying Agency.

Doniger, Wendy and Sudhir Kakar. 2002. *Vātsyāyana Kāmasūtra*. New York: Oxford University Press.

Elington, Sam and Sean Gammon. 2015. *Reading Landscape: Articulating a Non-Essentialist Representation of Space, Place and Identity in Leisure*. New York: Palgrave MacMillan.

Ghosh, Manmohan. 1972. *Rājśekhara's Karpūramañjarī*. Calcutta: The World Press Pvt. Ltd.

Giri, Kapil Deva. 1966. *Mattavilāsaprahasanam*. Varanasi: Chaukhambha Vidyabhavan.

Kale, M.R. 1928. *Bhavabhūti's Mālatīimādhava*. Mumbai: Messrs Gopal Narayen & Com.

———. 2011. *Ratnāvalī of Śri Harṣa-Devā*. New Delhi: Motilal Banarsidass.

———. 2015. *The Mṛcchakaṭika of Śūdraka*. New Delhi: Motilal Banarsidass.

Karmarkar, R.D. 1950. *Mṛcchakaṭika of Śūdraka*. Poona.

Kaul, Shonaleeka. 2006. 'Women about Town: An Exploration of the Sanskrit Kavaya Tradition'. *Studies in History*, Vol. 22 (1).

Kunbae, Bak. 1968. *Avimāraka*. New Delhi: Meharchand Lachhmandas Publications.

Lockwood, Michael and A. Vishnu Bhat. 1978. *Bhagavadajjuka-Prahasana: A Philosophical Farce*. Madras: Christian Literature Society.

Lockwood, Michael and A. Vishnu Bhat. 2005. *Mattavilāsa Prahasana (A Farce of Drunken Sport)*. Madras: Christian Literary Society. (Fourth revised edition)

Motichandra and Vasudeva Agrawal. 1960. *Caturbhani: A Collection of Four Sanskrit Bhanas, One-actor Plays, Viz., Padmaprabhrtaka, Dhurt-vita-samvada, Ubhayabhisarika and Padataditakam*. Bombay: Hindi Grantha Ratnakar Private Limited.

Nariman, G.K., A.V. Williams Jackson, Charles J. Ogden and G.C.O. Haas. 2000. *Harsha Priyadarśikā*. Cambridge: In Parentheses Publications, Sanskrit Drama Series, Ontario.

Nariman, G.K., A.V. Williams Jackson and Charles J. Ogden. 1923. *Priyadarśikā: A Sanskrit Drama by Harsha*. New York: Columbia University Press.

Olivelle, Patrick (trans.). 2005. *Manu's Code of Law*. New York: Oxford University Press.

Rai, Ganga Sagar. 2014. *Mālatīimādhavaṃ*. Varanasi: Chaukhambha Vidyabhawan.

Rangarajan. 1992. *The Arthaśāstra*. New Delhi: Penguin Books.

Sastri, Sakuntala Rao. 1952. *Kaumudī-Mahotsva*. Bombay: Bhartiya Vidya Bhawan.

Schopen, Gregory. 2006. 'The Buddhist Monastery and the Indian Garden: Aesthetics, Assimilations and the Siting of Monastic Establishments'. *Journal of American Oriental Society*, Vol. 126 (4).

Shamasastry, R. 1929. *Kauṭilya Arthaśāstra*. Mysore: Mysore Printing and Publishing House.

Shastri, Rakesh. 2019. *Ratnāvalī Nātikā*. Varanasi: Chaukhambha Orientalia.

Sheemar, Tara. 2008. 'Gardens in the Kathasaritasagara'. *Proceedings of the Indian History Congress*, Vol. 69.

Singh, Upinder. 2017. *Political Violence in Ancient India*. Harvard: Harvard University Press.

Sinha, Kanad. 2013. 'Sporting with Kama: Amusements, Games, Sports and Festivities in Early Indian Urban Culture'. *Journal of Asiatic Society*, Vol. LV (2): 73–120.

Spracklen, Karl. 2011. *Constructing Leisure: Historical and Philosophical Debate*. New York: Palgrave Macmillan.

Tawney, C.H. 1875. *Mālavikāgnimitra*. Calcutta: Thacker Spink and Co.

The Kāmasūtra of Vātsyāyana. 1883–1925. Translated from the Sanskrit by The Hindoo Kama Shastra Society. Benaras–New York: Printed for the Society of the Friends for India.

Venkatacharya, T. and A.K. Warder. 1967. *The Ubhayabhisarika Both Go to Meet*. Madras: G.S. Press

Woolner, A.C. and Lakshman Sarup. 1999. *Svapnavāsavadatta of Bhāṣa*. Cambridge: Parentheses Publications, Sanskrit Drama Series, Ontario.

10

SLEEP AS LEISURE: PERSPECTIVES FROM PERSIAN LITERATURE

Farhat Nasreen

I have gone mad and madmen never sleep.
A madman, what does he know about sleep?
You know: God doesn't sleep. So none of that!
You know: I'm mad with love, so I can't sleep.
(Rumi–Banani and Lee 2014, 56–57)

I

Sleep is the meta-key of the human mind. It is a reversible behavioural state of perceptual disengagement from and unresponsiveness to the environment. Non-Rapid Eye Movement (NREM) and Rapid Eye Movement (REM) are the two states identified within sleep by electromagnetic medico devices (Golbin et al. 2004). It is circardian in the sense that it occurs naturally in a twenty-four-hour cycle. Its timely recurrence sets the 'body clock' and then all neuro-hormonal cycles get tuned with this 'clock'. The ideal precision in this clockwork is determined by two factors: the total sleep time and the consolidation of that time in one continuous stretch. Due to their exceptional mental capabilities, the humans can ward off or postpone sleep even if the clock signals otherwise. Nightmares, sleepwalking, bed-wetting and harmfulness of oversleeping notwithstanding sleep's importance for living beings can never ever be overstated. It has a bearing on alertness, memorisation, motor-functions, etc. A tilt in the fine balance of its excess or denial can cause forgetfulness, fretfulness, anger, unease and even fatal illnesses.

Guilt around sleeping is hard to understand because rarely do things vital for life carry blameworthiness. The fact that sleep is not just about sleeping, it is about productive wakefulness is often lost in the long list of 'things to do'. The presumption that there is a conflict between work and sleep is erroneous. No matter how irreconcilable they might seem, they are peas of the same pod. In ecopolitical cases, collaborations are often made with apparent/immediate competitors to defeat bigger common enemies. Likewise, fraternisation is required between seeming contestants: wakefulness and sleep. Yet, the fixation on quick results labels sleep as a waste of time.

The curiosity around sleep mysteries prompted religions to offer explanations. This created sleep-cultures. Religions have many lives; they are resurrected in different forms time and again. The fluidity in lived religiosity changes sleep cultures within a single religious framework. The case of moral values is no different. Unlike laws, they only persuade people to behave in a certain manner. Laws force them. Since morals don't rest on legal pillars, they lean on religions for legitimisation. In this backdrop, the idea of sleep as leisure was usually bashed up by both, religions and the moral systems. Popular cultural perceptions drove choices around spending leisure. Sleep was never considered a good way to expend it, the halo of pleasure around it notwithstanding.

Religious righteousness attached shame with sleeping even before materialism did. Thus, the general feeling of guilt around sleeping for leisure stabilised in sleep cultures from a very early date. However, it is difficult to pin point exactly when, why or how sleep was huddled together with religious transgressions. Interestingly, Will Durant and Ariel Durant say that probably every vice was once a virtue. A quality which was needed for survival at a given point in time was a virtue at that time. Once its requirement ceased, it was forgotten or degenerated into a vice (Durant and Will 1968). Thus, vices and virtues were repeatedly redefined. Without artificial lights, sundown would imply closure of the day. Sleeping tight till sunrise would be a virtue and a boon. But, with artificial light, the day encroached upon the night. Sleep became a victim of the extended day and its ambitions. It became a vice to sleep from sunset to sunrise. Some relatable examples of vice–virtue shifts are those of intelligence becoming more important than just physicality or frugality and thrift giving way to the culture of 'YOLO' (you only live once) driven expenditures. For economic prosperity, peace has become more profitable than war and so on. Religions generally condemned sleeping for leisure almost in the same way as they were inclined to condemn sexual activity unless it was for procreation. As social formations matured, private ownership grew into the giant of greed. Sleep apparently inactivated human productivity and so the giant slayed it—piece by piece, hour by hour, minute by minute. After the Industrial Revolution, the machines were expected to gift leisure to the humans. However, whatever 'free-time' they created was spent either on making more machines or entertainment. Sleep continued and continues to strive for a fair share in leisure.

Bertland Russel in his timeless work *In Praise of Idleness* argues in favour of the availability of equal leisure for everyone. He laments that materialism and profit motive mess up the distribution of work and leisure. When money becomes a symbol of power, it changes the way people understand the value of things in life. To put it more simply, they forget that the most important things in life are not 'things'. There was a time when sleep was induced by the natural darkness after sunset but, with continuous scientific progression, man mastered the ability to elongate lighted hours, sun or no sun. As the world of daily life became increasingly 'manmade', man became trivial, arrogant and a little mad. Russel felt that the desire for wealth threatens the desire for peace and rest. So the road to happiness and prosperity lies in an organised diminution of work. But the reality is that the obsession with 'work' grew. No wonder Russel's idea of limiting working time to just four hours a day is yet to find serious takers (Russel 1935). With the growth of the idea that 'doing nothing' was equivalent to doing something harmful, sleep became synonymous with sin and stupidity. The cult of efficiency ambushed sleep.

Luckily, the spiritual language of dreams shielded sleep. It came to be universally believed that people could have spiritual or satanic experiences or get instructions, warnings, predictions, etc. while they slept. The idea washed off some disrepute from sleeping, but it wasn't entirely laundered. The receipt of mystic and divinely inspired dreams largely remained the prezzie of the spiritual, rich or powerful ones. So the justification for sleeping for dreaming depended on who was sleeping, who was dreaming and, more importantly, what did they usually do when awake. The contents of the dreams would be situated as a revelation, mystic experience, satanic prank or irrelevant nonsense accordingly.

Abraham/Ibrahim's dream forms the backbone of the Islamic idea of absolute surrender and submission to the will of god. He had dreamt that he is sacrificing his son. When he narrated this dream to his son, the latter requested his father to follow the command received in the dream. Accordingly, when he had laid his son down on his face, god stopped him and called out: 'Abraham you have fulfilled the dream' (*Quran*, 37). This encouraged the belief that divine orders could be received in sleep. The story of the prophet Yusuf shows that future could be predicted by a correct interpretation of dreams (*Quran*). He was imprisoned by the king of Egypt over some false charge. Two other men were also arrested on the same day as him. They were the king's cupbearer and a baker. Both of them were accused of trying to poison the king. One night, both of them dreamt. The cupbearer saw that he was pressing grapes to make wine and the baker saw that he was carrying bread over his head and birds were pecking at it. Yusuf interpreted these dreams. He predicted that the cupbearer would be released and will serve wine to the monarch. The baker would receive death sentence and birds would peck at his brains. This is exactly what happened. However, the cupbearer forgot Yusuf's request for intercession with the king for his freedom. One night, the king dreamt that seven weak cows devoured seven fat ones and seven green ears of corn were replaced by seven dry ones. Now the cupbearer remembered Yusuf and recommended him for decoding the dream. The latter was summoned and he interpreted that Egypt will have excellent yields for seven years followed by seven years of famine. The seven years of famine would empty the granaries and treasuries that had been accumulated in the seven years preceding them. To counter the situation, the Egyptians must prepare in the first seven years for the next seven. The king was convinced and he freed Yusuf from captivity to manage the finances and produce of his kingdom (*Quran*, S12). Thus, interpretation of dreams became a part of *istakhara* (divination; a word that emanates from *khair*; meaning good).

In the Islamic belief, Yusuf's good looks could never be surpassed by another. His and Zulaikha's love story is perhaps the only super intense romance which finds place in the *Quran*. Jami in a highly dramatised version which writes that Zulaikha was a chaste princess who had never seen a man in her waking hours. Once she saw Yusuf in a dream and fell in love with the unknown man of her dreams. As Jami puts it:

> It happened one sweet night, sweet as the dawn of life, full of the exhilaration of youth … Night like a thief had robbed the guards of all sensation. Sweet sleep weighed down Zulaikha's eyelids … The eyes that see the form of things were closed in sleep; but those other eyes the eyes of her heart, were wide open: and with them she suddenly saw a youth; or rather a pure spirit … No sooner had this vision appeared to Zulaikha … she fell in love with all her heart … God, What a vision! At length the graceful phantom vanished … Zulaikha in her waking life had never set eyes on a man, her companion thought that the present calamity must be the result of a dream. (Jami–Pendlebury 1980)

Before dreaming of Yusuf, Zulaikha used to sleep like a 'narcissus steeped in water; in the morning she opened up like a laughing blossom'. After the dream, her sleep was 'not a wholesome sleep: merely a state of crazed unconsciousness caused by her nocturnal vision' (ibid.).To cure her of lovesickness, her nurse told her that this dream is perhaps the work of spiteful and sly demons who want humans to go mad with love for the beautiful visions they show them in their dreams. However, this didn't work because Zulaikha continued to dream of Yusuf and communicate with him in her dreams. Eventually, she went to Egypt in his search and by mistake ended up marrying the wrong man—Al Aziz. Even marriage didn't deter her from pursuing the man of her dreams. In fact, when her extramarital advances towards Yusuf were spurned by the latter and the matter came to her husband's notice, she accused Yusuf of inappropriate behaviour. However, eventually, she told the truth. Years passed and she aged but could never get over her insanely helpless attraction and adoration for Yusuf. Interestingly, the *Quran* maintains a mysterious silence around the later part of her life but imaginative writers like Jami present powerful and allegorical account of her and Yusuf's connection from the world of dreams. That in a way redeems her of all lapses. Imam Ibn Kathir (d. 870 AD) notes that the legends about her were always afloat. Some said that she married Yusuf and was a virgin when she did. Others say that she lost her eyesight crying for him, abandoned the palace and wandered in the streets (*Quran*, S-12 and Kathir–Gemeiah 1997). One of the most famous dreams of Prophet Muhammad is when he saw that the Muslims had gone for a pilgrimage to Kabah in Mecca before their victory over Mecca. This dream did not materialise into reality immediately; nonetheless, its authenticity was validated in the *Quran* by the word of God: 'God has in all truth shown his Messenger a true vision in which he said, "God willing, you will most certainly enter the sacred mosque in safety and without fear, shaven headed or with hair cut short"—God knew what you did not; and has given you a victory beforehand' (*Quran*, S-48: 27).

According to *Fawaid ul Fuad*, Shaikh Nizamuddin Auliya narrated the sleep experience of a Turk called Tiklish. Once in a dream he saw god himself. He narrated this dream to Shaikh Najibuddin Mutawakkil but requested the Shaikh to keep it a secret till Tiklish lived. Forty years later, when he was close to death, Tiklish told the Shaikh that he is still frozen in the state of spirituality that he felt in that dream and that he would die in the same state. He had lived in one dream for forty years! That indeed was some fruit of sleep (Sijzi–Lawrence 1992).

In the *Tarikh-I Firozshahi*, Ziauddin Barani reports that Alauddin Khalji was worried when he didn't receive any news from his armies in the Deccan commanded by Malik Kafur. He sent Malik Qara Beg and Qazi Mughisuddin to Shaikh Nizamuddin Auliya to enquire whether the Shaikh had any divine intuition about some happy news (*basharat*) from Deccan. The messengers were instructed to hear each word of the Shaikh carefully and note it. The Shaikh replied: 'What to say of this victory, we expect many more victories.' When Alauddin heard of this, he was convinced that his armies had been successful. Barani notes that indeed the Shaikh was right because the

Fatehnamas (declaration of victories) arrived soon after (Barani–Zilli 2015). In fact, the relationship of the Shaikh with dreams and *Kashf* (revelation) seems to have been an inheritance from his mother. It is believed that in a dream someone had given his mother, Bibi Zulekha, a choice between the life of her husband and her son and she chose her son to survive. He did. Her husband, Khwaja Ahmad, fell ill soon after the dream and eventually passed away (Sijzi–Lawrence). Shaikh Nizamuddin Auliya claimed to have come very close to god in his sleep and felt an intense desire for Him in a dream. He narrated that this dream was like a blazing fire. He uttered in his sleep that he had been slain by his friend (Sijzi–Lawrence). Speaking of Qutubuddin Hyder, the founder of the Hyderi sect of mystics, Shaikh Nizamuddin said that he had dreamt of Mongol invasions much in advance of their actual occurrence. To authenticate the Syed (belonging to the Prophet's bloodline) lineage of Syed Tajuddin, the Qazi of Awadh and Badaun in the reign of Alauddin Khalji, Barani writes: 'A number of pious men and seekers of God had seen the Prophet in dream in his resemblance. His resemblance to the Prophet (in the dreams of pious people) is a clear evidence of his pure lineage' (Barani–Zilli 2015).

As David Lelyveld puts it, the dreams of an important person were remembered, narrated and interpreted within the boundaries of the dream culture in which he lived. He analyses the dreams of Sir Syed Ahmad Khan and concludes that Khan's dreams were instrumental in convincing self and the world that he was inspired and validated by Islam in the decisive moves that he made as a guide of his coreligionists (Lelyveld 2013).

Studies on how dreams and their interpretations were used for political or religious legitimisation give an insight into the value of sleep for the elite. Their extraordinary dreams were after all dependent on sleeping. In Persian texts, dreams predicting future greatness of great men when they were still 'ordinary' are quite popular. The *Hasht Bihisht* has narratives of many ancient dreams. Mirkhvand's *Rawzat al Safa* and Khvandmir's *Habib al Siyar* narrate dreams of Timur's ancestor Qachulay. *Akbarnama* has numerous dream narratives predicting the future greatness of the Mughal Emperor Akbar. As successive authors rewrote dreams of celebrated persons, they became increasingly sharp in matching narrative details and predictions with the place of that person in history. The increasing complexity of dream cultures was such that narratives of Mughal Emperor Jahangir's dreams were adamant in devising ways of making him seem more successful than his super-powerful father (Quinn 2021). Dream legitimisation was not limited only to the political arena, it crossed the spiritual perimeter as well. It is believed that the narration of his dream by Gisu Daraz prompted the

Chishti Sufi saint Nasiruddin to declare the former as his *sajjada-nashin* (spiritual heir) (Eaton 2005).

In the *Bakhtiyarnamah* is the story of a childless king. In his dream, an old man said to him: 'The Lord has complied with thy request and tomorrow thou shalt have a son, but in his seventh year a lion shall seize and carry him off to the top of a mountain from which he shall fall, rolling in blood and clay' (Clouston 1889, xxxviii). The interpreters of dreams said that it meant that the king will be killed by his own son after twenty years. The king's efforts to undo the *istakhara* notwithstanding in time the child was snatched by a lion and dropped off a hillock; rolling in blood and clay. However, the prince survived the fall. He was raised by one of the officers and later grew up to be an accomplished armour bearer for his biological father. The father and son were unaware about their personal relationship. As luck would have it, an accidental stroke from the prince's sword gave a deadly wound to the king. A suspicion arose that perhaps he is the lost prince. Investigations revealed that indeed he was. The king declared him to be his heir. The dream was their destiny (ibid., xxxix).

In Arabic, bad dreams are called *Hulum*; *Manaam* is used for ordinary dreams and *Ruyaa* for heavenly visions. It is reported in the *hadis* that the Prophet had said that a good dream denotes God's favour and a bad one signifies the devil's mischief. A pleasing dream should only be shared with a trusted friend or a well-wisher. A bad dream should not be narrated to anyone. In case of a nightmare, the concerned person must seek refuge in god's mercy from the wickedness of the Satan. He could spit three times over his left shoulder. The truest dreams are dreamt close to daybreak (Hughes 1993).

However, all this fuss over dreams was for the extraordinary; it was almost impossible for the ordinary to create a cultural commotion by just dreaming. So the massive majority of the sleepers found it difficult to justify sleeping for fun and being happy about it.

II

The *Atharvaveda* says that neither alive nor dead; Sleep is the immortal child of Varunani and Yama (the god of death). It is an ender; a temporary death. In a hymn, a devotee begs Sleep to save the sleeper from nightmares and transfer them to his enemies (Bulkeley 2008, 231 and 237). In the *Vishnu Purāṇa,* the *Yoga-nidra* (meditative-sleep) of Shri Vishnu is related to the dissolution and recreation of the world. It states that when the world nears dissolution, it rains so much that the whole of it becomes one large ocean. Then Shri Vishnu's breath becomes a strong wind that blows for a hundred years dispelling all the clouds. When the clouds clear, the wind is reabsorbed and Shri Vishnu goes off to sleep on the Shesha Naag—a massive cosmic snake resting on the cosmic waters. Later, when the universal spirit wakes, the world revives. When he closes his eyes, all things fall into the bed of a mystic slumber (*Vishnu Purāṇa*-Wilson 1895). This sleep of Shri Vishnu falls in the four rainy months of the Indian subcontinent and during this period pilgrimages and other activities which entail travel were stopped. Florae and faunae regenerate in this season. The idea of *Deva-shayani* (sleep of the divinity) gave an opportunity for the nature to revivify itself with the least of human intervention. Although religious systems recognised the essentiality of sleep to reawaken faculties, limits were set on it. In the *Bhagavad Gītā*, Shri Kṛṣṇa advices moderation in sleeping:

> He who eats too much food or too little, who is always drowsy or restless, will never succeed in the yoga of meditation.
>
> For the man who is moderate in food and pleasure, moderate in action, moderate in sleep and waking, yoga destroys all sorrow. (*Bhagavad Gītā*-Mitchell 2000)

Speaking of the qualities of men, Shri Kṛṣṇa says:

> The three *gunas*, born of Nature-*sattva*, *rajas*, *tamas*-bind to the mortal body the deathless embodied Self.
>
> Of the three, *sattva* untainted luminous, free from sorrow bind by means of attachment to knowledge and joy Arjuna.
>
> *Rajas* is marked by passion born of craving and attachment; it binds the embodied Self to never-ending activity.
>
> *Tamas* ignorance born deludes all embodied beings; it binds them Arjuna by means of dullness, indolence and sleep. (ibid.)

III

A large body of the medieval Persian writings on sleep are generated against the *Quranic* backdrop and the sleep culture which developed around the Muslim mystics. Sleep appears as a gift from god in the eighteenth surah of the *Quran*; entitled *Al-Kahaf* (The Cave). This narrative has a Christian version as well. In the reign of a Roman emperor who persecuted Christians, perhaps Emperor Decius,[1] seven Christian men of Ephesus[2] left the town and hid in a cave. They fell asleep and kept sleeping for a few centuries.[3] Finally, they were awakened by the demolition of the wall which had sealed the cave in which they slept. This probably happened in the reign of Theodosius II (408–450 AD). They felt that they had slept just for a bit, but when one of them went to buy provisions he realised that the world and its religious fads had changed. Christianity, their religion, was now the State religion. Their clothes and currency revealed that they belonged to a bygone era. This made news and the learned men of the times visited the cave for verification. They believed the men and perhaps something was inscribed at the mouth of the cave to preserve the spot and its history. The official version of the commentary on the *Quran*, published by the government of Saudi Arabia, states that hundreds of years later, Khalifa Wathiq (842–846 CE) had sent expeditions to examine and identify the locality of this cave (*Quran*, pp. 818–21). In the Quranic version, these men had begged God for protection and their prayers were answered in the form of a spell of sleep that lasted for centuries. They were divinely guided to the cave where they slept. The *Quran* states:

> *Thou wouldst have thought them awake, whilst they were asleep, and We turned them on their right and on their left sides ... If thou hadst looked at them, thou wouldst have certainly turned back from them in flight, and wouldst certainly have been filled with terror.* (*Quran*, S-18: 18)

Thus, sleep was God's tool to protect them (ibid.). They literally slept their troubles away. The surah besides other things speaks of the relativity of time. When these men woke up, they were in the same state of mind in which they had slept. For them time had not passed, but in fact it had. Indeed, such is the magic of sleep!

The idea of sleep as a reward from god occurs in the *Vishnu Purāṇa* as well. A man called Muchukunda had received a boon from a deity to sleep for extremely long periods of time. The blessing was fortified by a bonus that anyone who woke him would be consumed by a fire. Shri Kṛṣṇa tricked one of his enemies into waking Muchukunda (*Vishnu Purāṇa*). The case of Kumbha Karan, the brother of Ravan of Sri Lanka, is another instance of divinely induced sleep. He was cruel, but a tenacious devotee as well. After prolonged prayers, he planned to ask for the *Indra-Asan* (throne of god Indra) as a boon. To protect the realm from his oppression the gods intervened and made him ask for *Nidra-Asan* (seat of sleep) instead of *Indra-Asan*. Shaikh Sa'di reinforces the idea of the sleep of an oppressor being a blessing for the oppressed. He narrates that once a cruel king asked a hermit that what would be the best act of devotion that he could offer god. The reply was that, for him, the best act would be to sleep in the noon. It was implied that with the king sleeping in the peak business hours subjects would be spared of his ruthlessness. In fact, the Shaikh goes on to write that a man who is so evil that he is better asleep than awake, would be better off dead. Here sleep protects the world from the sleeper (Sa'di Shirazi–Thackston 2008). So, at least, the evil got a ticket to guilt-free sleep.

IV

For the common man, sleep meant by and large a pleasurable experience. Ibn Khaldun considered it to be a gift from God. When Al Ghizali wrote about the terror of death in his landmark work *Kitaab-Zirk Al-Maut-wa-ma-Bada-hu*, he said:

> *Death is the most fearsome terror that the believer will encounter in this world or in the next. It is worse than being carved up with saws, or being cut with scissors, or being boiled in cauldrons. If a dead man could be brought back to life to tell this world's people of death, they would find no profit in life and take no pleasure in sleeping.* (Al-Ghizali–Winter 1999)

Here sleep occurs on one side of the scale while on the other are the good things of the waking world. So, both the waking and sleeping worlds are equally precious and equally threatened by the thought of the eternal joy killer: death. Incidentally, the Prophet advised Muslims to remember death as often as they could.

The notion of sleep for the pleasure of sleeping was as loved as it was hated. The rich found it easier to brush aside the guilt around sleeping for fun. However, for the poor, sleep seemed to contribute to the causes of their poverty. Helping people sleep in leisure for pleasure was an industry in itself. Storytellers were employed to narrate soothing pre-sleep tales. Often, the story was left midway when the listener dozed off and was picked up from the same point later. If the storyteller was not a servant, he would usually expect the listener to indicate that he wasn't asleep yet by adding a word or two in the narration. Singing lullaby and reading books were all methods of putting people to a calm sleep. The rich even employed slaves to 'talk' them to sleep (Ali–Crooke 2020). The Persian text of *Qissa-i-Chahar-Darvesh*, a collection of stories, was translated by Mir Amman into Urdu in 1803 CE. He entitled the translation as *Bagh-o-Bahar* and attributed the original writing to Amir Khusroe (d. 1325 CE). Amman noted that the stories were narrated by Amir Khusroe to his spiritual guide Shaikh Nizamuddin Auliya while the latter was unwell and perhaps sleepless. It is a set of four stories with numerous complicated subplots (Mir Amman–Zakir 1994). The multitude of subplots indicates that the stories were to be narrated in small portions over many days. Speaking of the idea of sleep induction and dream incubation, the lore around these stories is classic, because they not only put the Shaikh to sleep but also cured him! This generated the belief that if a sick person listened to these stories before sleeping, he would recover by divine grace. He would be magically healed in his sleep.

In the *Baburnama*, Babur noted the death of the man who was employed to tell stories to his son and heir Humayun; the second Mughal emperor (Nasreen 2021). Many years later, when Humayun was well past forty years of age, he was betrayed by his brother Kamran. The realisation of the betrayal made him so sleepless that he laid his head in the lap of one of his nobles and asked the latter to sing him a lullaby (ibid.). In the *Haft Paikar*, Nizami Ganjavi narrates the story of an epileptic princess who just couldn't sleep: 'with eyes of ox, like lion all perturbed, by night not resting, sleeping not by day' (Nizami–Wilson 1914). Her father, the king, announced that whoever helped his daughter sleep would be given her hand in marriage. However, death would be the punishment if they tried and failed. Many lives were lost until the arrival of a mystic whose magical concoction made the princess sleep. This sleep physician was a selfless healer. He left the palace without claiming the prize—the princess. On waking up after three days, the first person whom she wished to meet was the magic medic. Learning of his vanishing act, she insisted that she will marry only if he is the groom. Now a royal search began. Finally, he was found and the princess married the man who made her sleep. In the description of the princess's sleep, Nizami emphasises that her perpetual wakefulness would have made her mad and perhaps eventually caused her death. He writes:

> *He (the mystic doctor) caused the princess (then) to drink the draught; and from the brain the rouble was dispelled; that tumult which was madness she escaped; as soon as she had drunk the draught she slept. When Good (the mystic) perceived that she a flowering spring slept quickly, from troubles onslaughts saved-He came from that celestial haram forth and towards his home returned with joyous heart. And she of fairy face slept on three days, her father unacquainted with her state. On the third day when she upraised her head, she ate such food as she found suitable.* (ibid.)

Thus, Ganjavi emphasised that none of the riches of the world could be a substitute for sleeping. Narratives of this kind created drama and romance around sleeping. In fact, Ganjavi artfully uses sleep or sleeplessness to denote many situations; here is a description of the beauty of sleepy eyes which steal the sleep of onlookers:

> *The fresh narcissus with (its) sleepy eyes; deprived of sleep the eyes of all it saw.*

Or

> *Her languorous drowsy glances by their spells banished from more than thousand lovers sleep.* (ibid.)

Contrast to this is the description of peaceful sleep in a lover's arms; he writes:

> Extending then his head to the red rose (his beautiful wife), he took her to his arms, in comfort slept.

Or

> Having these words of happy import spoken, they went to sleep in ease and cheerfulness. (ibid.)

V

Philosophers always recognised that sleep was the doorway to the world of unlimited possibilities. Although that world was not as easily understandable as the waking world but it was a world nonetheless. In this sense, sleep was liberating. It freed the soul from the physical chores of the everyday life. Even in very little time it could travel to go anywhere, see and do anything. The *Katha Upanishad* states:

> Sitting it (the soul) goes afar, sleeping it goes everywhere. (*Vishnu Purāṇa*)

No wonder, the limitlessness of possibilities in sleep were a matter of concern for the propriety driven waking world. The *Ṛig Veda* has a hymn summoning Agni, the killer of demons, to protect pregnant women and their unborn children as they sleep. The imagery of the demon who approaches these women in the dark is rather eerie:

> The one who bewitches you with sleep or darkness and lies with you- We will drive him away from here.... The one who spreads apart your two thighs, The one who lies between a married pair, who licks the inside of your womb—we will drive him away from here-the one who by changing into your brother or your husband or your lover

> lies with you, who wishes to kill your offspring-we will drive him away from here. (Bulkeley 2008, 231 and 237)

In a philosophical sense, sleep can have multiple implications: death, physical sleep, sheer ignorance, a low spiritual station, etc. In fact, we use a timeless cross-cultural metaphor when we speak of death as sleep or of ignorance as a slumber which can be ended only with enlightenment of some kind. For an example, Attar wrote:

> Heedless heart, don't sleep. Get up! The One we love is resting in those lover's breasts before us. (Lewisohn and Shackle 2006)

This 'getting up' is spiritual awakening. The urgency to wake up from spiritual sleep is justified by the unpredictability and suddenness of physical death. The spiritualists argue that, if someone dies physically without being spiritually awake, his losses will be eternal. While justifying the compilation of his famous *Mantiq-al tayr*, Attar wrote:

> So I as well like all the rest (writers on mysticism) have shown the sleepers how the bird of the soul has flown.

Attar noted that sleep too, like all other things, comes only by the will of god and so does awakening, both physical and spiritual. Speaking of a renowned Sufi, Abu-al-Husayn Nuri, he wrote:

> The Mighty and Glorious Lord has people who stand entirely through Him, who move and rest entirely through Him, who live through Him and who abide through the contemplation of Him. If they stop contemplating the real, their souls fly from them. They sleep through Him, they eat through Him. They hear through Him, they exist through Him. (ibid.)

Maulana Rumi equated death with awakening and the worldly life as sleeping:

> Evil and Good-Pure wine and dregs am I. Now old-now young-a new born babe am I. When I die, don't say that he died, just say: His lover woke him up, took him away. (Rumi–Banani and Lee 2014)

In Rumi's lines cited at the beginning of this write-up, madness is the code for real sanity. The distilled wisdom which comes with spiritual awakening only seems like madness to a 'mad' world. Once the mind is awakened, it cannot fall into the slumber of ignorance. Anyone who is truly awake cannot sleep. The sleepless madness is so vital in the metaphorical sense that Rumi goes on to write:

> If I am not mad by now then that is madness. (Rumi–Banani and Lee 2014)

Notwithstanding the metaphoric connection of death with sleep, it always has interesting conversations around it. The mystic writings in Persian judge an insomniac with different scales depending upon why he got insomnia. For example, insomnia for love of god is considered akin to an act of worship. Rumi lists sleep with seriously powerful things like patience, seas and mountains:

> Be patient and I'll tear your patience up!
> Sleep. Then I'll rip the sleep from your eye-cup.
> Be a mountain. I'll set you on fire.
> If you become the sea I'll drink you up. (ibid.)

And yet even he cannot ignore the pleasure of sleeping in leisure:

> Last night you left, had a good sleep out there. Tonight you are gone fooling around somewhere. I thought you will lie next to me forever-
> So where are all the drunken vows you swear? (ibid.)

Ziauddin Barani writes that great mystic spiritualists prayed right through the nights during the month of fasting, the nights of Fridays and on all the other special days which were considered to be important to please God. Even on usual days the devout ones offered prayers for two-thirds of the night and some one-third of the night. Some could even offer the morning prayers with the ablution of the night prayer, implying that they neither slept nor used the washroom throughout the night (Barani–Zilli 2015).

Paradoxically, the usefulness of physical sleep as a necessity to be alert in prayers is also recognised. The *Ilahinamah* mentions a man who was famous for his devotion to God. It was said of him:

> *He does not rest by day or sleep at night; he weeps so many tears that his eyes are dried out.*

When a more learned mystic heard of his condition, he went to meet the man. He said to the insomniac that by shunning sleep he had in reality missed the opportunity of being truly close and thankful to God.

When the sleepless man realised that his style of devotion was flawed, he dropped dead and slept; a sleep that could be interrupted only by God. (Lewisohn and Shackle 2006).

Nizami Ganjavi in the *Haft Paikar* writes about both, physical and spiritual sleep. A dying king counsels his son in the following words:

> My son I bid you earnestly take care that you be wakeful-I have gone to sleep. (Nizami–Wilson 1914)

The importance of alertness in a big bad world is emphasised by the metaphor of not sleeping:

> A friend whose breath is bad is better, far than one who speaking (only) nonsense talks. The vice of one associate is enough to give a bad name to a hundred men. The swallowing of coin by one who's poor tears many stomachs on the pilgrims road. On such a road (then) sleep not like the old; withdraw your skirt from those who seize the weak. (ibid.)

In context of physical sleep, Nizami counsels that sleep-induced laziness can increase dependence upon others and decrease self-respect:

> From your own tray it is better to give bread than to eat 'Halva' from the mean man's tray. Since sharp dagger has been drawn by dawn, how long Nizami will you sleep? Arise! Do miner's work and vex not at your toil: Open to men the door of hidden stores. (ibid.)

In a sequence when the protagonist of *Haft Paikar*, Bahram, pleads his case to secure the throne, he admits his mistake of over sleeping in the past and vows to be different. He says that there are some lucky people whose luck befriends their sleep. Although he had slept heavily and for long, his good fortune was still by his side. In fact, it is his good luck that has woken him and that he is happy to be awake (ibid.). It was argued that the price that one would pay for the sleep of negligence would eventually be decided by fate (ibid.). Indeed, fortune works even when we sleep:

> What do you (my faithful friends) well-wishers think? Think they the heavenly planets do not work? Though be drunk and sleep, fortune awake is (busied) with some work (on my behalf). Despite the sleep (in) which I was (immersed), behold how I disturbed the Khaqaan's (an enemy's) sleep! The man who through his weakness does not sleep at night upon his watch is (but) a dog. The lion through his bold can enter not the dragon's door, though in his cave he (the dragon) sleeps. (ibid.)

Appreciation for duty bound wakefulness is reflected in the protagonist's declaration that he has no share in any food or sleep. He stands all night (to pray) and always fasts. He doesn't eat in the day because he has no food and he doesn't sleep at night because he has no home (Nizami–Wilson 1914). Then there are other insomniacs in the narrative who were kept awake by worries of the day (ibid.). Nizami seemed to understand very well that fatigue is not equal to sleepiness and insomnia is not equal to alertness. Thus, he advised to use wisdom to safeguard oneself in a chaotic world where nights are risky, guards asleep and the robbers are out on the roads (ibid.).

VI

The Persian story titled Gulbakawali presents one of the most dramatic descriptions of sleeping in leisure.[4] Herein, the sleep of princess Gulbkawali is the pivot of the narrative. The story revolves around the life of Gulbakawali and prince Taj-ul Mulk. The latter was the fifth son of King Zayn-ul Muluk who ruled over eastern Hindustan. The astrologers had predicted that if the king saw Taj-ul Mulk he would turn blind. Thus, this prince was sent away to a secluded place where the king's sight would not fall on him. As luck would have it, during a hunt, the king and the prince accidentally came face to face. As predicted, the king turned blind. As a punishment, the prince was banished and his mother was demoted to be a maid of the royal harem. The healers opined that the king's eyes could be healed only with the rose of princess Bakawali; the Gul-Bakawali. Bakawali/Gulbakawali's father was a *Jinn* (Genii) and her garden was guarded by a thousand *devs* (giants). It was beyond the reach of mortals. Taj-ul-Mulk reached the princess' garden and plucked the rose as she slept. While sneaking out of the palace, he had a glimpse of the sleeping princess which left him mesmerised. The rose of Bakawali bloomed in a pond made of precious stones and filled with pure rosewater. The walls around the ponds were made of ruby and jasper. When he was leaving after stealing the rose, he saw a hall made entirely of ruby. The jewels in the window screens of this room glittered like stars. In this room on a magnificent couch slept Gulbakawali:

> A slender beauty fast locked in the arms of sleep. Her hair was dishevelled. Slight marks of the lamp black were observable round her closed eyes, her bodice was loosened, her waistband very much removed from its proper place and her trouser sleeves were pulled up and bunches of strings hanging loosely. With her fair hands gracefully laid upon her forehead, she was sleeping the sleep of innocent youth.

> The ruddiness of her cheeks brightened the world and cast the sun and moon into the shade. Those black eyes would have shamed even the narcissus and the redness of her lips would make the heart of the tulip bleed. The arch of her eyebrows made the crescent hide its face and the locks of night paled before the shady blackness of her raven hair.'
>
> The prince exchanged rings with the sleeping princess. Though he had got the flower, still he was saddened at the thought separation from the sleeping beauty. He said: 'In this garden I have entered and I go without a flower. (Clouston 1889)

Here the beauty of sleeping was in itself enchanting enough to make the prince fall in love with the sleeping beauty. The relaxed wakening of the princess was like an extension of her leisurely sleep:

> … she fastened her bodice, put her dress in order, drew the comb through her hair and went to the lake where her cherished rose grew. (ibid.)

The missing rose and the changed ring were noticed immediately. She instantly fell in love with the unseen stranger who had robbed her in her sleep. So, it wasn't just the flower that was stolen while she slept, her heart too was gone.

Later in the story, Gulbakawali left her palace in the search of her beloved. Adventures followed; she became a dancer in the court of Shri Indra, the king of Amravati. Eventually, she abandoned his court to be married to Taj-ul Mulk. On being informed that Gulbkawali has left without permission due to her love for a human being, an agitated Shri Indra summoned her to his presence immediately. Fairies arrived at Gulbakawali's residence while she was asleep in the arms of Taj-ul Mulk. They woke her and delivered Indra's summon. She had no choice but to leave with them. Asleep, Taj-ul Mulk didn't realise that Gulbakawli left his bedside. At Shri Indra's court, she had to be burnt to ashes to get rid of the fragrance of the human body which she had acquired due to her association with Taj-ul Mulk. The ashes were then brought to life again. Thereafter, she visited the court of Indra every night while Taj-ul Mulk slept. One night, he woke up and to his dismay realised that his wife was missing from the house. He didn't question her and just acted normally the whole day. At dusk he slashed his finger and stuffed salt in it so that the pain wouldn't let him sleep. He lay awake when the fairies arrived in a heavenly chariot to take Gulbakawali with them. He hung on to the chariot and reached Shri Indra's court. He witnessed Gulbakaali being burnt to ashes and then becoming alive again. He realised that she endured this torture just because she loved him. He quietly attended the court every night. Once he got an opportunity to play the music while Gulbakawali danced. Impressed, Shri Indra offered the musician to ask for a prize. He asked for Gulbakawali! The fulcrum of this story is sleep.

In a Persian folktale, three wives were challenged to trick their husbands. A precious ring was the prize for the greatest deception. The wife of the superintendent of police asked him to take a day off from work so that she could make a grand meal for him. He did as asked. Since he was tired and hadn't slept the night before, he dozed off while his wife cooked. His wife had expected this since her husband was usually overworked. She quickly mixed some opiate matter in a dish and fed him that for further sedation. She said:

> How long will you sleep? This is a day of feasting and pleasure, not of sleep and laziness. Lift up your head and see if I have made the sweets according to your taste. (Clouston 1889)

The poor fellow ate the drugged food and dozed off again; this time into a much deeper slumber. Now she shaved off his beard, tattooed his body and dressed him up in the robes of a Qalandar and had him dropped at a convent of qalandars. When the superintendent woke up and found himself amidst qalandars, he wasn't sure whether he was asleep or awake, conscious or dreaming. When he tried to find his way back home, his wife refused to accept him saying that this wasn't her husband; he was some stranger who was trying to sneak into her home. The confused superintendent, unsure of his reality, reconciled with the situation and started living with the qalandars. After a few days, his wife pitied his state and had him drugged again and brought him back home in a sleeping state. She wore the same clothes which she had worn on the day when he was initially put to sleep and the whole scenario of that day was recreated. Then she woke him up saying, 'O superintendent, do not sleep so much. I have told you that we are to spend the day in joy and festivity and it was not right for you to pass the time in this lazy manner. Lift up your head and see the beautiful sweetmeats I have baked for you.' When the superintendent woke up this time and found himself at home with his 'loving' wife, he thanked god for waking him from a terrible nightmare. His wife convinced him that his restless blabbering in his sleep had indicated that he was indeed seeing some 'strange dream' (ibid.). Anyway, the fear of nightmares notwithstanding, sleep was considered to be something that brought pleasure. It seemed like an easy-breezy, cost-free way to spend time.

According to Sa'di Shirazi, a thing worse than sleeping was eating. He writes that once there was an ascetic who ate ten maunds of food in a day and recited the whole *Quran* before the next dawn. The Shaikh opined that he would have been a much better person if he ate just half a loaf and went off to sleep. He advised his readers to keep their insides free from food so that they could see the light of gnosis. According to him, people are devoid of wisdom because they are full of food. It may be noted that for once the culprit here is food, not sleep (Sa'di Shirazi–Thackston 2008). The stubborn demands of the stomach were feared more than eyelids drooping with sleep. Sa'di wrote:

> *If there is no pillow stuffed with feathers, one can sleep with a stone under one's head.... It is only the useless good for nothing belly that cannot wait for anything.* (ibid.)

He describes how over eating is an enemy of sleep:

> *A prisoner of the gut has two nights in which he does not sleep: One night from a heavy stomach and one night from regret.* (ibid.)

In fact, Sa'di values sleeping at the right time and the right place, he recognises the physical need for sleep but feels that it should not be ill-timed. In one instance, a man fell asleep while travelling through the desert due to sheer fatigue. His guide woke him and said that safety is ahead and thieves are behind. If he moves, he lives and if he sleeps he dies.

Pretty much like a precursor of Robert Frost's poem:

> Woods are lovely dark and deep
> but I have promises to keep
> And miles to go before I sleep,
> And miles to go before I sleep.

Sa'di writes:

> It is pleasant to sleep under brambles on a desert road on the night of departure, but one must forfeit one's life. (ibid.)

He writes that, once due to his youthful naivety, he rode all day without taking a break. That evening, he fell asleep at the foot of a hill. Perhaps it wasn't a safe place to sleep but he was too tired to care. An old man woke him up and gave him an advice for future reference. He said that to walk and then sit is better than to run and then collapse. He went on:

who are yearning for the way-station hasten not. Put my advice into practice and learn patience. An Arabian steed gallops in haste and a camel proceeds slowly night and day. (Sa'di Shirazi–Thackston 2008)

Thus, the idea that sleep and work are each other's nemesis merits reconsideration. Reckless work schedules at the cost of sleep can be pretty expensive. Some people value wealth in its tangible form while others value the intangible happiness that spending it can buy. In his celebrated *Layla-Majnun*, Nizami Ganjavi writes that greed is a trap. Birds are caught when they become greedy. Human beings are no different. Fate entraps them into their unending hunger for more. The greedier they are the greater are the dangers for them. Those who are satisfied with their lot are truly free. They are the kings of their world (Ganjavi–Gelpke and Hill 1966). Sleeping in leisure or whenever one wants to sleep is, in fact, a priceless luxury which cannot be bought. No wonder sleep finds a place in all kinds of discourses, from religion to romance.

VII

In his book *Visionary Thinking*, Ashish Jaiswal argues that *prarabdh*, the sum total of a past life's karma, is carried over into a new life. Then *agami* (forthcoming), the ongoing deeds, are added to the *prarabdh* for the final result of the current life to occur. So, even if you have a great head start by having a good *prarabdh*, it is not enough for success in your new life unless you add good *agami* to it (Jaiswal 2022). Thus, the maintenance of work-life balance is to be a constant. There are duties towards others and there are duties towards your own self. In life, sleeping can be a sickness or a cure. It can be a lock or a key. It is the balance which decides what it is going to be. Ismail Meeruthi wrote a charged Urdu poem entitled 'Subh ki Aaamad' ('The Arrival of Dawn') in which the morning aggressively calls out to sleepers to get up and get going:

Utho-sonewaalon-ki main-aarahi-hoon,
Chaman-surkh-phoolon -se-dehka-diya-hai,
Magar-neend-ne tum-ko-behka-diya- hai,
Na-lo-karvaten-aur-na-bistar-tatolo,
Utho-sonewaalon-ki-main-aa-rahihoon.
(Wake up sleepers, I am here
The garden is brimming with Red flowers but sleep has misled you
don't twist and turn and don't hang around in your bed
Get up sleepers I am here) (Meeruthi 2008)

I recall that my mother recited Meeruthi's poem quite fondly but she also used a leisurely Bhojpuri couplet as equipoise to the wake and work call of the Dawn:

> *Padhalaka-likhlaka-aisi-taisi-cheelab-ghaans-charaib-bhainsii*
> (Let reading-writing go to hell
> Will clear grass and graze buffalos instead)

It might actually be interesting to imagine a shift in the symbol of success from mount of money to a comfortable peaceful sleep in leisure.

Clayton M. Christensen writes that, as youngsters, we have unlimited dreams. As we grow up, we limit them (Christensen et al. 2012). I fear that the ceiling applies not just to the waking world's dreams but also to the dreams in sleep. In fact, we don't sleep enough. It is sad to see that 'minimum sleeping hours' have become a goal to be achieved like other professional targets. At the end of the day, we must shut down our mind like we shut down the doors for our safety. There is usually a '*why*' attached with sleeping. Why should we sleep? But why can't we sleep? *Why not*?

Notes

1 The Arabic word '*daqyaanus*' is derived from the name of Decius. It means something/someone oppressive, unjust, old-fashioned or out of date.

2 This was a famous city on the west coast of Asia Minor; about 40 to 50 miles south of Smyrna.

3 The *Quran* mentions the debates around the number of men and the number of years for which they slept, but it advices to ignore those details and just focus on the lessons in the narrative.

4 It was originally written by Shaikh Izzatullah of Bengal in 1712. The Urdu translation was done by Nihal Chand lahori in the early 19thcentury. He gave it a new title: *Mazhab-e Ishq* (Doctrine of Love).

References

Ali, Meer Hassan. 2020. *Observations on the Mussalmauns of India*, edited by William Crooke. New Delhi: Manohar, pp. 81–82.

Al-Ghizali. 1999. '*Kitab dhikr al-mautwa-ma ba'dahu, The Remembrance of Death and the Afterlife*, Book XL of the Revival of The Religious Sciences, translated by T.J. Winter, United Kingdom: The Islamic Texts Society.

Awliya, Nizam Ad-Din, Amir Hasan Sijzi, *Fawaíd al-Fuad*. 1992. *Morals for the Heart*, translated by Bruce B. Lawrence. New York: Paulist Press International.

Barani, Ziauddin. 2015. *Tarikh-I Firoz Shahi*, translated by Ishtiyaq Ahmad Zilli. New Delhi: Primus Books, p. 203.

Bulkeley, Kelly. 2008. *Dreaming in the World's Religions—A Comparative History*. New York: New York University Press.

Christensen, Clayton M., James Allworth and Karen Dillon. 2012. *How Will You Measure Your Life*. London: HarperCollins Publishers.

Clouston, W.A. (trans.). 1889. *A Group of Eastern Romances and Stories: From the Persian, Tamil and Urdu*. Glasgow: privately printed.

Durant, Ariel and Will Durant. 1968. *The Lessons of History*. New York: Simon & Schuster Paperbacks.

Eaton, Richard M. 2005. *A Social History of Deccan, 1300–1761 Eight Indian Lives*. New York: Cambridge University Press, p. 36.

Golbin, Alexander Z., Howard M. Kravitz and Louis G. Keith (eds). 2004. *Sleep Psychiatry*. United Kingdom: Taylor & Francis.

Hughes, Thomas Patrick. 1993. *Dictionary of Islam*. New Delhi: Rupa & Co., p. 92.

Jami, Hakim Nuruddin Abdurrahman. 1980. Yusuf and Zulaikha—*An Allegorical Romance*, edited, translated and abridged by David Pendlebury. London: The Octagon Press.

Kathir, Imam Ibn. 1997. *Stories of the Prophets*, translated by Sheikh Muhammad Mustafa Gemeiah, edited by A. Elfwine Acelas Mischler. Egypt: El-Nour, p. 153.

Jaiswal, Ashish. 2022. *Visionary Thinking*. Wisdom Tree, p. 107.

Lewisohn, Leonard and Christopher Shackle (eds). 2006. *Attar and the Persisn Sufi Tradition—The Art of Spiritual Flight*. New York: I.B. Tauris Publishers.

Lelyveld, David. 2013. 'Young Man Sayyid-Dreams and Biographical Texts', *Muslim Voices—Community and the Self in South Asia*. New Delhi: Yoda Press, pp. 251–72.

Meeruthi, Ismail. 2008. *SubhkiAaamadi*. Available at: https://urdupoet.net>subhkiaamad.

Mir, Amman. 1994. *Bagh-o-Bahar (A Tale of Four Dervishes)*. Translated by Mohammed Zakir. New Delhi: Penguin Books, p. xiv.

Mitchell, Stephen (trans.). 2000. *Bhagavad Gita: A New Translation*. New York: Harmony Books.

Nasreen, Farhat. 2021. *The Great Mughals*. New Delhi: Rupa & Co., pp. 36, 62.

Nizami, Ganjavi. 1966. *The Story of Layla and Majnun*, translated by R. Gelpke, E. Mattin and G. Hill. London: Bruno Cassirer Publications Ltd.

Nizami of Ganja. 1914. *The Haft Paikar*, translated by C.E. Wilson. London: Arthur Probsthain & Co.

Quinn, Sholeh A. 2021. *Persian Historiography Across Empires, The Ottomans, Safavids and Mughals*. UK: Cambridge University Press.

Quran, revised and edited by The Presidency of Islamic Researches, King Fahad Complex, Saudi Arabia.

Quran, S12 and Imam Ibn Kathir. 1997. *Stories of the prophets*, translated by Sheikh Muhammad Mustafa Gemeiah, edited by A. Elfwine Acelas Mischler, El-Nour, Egypt, p. 153.

Rumi, Maulana Jalaluddin. 2014. *53 Secrets from the Tavern of Love-Poems from the Rubaiyat of Mowlana Rumi*, translated by Amin Banani and Anthony A. Lee. Ashland, Oregon: White Cloud Press.

Russel, Bertland. 1935. *In Praise of Idleness*. London: George Allen & Unwin Limited.

Shirazi, Shaikh Mushrifuddin Sa'di. 2008. *The Gulistan*, translated by Wheeler M. Thackston. Maryland: Ibex Publishers.

Wilson, H.H. (trans.). 1895. *The Vishnu Purāṇa*. Madras: Christian Literature.

11

POETIC PLEASURE, *SHE'R-O SHA'IRI*, IN WOMEN'S URDU COMPOSITIONS: A NEGLECTED CHAPTER AT THE MARGINS OF GENDERED HISTORIES

Raziuddin Aquil

I

A large corpus of Urdu poetry is deeply imbued with the spirit of love—*ishq* and *muhabbat*—free from gender barriers and above all kinds of social prejudice. Yet women poets dabbling in this emotional genre have been kept on the margins in the history of arts and literature. Some enchanting examples of the place of women poets in Urdu biographies will be presented in this chapter. These women were writing for pleasure or were articulating their emotional expressions through fine art of poetry—displaying their literary taste and flavour. In general, this was not their work; it was an activity in leisure.[1] For courtesans, some examples of whose lives and compositions will also be discussed here, it was an extension of their work, showcasing their excellent attributes to enhance their credentials as public figures, artists and performers. Some of these personalities—professional or otherwise—conformed to traditional ideals, but some others defied traditional norms and could be thoroughly subversive. The histories of lives of poets and other excellent men and women are called *tazkiras*. History provides an account of important events of the past and *tazkira* throws light on a particular time through the lives of extraordinary people of a particular period in different fields of expertise. In the context of the past, they together take the interesting form of literary-history, which is of special importance in our new historical understanding and practice. This fascinating blend of literature and history makes for a good example of interdisciplinary research and study. We are also adding their gendered perspective here. Indeed, historians are now increasingly reading the vast corpus of Urdu poetry to discover a whole cultural world that was previously outside their narrow frame.[2]

It is important to note here that, for long, historians and literary scholars would travel in separate boats, as it were, criss-crossing but never taking each other seriously; sometimes, even suspecting each other's credentials. Happily, researches and scholarships in the last couple of decades or so have ensured that historians and scholars of literature can now speak to each other comfortably; they can travel together onboard the same boat. Historians are now going beyond their conventional search for hard facts in government files to look for important clues to social and cultural realities of the past in the context of the production of literature and literature itself, whether literary masterpieces or even otherwise seemingly unimportant little and marginalised traditions of writings in regional vernaculars, as in this case fine expressions of emotions in women's Urdu poetry. Literary scholars are also increasingly looking at serious historical writings for the contexts of literary productions for understanding textual traditions better. Realising texts and contexts are made by each other, reflect on each other, made for each other as it were. In sum, it is a happy situation for all scholars of literary and intellectual practices, as in our Indian case going backward to close to two millennia now—surveying and studying literature in different languages and in a variety of genres.

Together, they reveal interesting ways in which literary works were produced, show how authors and reading publics resorted to intertextual cross-referencing and also understood the distinction between history and fiction. Current research also indicates the direction the emerging new literary histories can take for a more fruitful understanding of India's vast literary traditions, especially how its past has shaped the present. Historically, cultural diversity epitomises India's civilisational character. On the other hand, destructive pulls of communalism and bigotry continue to hurt the society fairly badly. However, for all we know, sanity prevails in the long run. Some key historical texts show enough light. They include many interesting versions of the epics, the *Rāmāyaṇa* and the *Mahābhārata* in Sanskrit and vernaculars. The Sikh scripture—*Adi Granth*, or Guru Granth Saheb, which comprises devotional compositions of not only Sikh Gurus, but also of such iconoclasts as Sant Kabir and Punjabi Chishti Sufi, Shaikh Farid, besides those of other *bhaktas* of the past—reveal the creation of a public soaked in Bhakti traditions of divergent kind and strive to coexist peacefully in a political environment in which regimes do not discriminate and pit them against each other. Example may also be given here of *Padmavat* of Malik Muhammad Jaisi, which was in the news in recent past; it is a fine sample of Sufi poetry of love in Hindi in a genre called the *premakhyan*. Also, it is important to recognise that the *Ramcharit Manas* of Tulsidas is a powerful expression of Ram-bhakti in Mughal India. Politically, *Akbarnama* and *Ain-i Akbari* of Abu'l Fazl articulated Mughal imperial ideology on how to govern a vast subcontinental country with so much diversity, especially for resolving the question of religious assertions through emphasis on broad-based governing principles, conceptualised as peace with all. Together, the literary and historical masterpieces showcase what is cherished as the best in India's inclusive political culture, devotional practices showing the way for peaceful coexistence and remarkable achievements in the cultural arena, including literary and historical practices.

Besides Sanskrit and Persian, the third set of historical literature is to be found in wide-ranging regional languages across the Indian subcontinent, from around the 14th century to the present. Unable to occupy a centre space in intellectual and political discourses, they flourish in the popular and public domain. It could be subversive and yet important in many ways. Mention may be made here of some fine piece of research and writing by Professor Partha Chatterjee, with whom this writer has coedited a book called *History in the Vernacular* (2008). In a sister publication, *History and the Present* (2002), Professor Chatterjee has also discussed historians' response to the postmodernist challenge to the writing of history, which is relevant to our conversation here, as much of the challenge came from literary scholars and writers who dabble in history, one of whom was recently heard saying that history was too important to be left to historians alone. In response, historians have begun to read literature and use the literary corpus as important texts and sources. This writer has previously analysed the historical significance of Mughal poets such as Ja'far Zatalli, Nazir Akbarabadi and Mirza Ghalib for a more informed historical analysis of their literary compositions. Previous generations of historians were not looking at popular Urdu poets seriously enough. Urdu histories with their precolonial roots were similarly marginalised.

The history of the lives of Urdu poets and their poetical compositions began to be written from the middle of the 18th century. The famous *tazkira* of Urdu poets in Persian, *Nikat-ush-Shu'ra* of Mir Taqi Mir (1724–1810), is a fine early example of this corpus.[3] A classic example of this artistic brilliance, Nawab Mustafa Khan Shaifta's *Gulshane Be-Khaar* (Thornless Garden), was published from Delhi in 1837. An Urdu translation of this book, originally written in Persian, was published by Hamida Khatoon from the National Council for Promotion of Urdu Language, New Delhi, in 1998.[4] Consolidating the glorious history of Urdu poetry over a hundred years through the biographies of hundreds of poets, Shaifta also did a commendable job of including the lives and compositions of some women poets as well. It is another matter that some exceptional personalities such as Mah Laqa Bai Chanda and Lutfun Nisa 'Imtiyaz', who had become famous in the last decades of the 18th century by completing their *diwans* (collections comprising at least one ghazal rhyming in each of the thirty-two letters of Urdu alphabet) full of touching ghazals, were kept out of this *tazkira*. Working on the lives and works of Shah Siraj (1715–63) of Aurangabad and Mah Laqa Bai Chanda (1768–1820/24) of Hyderabad, identified as Sun (Siraj) and Moon (Mah) respectively, Scott Kugle has offered an interesting discussion of Urdu literary and cultural milieu of 18th- and early decades of 19th-century Deccan. Outgrowing homosexual love in youth, Siraj styled himself as a Sunni Sufi-like poet. Rising above the filth around the life of a courtesan, Mah Laqa (literally moon-cheek) composed an elegant Urdu diwan of her own, once again anchoring herself in Sufi spirituality, revealing a disarming devotion (as a known Syed and Shi'i Muslim) for Imam Ali ibn abi Talib. Specialising in ghazal compositions, both the poets fused spiritual quest with erotic imagery for tantalising results.[5] Earlier, in the 17th century, the Mughal princesses had set high standards for themselves in scholarly activities, especially their poetic compositions, which would take a mystical turn, and in political interventions as in struggles for succession.[6]

II

It is well known that society and history have always enjoyed a peculiar pleasure in suppressing women. The lives of the few poets which Nawab Mustafa Khan Shaifta was magnanimous enough to include in his *Gulshane Be-Khaar* are being discussed here. Shaifta was one of Mirza Ghalib's acquaintances and among few whom the great poet respected. Indeed, the 1837 edition of *Gulshane Be-khaar* had also included Ghalib's praise for the book.[7] This was the period of the last Mughal emperors, when women were showing their flair as artists and performers on the cultural stage. But their roles were being restricted as courtesans, as professional dancers and singers attached to courts and salons, *kothas*, with some degree of stigma attached to the vocation. Professional or not, mostly not, but the society and the fraternity of the poets were not yet ready for women connoisseurs excelling in the art of poetry and preparing *diwans* and *kulliyats* of their own.

Even *rekhti* poetry, which expressed feminine emotions, was a form mainly deployed by male poets for the pleasure of writing and performance for appreciation in *mushairās*, which were poetical assemblies for live and public presentations by accomplished poets.[8] In such a context, it is commendable for Shaifta to have included discussions on the lives of women poets in his *tazkira*. Conforming to the usual male gaze and typical attitudes of the time, Shaifta has generally praised the pretty physical attributes of the poets focusing less on their Kalam, poetical compositions. Yet he has presented their work in such a way that the reader could easily understand their value. He has also very well illustrated the poets' independent mindedness and free flow of imagination, feelings and emotions in their poetry. Some of these were wives and daughters of Mughal nobles, some worked as courtesan and were independent women known for their taste for nicer aspects of life such as poetry, music, dance and other art forms. For our purpose, they composed poetry in leisure and impromptu, when situation demanded—for pleasure or as critical comments on conditions they were confronted with. It could be highly romantic, less devotional and certainly not prudish.[9]

Shaifta mentions in *Gulshane Be-Khaar* (p. 119) that the poetess, popularly known as Bahu Begam, whose *nom de plume* was Jani and name Begam Jan, was daughter of Nawab Qamar-ud-Din Khan and wife of Nawab Asaf-ud-Daula Bahadur. Shaifta has written that once she was troubled by several diseases and a Khwaja-Sira, *Hijra*, eunuch, named Hamdam, came to inquire about her condition. Related to her condition and Hamdam's concern, Jani Bahu Begam immediately recited this *matala*, the first *she'r* of the *nazm*:

کیا پوچھتا ہے ہمدم اس جسم ناتواں کی
ہر رگ میں نیش غم ہے کہئیے کہاں کہاں کی

Kya puchhta hai hamdam iss jism natawan ki
Har rag mein nish gham hai kahiye kahan kahan ki

What do you ask about this weak body, my breath (Hamdam)
Every vein is hurting with sorrows, where all I lament about

Shaifta has also included this *she'r* by Jani:

دل جس سے لگایا وہ ہوا دشمن جانی
کچھ دل کا لگانا ہی ہمیں راس نہیں ہے

Dil jisse lagaya woh hua dushman Jaani
Kuchh dil ka lagana he hamen raas nahin hai

Whoever I attach my heart with turns into an enemy of life (Jaani)
Attachments of the heart don't seem to suit me somehow.
(*Gulshane Be-Khaar*)

Shaifta (*Gulshane Be-Khaar*, 131) writes about another poetess, Jina Begam, that, like her beauty, her circumstances remained in purdah. Justifying this, Shaifta notes that this was an obvious implication of her amazing presence. Look at this example of her poetry:

یہ کس کے آتش غم نے جگر جلایا ہے
کہ تا فلک میرے شعلے نے سر اٹھایا ہے

Yeh kiske aatishe gham ne jigar jalaya hai
Ke ta falak mere sholay ne sar uthaya hai

Whose love's sorrow has burnt the liver/heart
That the flame has raised its head to the horizon

Similarly, a poet named Dulhan Begam is briefly introduced be Shaifta (*Gulshane Be-Khaar*, p. 161), in such a way that her condition was similar to that of her face covered in veil. Here are two couplets by that poet, who epitomised chastity:

بہا ہے پھوٹ کے آنکھوں سے آبلہ دل کا
تری کی راہ سے جاتا ہے قافلہ دل کا

Baha hai phoot ke aankhon se aabla dil ka
Tari ki raah se jata hai qafila dil ka

The blister of my heart bursts through my eyes
The convoy of the heart passes through the moistened path.

Dulhan Begam also proclaimed:

جہاں کے باغ میں ہم بھی بہار رکھتے ہیں
مثال لالہ کے دل داغدار رکھتے ہیں

Jahan ke bagh mein ham bhi bahaar rakhte hain
Misaal lala ke dile daghdaar rakhte hain

We also have a spring in the garden of life
Like laleh we have a wounded heart.

In contrast to the simplicity of the above-mentioned noble-tempered poetesses and their style protected by *hijab*, Shaifta has described the condition of a *bindas* poetess named Zinat in the following manner (*Gulshane Be-Khaar*, p. 190): Her *nom de plume* is Zinat. She is one of the women of the *bazaar*. She is lovelorn by temperament. In the city of Shahjahanabad, which matched with the paradise, there was a poet called Mirza Ibrahim Beg, whose *takhallus*, *nom de plume*, was Maqtul, that is, someone who was killed. He was so enchanted that he sank himself in love for her. According to Shaifta, he was so enamoured by Zinat's awe and *naaz* that he disregarded established social conventions for proper conduct and shamelessly left with her to Lucknow. As if, Maqtul was killed for love! An example of the absolutely maddening poetry of Zinat is given here:

شب مہتاب میں تا صبح زینت
خیال مہ رو ہے اور ہم ہیں

Shabe mahtaab mein ta subah Zinat
Khayale maah ru hai or ham hain

Till the morning of the moonlit night, Zinat
We are together sunk in thoughts of the moon-cheeked one.

Further, according to Shaifta (*Gulshane Be-Khaar*, 234–35), a poet named Ummatul Fatima Begam preferred to adopt a masculine *takhallus*, Saheb, and became famous as Saheb-ji! She was also going places. In Delhi, she had a close acquaintance, indeed a special relationship, with the famous poet Mu'min Khan Mu'min.[10] She was from Lucknow and earned a big name for herself after returning. Look at Shaifta's eulogy: She is the moon of the heavens of righteousness; the sun which rises from the east, coming out of the west for a change. In connection with the treatment for an illness, she needed Mu'min Khan's help. This led, within a month, to many opportunities for sharing pain and medicine.

Shaifta speculates that the plot of sorrows in Mu'min's long poem (*masnavi*), *Qaule Ghamgin*, or Sorrowful Utterances, is inspired by the tremors caused by Saheb's grace and beauty. There was some fire at the other side also. After a while, the matters of heart do not remain one sided. Because of this inspired association with Mu'min Khan, Saheb's heart also moved towards poetry of love, *she'r-o sha'iri*, and the pain associated with the youthful physical beauty transformed itself into a graceful poetic style. Thus, while taking care of the demands of the curls and curves of the time, bodily and emotional requirements, *zulf-i parishan*, Saheb learned to untie the knots of the complex and tangled poetry as it were. Some couplets of a ghazal by Saheb, reproduced by Shaifta, may be presented here:

رقیبوں کا جلنا کہاں دیکھتا تو
سماں یہ میرے گھر میں آیا تو دیکھا

گنہ کیا صنم کے نظارے میں زاہد
یہ جلوہ خدا نے دکھایا تو دیکھا

صاحب جو بنایا ہے تو مانند زلیخا
یوسف سا غلام ایک مجھے دے ڈال الہی

Raqibon ka jalna kahan dekhta tu
Saman yeh mere ghar mein aaya tow dekha

Gunah kya sanam ke nazare mein zahid
Yeh jalwa khuda ne dikhaya tow dekha

Saheb jo banaya hai tu manind zulaikha
Yusuf sa ghulam ek mujhe de daal ilahi

Where would you see the jealous rivals burning
You saw this when you came to my place

What sin it is to witness the sight of the idol, the pious man
We saw this when God showed this light

You have made Saheb like a Zulaikha
Give me a slave like Yusuf, O God.

No custodian of patriarchal religion could have run amok armed with a *fatwa* or religious decree, condemning such fine poetry as indecent. The poetry of this kind symbolised frankness and sincerity in literary endeavours. The people involved in the production of literature were aware of the mood of the times and represented it. They themselves were the product of the times and, thus, the compositions of women poets and their context—time and space—complemented each other. In other words, they constructed each other. The political context which encouraged and supported cultural activities and influence and clout which some literary figures could enjoy meant that they had artistic license to excel in their compositions.

Look at one such example: Shaifta has written (*Gulshane Be-Khaar*, p. 298) that Gana Begam belonged to a noble family. She was married to Nawab Itamad-ud-Daula Ghaziuddin Khan, who was known with the *takhallus*, Nizam. With her husband's permission, Gana Begam got her Kalam corrected by Mir Qamr-ud-Din Minnat, that is, the latter was her *ustaad*. Her poetic style was *bindas*, though deploying a lot of interesting metaphors and sometimes resorting to euphemism as well. In the couplets given below, Gana Begam referred to chewing the sugar candy like lips of the beloved and compared exchanging loving glances with enjoying the pleasure of munching almonds!

مقابل ہو اگر لب کے تیرے مصری چبا جاؤں
تیری آنکھوں سے ہم چشمی کرے بادام کھا جاؤں

Muqqabil ho agar lab ke tere misri chaba jaaun
Teri aankhon se ham chashmi kare badaam kha jaaun

Were the lips to be encountered, I would partake a sugar-sweet bite
If eyes locked glances, I would devour those almonds.

And:

تیرے منہ کی تجلّی دیکھ کر کل رات حسرت سے
زمیں پر لوٹتی تھی چاندنی اور شمع جلتی تھی

Tere munh ki tajalli dekhkar kal raat hasrat se
Zamin par lotti thee chandni aur shamma jalti thee

Looking at your glowing face last night with a sense of deprivation
Moonlight rolled on the ground with the light burning.

Shefta (*Gulshane Be-Khaar*, 375–76) also mentions Zinat as 'one of the beautiful *tawaifs*', who used to do poetry and adopted *nazuk*, delicate, as *takhallus*. These *asha'ar* couplets by her are also given:

یاد آتی ہے ان آنکھوں میں آمد وہ نشوں کی
ساقی مے گلرنگ سے جب جام بھرے ہے

ہے نالہ و زاری کا میرے شور فلک تک
پر وہ بت مغرور کوئی کان دھرے ہے

Yaad aati hai in aankhon mein woh aamad nashon ki
Saaqi maye gulrang se jab jaam bhare hai

Hai nala o zaari ka mere shor falak tak
Par woh bute maghrur koyi kaan dhare hai

I remember the arrival of drunkenness in these eyes
When the cupbearer fills the goblet with the rose-coloured wine

My shouting and wailing has reached the sky
But that arrogant idol has refused to hear.

The poetess who robbed the heart of Shaifta (*Gulshane Be-Khaar*, 386–88) was known by the *takhallus*, Nazakat. The author has given a detailed description of both her exceptional beauty and excellent character. Here are some excerpts from the way Shaifta has praised her: The name of this poetess resembling the moon and sun together, terribly pretty, life-giving and comfort for the heart is Ramju and her *takhallus* is Nazakat. Her family is from the town of Narnaul. Like the morning queen, she has suddenly risen and is shining in the city with the blessed foundation, Shahjahanabad. In other words, she is taking the city by a storm and blowing away the best of the celebrities. She is a fantastic combination of a sweet lover and a salted beloved!

The generous heart and creative imagination with which Shaifta has heaped praises on Nazakat from head to toe was beyond the literary tropes deployed by the best of the poets immersed in traditional Indian *sringar-rasa*.[11] The prudish reader will be aghast at Shaifta's language, but a sentence can still be quoted here: she is the newly blown rose in the garden of youth and juicy fruit of the garden of life, and a just rising ecstasy of the garden of grace and beauty. Shaifta further adds that, as part of her temperament, she distastes the disgusting ways of people and loves fine characteristics she likes. She was fully aware of and adorned with the virtues of sagacity, intelligence, humour and playfulness as well as gravity and seriousness. She was also fully acquainted with emotions and feelings associated with compassion, empathy and loyalty on the one hand and cruelty and tyranny on the other.

Noting that she sometimes expressed delightful poetical thoughts in a commendable style of poetry, Shaifta has presented some of her touching verses. See, for instance:

بس کہ رہتا ہے یار آنکھوں میں
بے نظر بے قرار آنکھوں میں

Bas ke rahta hai yaar aankhon mein
Be nazar be qaraar aankhon mein

The friend just stays in the eyes
Invisible and restless eyes.

And this:

کیوں نہ میں قربان ہوں جب وہ کہے ناز سے
ہم کو جفا کا ہے شوق اہل وفا کون ہے

Kyon na mayen qurbaan hun jab woh kahe naaz se
Hamko jafa ka hai shauq ahle wafa kaun hai

Why shouldn't I sacrifice myself when he says with playful dalliance
We long for cruelty of unrequited love, where are the faithful ones after all?

Also:

کیا کیا عذاب اٹھائے ہیں اندوہ عشق کے
جز نام اب تو کچھ بھی نزاکت نہیں رہی

Kya kya azaab uthaye hain andoh ishq ke
Juz naam ab tow kuchh bhi Nazakat nahin rahi

What torments one has endured as pain of love
Except for her name, delicate Nazakat is no more.

III

Where did these women disappear in the subsequent decades? The world around them was changing rapidly. In the 1830s, the decade in which Shaifta was preparing his book for publication, an aggressive colonial regime and its associated trope of modernity was tearing apart older values attached with politics, economy, society and culture.[12]

Indeed, colonialism sought to completely transform the conquered people, delegitimising and making redundant early modern cultural practices and worldviews. Conquerors and new ruling elites want to write history on the body of the people and society they subjugate. Women are also dragged into this, with the presumption that the older customs and traditions had suppressed women and injustices meted out to them will be corrected through legal means now. Undoubtedly, some of the policies of the new colonial regime were empowering women and providing scope for some agency for them. Education, jobs, equality before law and right to inherit property were creating conditions for change in the life of the women. Rise of women reformist leaders in the middle of the 19th century is, indeed, understood as the necessary and welcome change caused by the colonial rule and institutions.[13]

However, as Partha Chatterjee has shown, subsequent decades witnessed the Indian nationalist discourse managing to deal with the colonial assault in the name of justice for women. Colonialism was an all-pervasive reality, but it could be stopped at the doorstep of the homes, even while compromising with colonial modernity associated with the government apparatus. In this way, indigenous customs and traditions could be preserved, while keeping pace with the times. Professor Chatterjee has termed the new process of reforming the society, balancing differences between the Indian traditional world at home and the new Western world outside as the 'Nationalist Resolution of the Women's Question'.[14] A recourse could be made for ideas and inspirations from the ancient Hindu texts. This would also mean that the recent historical experience of the country ruled by generations of Muslim dynasties were to be condemned as a dark age responsible for all the ills facing the society. This was once again a result of the colonial regime that wanted people to believe in the canard that they were there to liberate Hindus from the precolonial Muslim onslaught—typically imagined as widespread loot, rape and murder for several centuries.[15]

Since the British had captured power by defeating Muslim dynasties all around, they especially targeted Muslims for special chastisement. The latter needed time to recover from the shock of the new revolution of sorts. Commitments to various kinds of religious conservatism and orthodoxy also meant it was not easy for them to move with time. The question of reform for women did become a major concern in Muslim communities, but the pace and form of change was obviously running late by fifty to sixty years, especially when compared to the quick response in other communities such as the Bengali Hindus. This also meant that women could be invisibilised under the garb of religion and customary practices, resorting to some misplaced invocation of *shari'at*, which was presented as Islamic law governing the life of the people.

Some people were definitely raising questions against the patriarchal machinations to suppress women. The poet inside the heart of many women may also be dying in despair. They had nothing to do. The reformists and revivalists who came to the centre stage in different garbs were also against their singing and dancing. They could be encouraged to knit and sew clothes as part of their responsibility to manage the household and keep men satisfied and happy. Or, they could do it for leisure. Their composing poetry as part of the murmurs of heart was suspected and questioned. Poet Nazakat had already complained in no uncertain terms (*Gulshane Be-Khaar*, 388):

کہتا ہے آپ کی بھی ہے کیا عاشقی غلط
گر کہئے تیرے عہد میں الفت نہیں رہی

Kahta hai aapki bhi hai kya aashiqi ghalat
Gar kahiye tere ahad mein ulfat nahin rahi

Says you have an utterly misplaced sense of the idea of love
If you point out love is lost in your realm.

In our times, despite different kinds of challenges, historians and literary scholars have been able to do interesting new research, often in conversation with each other and sometimes from their own distinct disciplinary stances. Scholars of allied disciplines in the Social Sciences and Humanities bring in their own expertise and results of their research. Together, and separately, they have pushed frontiers of research and knowledge production on a scale that matches the best in the world of contemporary global scholarship in respective fields. Our new historical research is offering a more decentred view of the past perhaps, and, therefore, presenting richer accounts, bringing in themes and issues which were previously marginalised, even ignored altogether. The combined efforts of historians and literary scholars have been particularly fortuitous. The critics of history might think of traditional history being supplanted by historical fiction, novel, etc., but history as an academic discipline does not need anything outside of it to assert itself in relation to other scholarly activities, working with historical evidence and analysis as a well-established method and practice. History departments of our universities are not going to be shut down any time in the foreseeable future, even though disciplinary boundaries are being continuously crossed. Women poets had long shown the way—crossing boundaries, questioning and critiquing. Perhaps, some did it for leisure only, in the language of pleasure, and some sounded subversive indeed.

Acknowledgement

This chapter is part of my larger book-length project on the intersection of literature, culture and history. Thanks are due to Professor Seema Bawa for inviting me to contribute this chapter in the volume on leisure she is editing, and also for patiently tolerating the delay in its submission.

Notes

1 For an important introduction to women's studies or leisure studies from a North American perspective, with women constrained in their lives—affecting their leisure, which can make a difference to lives and politics around them, at least for a right to free-time, see Henderson et al. (1989). For a discussion of gendered leisure activities, see Harris (2005).

2 For some recent discussion on the literary excellence in Urdu, including the more mixed and early form, *rekhta*, in the 18th and early 19th centuries, see Aquil (2021); idem, Aquil (2017). Also see, Naim (2004). Carla Petievich has noted that 'Urdu literature, with all its elegance and refinement, has been widely chosen as the medium through which Indian Muslims projected a self-image of cultural accomplishment. It went hand in hand with the political and military achievements of the great Mughal empire', adding that the 'political upheaval' of the late 18th and early 19th centuries 'sought expression in an appropriate literary form', the genre of classical Urdu poetry known as *shahr ashob* (literally, the city's misfortune), lamenting the decline of Delhi and its inability to provide patronage to scholars, poets and artists, 'Poetry of the Declining Mughal: The "*Shar ashob*"', *Journal of South Asian Literature*, Vol. 25, No, 1, 1990, pp. 99–110. Also see, for a good early use of Urdu poetry by a historian, Mukhia (1999).

3 Mir Taqi Mir's own life witnessing the tumultuous 18th century is instructive and is best described by himself in his, *Remembrances* [autobiographical narrative], Persian text with English translation. Edited and translated by C.M. Naim. Murty Classical Library of India. Cambridge, MA: Harvard University Press, 2019.

4 Nawab Mustafa Khan Shaifta, *Gulshane Be-Khaar*. Lucknow: Munshi Nawal Kishore, 1874; Urdu translation, Karachi: Nafis Academy, 1963; we will be citing here from the Urdu translation published by the National Council for Promotion of Urdu Language, New Delhi, 1998.

5 Their Urdu *diwans* should be a veritable treat. Knowing Kugle as an accomplished scholar of bodily practices in Sufism and Deccani Urdu literature, it is worth discussing the book, even if briefly. First treating the two poets (Sun and Moon) separately as two orbits of the cultural planet, Kugle eventually brings them together in a literary Conjunction—When Sun Meets Moon. The author has provided English translations of a number of verses, but we may look at the original Urdu for the sheer linguistic charm of it. Happily, some of the *she'rs* are quoted in the endnotes packed together at the end of the book, Kugle (2016).

6 For some recent discussion, see Alam (2021, Ch. 7). Also see, the celebration of the extraordinary life and career of Nur Jahan, Lal (2018).

7 For Mirza Ghalib's tough life, especially his painful reflection on 1857 and its aftermath in *Dastanbu*, Urdu translation from original Persian, New Delhi: Taraqqi Urdu Bureau, 2000; Raziuddin Aquil, 'Mirza Ghalib and the Tragedy of 1857', in idem, Aquil (2023, 219–25). Also see, for current appreciation of Mirza Ghalib's fine work, Narang (2017); Farooqi (2021).

8 For *rekhti* poetry and performance, see Petievich (2007); Vanita (2012). For a recent study of the political contents of the *mushairās*, see Mahmudabad (2020).

9 Even as Mughal political power was declining, cultural practices were taking a fantastic turn, see Khan (1993). For a new account of the early decades of the 19th century, see Liddle (2022). Also see, the classic work of Gupta (1981).

10 Mirza Ghalib was particularly fond of one of the couplets of Mu'mim Khan Mu'min: *tum mere paas hote ho goya / jab koyi dusra nahin hota* (You are close to me, as if / only when no one else was around). It is circulated in the literary circles from Ghalib's time that the veteran poet found the lines so touching that he wished how Mu'min could agree to exchange them with an entire *diwan* of his, see Hali (2012, 83).

11 Mention may be made here of Sayyid Ghulam Nabi Raslin's work in Braj, namely *Angdarpan* (1737) and *Rasprabodh* (1742), which point to the intricacies of gender and culture in the 18th century. They offer substantial information on genre such as *nayak-nayika bhed*, *barahmasa*, *shad-ritu*, and *shikh-nakh*, referring to male-female relationships, male gaze, love, erotics, sexual and non-sexual intimacies, bodily practices, etc. For more details, see Singh (2017).

12 See for an important discussion on colonial violence and transformations, Chatterjee (2012); and a more recent analysis of violence and resistance, Farooqui (2022).

13 The appreciation of this change does not mean supporting colonial instruments of subjugation, see Anagol (2008, 603–27). Also see, Gupta (2012); Malhotra (2017).

14 Chatterjee (2010).

15 For a critical analysis of these outlandish propositions, see Sarkar (2017).

References

Alam, Muzaffar. 2021. *The Mughals and the Sufis: Islam and Political Imagination in India, 1500–1750*. Ranikhet: Permanent Black.

Anagol, Padma. 2008. 'Agency, Periodization and Change in the Gender and Women's History of Colonial India'. *Gender and History*, Vol. 20(3): 603–27.

Aquil, Raziuddin and Partha Chatterjee (eds). 2008. *History in the Vernacular*. Ranikhet: Permanent Black.

Aquil, Raziuddin. 2017. *The Muslim Question: Understanding Islam and Indian History*. New Delhi: Penguin Books.

———. 2021. '"Aashiq ko tow Allah na dikhlaai budhapa": Nazir Akbarabadi and the Little Pleasure of Life in Urdu Poetry'. In *Locating Pleasure in Indian History: Prescribed and Proscribed Desires in Visual and Literary Cultures*, edited by Seema Bawa. New Delhi: Bloomsbury Publishing.

———. 2023. *History in the Public Domain*. New Delhi: Manohar.

Chatterjee, Partha and Anjan Ghosh (eds). 2002. *History and the Present*. New Delhi: Permanent Black.

Chatterjee, Partha. 2010. 'The Nationalist Resolution of the Women's Question', *Empire and Nation*. New York: Columbia University Press.

———. 2012. *The Black Hole of Empire: History of a Global Practice of Power*. Ranikhet: Permanent Black..

Farooqi, Mehr Afshan. 2021. *Ghalib: A Wilderness at My Doorstep*. Gurgaon: Penguin Books.

Farooqui, Amar. 2022. *The Colonial Subjugation of India*. New Delhi: Aleph Book Company.

Ghalib, Mirza. 2000. *Dastanbu*. Urdu translation from original Persian. New Delhi: Taraqqi Urdu Bureau.

Gulshane Be-Khaar of Nawab Mustafa Khan Shaifta. 1998. Lucknow: Munshi Nawal Kishore, 1874; Urdu translation, Karachi: Nafis Academy, 1963; Urdu translation, New Delhi: National Council for Promotion of Urdu Language.

Gupta, Charu (ed.). 2012. *Gendering Colonial India*. New Delhi: Orient Blackswan.

Gupta, Narayani. 1981. *Delhi between Two Empires, 1803–1931: Society, Government and Urban Growth*. New Delhi: Oxford University Press.

Hali, Altaf Husain. 2012. *Yadgar-i Ghalib*, reprint, New Delhi: Ghalib Institute.

Harris, David. 2005. *Key Concepts in Leisure Studies*. London: Sage, pp. 125–30.

Henderson, Karla A., M. Deborah Bialeschki, Susan M. Shaw and Valeria J. Freysinger. 1989. *A Leisure of One's Own: A Feminist Perspective on Women's Leisure*. State College, PA: Venture Publishing.

Khan, Dargah Quli. 1993. *Muraqqa-i Dehli*, Persian text with Urdu translation. Edited and translated by Khaliq Anjum. New Delhi: Anjuman Taraqqi Urdu (Hind).

Kugle, Scott. 2016. *When Sun Meets Moon: Gender, Eros, and Ecstasy in Urdu Poetry*. New Delhi: Orient Blackswan.

Lal, Ruby. 2018. *Empress: The Astonishing Reign of Nur Jahan*. New Delhi: Penguin Books.

Liddle, Swapna. 2022. *The Broken Script: Delhi under the East India Company and the Fall of the Mughal Dynasty, 1803–1857*. New Delhi: The Speaking Tiger.

Mahmudabad, Ali Khan. 2020. *Poetry of Belonging: Muslim Imaginings of India, 1850–1950*. New Delhi: Oxford University Press.

Malhotra, Anshu. 2017. *Piro and the Gulabdasis: Gender, Sect and Society in Punjab*. New Delhi: Oxford University Press.

Mir, Mir Taqi. 2019. *Remembrances* [autobiographical narrative], Persian text with English translation. Edited and translated by C.M. Naim. Murty Classical Library of India. Cambridge, MA: Harvard University Press.

Mukhia, Harbans. 1999. 'The Celebration of Failure as Dissent in Urdu Ghazal', *Modern Asian Studies*, Vol. 33 (1): 861–81.

Naim, C.M. 2004. *Urdu Texts and Contexts: The Selected Essays of CM Naim*. New Delhi: Permanent Black.

Narang, Gopi Chand. 2017. *Ghalib: Innovative Meanings and the Ingenious Mind*, translated from the Urdu by Surinder Deol. New Delhi: Oxford University Press.

Petievich, Carla. 1990. 'Poetry of the Declining Mughal: The "*Shar Ashob*"', *Journal of South Asian Literature*, Vol. 25 (1): 99–110.

———. 2007. *When Men Speak as Women: Vocal Masquerade in Indo-Muslim Poetry*. New Delhi: Oxford University Press.

Sarkar, Sumit. 2017. *Essays of a Lifetime: Reformers, Nationalists, Subalterns*. Ranikhet: Permanent Black.

Singh, Nagwant. 2017. 'Sayyid Ghulam Nabi Raslin and His Works: A Historical Analysis of Gender and Culture in the Eighteenth Century', M.Phil. Dissertation, Department of History, University of Delhi.

Vanita, Ruth. 2012. *Gender, Sex and the City: Urdu Rekhti Poetry, 1780–1870*. New Delhi: Orient Blackswan.

12

THE LAST *MUSHAIRĀ* OF DELHI: A STUDY OF A TEXT AND RECREATION OF A PAST

Rakhshanda Jalil

Imagine, if you will, that you are in the *haveli* of Mubarakunnisa Begum in Hauz Qazi. Outside, the *gali*, *kucha* and *bazaar* of 'Dehli' are abuzz with excitement. Word has spread about the *mushairā* that is about to take place. The greatest poets of this age are about to come together—a bit like a rare astronomical alignment. This *haveli*, which once housed a printing press, has been cleared of its clutter and transformed into a magical space filled with the dazzling light from countless candles, lamps, lanterns. Expensive woolen carpets, *gao-takhiya* and cushions are scattered on the spotless white *chandni*-covered *farsh*. Burnished *huqqās*, polished *pīkdān*, *khāsdan* and *pāndān* await the honoured guests. The mingled scent of musk, amber and *kewra* delights the senses. The stage is set for the last *mushairā* of Delhi. The date is 14th of Rajab (corresponding with 20th July), the year 1845. The above description is found in Farhatullah Baig's modern Urdu classic, *Dehli ki Aakhri Shama* (literally meaning 'the last candle of Delhi').[1]

But there is something that we know with the benefit of hindsight, something that the fifty-nine poets who will come to occupy their places on the *chandni*-covered *farsh* have no inkling of. It is this knowledge that makes us at once privileged and poignant. For, we know that dark clouds are gathering on the not-so-distant horizon and the shadows are lengthening. We know that a way of life is about to come to an end. We know that the *ghadar* (revolt) of 1857 shall change things irrevocably. But the poets seated in the *haveli* of Mubarakunnisa Begum are serenely unconcerned. Tonight, it matters little to them that their Badshah's empire extends no further than the shabby grandeur of the *Quila-e Moalla*, or the 'Exalted Fort' as the Red Fort was then called. Or that the British Resident is tightening his hold imperceptibly over not just Delhi but all of Hindustan. Or, for that matter, that their beloved 'Dehli' (as the residents called their city) is on the verge of being eclipsed by the far more glamorous and wealthier cities of Lucknow and Hyderabad. Tonight, they have come to savour what the best and brightest among them have to offer. Tonight, they have come to indulge in a favourite leisure-time activity, namely, listening and reciting poetry in a *mushairā*.

For the middle of the 19th century, it could be well said: 'Those were the best of times; those were the worst of times.' One way of life was coming to an inexorable end; the other was waiting to be born. The Rebellion of 1857, considered by many as the First War of Independence, did not merely mark the end of a way of life; it also, in a sense, marked a departure in a way of *seeing* things. While the Indian response(s) to the events of 1857, the effect on Indians in general and the Urdu-speaking intelligentsia in particular and the changes ushered in their life and literature as a direct result of this cataclysmic event have been studied by scholars and historians;[2] perhaps no one can fully enunciate the effect of these changes than those who lived through these trying times and were directly affected by these events. Also, given the close relationship between social reality and literary texts, it is important to revisit and reexamine the literature(s) produced during times of great social upheaval. Doing so can provide a far more nuanced understanding of historical events than official records and documents.

Dehli ki Aakhri Shama, therefore, needs to be read in conjunction with other texts from the same period, namely: *Asar-us-Sanadid* (literally meaning 'Remains of the Past') by Sir Syed Ahmad Khan; *Bazm-i Aakhir* by Munshi Faizuddin and *Twilight in Delhi* by Ahmed Ali which is a later book but nevertheless important for its evocation of a fading Delhi.

The first, *Asar-us-Sanadid*, was originally written in 1847 and subsequently revised and published by the Asiatic Society in 1862.[3] In its first edition, the six hundred pages of text were illustrated with over a hundred lithographic illustrations. It listed not just the monuments that lay scattered across the many 'Delhis', but also described the city's fairs, festivals and included a lengthy account of the city's vibrant cultural life. Compiled at real physical risk to life and limb (for its compilation required the venerable and lugubriously well-built Sir Syed to be dexterously raised and lowered by an ingenious pulley in order to be able to read the plaques and engravings), the four-volume work can be regarded as a lasting monument not only to the author's industry but also to his sense of culture and history and his realisation, well ahead of his times, of the need to record and preserve the monuments of Delhi and their inscriptions.

The first edition also contained a large section on the sufis, men of learning, and poets and artists of contemporary Delhi. Divided under ten headings, it also included a listing of 118 eminent citizens of Delhi. Its French translation by Garcin de Tassy was brought out in 1861. Its second edition in 1854 deleted the cultural references and retained only the descriptions of the historical monuments, translations of the epitaphs and plaques as well as measurements and architectural details of the actual building and some pen portraits.[4] Scholars such as David Lelyveld and Shamsur Rahman Faruqi have remarked upon this curious deletion from the second edition and attributed it to Syed Ahmad's pragmatic reassessment of the significance of 'culture' in the life of Indian Muslims. It is noteworthy that Syed Ahmad undertook this 'reassessment' well before the Revolt.

First published in 1885, *Bazm-i Aakhir*[5] is a rich and lively first-hand account of life in the royal court of the last Mughal emperor in Red Fort, Bahadur Shah Zafar. From meticulous details of the day-to-day happenings inside the fort-palace and the royal protocols to the celebration of festivals such as Eid, Nauroz, Diwali, Rakhshabandhan, Muharram, the various *urs* of the Sufi saints revered by the people of Delhi, this gives us a glimpse into the life in Delhi in the mid- 19th century. There are vivid descriptions of the games in the ladies' garden and the various leisure-time activities of the inhabitants of the Red Fort.

Ahmed Ali's epochal novel, *Twilight in Delhi*, originally published in English in 1940, is indeed the furthest removed in terms for time but it nevertheless conveys to the English reader a luminous account of the decay and downfall of a genteel Muslim family from Delhi. More importantly, for the purpose of this volume on leisure, this novel contains many vivid descriptions of leisure activities such as kite-flying, pigeon-racing, cock-fighting as well as the favourite pastime of the people of Delhi, namely, people gazing while sitting on the steps of the Jama Masjid and watching the world go by. The entire hustle and bustle in Delhi was centred around five features: the Red Fort, Chandni Chowk, the Jama Masjid, the Jamuna river and the much-awaited annual carnival of *Phoolwalan-ki-Sair* ('The Flower-sellers' Festival). They were the pivots of social and cultural life in Delhi. The *ghadar* of 1857 would change this irrevocably.

In Urdu, there are several accounts that provide delightful vignettes of life and manners in the Delhi of the mid-19th century. A serious reader might as well read some of these alongside Baig's *Dehli ki Aakhri Shama*: Nawab Quli Khan's *Muraqqua-e Dehli* ('An Album of Delhi') detailing the sack and plunder of Delhi by Nadir Shah in 1739; Abdul Latif's *1857 ka Tareekhi Roznamcha* ('A Historical Diary from 1857'); Hasan Nizami's *Dehli ki Akhri Saans* ('The Last Breath of Delhi'); Altaf Husain Hali's biography written in 1897 *Yaadgar-e Ghalib* ('A Reminiscence of Ghalib'); Ghalib's own poetry which contains many a reference to his changed world and, most pertinently, Ghalib's letters collected and edited by Khaliq Anjum as *Ghalib ke Khutoot*. Taken together, they serve to give an insight into a way of life that was threatened by a fast-overwhelming colonialism that was nibbling away at a city and a way of life.

Always a diligent and prolific letter writer, the post-1857 letters show not merely Ghalib's agony but the trials and tribulations of his beloved city. In a letter to Hargopal Tafta, Ghalib writes: '... the city where I am bears the name of Delhi and the locality of Ballimaran is also the same, but I do not find the friends of my earlier birth.' Ghalib lived another twelve years after the Revolt and witnessed the confusion and disarray that followed the loss of power and patronage. The Hindus were permitted to return to Delhi in June 1858 and the Muslims in August 1859, almost two years after the uprise. But the Delhi they returned to was a transformed city. Two worlds—the decaying and the emergent—fused and merged. Pathos, confusion and conflict reigned supreme. Ghalib's Delhi was but a shadow of its former self causing him to cry out:

> *Dekho mujhe jo deeda-e-ibrat-nigah ho*
> *Meri suno jo gosh-e-nasihat-neosh hai*
> Observe me and be warned if you are wise
> And be prepared if you are to heed my advice.

***

Just as the candle burns brightest at dawn before being snuffed out, so did the city of Delhi just before it was ravaged by the Mutiny. And it is this city poised on the brink of disaster, its culture, its poets and above all its language, the *zabaan-e-Dehli,* threatened by extinction that Farhatullah Baig captures in his book, initially titled *Dehli ka Eik Yaadgaar Mushairā* ('A Memorable Mushairā of Delhi'), later changed to the more apt *Dehli ki Aakhri Shama*. Born in 1883 Farhatullah Baig felt sufficiently close in time to attempt a fictional-historical account of what *might* have been the last *mushairā* of its kind held in Delhi. Rather ingeniously he makes the narrator a certain Maulvi Karimuddin Maghfoor who actually wrote a florid account of a *mushairā* that is said to have taken place in 1845.

A *mushairā* is a poetic symposium, a soiree at which poets of the day read their original works purely for their own and their listeners' pleasure. To quote from Akhtar Qamber's excellent Introduction to *The Last Mushairā of Delhi*:

> The mushairā is not an easy form of entertainment. It demands full intellectual and emotional participation within the prescribed framework of aesthetic conventions set by the masters long ago. In

> course of time mushairās became, in addition, excellent forums for literary criticism, disputation and, sometimes, on-the-spot poetic compositions. But the main purpose of the mushairā is to offer opportunities for the enjoyment of reciting and listening to selected ghazal poetry.[6]

In India, the *mushairā* tradition is said to go back to the 16th century when, often under royal patronage, poets would assemble to recite their poetry to each other but more often than not in a large enough public space where ordinary citizens could listen, if not join. At its simplest, a *mushairā* offers a space for the enjoyment of reciting and, in turn, listening and savoring poetry; in traditional *mushairās*, it was only ever the ghazal and the *qata* or *rubai*, the *nazm* not having been born yet. Modern *mushairās* have all forms of Urdu poetry read from the stage or podium including the *nazm* and the *geet*. The mike has replaced the lit candle, *shama* that would be placed, in turn, before each poet under the direction of the person doing the *nizamat* of the *mushairā*, a sort of referee, umpire, organiser, master of ceremonies rolled into one. What is more, modern-day *mushairās* have a fair representation of women—both as poets and in the audience—something that could not have been imagined in the all-male domain that any public space once was by its very definition.

From marketplaces and city-squares where poets met and recited their poetry in small groups, these gatherings moved to the homes of the nobility. Given the importance of poetry as a means of communication, soon rulers and princes began to host these soirees. Quili Qutub Shah began to hold *mushairās* in his capital city, Golconda, in the Deccan. As Urdu travelled north, soon *mushairās* became common in Delhi and its environs. Noted 18th-century poets such as Khwaja Mir Dard and Mir Taqi Mir hosted these poetic gatherings in their homes. With time, the nawabs and talukdars of Rampur, Awadh and other big and small principalities, who saw themselves as arbiters of good taste, began to organise *mushairās* where poets from outside the state were invited as royal guests. During Bahadurshah Zafar's reign, *mushairās* came to be organised on the 15th and 29th of each month in the Diwan-e Aam. By the time of Karimuddin's *mushairā*, which takes place outside the fort, however a template is in place. The seating, the sequence, the stylized manner of recitation—be it in *tarranum* (singing or, rather, reciting in a sing-song manner) or *tahat-ul lafz* (a sonorous but not song-like manner with due emphasis on each word)—has been perfected. Elaborate courtesies have evolved and are known to each participant and viewer; any deviation from time-honoured rules is frowned upon as discourtesy. Elegance of speech, immaculate voice modulation, due deference to seniors and peers, these have codified into the template of the *mushairā*. Nuance and subtlety reign supreme.

Mushairā (literally meaning 'vying poetry' from the Arabic word *musa'ara*) was, in its own way, a democratic space or as democratic as it was possible to be in a feudal world. For one, it drew poets and non-poets, reciters and listeners, patrons and performers to a common, shared space. A listener, or a fellow poet, was free to be as liberal or as parsimonious with his praise as he wished to be. Ovation could not be demanded; it had to be earned. What is more, the *daad* or praise had to be just so appropriate to the occasion. To be asked to repeat a line or two, or hear the entire ghazal without asking for any such repeats could means approval or its opposite: a silent, unspoken disapproval. A good couplet caused everyone—the poets as well as the non-poets among the listeners—to chorus their approval. These gatherings of soirees have been likened to an instance of 'being and belonging',[7] where the poetic space gradually transforms from a purely leisurely activity to one that has a strong political and social commitment.

By the turn of the century, with the spirit and essence of Western imagination seeping into Urdu literature, literary tastes too began to be transformed. In Lahore, Colonel W.R.M. Holroyd, Director of Public Instruction in the Punjab, began to organise new kinds of *mushairās* that weaned Urdu poetry away from preoccupations with courtly love and turned it towards facts and events.[8] Under his influence, a new breed of modernists and prose-stylists such as Muhammad Husain Azad and Altaf Husain Hali too began to exhort poets to look for 'radically new vision of the nature and goal of poetry'. On 9 May 1874, speaking at the Anjuman-e-Punjab in Lahore, Azad stressed the need for naturalism and realism in poetry. The new kind of *mushairās* lasted barely a year but their influence lived on in the new sort of poetry being written. With time, the leisurely aspect of the *mushairā* gradually began to leach out, giving way to didacticism and even political rhetoric and the occasional bombast.

***

'My name is Karimuddin. I am a native of Panipat,' begins Farhatullah Baig's narrative. 'As the mullah heads for the masjid, so scholars flocked to Delhi,' he says. Like so many others, Maulvi Karimuddin too came to Delhi with stars in his eyes, set up a printing press but, when that floundered, he decided to organise a *mushairā*, publish its proceedings and make some money. What follows is entirely conjecture on the part of a man who has the gift of a brilliant imagination but certainly no proof that a *mushairā*, said to be the last of its kind, was held at a particular place on a particular date where a certain number of poets were present who recited a particular set of ghazals.

Fact and fiction blend seamlessly in a narrative that is not only a highly entertaining account of historical personages and their distinctive literary styles but is also a valuable document of a society, its morals and manners. Farhatullah Baig's book transports us to an age when everyone—from the Mughal Emperor Bahadurshah Zafar to the poorest beggar—cherished and adored Urdu. Polished and perfected by Delhi *ustads*, such as Mir, Sauda and Dard, it shone like burnished gold by the time of Karimuddin's *mushairā*. And, like gold, it could be fashioned into exquisitely delicate ghazals that could be light as gossamer yet fulsome with metaphysical import. For as long as they were able, the Mughal emperors and *salatin* (princes of royal blood), many of whom wrote tolerably good poetry themselves, organised *mushairās* within the fort. Later, as they became steadily more impoverished, *mushairās* and *mehfils* (soirees) came to be organised in different parts of the city such as Ghaziuddin Khan's madrasa and the homes of the nobility as also the wealthier among the city's bankers and financiers.

Farhatullah Baig's book provides a vivid account of the development of not just the Urdu ghazal but the Urdu language itself. His narrative is studded with lively pen portraits of the *ustads* Zauq, Ghalib, Momin, Dagh, Sheftah, Azurdah as well as their *shagirds* (disciples) who were popular figures in the *mushairā* circuit, such as, the French army captain Alexander Heatherley Azad who always came to Delhi whenever he heard of a *mushairā* being organised; Hakim Sakhanand Raqam who was an ardent devotee of Momin and the colourful Nazneen who wrote in the women's dialect *rekhti*, using women's idiom and slang and recited with great coquetry and coy playfulness wearing an *odhni*. The masters of *rekhta* would listen in stony silence as the crowd went into raptures over Nazneen's histrionics. 'There were some rather droll celebrities,' Qamber summarises in her Introduction,

> Like the saintly, senile, unknown muddle-headed Mir Sahib with the aura of his seventy years of grand old age and Mirza Rasa, another near veteran. Ghulam Rasool Shauq was so old that he was Shah Naseer's shagird and himself an ustad of Ustad Zauq. The rather crotchety Hafiz Ghulam Rasool Veeran was blind and was always on the offensive taking up cudgels on behalf of his ustad Zauq. Among the young set were the mischievous, arrogant Abdur Rehman Hud Hud, and some promising youth not without beauty and romance like the fifteen-year-old Tamkeen as yet a student at the Delhi Madarssa or the brilliant Khan Dagh of the royal household....[9]

Then there was the mystical Tashnah who arrived at *mushairās* not only drunk but also completely naked. In the *mushairā* described by Karimuddin, he absentmindedly snuffs out the *shama* placed before him before reading a ghazal that carries the only portent of disaster in its refrain of the nothingness that awaits them all and their beloved city a few short years away after the *ghadar* of 1857. Tashnah and Zauq sound the only note of sadness in this assembly that is otherwise complacent in its sense of well-being.

A *mushairā* such as the one described in Baig's book would usually begin after the last of the five prescribed prayer, the *Isha* prayer, say about nine or ten and go on till the predawn hour when the call for the *Fajr* prayer would cause the assembly to disperse. The patron, in this case Mirza Arif, would welcome the poets and tactfully handle the ticklish issues of seating the poets and the order in which they would be invited to recite according to a complicated system governed by etiquette, seniority and affiliation. Touchy and temperamental, the poets could take offense at the smallest misdemeanour; it could well be the *daad* or ovation given sparingly or too well. The readings would be interspersed with wit and repartee, both personal and poetic. Ordinarily, the patron would announce the *tarah* or rhyme pattern at the time of extending the invitation. Baig's *mushairā* has been decreed *be-tarah* by the emperor himself and, thus, free from the vexing issue that caused many squabbles to break out among rival literary camps. The only request made by the emperor to Karimuddin, when he went to solicit his permission, was that he'd (Karimuddin) personally invite the great poets of Delhi, namely, Momin, Ghalib and Zauq (the latter being the emperor's *ustad*) as a gesture of courtesy. Royal protocol forbade the emperor himself and the heir apparent to attend a *mushairā* in the city but he was pleased to send his ghazal (which was read by an emissary on his behalf) and his younger son, Mirza Fakhru, in his stead.

A venue was finalised, a list of fifty-nine poets was drawn up and all arrangements were made within nine days from the date Karimuddin succeeds in gaining the emperor's consent. The day of the *mushairā* arrived. The street leading up to the venue, the *haveli* of Mubarakunnisa Begum, was fixed with so many lights that it seemed like 'night is turned into day'. Thick wads of fragrant *khus* send out cool wafts of air. Karimuddin's friend and benefactor, Arif, had wrought a wonder. One by one, the *utsads* came in, accompanied by their *shagirds*. In Baig's own words:

> The seating pattern was such that those assigned places to the right of the presiding poet (in this case Mirza Fakhru) had connections with the Lucknow Court and on the left were seated the Delhi ustads

> and their shagirds. One thing that struck me as rather strange was that those who came from the Fort held quails in their hands. The craze for quail-shooting and cock-fighting was very strong at the Fort. There were quail, partridge and cock-fighting rounds every day. One of the princes has outdone all the rest in this sport. On a two-wheeled bullock cart he has built a little hut with a thatched roof of small bamboo shoots and strewn the floor with soil in which he has sown birdseeds. Believe it or not, the roof invites literally thousands of titlarks and small singing wren. The prince carts them around wherever he likes....[10]

Replete with asides such as the one above that shed light on the idea of leisure and entertainment in the city at the time, the narrative continues at a leisurely pace. Soon, it was time for the *mushairā* to begin. Upon receiving a sign from the prince, two mace bearers announced: 'Your lordships, the *mushairā* commences.' The emperor's page took out Zafar's ghazal from a silken case and read it aloud in a sonorous voice. This was followed by Mirza Fakhru who, in choosing to read his own poem first, was removing the difference between the first and the last. A lighted *shama* was placed before each poet, beginning with the younger and lesser-known ones and ending with Zauq, the emperor's *ustad*. The *ustads* lavished generous praise on their own *shagird* as well as genuinely talented younger poets such as Dagh but remained silent when they wished to show either disapproval or disappointment. Mirza Fakhru, the presiding poet in Baig's fictitious *mushairā*, was not just the emperor's son and representative and a fine poet himself but also a deeply religious man. He said the *fateha* before lighting the *shama*. As the last poet, Ustad Zauq, was reading his *qata*, the call for *Fajir* prayer was heard, and the *mushairā* ended with the assembly once again raising its hand in prayer.

And, finally, to come to the author of this remarkable book—Farhaullah Baig, or to give him his full name, Mirza Farhatullah Baig Dehalvi (1883–1948), he was educated first at the Delhi madrassah (or 'Dilli Kalege' as it was called), and later at Hindu College and St Stephens College. He studied science, played cricket and football, moved to Hyderabad in 1907 where he later became the Registrar of the Hyderabad High Court. Despite moving to the Deccan, he remained faithful to the Urdu vocabulary and register of the Delhi style. He wrote this book 'to light the last lamp of Urdu poetry and to honour and immortalize the Urdu poets of the last days of Mughal splendour.'[11] Apart from the seminal *Dilli ki Aakhri Shama*, he also wrote a tribute to his teacher, *Dr Nazeer Ahmad ki Kahani: Kuch Meri aur Kuch Unki Zubani* ('The Story of Dr Nazeer Ahmad: Some in His Own Words and Some in Mine').

Baig presents himself to the readers in the guise of a real person, Maulvi Karimuddin 'Maghfoor', who wrote an actual book, *Tabquat-e Shora-e Hind*. From this, he draws inspiration but adds heavily from his own imagination. From a *tazkira* or description of the poets and an analysis of their poetry, he ends up not just describing a 'mushairā in the old traditional style' but in the process also describing an entire way of life in which the *mushairā* fitted in seamlessly. Had the impulse behind *Dilli ki Aakhri Shama* been mere nostalgia and a scraping of the past, this text would never have acquired the iconic status it has. The idea behind the book is best described by Baig himself:

> Looking at the flickering light of the morning star I conceived an idea and the idea was stimulated by the image in my mind of the late Momin, that I should light such a lamp for Urdu with the help of which future generations might behold, howsoever dimly, the figures and faces of the benefactors and sponsors of the Urdu tongue and while reading their works might have, at least, a dim vision of their individual personalities.[12]

Afterword

I had the singular pleasure of 'directing' Farhatullah Baig's book *Dilli ki Aakhri Shama* like a stage play on 23 April 2007. I was working at the Jamia Millia Islamia then and had ready access to a pool of Urdu-speaking talent of varying age groups. Of the fifty-nine poets assembled by Farhatullah Baig in his imaginary *mushairā*, I chose eleven, the twelfth being the royal emissary who read the Emperor's ghazal. I followed the seating plan provided by Baig in his book in seating the poets on stage. I chose a motley 'cast' of serving university professors, students, Old Boys as well as members of the non-teaching staff. The play was staged at the Stein Auditorium of the India International Centre as part of the 'Delhi series', organised by Parminder Singh of The Attic, New Delhi. Needless to say, it was extremely well received.

I have had the occasion to attend several *mushairās* in different cities: Delhi, Aligarh, Lucknow, Patna, among others. I have also had the honour of organising *mushairās* while I worked at the Jamia. For the past several years I serve as Trustee of the annual Shankar-Shad Mushairā in Modern School, Barakhamba Road, Delhi, which is a highpoint in the city's cultural calendar. The dynamics of a *mushairā*, its composition, its template, the judicious mix of poetry ranging from political to romantic to humorous, whom to invite, in which order to seat a poet or ask him/her to recite is by now well known to me. You could say, I am a latter-day Maulvi Karimuddin. However, for me, personally, the most memorable *mushairās* are the ones I attended as a child when I visited my grandparents in the university town of Aligarh. The city would play host to many *mushairās* throughout the year: in its big auditoriums, its smaller seminar rooms, in the cozy drawing rooms of the university teachers many of whom were fine poets themselves. It was here that, from a young age, one learnt to give *daad* in the correct manner hearing elders say '*Wah! Wah!*' or '*subhan Allah*', '*Marhaba*', '*Mukarrar Irshad!*' It was here that one learnt the art of *misra uthana*, that is, repeating the *misra* or the first line of the two-line *she'r* in a ghazal.

By far, the most memorable and the most raucous were the *mushairās* organised by the city administration (as distinct from the university administration), especially the annual *mushairā* during the yearly *numiash*. Literally meaning 'exhibition', the *numaish* is a travelling fair or carnival that winds its way across multiple cities in western Uttar Pradesh. Along with the usual stalls selling food, clothes, consumer goods, it also has daily cultural shows. The showstopper is invariably the *mushairā*. Less sedate than the *mushairās* organised in the university, these are crowded, clamorous events. The audience is excitable, as willing to boo, hiss, jeer and hoot as to approve, applaud, cheer and clap—doing both with equal abandon! Only the best and bravest are known to survive a *mushairā* at the Aligarh *numaish*.

Notes

1 I have read both the original Urdu and the excellent translation by Akhtar Qamber published as *The Last Mushairā of Delhi* by Orient Longman. All translations in English from this text are by Akhtar Qamber. She has chosen to tweak Baig's title choosing to use the word '*mushairā*' instead of the 'candle' in the original.

2 Most notably, Hardy (1972); Mushirul Hasan, *A Moral Reckoning: Muslim Intellectuals in 19th Century Delhi*, New Delhi, Oxford University Press; Perceval Spear, *Twilight of the Mughals*, New Delhi, Oriental Books Reprint Corporation, 1969; among others.

3 I have relied on this edition: *Asar-us-Sanadid* by Sir Syed Ahmad Khan, (reprint), New Delhi, Urdu Akademi, 2006.

4 See C.M. Naim, 'Syed Ahmad and His Two Books called *Asar-al-Sanadid*', *Modern Asian Studies*, Vol. 45 (3) May 2011, pp. 669–708. Naim views the two versions as two separate books.

5 Translated as *The Last Gathering: A Vivid Portrait of Life in the Red Fort* by Ather Farouqui, New Delhi: Roli Books, 2021.

6 Akhtar Qamber, op. cit., p. 18.

7 See an excellent study of the *mushairā* as in it evolved from Mughal to modern times in Mahmudabad (2020).

8 See Frances Pritchett, *Nets of Awareness: Urdu Poetry and its Critics*, Berkeley, University of California Press, 1994.

9 Qamber, op. cit., p. 31.

10 Ibid., p. 68.

11 Ibid., p. 1.

12 Ibid., p. 36.

References

Ali, Ahmed. 2007. *Twilight in Delhi: A Novel* (second impression). New Delhi: Rupa & Co.

Azad, Muhammad Husain. 2001. *Ab-e Hayat: Shaping the Canon of Urdu Poetry*, translated by F.W. Pritchett, in association with S.R. Faruqi. New Delhi: Oxford University Press.

Faizuddin, Munshi. 2021. *Bazm-i Aakhir*, translated by Ather Farouqui as *The Last Gathering: A Vivid Portrait of Life in the Red Fort*. New Delhi: Lotus Collection/Roli, p. 202.

Farouqi, Khwaja Ahmad (Trans.). 1970. *Dastambu of Mirza Ahsanullah Ghalib*. Bombay: Asia Publishing House.

Faruqi, Shamsur Rahman. 2001. *Early Urdu Literary Culture and History*. New Delhi: Oxford University Press.

Gupta, Narayani. 1997. *Delhi between Two Empires 1803–1831: Society, Government and Urban Growth*. New Delhi: Oxford University Press.

Hardy, Peter. 1972. *The Muslims of British India*. Cambridge: Cambridge University Press.

Hasan, Mushirul and Asim Roy (eds). 2005. *Living Together Separately: Cultural India in History and Politics*. New Delhi: Oxford University Press.

Mahmudabad, Ali Khan. 2020. *Poetry of Belonging: Muslim Imaginings of India, 1850–1950*. New Delhi: Oxford University Press.

Minault, Gail. 2003. 'Delhi College and Urdu', *Annual of Urdu Studies*, Vol. 18. Chicago: University of Wisconsin-Madison.

Naim, C.M. 1989. 'Poet-Audience Interaction at Urdu Mushairās', *Urdu and Muslim South Asia: Studies in Honour of Ralph Russell*. New Delhi: Oxford University Press.

Narang, Gopichand. 2005. *Urdu Ghazal aur Hindustani Zahn-o-Tahzib*. Lahore: Sang-e Meel Publication.

Sadiq, Muhammad. 1984. *A History of Urdu Literature* (revised and enlarged). New Delhi: Oxford University Press.

ABOUT THE EDITOR AND CONTRIBUTORS

The Editor

Seema Bawa is a professor specialising in the history of South Asian art and culture at Department of History, University of Delhi. Books written by her include *Gods, Men and Women: Gender and Sexuality in Early Indian Art* and *Religion and Art of the Chamba Valley, A.D. 700–1300*. She has edited *Locating Pleasure in Indian History: Prescribed and Proscribed Desires in Visual and Literary Cultures* (Bloomsburty India). The areas of research focus on Indian Art, Ancient Indian Art and Iconography; Western Himalayan Art; and Religion and Modern and Contemporary Indian Art. She was the recipient of DAAD Fellowship to read at the University of Bonn. Her research includes narrative depiction of *Rāmāyaṇa* and visual hagiographies of Gandhi, Gupta and Post Gupta Shivaism in Northern India. Her research papers on early Indian sculptures and architecture have been published in many journals. She writes on contemporary Indian art and culture for national newspapers, specialised journals and magazines; she has edited *ARTimes* and curated shows including the *Decorated Cow: Sidharth* and *Shatadru: Feminine Sensibilities in Indian Art* for Lalit Kala Akademi.

The Contributors

Suchandra Ghosh is a professor at Department of History, University of Hyderabad. She specialises in early Indian history, with a focus on epigraphy and numismatics. Before joining University of Hyderabad, she was a professor in the department of Ancient Indian History & Culture, University of Calcutta (November 2000–June 2020). She is the Area Editor of *The Encyclopaedia of Ancient History: Asia and Africa*, Wiley Blackwell. Her publications include works like *Exploring Connectivity: South-Eastern Bengal and Beyond* (Institute of Social and Cultural Studies, Kolkata, 2015); *From the Oxus to the Indus: A Political and Cultural Study, c.300 BCE to c.100 BCE* (Primus Books, Delhi, 2017).

Smita Sahgal is a professor at Department of History, Lady Shri Ram College, University of Delhi. She did post-doctoral research project, on 'Niyoga: Commissioned Procreation and Sexual Regulation in Early India [A Socio-Historical Study in North India between 1500 BCE and

700 CE]' and on 'Masculinities in early India: Exploring the possibility of a Discourse'. She has authored a monograph titled *Niyoga: Alternative Mechanism to Lineage Perpetuation in Early India: A Socio-Historical Enquiry* (Delhi, ICHR and Primus Books, 2017) and co-authored with K.M. Shrimali et al., *Teaching History*. She chaired a short-term course on Early Indian Religions at University of Haifa, Israel, 2018. Prof. Sahgal was felicitated by the Romanian Embassy for promotion of Indo-European cultural ties, 2007, and received Best Paper Award from Indian History Congress in 2006. She has around forty publications to her credit in international and national journals and has been keynote speaker/invited speaker to many conferences.

Marion Frenger has studied Oriental Art History and Indology at the Rheinische Friedrich-Wilhelms-Universität Bonn with T.S. Maxwell and Claus Vogel. She has taught courses on ancient and contemporary arts of South and Southeast Asia in Bonn and at the Frieie Universität Berlin and has worked for several museums and private collections in Germany, Spain and Switzerland. In recent years, she has worked as a freelance editor and consultant for different academic projects on Asian art. Most recently, she was part of the curatorial team of a major exhibition on Jainism organised by Museum Rietberg, Zurich. Her research interests include the art and architecture of northern India in the 1st millennium CE, the exchange and adaptation of visual models between South and Southeast Asia and the repercussions of 18th and 19th century scholarship in modern perceptions of South Asia and its arts.

Mrityunjay Prabhakar, an avid theatre-maker as well as theoretician, has been active in the field of theatre, literature, media and culture for over two decades. He is a celebrated poet, playwright, theatre trainer and a director. Prabhakar is also a screenwriter and have been a film critic for many years. Currently, he is working as an assistant professor of Drama and Theatre Arts at Visva-Bharati University, Shantiniketan, India.

T.K. Venkatasubramanian joined Delhi University in 1984 as reader and became a professor in 1994. He was also the Head of Department and Dean of the social sciences in 2001–2004. He completed his PhD from Madras University in the year 1979. He was head of the department and Dean of the *Social Sciences* in 2001–2004. His major interest areas are social and economic history of the peninsular India in addition to performing arts. Some of his published works includes *Political Change and Agrarian Tradition in South India (1600–1801)* (Mittal Publications,

Delhi, 1986); *Environment and Urbanization in Early Tamilakam* (Tamil University, Thanjavur, 1988); *Evolution of Political Society in South India* (Kalinga Publications, New Delhi, 1993) and *Music as History in Tamil Nadu* (Primus Publications, New Delhi, 2010).

Patrick Krüger studied Art History of South and East Asia at Freie Universität Berlin and Ancient and Medieval History of South Asia at Humboldt-Universität zu Berlin. He received his PhD degree in Art History of South Asia with a thesis on illustrated Jain manuscripts from the early modern period. In 2016, he was Research Fellow of the Käte Hamburger Kolleg Dynamics in the History of Religion between Asia and Europe at the Center for Religious Studies (CERES), University of Bochumand, where he currently works as a research associate. He also served as Interim Professor of Religious Studies at the University of Münster. He has curated exhibitions on the history of religion, Jain miniatures and Jain art and religion in Münster, Cologne and Zurich.

Vipul Singh is a professor at the Department of History, University of Delhi. He is an alumnus Carson Fellow of the Rachel Carson Center for Environment and Society, Munich, Germany. His most recent publications include a book titled *Speaking Rivers: Environmental History of a Mid-Ganga Flood Country* (2018), and research papers titled 'Cyclones, Shipwrecks and Environmental Anxiety: British Rule and Ecological Change in the Andaman Islands, the 1780s to 1900s', 'Global Environment' (2020) and 'Governing Fluvial Commons in Colonial Bihar: Alluvion and Diluvion Regulation and Decommonisation' (Routledge, 2021). He is currently working on a book project on the effects of global climate anomalies and oceanic circulations in early modern India. He is on the editorial board of the *Water History Journal* published by Springer, and a member of the Association for East Asia Environmental History.

Prem Kumar is an associate professor at the Department of History, Motilal Nehru College (Evening), University of Delhi. He has received his BA, MA and PhD degrees from the University of Delhi. He has interests in urban history, dramas, social histories, religion, ecology and cityscapes. He has published several research papers and chapters in several national and international journals and books.

Farhat Nasreen is a professor of History and is heading the department of History and Culture at Jamia Millia Islamia, New Delhi. Her recent books include *If History Has Taught Us Anything* and *The Great Mughals*, published by the Rupa Publications, have been very well received in both academic and commercial sectors. She has presented papers in fifty-nine seminars and conferences and has delivered talks in 128 forums of repute. She has served as the Honorary Director of the Centre of Jawaharlal Nehru Studies of Jamia Millia Islamia and has officiated as the Honorary Director of the following from time to time: Centre for the Study of Social Exclusion and Inclusive Policy, Centre for Innovation and Entrepreneurship, Centre for Jawaharlal Nehru Studies, India-Arab Cultural Centre and Sarojini Naidu Centre for Women's Studies. Besides being a member of various administrative boards of her University, she is a member of the following: Board of the School of Social Sciences, Mizoram University, Board of Studies of the Department of History, Aligarh Muslim University and External Member of the Full Centre's Committee of the Centre for Historical Studies, Jawaharlal Nehru University. She has served as the editor of the journal *History and Sociology of South Asia* (Sage).

Raziuddin Aquil teaches History at the University of Delhi. His research and teaching interests include literary and historical traditions, religious practices and political cultures in medieval and early modern India. His books include *Sufism, Culture, and Politics: Afghans and Islam in Medieval North India* (Oxford University Press), *The Muslim Question: Understanding Islam and Indian History* (Penguin Books) and *History in the Public Domain* (Manohar). He has also edited with Partha Chatterjee on *History in the Vernacular* (Permanent Black), with David L. Curley on *Literary and Religious Practices in Medieval and Early Modern India* (Manohar and Routledge) and with Tilottama Mukherjee on *An Earthly Paradise: Trade, Politics and Culture in Early Modern Bengal* (Manohar and Routledge).

Rakhshanda Jalil is a multi-award-winning translator, writer and literary historian. She has published over thirty books and written over fifty academic papers and essays. Her book on the lesser-known monuments of Delhi, *Invisible City* (2008), *Liking Progress, Loving Change: A Literary History of the Progressive Writers Movement in Urdu* (Oxford University Press, 2014); *A Rebel and Her Cause* (Women Unlimited, 2014); an edited volume called *An Uncivil Woman* (Oxford University Press, 2017); a literary biography of Shahryar: *A Life in Poetry*, *The Great War: Indian Writings on the First World War* (Bloomsbury Publishing); *Preeto & Other Stories: The Male Gaze in Urdu* (Niyogi Books); *Kaifiyat, Jallianwala Bagh: Literary Responses in Prose & Poetry* (Niyogi Books) among others. Her recent books include *Looking Back: The 1947 Partition of India, 70 Years On*, co-edited with Tarun K. Saint and Debjani Sengupta (Orient Blackswan, 2017); *Footprints on*

Zero Line: Writings on the Partition, *But You Don't Look Like a Muslim* (HarperCollins, 2019), *Bangladesh: Writings on 1971 Across Borders* (co-edited with Debjani Sengupta, Orient Blackswan, 2022). She runs an organisation called Hindustani Awaaz, devoted to the popularisation of Hindi–Urdu literature and culture.

INDEX

T